Python Web Development
with Django®

Developer's Library

ESSENTIAL REFERENCES FOR PROGRAMMING PROFESSIONALS

Developer's Library books are designed to provide practicing programmers with unique, high-quality references and tutorials on the programming languages and technologies they use in their daily work.

All books in the *Developer's Library* are written by expert technology practitioners who are especially skilled at organizing and presenting information in a way that's useful for other programmers.

Key titles include some of the best, most widely acclaimed books within their topic areas:

PHP & MySQL Web Development
Luke Welling & Laura Thomson
ISBN 978-0-672-32916-6

MySQL
Paul DuBois
ISBN-13: 978-0-672-32938-8

Linux Kernel Development
Robert Love
ISBN-13: 978-0-672-32946-3

Python Essential Reference
David Beazley
ISBN-13: 978-0-672-32862-6

Programming in Objective-C
Stephen G. Kochan
ISBN-13: 978-0-321-56615-7

PostgreSQL
Korry Douglas
ISBN-13: 978-0-672-33015-5

Developer's Library books are available at most retail and online bookstores, as well as by subscription from Safari Books Online at **safari.informit.com**

**Developer's
Library**

informit.com/devlibrary

Python Web Development with Django®

Jeff Forcier, Paul Bissex, Wesley Chun

♦♦Addison-Wesley

Upper Saddle River, NJ · Boston · Indianapolis · San Francisco
New York · Toronto · Montreal · London · Munich · Paris · Madrid
Cape Town · Sydney · Tokyo · Singapore · Mexico City

Many of the designations used by manufacturers and sellers to distinguish their products are claimed as trademarks. Where those designations appear in this book, and the publisher was aware of a trademark claim, the designations have been printed with initial capital letters or in all capitals.

The authors and publisher have taken care in the preparation of this book, but make no expressed or implied warranty of any kind and assume no responsibility for errors or omissions. No liability is assumed for incidental or consequential damages in connection with or arising out of the use of the information or programs contained herein.

The publisher offers excellent discounts on this book when ordered in quantity for bulk purchases or special sales, which may include electronic versions and/or custom covers and content particular to your business, training goals, marketing focus, and branding interests. For more information, please contact:

U.S. Corporate and Government Sales
(800) 382-3419
corpsales@pearsontechgroup.com

For sales outside the United States, please contact:

International Sales
international@pearson.com

Visit us on the Web: informit.com/aw

Library of Congress Cataloging-in-Publication Data:

Forcier, Jeff, 1982-
 Python web development with Django / Jeff Forcier, Paul Bissex, Wesley Chun.
    p. cm.
 Includes index.
 ISBN-10: 0-13-235613-9 (pbk. : alk. paper)
 ISBN-13: 978-0-13-235613-8 (pbk. : alk. paper) 1. Web site development. 2. Django (Electronic resource) 3. Python (Computer program language) 4. Web sites—Authoring programs. I. Bissex, Paul. II. Chun, Wesley. III. Title.
 TK5105.8885.D54F68 2009
 006.7'6—dc22

                         2008037134

ISBN-13: 978-0-13-235613-8
ISBN-10: 0-13-235613-9
Text printed in the United States on recycled paper at RR Donnelley in Crawfordsville, Indiana.
First printing October 2008

Editor-In-Chief
Mark Taub

Acquisitions Editor
Debra Williams Cauley

Development Editor
Michael Thurston

Managing Editor
Kristy Hart

Project Editor and Copy Editor
Jovana San Nicolas-Shirley

Indexer
Cheryl Lenser

Proofreader
Geneil Breeze

Publishing Coordinator
Kim Boedigheimer

Cover Designer
Gary Adair

Compositor
Jake McFarland

❖

To Brian Levine, for introducing me to Python, a small thing that has made a big difference. To my parents, for allowing me to monopolize the family computer while growing up. And to my wife, for her loving support and understanding.

—Jeff Forcier

To my late father Henry, who taught me to tinker; to my mother Glenda, who taught me to write; and to my wife Kathleen, a brilliant star in my life.

—Paul Bissex

To my wonderful children, Leanna Xin-Yi and Daylen Xin-Zhi, for whom I've had to develop multiple pairs of eyes with which to keep watch over, and who are miraculously able to temporarily transport me back in time to remind me of what childhood and its amazing wonders were like.

—Wesley Chun

❖

Table of Contents

Preface

Welcome to Django!

Greetings, and welcome to Django! We're glad to have you along on our journey. You will discover a powerful Web application framework that lets you do everything rapidly—from designing and developing the original application to updating its features and functionality without requiring major changes to the codebase.

About This Book

Several Django books are already on the market, but ours differs from most in that we focus equally on three areas: Django basics, a variety of example applications, and advanced Django topics. Our intent is to make this the most well-rounded book on the subject, one you find useful regardless of background, and which will give you a complete picture of the framework and what you can do with it.

Chapter Guide

In Figure 0.1, you see recommended starting points for your reading depending on your Python and Django experience. Of course, we recommend a cover-to-cover treatment, but the diagram will help if time is not on your side. Regardless of your experience, you are always welcome to look at the applications because reading and studying code is one of the best ways to learn. We also provide this chapter-by-chapter reading guide to further help direct you to where you need to read.

Part I, "Getting Started"

Part I covers the basic material needed to introduce users new to Django and/or Python, although we recommend Chapter 3, "Starting Out," even to advanced readers.

Chapter 1, "Practical Python for Django"

This chapter is an introduction for readers who are new to Python. In one comprehensive chapter, we show you not only the syntax, but also go a bit more in-depth and expose you to Python's memory model and data types, especially constructs commonly used in Django.

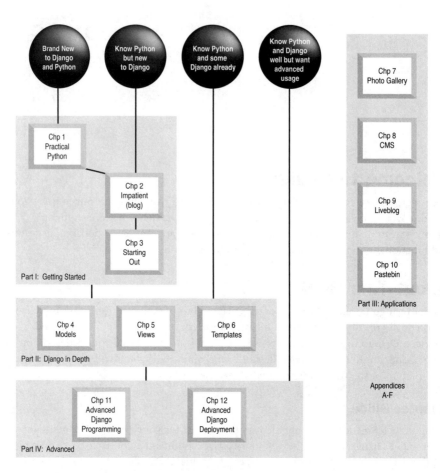

Figure 0.1   Suggested reading guide based on your Python and/or Django experience

Chapter 2, "Django for the Impatient: Building a Blog"

This is a chapter for those who want to skip any Python introduction and want to dive immediately into a Django application that can be completed in 15-20 minutes. It gives a good overview of what's possible with the framework.

Chapter 3, "Starting Out"

For those with a bit more patience, this chapter serves as an introduction to all the foundations of developing Web-based applications (useful both for newbies and experienced coders alike). Once the formalities are over, we describe how each concept fits into the world of Django as well as what its philosophies are and how it may differ from other Web application frameworks.

Part II, "Django in Depth"

Part II covers all the basic components of the framework, laying the foundation for the example applications in Part III, "Django Applications by Example."

Chapter 4, "Defining and Using Models"

In Chapter 4, learn how to define and work with your data model, including the basics of Django's object-relational mapper (ORM) from simple fields up to complex relations.

Chapter 5, "URLs, HTTP Mechanisms, and Views"

This chapter goes into detail on how Django handles URL processing and the rest of the HTTP protocol, including middleware layers, as well as how to use Django's time-saving generic views, and how to write custom or partially custom views from scratch.

Chapter 6, "Templates and Form Processing"

Chapter 6 covers the final major piece of the framework, where we explore Django's template language and its form-handling mechanisms. It covers how to display data to your users and get data back from them.

Part III, "Django Applications by Example"

In Part III, we create four distinct applications, each highlighting a different aspect or component of Django development, both to introduce new general ideas and to expand on the concepts found in Parts I and II.

Chapter 7, "Photo Gallery"

In Chapter 7, learn how to apply the "Don't Repeat Yourself" convention to your URL structure and create a new thumbnail-creating image form field, while you make a simple photo gallery application.

Chapter 8, "Content Management System"

Chapter 8 contains two related approaches to creating a CMS or CMS-like system and covers the use of a number of "contrib" Django applications.

Chapter 9, "Liveblog"

Chapter 9 covers writing a "liveblog"—a site that makes use of advanced JavaScript techniques, serves as a backdrop for applying AJAX to a Django project, and shows how easy it is to use any AJAX toolkit you want.

Chapter 10, "Pastebin"

In Chapter 10, learn the power of Django's generic views as we create a pastebin using almost no custom logic whatsoever.

Part IV, "Advanced Django Techniques and Features"

Part IV is a collection of advanced topics, ranging from customizing Django's admin application to writing command-line scripts that interface with your Django applications.

Chapter 11, "Advanced Django Programming"

Chapter 11 covers a number of topics related to fleshing out your own application's code, such as RSS generation, extending the template language, or making better use of the Django admin application.

Chapter 12, "Advanced Django Deployment"

In Chapter 12, learn a number of tricks related to deploying Django applications or working with your app from outside your Django project's core code, such as command-line scripts, cron jobs, testing, or data import.

Part V, "Appendices"

Part V fills in the remaining gaps or addresses topics relevant to the rest of the book but that don't fit in well as full chapters. Learn the basics of the Unix command line, Django installation and deployment strategies, tools for development, and more.

Appendix A, "Command Line Basics"

Appendix A is an introduction to the Unix command line for those who haven't been exposed to it before now. Trust us—it's useful!

Appendix B, "Installing and Running Django"

In Appendix B, learn how to install all the necessary components for running Django, including the various options for database and Web servers, as well as some tips on specific deployment strategies.

Appendix C, " Tools for Practical Django Development"

Appendix C outlines some basic development tools you may or may not be familiar with, including source control, text editors, and more.

Appendix D, "Finding, Evaluating, and Using Django Applications"

Good developers write code, but great developers reuse somebody else's code! In Appendix D, we share some tips on the where and how of finding reusable Django applications.

Appendix E, "Django on the Google App Engine"

Appendix E provides an exclusive look at how Google's new App Engine leverages Django, and you can also learn how to enable your Django applications to run under the App Engine framework.

Appendix F, "Getting Involved in the Django Project"

In Appendix F, learn how to contribute to Django and become a part of the community.

Conventions

Throughout this book, we use **bold** to introduce new or important terms, *italics* for emphasis, http://links/ for URLs, and `monospacing` to delineate Python and command line material such as variable names or commands. Multiline blocks of code or command examples are in monospaced blocks, like so:

```
>>> print "This is Python!"
This is Python!
```

We have made use of all three major platforms—Mac OS X, Linux, and Windows—when writing this book and the example applications. In addition, we've used all major browsers (although not all may be present in our screenshots), namely Firefox, Safari, Opera, and Internet Explorer.

Book Resources

You can contact the authors collectively at authors@withdjango.com. Our Web site, http://withdjango.com, contains a large amount of auxiliary material and is referenced in a number of places throughout the book.

Acknowledgments

My name may have ended up first in the author list, but this book wouldn't be here without the effort and dedication of the other two. Paul and Wesley are scholars and gentlemen of the highest caliber, and working with them has been an awesome experience.

Speaking of scholars and gentlemen, the Django core team is filled to the brim. The original four—Adrian Holovaty, Jacob Kaplan-Moss, Simon Willison, and Wilson Miner—have laid (and continue to lay) an incredible groundwork, which has been expanded on by Malcolm Tredinnick, Georg Bauer, Luke Plant, Russell Keith-Magee, and Robert Wittams. Each one of these guys is an inspiration to me, and I'm not easily inspired.

I'd also like to acknowledge two fellow "Djangonauts" and IRC veterans, Kevin Menard and James Bennett, as well as the NYCDjango group, as stellar examples of the kinds of talented people found in the Django community.

Finally, a big thanks to the staff at Pearson, including our editors and technical reviewers (Wesley will fill you in on these folks below!) and especially the copyediting staff, whose careful eye to detail is greatly appreciated.

Jeff Forcier
New York, NY
August 2008

Thanks are due to the communities surrounding Django, Python, and other open source infrastructure for web applications. The work of thousands of dedicated developers and maintainers makes powerful software stacks freely available worldwide.

My coauthors have been a boon, bringing essential knowledge and skills to the task as well as serious dedication. Despite the fact that we are spread across a continent, I have been lucky enough to meet face-to-face with both Jeff and Wes.

Thanks to the Western Massachusetts Developers Group for many interesting geeky discussions and much enthusiasm about the book project.

Thanks to George J. Rosa III, President of Hallmark Institute of Photography, for bringing me on and trusting me to choose the best tools—including, of course, Django—to do the best job possible.

In the summer of 2008, after a serious automobile accident, I received an amazing surge of attention and support from family, friends, and community. Every good wish, card, dollar, and meal made a difference. You know who you are, and I thank you again.

And to my wonderful wife Kathleen, thank you for your support, smarts, vision, and love.

Paul Bissex
Northampton, MA
September 2008

Writing my second book was a great experience. I'd like to salute the two wonderful coauthors whom I've had the pleasure of working with. They were able to take someone with some preexisting Python skills and introduce Django as an experience. I'm glad to be able to contribute to producing this great Django book and look forward to working with them again on future writings or in the classroom. It was also extremely gratifying to write the entire book as if it were an open source project, using the same tools that developers use every day to develop game-changing software.

I'd like to thank Debra Williams Cauley for helping us manage the entire process, since I was first approached with this project. We had numerous changes in personnel, and she kept us focused on the manuscript. It wasn't enough to deliver just any ol' Django book to meet market demand, as she subscribed to believing in our philosophy of releasing the "right book" for the community as a whole. Thanks to all of our technical reviewers, Michael Thurston (development editor), Joe Blaylock, and Antonio Cangiano, as well as those who submitted Rough Cuts feedback to make this book better than it was when first introduced. I'd also like to thank Matt Brown, lead maintainer of the Django Helper for Google App Engine, for his assistance in reviewing Appendix E, and Eric Walstad and Eric Evenson for their last-minute overall review and commentary.

Finally, without the support of our collective families, this book would not have been possible.

Wesley Chun
Silicon Valley, CA
August 2008

About the Authors

Jeffrey E. Forcier currently works as a systems administrator and backend Web developer at Digital Pulp, Inc., a New York–based interactive agency and Web development company. He has 7 years experience in Web development with PHP and Python, including professional and personal use of the Django framework since its public release in 2005. He holds a degree in Computer Science from the University of Massachusetts.

Paul Bissex has worked as a graphic designer, writer, teacher, babysitter, and software developer. He was an early adopter of Django and is the creator and maintainer of dpaste.com, the Django community pastebin site. From September to June, he can be found at the Hallmark Institute of Photography (hallmark.edu), teaching Web development and using Python and Django to build everything from attendance systems to housing databases to image processing utilities. His writings on technology have appeared in *Wired*, Salon.com, and the *Chicago Tribune*. Since 1996, he has served as a conference host for The Well (well.com), which *Wired* magazine called "the world's most influential online community," and currently hosts the Web conference there. He lives in Northampton, Massachusetts, with his wife Kathleen.

Wesley J. Chun is author of Prentice Hall's bestseller, *Core Python Programming* (corepython.com), its video training course, *Python Fundamentals* (LiveLessons DVD), and coauthor of *Python Web Development with Django* (withdjango.com). In addition to being a senior software architect, he runs CyberWeb (cyberwebconsulting.com), a consulting business specializing in Python software engineering and technical training. He has more than 25 years of programming, teaching, and writing experience, including more than a decade of Python. While at Yahoo!, he helped create Yahoo! Mail and Yahoo! People Search using Python. He holds degrees in Computer Science, Mathematics, and Music from the University of California.

Introduction

If you're a Web developer, a programmer who creates Web sites, then Django just might change your life. It has certainly changed ours.

Anyone with even a little experience building dynamic Web sites knows the pain of reinventing certain standard features over and over. You need to create database schemas. You need to get data into and out of the database. You need to parse URLs. You need to sanitize input. You need to provide content-editing tools. You need to attend to security and usability. And so on.

Where Web Frameworks Come From

At some point you realize the wastefulness of reimplementing all these features on every new project; you decide to code your own libraries from scratch to provide them—or, more likely, you extract those libraries from your latest and greatest creation. Thereafter, when you start a new project, the first thing you do is install your library code. It saves you work and time.

However, there are still rough spots. Clients want features that aren't provided by your library code, so you add these. Different clients need different things, so you end up with different versions of your library installed on different servers. Maintenance becomes hell.

So then, seasoned with experience, you take your base library and all the best add-ons from your various projects and combine them. For most projects you no longer have to tweak your library code directly; you alter a configuration file instead. Your codebase is bigger and more complicated, but it's also more powerful.

Congratulations, you've written a Web framework.

And as long as you (or your team, or your company, or your clients) keep on using it, you're responsible for keeping it working. Will the next upgrade of your OS, your Web server, or your programming language break it? Will it be flexible enough to accommodate future changes without great pain? Does it support difficult but important features like session management, localization, and database transactions? And how's your test coverage?

A Better Way

You have this book in your hands because you want something better. You want a powerful, flexible, elegant, well-tested framework *you don't have to maintain yourself.*

You want to write your code in a real programming language; one that is powerful, clean, mature, and extensively documented. You want it to have a great standard library and a huge selection of high-quality third-party packages for whatever needs arise, from generating a CSV or a pie chart to scientific computations or image file processing.

You want a framework that has a vibrant, helpful community of users and developers; one that is designed to function smoothly as an integrated stack, but whose components are loosely coupled, so you can make substitutions if circumstances require.

In short, you want Python, and you want Django. We wrote this book to help you learn and use Django in real-world settings as easily, quickly, and smartly as possible.

We're Not in Kansas Anymore

Django was originally written by Adrian Holovaty and Simon Willison at World Online, the Web arm of a family-owned media company in Lawrence, Kansas. It was born out of a need to quickly develop database-driven applications tied into news content.

After proving itself in the field, Django was released as an open source project in July 2005—a time, ironically, when it was widely felt that Python had far *too many* Web frameworks—and rapidly gained a strong following. Today, it is one of the leaders not just among Python frameworks, but among Web frameworks in general.

Django is still heavily used at World Online of course, and some of its core developers work there and use it daily. But since Django's open source release, companies and organizations around the world have picked it up for use in projects large and small. A partial list includes

- The *Washington Post*
- The *Lawrence Journal-World*
- Google
- EveryBlock
- Newsvine
- Curse Gaming
- Tabblo
- Pownce

There are, of course, thousands of other Django sites that are not (yet) household names. It's inevitable that as Django spreads and grows that an increasing number of popular sites will be powered by it. We hope that yours is one of them.

Web Development Is Better with Python and Django

Web development is generally messy business. You have to contend with browser incompatibilities, rogue bots, bandwidth and server limitations, and an overall architecture that seems to defy thorough testing.

Of course, we believe our book is an excellent introduction to the basics of Django, but we also aim to address many of those messy spots—the 20 percent of your work that can take 80 percent of your time. We've worked with, listened to, and helped many developers using Django and have kept their questions and challenges in mind while writing this book.

If we didn't think that Django and Python were great, we wouldn't have gone to the trouble of writing a whole book about them. But when there are limitations you should know about or sharp edges you should watch out for, we'll tell you. Our goal is to help you get things done.

Getting Started

Practical Python for Django

Welcome to Django, and in this case, perhaps Python as well! Before jumping straight into Django, we give you an in-depth overview of the language that is the foundation of the Django applications you will develop. Programming experience with another high-level language (C/C++, Java, Perl, Ruby, and so forth) makes it easier to absorb the material in this chapter.

However, if you have never programmed before, Python itself is a great first language, and several books out there teach you how to program using Python. Those references are provided at the end of this chapter. We recommend those new to programming check out some of those resources; once you've gotten your feet wet, return here, and then you'll get more out of the following sections.

We introduce you to Python in this chapter, focusing on the core features of the language and specific skills related to Django development. To develop effectively in Django, not only do you need basic Python skills, but you need to know a bit more about how Python works under the covers so when you come across certain features, aspects, or requirements of Django, you won't be left high and dry. Those new to Python or to programming in general can benefit from reading other general Python material first or following such materials along with this chapter—whichever suits your learning style best.

Python Skills Are Django Skills

Django provides a high-level framework that enables you to build Web applications with relatively few lines of code. It is simple, robust, and flexible, allowing you to design solutions without much overhead. Django was built using Python, an object-oriented applications development language which combines the power of systems languages, such as C/C++ and Java, with the ease and rapid development of scripting languages, such as Ruby and Visual Basic. This gives its users the ability to create applications that solve many different types of problems.

In this chapter, we show you what we believe are some of the necessary Python skills you should have to be an effective Django developer. Rather than regurgitating a generic Python tutorial, we focus on those concepts of Python which are "must-haves" for the

Django developer. In fact, you find Django code scattered throughout the chapter.

> **Python 2.x Versus 3.x**
>
> At the time of this writing, Python is transitioning from the 2.x series to a new generation starting with version 3.0. The 3.x family does not guarantee backward-compatibility with older releases, so it's entirely possible code written for 2.x doesn't work under 3.x. However, the core Python development team is making the switch as painless as possible: There will be solid 2.x-to-3.x conversion tools available, and the switch itself is set to take enough time so nobody is left behind.
>
> The Django core team does not plan to switch to 3.0 right away—as with most large or framework-oriented projects, such a switch can be disruptive and must be taken with care— so we're only mentioning this transition in passing. Chances are good Django will only take the leap when the majority of the user-base (that's you!) is ready for it.

Getting Started: Python's Interactive Interpreter

The interactive interpreter is one of the most powerful tools used in everyday Python development, enabling you to test a few lines of code without needing to create, edit, save, and run a source file. Not only will a language shell such as Python's verify your code's correctness, but it also enables you to try out different things with new code, such as inspecting data structures or altering key values, prior to adding it to your source files.

While reading this chapter, we suggest you launch an interactive Python interpreter to try code snippets right away; most Python Integrated Development Environments (IDEs) make it easily accessible, and it can also be run on its own from the command line or your operating system's (OS) applications menu. By using it, you see an immediate impact and become more comfortable with Python and Django in a very short amount of time. Python veterans, such as your authors, still use the Python shell daily, even after a decade of Python programming experience!

Throughout this book, you see code snippets that are prefixed with the Python shell's interactive prompt: >>>. You can try these examples directly in your interpreter while reading the book. They look something like this:

```
>>> print 'Hello World!'
Hello World!
>>> 'Hello World!'
'Hello World!'
```

print is your friend. It not only provides relevant application information to your users, but also is an invaluable debugging tool. It's often possible to "print" the value of variables without explicitly calling print, as we just did, but note this often results in different output than when print is involved.

Notice the difference in our Hello World example. When you "dump the object" in the interactive interpreter, it shows the quotation marks that tell you it is a string. When using the `print` statement, it doesn't do that because you told it to display the *contents* of the string, which of course, does *not* include the quotes. This specific example is a subtle difference that applies only for strings—there's no difference for numbers.

```
>>> 10
10
>>> print 10
10
```

However, for complex objects, which we get to later, the difference can be quite pronounced—this is because Python gives you a lot of control over how objects behave when used with or without `print`.

Although we go over the details of variables and looping later on, the following is a quick taste of some slightly more complex Python, involving a couple of `for` loops.

```
>>> for word in ['capitalize', 'these', 'words']:
...     print word.upper()
...
CAPITALIZE
THESE
WORDS
>>> for i in range(0, 5):
...     print i
...
0
1
2
3
4
```

An important aspect of Python's syntax is the absence of curly braces ({ }) for delimiting blocks of code. Instead of braces, we use indentation: Within a given chunk of Python code, there must be distinct levels of indentation, typically four spaces per indent (although a different number of spaces, or tabs, can also be used). If you're used to other languages, this can take a bit of time to adjust to; however, after a short period, you realize it is not as bad as it seems.

A final note about the interpreter: Once you become familiar with using it, you should consider a similar tool called IPython. If you're already sold by the concept of an interactive interpreter, IPython is an order of more powerful magnitude! It provides numerous features such as system shell access, command-line numbering, automatic indentation, command history, and much more. You can find out more about IPython at http://ipython. scipy.org. It does not ship with Python, but it is available as a third-party download.

Using the Interpreter with Django

It can be handy to use Python's interactive interpreter to experiment with your Django application code or aspects of the framework itself. But if you just launch the interpreter normally and try to import your Django modules, you get an error about DJANGO_SETTINGS_MODULE

> not being set. As a convenience, Django provides the `manage.py shell` command, which performs the necessary environment setup to avoid this problem.
>
> `manage.py shell` uses iPython by default if you have it installed. If you do have iPython installed but want to use the standard Python interpreter, run `manage.py shell plain` instead. We continue to use the default interpreter in our examples, but highly recommend the use of iPython.

Python Basics

We introduce several basic aspects of Python in this section. We talk about comments, variables, operators, and basic Python types. The next few sections go into even more detail about the main Python types. Most Python (and Django) source code goes into text files that have a `.py` extension—that is the standard way of telling your system it is a Python file. You can also see files with related extensions such as `.pyc` or `.pyo`—these don't cause a problem on your system, and you see them, but you do not need to be distracted by them at this time.

Comments

Comments in Python are denoted with the pound or hash mark (#). When that is the first character of a line of code, the entire line is deemed a comment. The # can also appear in the middle of the line; this means from the point where it is found, the rest of the same line is a comment. For example:

```
# this entire line is a comment
foo = 1          # short comment: assign int 1 to 'foo'
print 'Python and %s are number %d' % ('Django', foo)
```

Comments are not only used to explain nearby code, but also to prevent what would otherwise be working code from executing. A good example of this is in configuration files like Django's `settings.py`—common options that are not absolutely necessary, or that have differing values than the default, are commented out, making it easy to re-enable them or to make configuration choices obvious.

Variables and Assignment

Python's variables do not need to be "declared" as holding a specific type of value, as in some languages. Python is a "dynamically typed" language. Variables can be thought of as names that refer to otherwise anonymous objects, which contain the actual values involved—and thus, any given variable can have its value altered at any time, like so

```
>>> foo = 'bar'
>>> foo
'bar'
>>> foo = 1
>>> foo
1
```

In this example, the variable foo is mapped to a string object, 'bar', but is then remapped to an integer object, 1. Note the string that foo used to refer to disappears, unless other variables are also referring to it (which is entirely possible!).

Because you can remap variable names like this, you are never really 100 percent sure what type of object a variable is pointing to at any given time, unless you ask the interpreter for more information. However, as long as a given variable behaves like a certain type (for example, if it has all the methods a string normally has), it can be considered to be of that type, even if it has extra attributes. This is referred to as "duck-typing"—if it waddles like a duck and quacks like a duck, then we can treat it as a duck.

Operators

As far as operators in general go, Python supports pretty much the same ones you're used to from other programming languages. These include arithmetic operators, such as +, -, and *, and so on, and this includes their corresponding *augmented assignment* operators, +=, -=, *=, and so forth. This just means instead of x = x + 1, you can use x += 1. Absent are the increment/decrement operators (++ and --) you may have used in other languages.

The standard comparison operators, such as <, >=, ==, !=, and so on, are also available, and you can group clauses together with Boolean AND and OR with and and or, respectively. There is also a not operator that negates the Boolean value of a comparison. The following is what an example grouping using and would look like:

```
show_output = True
if show_output and foo == 1:
    print 'Python and %s are number %d' % ('Django', foo)
```
Py 2

As far as Python syntax goes, you already know code blocks are delimited by indentation rather than curly braces. We previously mentioned it becomes fairly easy to identify where blocks of code belong, and to take it one step further, you realize it is *impossible* to have a "dangling-else" problem, simply because an else clearly belongs to one if or the other—there is no ambiguity.

On the same note, Python has an absence of symbols in general. Not only are there no delimiting braces, but no trailing semicolon (;) to end lines of code with, no dollar signs ($), and no required parentheses (( )) for conditional statements (such as the preceding if). You notice the occasional "at" (@) sign for decorators and an abundance of underscores (_), but that's really about it. The creator of Python believes less clutter means code is clearer and easier to read.

Python Standard Types

We now introduce you to the standard types you are working with as a Django programmer. They include scalars or literals (such as numbers and strings), or they are "containers," or data structures, used to group together multiple Python objects. Before we introduce you to the main data types, it is worth first noting all Python objects have some inherent Boolean value.

Object Boolean Values

Like most other languages, exactly two Boolean values can be expressed: `True and False`. All Python values can be represented as a Boolean value, regardless of their data values. For example, any numeric type equal to zero is considered `False` while all nonzero numeric values are `True`. Similarly, empty containers are `False` while nonempty containers are `True`.

You can use the `bool` function to determine the Boolean value of any Python object; furthermore, `True` and `False` are legitimate values of their own and can be explicitly assigned as a variable's value.

```
>>> download_complete = False
>>> bool(download_complete)
False
>>> bool(-1.23)
True
>>> bool(0.0)
False
>>> bool("")
False
>>> bool([None, 0])
True
```

The previous examples and the output of `bool` should all make sense. The final example can be a bit trickier: Although both list elements have `False` values, a nonempty list has a `True` value. The "truthfulness" of Python objects comes into play when you use them in *conditionals* such as `if` and `while` statements where the path of execution depends on the Boolean value of those objects.

You should also note in the final example, the value `None`. That is Python's special value which is equivalent to `NULL` or `void` values found in other languages. `None` always evaluates to `False` when treated as a boolean.

Booleans are literals just like numbers are; speaking of numbers, they're our next topic.

Numbers

Python has two primary numeric types: `int` (for integer) and `float` (for floating point number). In following its mantra of keeping it simple, Python has only one integer type, `int`, as opposed to many other languages that have multiple integer types.[1] In addition to normal base-10 notation, integers can be represented in hexadecimal (base 16) and octal (base 8). `float`s are double-precision floating-point real numbers you should be familiar

---

[1] Python used to have another integer type called `long`, but its functionality has been merged into today's `int`. You can still see a trailing `'L'` representing long integers in various bits of old code and documentation though. It looks like this: `1L`, `-42L`, `99999999999999999L`, and so on.

with from other languages. The following are some examples of ints and floats as well as some interactive interpreter operators using them:

```
>>> 1.25 + 2.5
3.75
>>> -9 - 4
-13
>>> 1.1
1.1000000000000001
```

Whoops, what's going on with the last example? floats have a large range; however, they are not very accurate in terms of representing rational numbers with a repeating fraction. Because of this, there is another floating point type called Decimal—which is not a built-in type and must be accessed via the decimal module—with a smaller value range, but better accuracy. Python also features a built-in complex number type for scientific calculations.

Table 1.1 summarizes these numeric types as well as gives a few more examples.

Table 1.1   **Python Built-in Numeric Types**

Type	Description	Examples
int	Signed Integers (no size limit)	-1, 0, 0xE8C6, 0377, 42
float	Double-precision Floating-Point Numbers	1.25, 4.3e+2, -5., -9.3e, 0.375
complex	Complex (Real+Imaginary) Numbers	2+2j, .3-j, -10.3e+5-60j

Numeric Operators

Numbers support the basic arithmetic operations you are familiar with from other languages: addition (+), subtraction (-), multiplication (*), division (/ and //), modulus (%), and exponentiation (**).

The division operator / represents "classic division," meaning truncation when both operands are integers (floor division) but "true division" for floats. Python also features an explicit "floor division" operator that always returns an integer result regardless of its operand types:

```
>>> 1 / 2          # floor division (int operands)
0
>>> 1.0 / 2.0      # true division (float operands)
0.5
>>> 1 // 2         # floor division (// operator)
0
>>> 1.0 // 2.0     # floor division (// operator)
0.0
```

Finally, Python integers have bitwise operators for binary AND (&), OR (|), XOR (^), bit inversion (~), and left and right shift (<< and >>), as well as their augmented assignment equivalents, such as, &=, <<=, and so forth.

Numeric Built-in and Factory Functions

Each of the numeric types has a *factory* function that enables users to convert from one numeric type to another. Some readers say "conversion" and "casting," but we don't use those terms in Python because you are not *changing* the type of an existing object. You are returning a new object based on the original (hence the term "factory"). It is as simple as telling int(12.34) to create a new integer object with value 12 (with the expected fraction truncation) while float(12) returns 12.0. Finally, we have complex and bool.

Python also features a handful of operational *built-in* functions that apply to numbers, such as round to round floats to a specified number of digits or abs for the absolute value of a number. The following are a few examples of these and other built-ins:

```
>>> int('123')
123
>>> int(45.67)
45
>>> round(1.15, 1)
1.2
>>> float(10)
10.0
>>> divmod(15, 6)
(2, 3)
>>> ord('a')
97
>>> chr(65)
'A'
```

For more information on the previous number-related functions and others, see the Numbers chapter in *Core Python Programming* (Prentice Hall, 2006), check out any of the pure reference books, or search Python documentation online. Now let's look at strings and Python's key container types.

Sequences and Iterables

Many programming languages feature arrays as data structures, which are typically of fixed size, and tie together a group of like objects, accessible sequentially by index. Python's sequence types serve the same purpose, but can contain objects of differing types and can grow and shrink in size. In this section, we discuss two very popular Python types: **lists** ([1,2,3]) and **strings** ('python'). They are part of a broader set of data structures called **sequences**.

Sequences are one example of a Python type that is an **iterable**: a data structure you can "traverse" or "iterate," one element at a time. The basic idea behind an iterable is you can continually ask it for the next object via a next method, and it continues to "read off" its internal collection of objects until it's exhausted. Python sequences are not only itera-tors in this way (although 99 percent of the time you are using `for` loops instead of the `next` method), but also support random access—the capability to ask for the object at a specific spot in the sequence. For example, use `my_list[2]` to retrieve the third item in a list (given indexes begin at 0).

There is a third sequence type called **tuples**. They can most easily be described as "handicapped read-only lists" because they don't seem like more than that—they serve a very different purpose. They are not going to be your first choice as an application data structure, but we do need to tell you what they are and what they're used for. Because you probably already know what a string is, we'll start with lists first and cover tuples last. Table 1.2 itemizes each sequence type we discuss and gives some examples.

Table 1.2   **Examples of Sequence Types**

Type	Examples
str	`'django'`, `'\n'`, `""`, `"%s is number %d" % ('Python', 1)`, `"""hey there"""`
list	`[123, 'foo', 3.14159]`, `[]`, `[x.upper() for x in words]`
tuple	`(456, 2.71828)`, `()`, `('need a comma even with just 1 item',)`

Sequence Slicing

A minute ago, we mentioned the capability to directly index a sequence; the following are some examples of this operating on a string. Unlike many other languages, Python's strings can be treated both as discrete objects and as if they were lists of individual characters.

```
>>> s = 'Python'
>>> s[0]
'P'
>>> s[4]
'o'
>>> s[-1]
'n'
```

Python also offers the flexibility of negative indices. How many of you have ever coded something like `data[len(data)-1]` or `data[data.length-1]` to get the last element of some sort of array? As in the final example of the preceding snippet, a simple -1 suffices.

You are also able to index multiple elements of a sequence at once, called **slicing** in Python. Slicing is represented by a pair of indices, say *i* and *j*, delimited by a single colon (`:`). When a slice of a sequence is requested, the interpreter takes the subset of elements beginning at the first index *i* and goes up to but not including the second index *j*.

```
>>> s = 'Python'
>>> s[1:4]
'yth'
```

```
>>> s[2:4]
'th'
>>> s[:4]
'Pyth'
>>> s[3:]
'hon'
>>> s[3:-1]
'ho'
>>> s[:]
'Python'
>>> str(s)
'Python'
```

The absence of an index means either from the beginning or through to the end, depending on which index is missing. An **improper slice** (meaning to return a copy[2] of the entire sequence) can be designated with [:]. Finally, please note although all our previous examples feature strings, the slicing syntax is applicable to lists and all other sequence types.

Other Sequence Operators

We saw the slicing operation in the previous section using the [] and [:] operators. Other operations you can perform on sequences include concatenation (+), repetition/duplication (*), and membership (in) or nonmembership (not in). As before, we'll use strings in our examples, but these operations apply to other sequences as well.

```
>>> 'Python and' + 'Django are cool!'
'Python andDjango are cool!'
>>> 'Python and' + ' ' + 'Django are cool!'
'Python and Django are cool!'
>>> '-' * 40
'----------------------------------------'
>>> 'an' in 'Django'
True
>>> 'xyz' not in 'Django'
True
```

> ## Alternatives to Concatenation
>
> One caveat is we recommend avoiding the use of the + operator with sequences. When you're new to the language, it does solve the problem of putting a pair of strings together; however, it's not a solution that provides the best performance. (The details on why would involve explanation of Python's C underpinnings, which we don't go into here—you just have to trust us.)

---

[2] When we say "copy," we mean a copy of the references and not of the objects themselves. This is more correctly described as a **shallow copy**. See the following section on mutability for more information on copying objects.

For example, with strings, instead of `'foo'+'bar'`, you can use the string format operator (%) discussed in the following strings section, as in `'%s%s' % ('foo', 'bar')`. Another way of putting strings together, especially given a list of strings to merge together, is the string `join` method, such as, `''.join(['foo', 'bar'])`. For lists, there is the `extend` method, which adds the contents of another list to the current (as opposed to `list1 += list2`)—yes, `list1.extend(list2)` is better.

Lists

The Python type that acts most like other languages' arrays is the list. Lists are mutable, resizable sequences that can hold any data type. Next we present an example of how to create a list and what you can do with it.

```
>>> book = ['Python', 'Development', 8]        # 1) create list
>>> book.append(2008)                          # 2) append obj
>>> book.insert(1, 'Web')                      # 3) insert obj
>>> book
['Python', 'Web', 'Development', 8, 2008]
>>> book[:3]                                    # 4) first three slice
['Python', 'Web', 'Development']
>>> 'Django' in book                            # 5) is obj in list?
False
>>> book.remove(8)                              # 6) remove obj explicitly
>>> book.pop(-1)                                # 7) remove obj by index
2008
>>> book
['Python', 'Web', 'Development']
>>> book * 2                                    # 8) repetition/duplication
['Python', 'Web', 'Development', 'Python', 'Web', 'Development']
>>> book.extend(['with', 'Django'])            # 9) merge list into current one
>>> book
['Python', 'Web', 'Development', 'with', 'Django']
```

What happened in the previous example? The rundown:

1. Create list initially with a pair of strings and an integer.

2. Add another int to the end of the list.

3. Insert a string into the second position (at index 1).

4. Pull out a slice of the first three elements.

5. Membership check. (Is an item in the list?)

6. Remove an item regardless of its location in the list.

7. Remove (and return) an item by its location (index).

8. Demonstrate the repetition/duplication operator *.

9. Extend this list with another one.

As you can see, lists are very flexible objects. Let's discuss their methods further.

List Methods

Let's reset the list back to what we had in the middle of the previous set of examples. We then sort the list but with some follow-up discussion afterward.

```
>>> book = ['Python', 'Web', 'Development', 8, 2008]
>>> book.sort()          # NOTE: in-place sort... no return value!
>>> book
[8, 2008, 'Development', 'Python', 'Web']
```

A "sort" on mixed types is really something that is undefined. How can you compare objects (for example strings versus numbers) that have no relationship? The algorithm Python uses is a "best guess" as to what is the "right thing to do": Sort all the numeric values first (smallest to largest) followed by a lexicographic sort of the strings. This example can make a bit of sense, but if you start throwing files and class instances in there, it becomes more undefined.

List built-in methods such as sort, append, and insert modify the object directly and do not have a return value. Newcomers to Python can find it strange that sort does not return a sorted copy of the list, so beware. In contrast, the string method upper we saw earlier returned a string (consisting of a copy of the original string but in all UPPER-CASE). This is because unlike lists, strings are *not* mutable, thus the reason why upper returned a (modified) copy. See the following for more on mutability.

Of course, it's often desirable to obtain a sorted copy of a given list instead of sorting in-place; Python 2.4 and up provide the built-in functions sorted and reversed, which take a list as an argument and returns a sorted or reversed copy.

List Comprehensions

A **list comprehension** is a construct (borrowed from another programming language called Haskell) consisting of logic that builds a list containing the values/objects generated by the logic. For example, let's say we have a list containing the integers 0 through 9. What if we wanted to increment each number and get all the results back in a list? With list comprehensions (or "listcomps" for short), we can do just that.

```
>>> data = [x + 1 for x in range(10)]
>>> data
[1, 2, 3, 4, 5, 6, 7, 8, 9, 10]
```

Listcomps, like lists, use the square bracket notation and a shortened version of Python's for loop. Even though we haven't formally covered loops yet—we'll get to them soon—you can see how easy a listcomp is to read. The first part is an expression generating the resulting list items with the second being a loop over an input expression (which must evaluate to a sequence).

The recommended way of "reading listcomps" is to start from the inner `for` loop, glance to the right for any `if` conditional next to it—our first example did not have one of these—and then map the expression at the beginning of the listcomp to each matching element. See if you can read this one.

```
>>> even_numbers = [x for x in range(10) if x % 2 == 0]
>>> even_numbers
[0, 2, 4, 6, 8]
```

This second example demonstrates the use of an additional filtering `if` clause at the end. It also omits any actual modifying logic—x by itself is a perfectly valid expression (evaluating, of course, to the value of x) and is useful for using list comprehensions to filter sequences.

Generator Expressions

Python also features a construct similar to list comprehensions, called a **generator expression**. It works in nearly the same way as a list comprehension, except it performs what is called "lazy evaluation." Rather than processing and building an entire data structure with all the resulting objects, it performs the work on a single object at a time, thus potentially saving a lot of memory (although sometimes taking a speed hit instead).

In our last example, we used a listcomp to identify even numbers out of a list of ten—but what if our list of numbers was ten thousand or ten million? What if the list contents were not simple integers, but complex or large data structures? In such cases, generator expressions' memory-saving behavior can save the day. We can tweak the syntax of a listcomp to make it a "genexp" by replacing the square brackets with parentheses.

```
>>> even_numbers = (x for x in range(10000) if x % 2 == 0)
>>> even_numbers
<generator object at 0x ...>
```

Generator expressions are new as of Python 2.4, so if you're stuck with Python 2.3 they won't be available, and they're still gaining steam in the collective consciousness of Python programmers. However, for any case where your input sequence has a chance of becoming nontrivial in size, it's smart to form a habit of using generator expressions instead of list comprehensions.

Strings

Another Python sequence type is the string, which you can think of as an array of characters, although they are specified with single- or double-quotes (`'this is a string'` or `"this is a string"`). Also unlike lists, strings are not mutable or resizable. The act of resizing or modifying strings actually creates a new, altered one from the original. However, this act is generally transparent in normal usage, and only becomes important when dealing with memory issues and similar problems.

Like lists, strings also have methods, but again, because strings are immutable, none of them modify the existing string, instead returning a modified copy. At the time of this writing, strings had no less than *37* methods! We focus only on the ones you're more likely to use with Django. Next are some examples.

```
>>> s = 'Django is cool'               # 1
>>> words = s.split()                  # 2
>>> words
['Django', 'is', 'cool']
>>> ' '.join(words)                    # 3
'Django is cool'
>>> '::'.join(words)                   # 4
'Django::is::cool'
>>> ''.join(words)                     # 5
'Djangoiscool'
>>> s.upper()                          # 6
'DJANGO IS COOL'
>>> s.upper().isupper()                # 7
True
>>> s.title()                          # 8
'Django Is Cool'
>>> s.capitalize()                     # 9
'Django is cool'
>>> s.count('o')                       # 10
3
>>> s.find('go')                       # 11
4
>>> s.find('xxx')                      # 11
-1
>>> s.startswith('Python')             # 12
False
>>> s.replace('Django', 'Python')      # 13
'Python is cool'
```

The following is a summary of what went on in the previous examples:

1. Create initial string.

2. Split up string delimited by any whitespace into a list of substrings.

3. Inverse of #2. (Join a list of substrings into a single string delimited with a space.)

4. Same as #3 but delimited by a pair of semicolons.

5. Same as #3 but with no delimiter (merges all substrings together).

6. Create (and discard) new string that is an all-CAPS version of original [also see `lower`].

7. Demonstrate chaining calls to confirm a string made of all CAPS [also see `islower`, and others].

8. Convert string to being title-cased. Capitalize first letter of each word; the rest in lowercase.

9. Capitalize only first word; the rest in lowercase.

10. Count the number of times substring `'o'` appears in string.

11. Index where substring `'go'` is found in string (at index 4) [also see `index`].

12. Same as #10 but when no match is found, returns `-1`.

13. Check to see if a string starts with given substring; it doesn't [also see `endswith`].

14. Simple search and replace.

Similar to `split`, there is `splitlines`, which looks specifically for end-of-line characters (instead of just whitespace). If you have a string containing these characters, such as when you're reading lines in from a file, you can use `rstrip` to remove all trailing whitespace characters (or even `strip`, which deletes both leading *and* trailing whitespace).

Another example, #7, shows how we can chain methods together, as long as you are fully aware of what object is coming back as a result of the first method call. Because we know `upper` returns a string, there's nothing wrong with immediately calling another string method on the new string. In our case, we call the `isupper` method, which is a Boolean indicating whether (or not) a string is comprised of all CAPS. For example, if the object returned instead was a list, then you could call a list method.

Aside from `isupper`, many other string methods start with `is-.`, such as, `isalnum`, `isalpha`, and so forth. Table 1.3 summarizes the methods presented in this section. There are plenty of others, as you can surmise, so we refer you to your favorite Python text to find out about all the other string methods available.

Table 1.3 **Popular Python String Methods**

String Method	Description
count	Number of occurrences of substring in string
find	Search for substring [also see `index`, `rfind`, `rindex`]
join	Merge substrings into single delimited string
replace	Search and replace (sub)string
split	Split delimited string into substrings [also see `splitlines`]
startswith	Does string start with substring [also see `endswith`]
strip	Remove leading and trailing whitespace [also see `rstrip`, `lstrip`]
title	Title-case string [also see `capitalize`, `swapcase`]
upper	UPPERCASE string [also see `lower`]
isupper	Is string all UPPERCASE? [also see `islower`, and so forth]

String Designators

Python strings enable annotations placed before the opening quote: r for raw strings and u for Unicode strings. These designators are used both when writing code and displaying the value of strings in the interpreter.

```
>>> mystring = u'This is Unicode!'
>>> mystring
u'This is Unicode!'
```

However, the act of print-ing or converting raw or Unicode strings does not print the designator:

```
>>> mystring = u'This is Unicode!'
>>> print mystring
This is Unicode!
>>> str(mystring)
'This is Unicode!'
```

The "raw" designator tells the interpreter not to transform any special characters inside the string. For example, the special string character \n typically stands for a newline, but there can be times where you *don't* want such a transformation, such as in a DOS file-name: filename = r'C:\temp\newfolder\robots.txt'.

Another use-case for raw strings is regular expressions, due to their heavy use of otherwise special characters such as the backslash (\). In the regular expressions section, we feature a raw string regular expression, r'\w+@\w+\.\w+', which is easier to read than the normal (and thus escaped) string, '\\w+@\\w+\\.\\w+'.

Raw Strings in Django

Raw strings are often seen in Python code wherever regular expressions are used. In the case of Django, that's in your URL configuration rules, where Django dispatches control to various parts of your application based on matching the requested URL against regular expression rules you provide. Using raw strings for these rules keeps their representation a little cleaner, and for consistency, it is typically used for all regular expression strings, regard-less of whether they contain a backslash.

Because normal Python strings are typically in a limited character set—one including a Western alphabet plus a few special characters—they're not capable of displaying the wide range of characters used in non-English languages. Unicode is a newer string encoding with extremely wide support that lacks this limitation. Django has (as of this writing) fairly recently taken steps to ensure every part of the framework is Unicode-capable. As such, you see a number of Unicode string objects when developing with Django.

String Format Operator and Triple Quotes

You've seen the string format operator (%) in previous examples in this chapter; it's used to prepare different input types for printing in a string via the use of a *format string*, which contains special directives. Here's another example to refresh your memory.

```
>>> '%s is number %d' % (s[:6], 1)
'Django is number 1'
>>> hi = '''hi
there'''
>>> hi
'hi\nthere'
>>> print hi
hi
there
```

In the previous example, we had a string (whose format-string directive is `%s`) and an integer (`%d`). The format operator joins this format string on the left with a tuple (not a list) of arguments on the right; the arguments must match one-to-one with the directives. We refer you to your favorite Python reference for all the other format directives you have access to.

The use of triple quotes, also featured in the previous example, is a feature unique to Python. It enables you to embed special characters inside your string that are taken verbatim. If you have a long string that you have to generate, you no longer have to worry about slipping end-of-line characters, such as \\n or \\r\\n, into all your strings to make them wrap; instead, you can simply use triple quotes, such as in this XML snippet.

```
xml = '''
<?xml version="1.0"?>
<Request version="%.1f">
    <Header>
        <APIName>PWDDapp</APIName>
        <APIPassword>youllneverguess</APIPassword>
    </Header>
    <Data>
        <Payload>%s</Payload>
        <Timestamp>%s</Timestamp>
    </Data>
</Request>
'''
```

Finally, note the previous example uses formatting directives, but lacks the string format operator and matching tuple. This is because the string format operator is just that—an operator—and so it's possible to define a format string in one part of your code, and fill it out with the operator and tuple of arguments later on.

```
import time          # use time.ctime() for timestamp
VERSION = 1.2        # set application version number

# [...]

def sendXML(data):   # define some sendXML() function
    'sendXML() - transmit XML data'

# [...]
```

```
payload = 'super top-secret information'
sendXML(xml % (VERSION, payload, time.ctime()))
```

Tuples

Tuples (pronounced either "TOO-ples" or "TUP-ples") are a close cousin to lists as we've been discussing on the side in the last several sections. The one obvious difference is lists use square brackets and tuples uses parentheses, but beyond that, you have to consider Python's object model again. Although lists enable their values to be changed and have methods that do so, tuples are immutable, meaning you cannot change their values—and, partly because of this, they do not have methods.

On first glance, new Python programmers can wonder why it is a separate data type; in other words, why not just have a "read-only" list? On the surface, you may have an argument; however, tuples serve a more useful purpose than merely being "read-only" lists. Their main purpose is to get parameters to and from functions (actually function calls) and protecting their contents from being modified by foreign interfaces.

This doesn't mean they're not useful to the programmer—far from it. They just aren't used as much on the main stage, but instead are there for more of the behind-the-scenes action. You see a lot of tuples in Django configuration files, for example. Although they do not have methods, they still work with the general sequence operators and built-in functions.

Tuple-Related Gotchas in Django

You see tuples frequently in a typical Django application. For relative newcomers to Python, they tend to be the trickiest sequence type—in particular, the single-item tuple with its *required* trailing comma. See if you understand what's happening in the following examples:

```
>>> a = ("one", "two")
>>> a[0]
'one'
>>> b = ("just-one")
>>> b[0]
'j'
>>> c = ("just-one",)
>>> c[0]
'just-one'
>>> d = "just-one",
>>> d[0]
'just-one'
```

What went wrong in the second example? Remember, it's the commas, not the parentheses, that make a tuple. So b was really just a string, and b[0] gave us the first character of that string as we saw previously. The trailing comma inside the parentheses in the assignment to c gives us a tuple, and so c[0] yields the value we expect. We can even leave off the parentheses entirely, as in the previous assignment to d—but it's generally better not to. A core tenet of Python is being explicit is better than relying on implicit behavior.

Many Django config values are specified as tuples—admin options, URLconf rules, and many settings in settings.py. Some parts of Django are better than others at telling you what's wrong. If you set an admin option to be a string when it's supposed to be a tuple, you can get a helpful message such as "admin.list_display", if given, must be set to a list or tuple. On the other hand, if your ADMINS or MANAGERS setting is missing its trailing comma, you can find your server tries to e-mail error notices to every letter in your first name! Because this is a common issue for new Django developers, we rehash this issue later in the "Common Gotchas" section.

Sequence Built-ins and Factory Functions

Like numbers, all sequence types have a special factory function that creates an instance of the type requested: list, tuple, and str. There is also a unicode for Unicode strings. Usually str is responsible for providing a human-friendly or *printable* string representation of an object. There is another function in Python called repr that is similar but produces an *evaluatable* string representation of an object. What this typically means is that it is the pure representation of a Python object as a string, and it should be possible to run the eval statement on that string to turn it into the object in question.

The len built-in function tells you how many elements a sequence has. max and min return the "largest" and "smallest" object in a sequence, respectively. any and all make up another pair that tells you whether any or all elements of a sequence evaluate to True.

You've already seen how range helps a Python for loop gain some of the counting skills that its cousins from other languages do natively while Python's is more iterator-style. However, a built-in function called enumerate combines the two styles together; it returns a special iterator that emits both the traversed sequence's index as well as its corresponding item at that index.

We present all these common sequence functions in Table 1.4.

Table 1.4 **Sequence Built-in and Factory Functions**

Function	Description[3]
str	(Printable) string representation [also see repr, unicode]
list	List representation
tuple	Tuple representation

[3] Although many of the function descriptions state "sequence," it is likely such functions are applicable across all *iterables*, meaning any sequence-like data structure you can iterate over, such as, sequences, iterators, generators, keys of a dictionary, lines of a file, and so forth.

Table 1.4   **Sequence Built-in and Factory Functions**

Function	Description[3]
`len`	Object cardinality
`max`	"Largest" object in sequence [also see `min`]
`range`	Iterable of numbers in given range [also see `enumerate`, `xrange`]
`sorted`	Sorted list of sequence members [also see `reversed`]
`sum`	Sum (numerical) sequence values
`any`	Is any sequence element `True`? [also see `all`]
`zip`	Iterator of N-tuples for each corresponding element of N sequences

Mapping Type: Dictionaries

Dictionaries are Python's sole mapping type. They are mutable, unordered, resizable mappings of keys to values, and are sometimes alternatively called hash tables ("hashes") or associative arrays. The syntax is otherwise similar to sequences, but instead of an index to access the value, you use a key, and rather than square brackets (lists) or parentheses (tuples), they are defined with curly braces ({ }).

Dictionaries are by far the most important data structure in the language. They are the secret sauce for most of Python's objects. Regardless of what types of objects they are or how you use them, there's a high likelihood that under the covers, there's a dictionary managing that object's attributes. Without further ado, let's take a look at what they are and what they can do.

Dictionary Operations, Methods, and Mapping Functions

The following are some examples of how to use a dictionary. We discuss what happens in this code as well as describe the operators, methods, or functions used.

```
>>> book = { 'title': 'Python Web Development', 'year': 2008 }
>>> book
{'year': 2008, 'title': 'Python Web Development'}
>>> 'year' in book
True
>>> 'pub' in book
False
>>> book.get('pub', 'N/A')          # where book['pub'] would get an error
'N/A'
>>> book['pub'] = 'Addison Wesley'
>>> book.get('pub', 'N/A')          # no error for book['pub'] now
'Addison Wesley'
>>> for key in book:
...     print key, ':', book[key]
...
year : 2008
```

```
pub : Addison Wesley
title : Python Web Development
```

So what did we do? Here's a summary:

1. Create initial dictionary with a string and an integer; both keys are strings.

2. Dump out the object.

3. Check to see if the dictionary has a particular key (twice; once yes, once no).

4. Use the `get` method to fetch a value using the given key (gets default here).

5. Assign a new key-value pair.

6. Perform the same `get` call but with success this time.

7. Iterate through the dictionary and display each key-value pair.

Let's take things slightly out-of-turn. In the final code segment, we used a `for` loop to iterate through a dictionary's keys. This is the typical way of doing it. You can also confirm what we said previously; the dictionary keys are *not* ordered (if we cared about order, we'd be using a sequence!), and it is this (lack of) ordering of keys that enables hashes to be very quick in the lookup of values.

Backtracking to Step 4, if the key passed to `get` doesn't exist in the dict, it returns the second argument (or `None` if you don't specify such a default). Alternately, you can use square-bracket notation, similar to retrieving a single element of a sequence, `d['pub']`. The difference in this case is that `'pub'` was not yet a member of the dictionary, so `d['pub']` would have resulted in an error. The `get` method is safer as it always returns a value instead of raising an error.

There's another, even more powerful method called `setdefault`. It does the same thing as `get`, but if you provide a default and the key doesn't exist yet, it creates the key with that default value so that "`dict.get(key)`" or `dict[key]` is valid afterward.

```
>>> d = { 'title': 'Python Web Development', 'year': 2008 }
>>> d.setdefault('pub', 'Addison Wesley')
'Addison Wesley'
>>> d
{'year': 2008, 'pub': 'Addison Wesley', 'title': 'Python Web Development'}
```

Now, those of you who already know what hashes are should be familiar with the term *key collision*. That is where you try to save a different value using a key that is already in the table. Python does not enable such a collision, so you assign another object to the dictionary with a key that's already there; then it overwrites the previous value. We also demonstrate how to remove a key-value pair using the `del` keyword to get the dictionary back to the way we had it in the beginning:

```
>>> del d['pub']
>>> d['title'] = 'Python Web Development with Django'
>>> d
{'year': 2008, 'title': 'Python Web Development with Django'}
```

```
>>> len(d)
2
```

The first line uses the `del` command to get rid of a key-value pair. We then save a different string using an existing key, `title`, to replace the value that was previously there. Finally, we use the generic `len` built-in function to tell us how many key-value pairs are in our dictionary. Table 1.5 summarizes some common dictionary methods.

Table 1.5   **Popular Python Dictionary Methods**

Dictionary Method	Description
keys	Keys (also see `iterkeys`)
values	Values (also see `itervalues`)
items	Key-value pairs (also see `iteritems`)
get	Get value given key else default [also see `setdefault`, `fromkeys`]
pop	Remove key from dict and return value [also see `clear`, `popitem`]
update	Update dict with contents of (an)other dict

"Dictionary-like" Data Types in Django

The dictionary (or "dict") is a Python standby, so naturally it's used many places in Django. However, some of the places where we want the key-value behavior of a dict also require other things a dict doesn't provide. The most prominent example is the `QueryDict` object that holds `GET` and `POST` parameters in `HttpRequest` objects. Because it's legal to submit more than one value for a given parameter (dictionary key) and a normal Python dict can't do that, a special structure is needed. If you have an application that takes advantage of this somewhat obscure feature of HTTP requests, see the official Django documentation on Request and Response Objects.

Standard Type Summary

You find that of all these standard data types, lists and dictionaries ("dicts") are the most highly used data structures for your application. Tuples and dicts are primarily used for exchanging parameters and return values to/from function calls; strings and numbers are used as needed. Python has plenty more data types for you to use, but we have highlighted the ones you use most frequently when writing Django applications.

Flow Control

Now that you know the basics of Python's variables, we need to explore how to do more than just assign values to them. Data, in the form of variables, doesn't mean much unless you can apply logic to it in the form of conditionals (taking different "paths" in the code depending on certain conditions) and loops (repeating a chunk of code a number of times, usually based on a list or tuple of some kind).

Conditionals

Like other languages, Python features `if` and `else` statements. Python's "else-if" is actually spelled `elif`, just like in the Bourne family of shell script languages (`sh`, `ksh`, and `bash`). It's so simple in Python we feel a single example conveys to you how they work.

```
data = raw_input("Enter 'y' or 'n': ")
if data[0] == 'y':
    print "You typed 'y'."
elif data[0] == 'n':
    print "You typed 'n'."
else:
    print 'Invalid key entered!'
```

Loops

Like other high-level languages, Python has a `while` loop. `while` continues to execute the same body of code until the conditional statement is no longer `True`:

```
>>> i = 0
>>> while i < 5:
...     print i
...     i += 1
...
0
1
2
3
4
```

But to be quite honest, you don't need to use the `while` loop very much as Python's most powerful looping mechanism is `for`. A `for` loop in other languages serves only as a counting loop, much like its companion `while`. However, Python's `for` is much more like a shell scripting `foreach` loop and fits in with the language's emphasis on letting you solve the problem at hand instead of babysitting counter variables and so forth.

```
for line in open('/tmp/some_file.txt'):
    if 'error' in line:
        print line
```

Of course, if you recall list comprehensions, you realize this could be turned into one. Many simple loops work as well (or better!) as list comprehensions; however, there are still times when even a simple `for` loop is still preferable, such as during debugging when you can't use a `print` statement in a listcomp. Figuring out where to use list comprehensions and where to use `for` loops is a skill that comes with time.

For example, `enumerate` is a built-in function enabling you to iterate and count at the same time (because the latter isn't possible with `for` by itself), as shown here:

```
>>> data = (123, 'abc', 3.14)
>>> for i, value in enumerate(data):
...   print i, value
...
0 123
1 abc
2 3.14
```

Using enumerate in Django Models

A handy place to use enumerate when writing Django code is in your model definitions, specifically for fields utilizing the choices keyword argument—see Chapter 4, "Defining and Using Models," for details on that particular model field argument. Such a use can look like this:

```
STATUS_CHOICES = enumerate(("solid", "squishy", "liquid"))

class IceCream(models.Model):
    flavor = models.CharField(max_length=50)
    status = models.IntegerField(choices=STATUS_CHOICES)
```

In the database, your ice cream status values are stored as integers (0, 1, 2), but in the Django admin interface, the textual labels are displayed. This is an efficient use of database storage (if that matters to you) and also a nice convenience in cases like this where alphanumeric sorting can't produce the desired order.

Exception Handling

Like other modern-day languages such as C++ and Java, Python offers exception handling. As we saw in the first example at the beginning of this chapter, it gives the programmer the ability to detect errors at runtime, opening the door to taking some action and/or use recovery step(s) to continue execution. Python's try-except looks similar to the try-catch blocks found in other languages.

What happens is that during runtime, if an exception occurs, the interpreter looks for a handler for it. If it cannot find one in the current function, it propagates the exception upward to the calling function to see if there's a handler *there* and so on. If we are at the topmost level (global "main," unindented code) and no handler is found, this is when the interpreter exits, dumping a traceback for the user to figure out what went wrong.

One thing to keep in mind is that although most errors result in exceptions, an exception doesn't necessarily mean an error has occurred. Sometimes they are only meant as warnings, and other times they can act as signals to functions higher up the call stack, such as signaling the end of an iteration loop.

Exception handling can range from a single, specific case up to a series of different blocks handling multiple different exception types. Reprising our earlier example, you can see here we have one handler (the code in the except block):

```
# attempt to open file, return on error
try:
    f = open(filename, 'r')
```

```
except IOError, e:
    return False, str(e)
```

You can also have the same handler take care of more than one exception type—just put them inside a tuple.

```
try:
    process_some_data()
except (TypeError, ValueError), e:
    print "ERROR: you provide invalid data", e
```

Our example handles two exceptions, and you can place more inside that tuple.

It is also possible to create multiple handlers for multiple exceptions.

```
try:
    process_some_data()
except (TypeError, ValueError), e:
    print "ERROR: you provide invalid data", e
except ArithmeticError, e:
    print "ERROR: some math error occurred", e
except Exception, e:
    print "ERROR: you provide invalid data", e
```

The final `except` takes advantage of the fact that `Exception` is the root class for (almost) all exceptions, so if a thrown exception wasn't caught by one of the earlier handlers, it would be taken care of in that last statement.

The `finally` Clause

Python also features a `try-finally` statement. We are not as focused on catching errors as we are in executing code that *must* run, regardless of whether an exception has occurred or not, as in the closing of files, releasing of a lock, throwing a database connection back into the pool, and so forth. For example:

```
try:
    get_mutex()
    do_some_stuff()
finally:
    free_mutex()
```

When no exception has been raised, the code in the `finally` suite is executed right after the `try` block has completed. If an error does happen, then the `finally` block still executes, but does not suppress the exception, which continues to bubble up the call chain looking for a handler.

As of Python 2.5, `try-finally` can be used alongside `except`. (This tactic does not work in previous versions.)

```
try:
    get_mutex()
    do_some_stuff()
```

```
except (IndexError, KeyError, AttributeError), e:
    log("ERORR: data retrieval accessing a non-existent element")
finally:
    free_mutex()
```

Throwing Exceptions with `raise`

So far, we've only discussed catching of exceptions; how do you throw them? You use the `raise` statement. Let's assume you created an API call that requires those writing against your library to send in a positive integer greater than 0. With the help of the `isinstance` built-in function that verifies the type of an object, your code can look something like this:

```
def foo(must_be_positive_int):
    """foo() -- take positive integer and process it"""

    # check if integer
    if not isinstance(must_be_positive_int, int):
        raise TypeError("ERROR foo(): must pass in an integer!")

    # check if positive
    if must_be_positive_int < 1:
        raise ValueError("ERROR foo(): integer must be greater than zero!")

    # normal processing here
```

In Table 1.6 is a short list of the most common exceptions and ones that you most likely run into when learning Python.

Table 1.6   **Common Python Exceptions**

Exception	Description
AssertionError	assert statement failed.
AttributeError	Tried to access an attribute that the object does not have, such as `foo.x` where `foo` does not have an attribute `x`.
IOError	Some input/output error; most likely a file that could not be opened.
ImportError	Could not import module or package; most likely a path issue.
IndentationError	Syntax error; code not indented properly.
IndexError	Tried to use index larger than sequence size, such as, `x[5]` when `x` only has three elements.
KeyError	Attempted to access key not in dictionary.
KeyboardInterrupt	CTRL-C pressed.
NameError	Used a variable that hasn't been assigned to an object yet.

Table 1.6   **Common Python Exceptions**

Exception	Description
SyntaxError	Code does not compile due to invalid Python code.
TypeError	Passed in object of type different from expected.
UnboundLocalError	Tried to access local variable that has not been set yet, likely because you have global of the same name and thought you were accessing *that* one.
ValueError	Passed in value that caller was not expecting, even though the type can be correct.

For a complete list of the current exceptions, see the documentation for the exceptions module at http://docs.python.org/lib/module-exceptions.html.

Exceptions in Django

Like any complex Python program, Django uses exceptions extensively. For the most part, these are internal and are not part of your regular use of Django. However, a few exceptions are designed to be used directly in your Django applications. For example, raising an exception named Http404 triggers Django's handling of an HTTP 404 "Not Found" error. Being able to raise Http404 as soon as you know something is wrong—rather than, say, carefully propagating a special flag all the way back up through your code—turns out to be a significant convenience when creating Web applications.

Files

You have already seen a few examples of the open built-in function in earlier code segments; it is used to open files for reading or writing:

```
>>> f = open('test.txt', 'w')
>>> f.write('foo\n')
>>> f.write('bar\n')
>>> f.close()
>>> f = open('test.txt', 'r')
>>> for line in f:
...     print line.rstrip()
...
foo
bar
>>> f.close()
```

In addition to the `write` method, there is `read` to read in the entire contents of a file as a single string. For text files, `readlines` reads all lines of a file into a list, and similarly `writelines` outputs a list of strings to a file with appropriate linebreaks.

A file object itself is an iterator, so there is often no need to use `read` or `readlines` directly. Just a simple `for` loop as in the previous code sample suffices most of the time.

The line termination characters (`\n`, `\r\n`, or `\r`, depending on your operating system) are preserved, hence the reason why we had to call the string `rstrip` method to take it off incoming strings. (Otherwise, the output would be double-spaced because `print` automatically adds one.) Similarly, all outbound strings sent to a file via `write` or `writelines` require line termination characters, lest they all be merged into a single line.

Finally, a few other less-commonly used auxiliary file methods are not discussed here but can easily be looked up in a reference or in the Files and I/O chapter of *Core Python Programming*.

Functions

Creating functions in Python is straightforward. We have seen several function declarations already in this chapter. In this section, we also present slightly more advanced usage, including (but not limited to)

- Declaring and calling functions
- Keyword arguments (in function calls)
- Default arguments (in function signatures)
- Functions are first-class objects
- Anonymous Functions and `lambda`
- Parameter containers (in function calls)
- Variable arguments (in function signatures)
- Decorators

Declaring and Calling Functions

Using the `def` keyword, you provide the name of your function with any parameters in parentheses. (Parameterless functions simply use an empty pair of parentheses.)

```
>>> def foo(x):
...     print x
...
>>> foo(123)
123
```

As you can see, calling a function is even easier: Give the function name and a pair of parentheses, putting any requirement arguments inside. Now let's take a look at a more useful example.

host name or ip addr

```
import httplib
def check_web_server(host, port, path):
    h = httplib.HTTPConnection(host, port)      # connect to web server
    h.request('GET', path)                       # make get request
    resp = h.getresponse()
    print 'HTTP Response:'
    print '    status =', resp.status
    print '    reason =', resp.reason
    print 'HTTP Headers:'
    for hdr in resp.getheaders():
        print '    %s: %s' % hdr
```

What does this do? It takes a hostname or IP address (host), server port number (port), and a pathname (path) and attempts to contact the Web server running on the specified host at the given port number. If that is successful, it issues a GET request on the provided path. You can execute it and get the following output for checking the main Python Web site's server:

```
>>> check_web_server('www.python.org', 80, '/')
HTTP Response:
    status = 200
    reason = OK
HTTP Headers:
    content-length: 16793
    accept-ranges: bytes
    server: Apache/2.2.3 (Debian) DAV/2 SVN/1.4.2 mod_ssl/2.2.3 OpenSSL/0.9.8c
    last-modified: Sun, 27 Apr 2008 00:28:02 GMT
    etag: "6008a-4199-df35c880"
    date: Sun, 27 Apr 2008 08:51:34 GMT
    content-type: text/html
```

Keyword Arguments (in Function Calls)

In addition to this "regular" calling convention, Python also enables you to specify named *keyword arguments*, which makes code using the function clearer and makes it easier to use functions—also, there's no need to remember a fixed parameter order. Keyword arguments are specified as key=value, as in the following modification of our earlier example (output omitted for brevity):

```
>>> check_web_server(port=80, path='/', host='www.python.org')
```

Based on the keyword names given, Python assigns the corresponding objects to those variables when executing the function.

Default Arguments (in Function Signatures)

Another feature of Python functions is the capability to specify default values for parameters so that passing them in as arguments is optional. Many functions have variables that are often the same value for every call, so defining those default values makes using the function a bit easier in that common case.

Default values can be assigned to parameters using an equal sign directly in the function signature. In our ongoing Web-server-checking example, most Web servers run on port 80, and when running a simple "is the Web server up" one typically just tests the top-level page. We can encode these defaults like so:

```
def check_web_server(host, port=80, path='/'):
```

This is not to be confused with keyword arguments because those are only for *function calls*, and default arguments only apply to the *function declaration*. All required parameters must come before any optional ones; they cannot be mixed or in the opposite order.

```
def check_web_server(host, port=80, path):        # INVALID
```

Lists and dicts as Default Arguments

We'd like to warn you about a common mistake some Python users tend to make; recall our earlier discussion about mutable versus immutable variables, specifically how lists and dicts are mutable whereas strings and integers are not. Because of this, specifying lists or dicts as default arguments can be very dangerous, as they persist across multiple function calls, like so:

```
>>> def func(arg=[]):
...     arg.append(1)
...     print arg
...
>>> func()
[1]
>>> func()
[1, 1]
>>> func()
[1, 1, 1]
```

This particular tendency of mutable objects is not terribly intuitive, which is why we mention it here. Try to keep it in mind, or you can find yourself with odd behavior in some functions down the road!

Functions Are First-Class Objects

In Python, you can treat functions (and methods) as any other object, such as, store them in containers, assign them to different variables, pass them in as arguments to functions, and so forth. The only difference is you can execute function objects, meaning you treat them as a function by appending the usual parentheses and arguments. To discuss this further, we need to understand what object references are.

References

When you execute the `def` statement, you are creating a function object and assigning and/or binding it to a name in the current namespace, but that can be just the first reference or *alias* of many. Every time you pass a function object in a call to another function, put it in a container, assign it to a local variable, and so forth, you are creating an additional reference or *alias* to that object.

By way of example, the following snippet creates not one, but *two* variables in the global namespace because once defined, a function is a normal variable like any other:

```
>>> foo = 42                    # Foo, bar become vars in global namespace
>>> def bar():
...     print "bar"
...
```

Just like other Python objects, functions can have as many references as you like. The following are a few examples to make this a little more obvious. First, normal usage of bar:

```
>>> bar()
bar
```

Next, we assign bar to another name, baz, so the function formerly known just as bar can now be referenced as baz too.

```
>>> baz = bar
>>> bar()
bar
>>> baz()
bar
```

To use a function object that has been saved in a container, you just reference it as any other object, place the parentheses after it, and pass it in any parameters. For example:

```
>>> function_list = [bar, baz]
>>> for function in function_list:
...     function()
...
bar
bar
```

Note we only put the parentheses in there when we want to *call* the function. When passing it around like a variable or object, you only use the function's name (like we did previously when creating function_list). This highlights the difference between referring to the *name* of the function object or objects—for example, bar—and actually calling or executing it—for example, bar().

First-Class Functions in Django

The fact that Python function objects can be passed around just like other values is leveraged effectively in Django. One common example is assigning Django views in URLconf files.

```
from django.conf.urls.defaults import *
from myproject.myapp.views import listview

urlpatterns = patterns('',
```

```
        url(r'^list/', listview),
)
```

In this code snippet, `listview` is being used to pass a function object directly, rather than a string containing the name of the function.

Another spot where function objects are used to good effect is in default arguments for model fields. For example, if you want a `DateField` to receive the creation date by default, you can pass a standard library function object that generates that value when called.

```
import datetime

class DiaryEntry(models.Model):
    entry = models.TextField()
    date = models.DateField(default=datetime.date.today)
```
func ref: called dyn. who arg

This is tricky. If we had set `default` to `datetime.date.today()`—note the parentheses—the function would be called at the time the model was *defined*, which is not what we want. Instead, we pass the function *object*; Django is aware of this and calls the function at instance-creation time to generate the value for us.

Anonymous Functions

Anonymous functions are another functional programming feature of Python. They are created using the `lambda` keyword and consist of a single expression, which represents the "return value" of the function. Such functions are not declared like a typical function and thus do not receive a name, hence the term *anonymous function*. They are usually single-line expressions that are meant to be created, used, and discarded in a general fashion. We should point out the distinction between "expressions" and "statements" so there is no confusion.

anon = lambda x, y : x + y
anon(2, 3) → 5

Expressions Versus Statements

Python code is made up of both expressions and statements which are executed by the Python interpreter. The major difference is an *expression* has a value; its result is always a Python object. When evaluated by the Python interpreter, it results in some object, any object; for example, `42`, `1 + 2`, `int('123')`, `range(10)`, and so forth.

Lines of code that do *not* result in objects are called *statements*; for example, `if` or `print` statements, `for` and `while` loops, and so forth. You get the idea—they perform an action instead of returning or generating a value.

Using `lambda`

The syntax for `lambda` is the following: `lambda args: expression`. Upon execution, `lambda` returns a function object that can be used right away, or you can choose to save a reference by assigning to a variable or by passing it to be saved off as a callback to be executed later.

One common use of lambdas is to provide a function object to functional tools such as `sorted`, which among other things takes a `key` argument; `key` needs to be a function which, when applied to the items in the list to be sorted, yields the value to sort by. For example, if we had a list of complex objects representing people and we wanted to sort by their last name attribute, we could do the following:

```
sorted(list_of_people, key=lambda person: person.last_name)
```
(a)
arg : val

This works because key expects a function object, and lambda returns an anonymous one. We could also have done the following, which would have been directly equivalent:

```
def get_last_name(person):
    return person.last_name

sorted(list_of_people, key=get_last_name)
```
(b)   *(a) equiv to (b)*
equiv to (c)

In fact, we could even do something like this:

```
get_last_name = lambda person: person.last_name
sorted(list_of_people, key=get_last_name)
```
(c)

The difference between those three statements is largely that of readability and reusability. The first example is much more compact and still pretty obvious and is generally the best way to solve the problem at hand. However, many lambdas eventually "grow up" to become regular functions (such as when the programmer realizes she needs to use it more than once), in which case we would be looking at the second example.

The third example isn't really practical—we just wanted to make it clear that lambda is exactly equivalent to a one-off function definition—but it further highlights the first-class nature of Python functions.

Lambda Functions in Django

Lambda functions are not commonplace in Django, but there is one spot where they seem to be especially handy: the so-called "authentication decorators," which identify pages that should only be seen by users with certain permissions. One way to perform this gatekeeping *✱* is to take the User object representing the logged-in user and pass it to a function that returns True if the user should be allowed to see the page and False otherwise.

Such a function could be defined with the usual def foo(): construct, but lambda gives us a more compact way to do it. You don't have all the pieces necessary to completely understand this example until later, but the identifier names should make it clear enough.

```
@user_passes_test(lambda u: u.is_allowed_to_vote)
def vote(request):
    """Process a user's vote"""
```
p 43 : a decorator that takes an arg

That line beginning with the @ is a **function decorator**, which you learn about later in this chapter. Decorators "wrap" functions (such as our vote function here) to change their behavior. The user_passes_test decorator, a built-in feature of Django, takes as an argument any function that accepts a Django User object and returns a Boolean (True or False) value. Because our test is so simple—we simply return the value of a particular attribute on a User object—it works tidily on one line. *✱*

*args and **kwargs

In this section, we discuss the special meaning of the * and ** characters in Python, both related to functions but which exhibit different behavior when used in function calls versus function declarations. Before we go any further, we want to be absolutely clear to all the C/C++ programmers out there the asterisks have nothing to do with pointers!

In general, whether tied to function calls or declarations, when you see a single *, this means a `tuple` (or `list`) is involved, and a double ** means there is a `dict` nearby. We start with function calls first.

* and ** in Function Calls

Let's reuse our `check_web_server` function that we studied earlier. The following shows the signature again:

```
def check_web_server(host, port, path):
```

To call this function, we issued `check_web_server('127.0.0.1', 8000, '/admin/')`. What if you had this information in a three-tuple instead? For example:

```
host_info = ('www.python.org', 80, '/')      # http://www.python.org/
```

Our call would then look like this:

```
check_web_server(host_info[0], host_info[1], host_info[2])
```

However, that method of doing things is neither scalable (what if the function in question had a dozen arguments?) nor desirable. Using a single * can solve our problem because when calling a function, an expression evaluating to a tuple or list is **unpacked** if prefixed by an asterisk. The following snippet is exactly equivalent to the previous line of code:

```
check_web_server(*host_info)
```

As you can see, this is a clean and elegant solution and using ** with dictionaries is similar. Instead of (`'www.python.org'`, `80`, `'/'`), let's create a dictionary with similar content.

```
host_info = {'host': 'www.python.org', 'port': 80, 'path': '/'}
```

You would then call the function like this:

```
check_web_server(**host_info)
```

This tells the function to unpack the dictionary where each key is the name of the parameter and its corresponding value should be the argument to the function call. In other words, it's equivalent to the following:

```
check_web_server(host='www.python.org', port=80, path='/')
```

You are able to use one or both of these techniques at the same time, in the same way that it's possible to manually call a function with positional and/or keyword arguments.

(2)

* and ** in Function Signatures

Using * and ** in function signatures has a similar but different purpose: enable Python functions to support *variable arguments*, sometimes known as "varargs." This gives functions the capability to accept *any number of arguments* passed to them via function calls.

When defining a function with three required arguments (such as arguments with no default value), that exact number must be passed in by the caller. Use of default arguments adds a little flexibility, but one is still limited by the maximum number of defined arguments.

For increased flexibility, it's possible to define a vararg using a single * representing a tuple, as a "shopping bag" that holds each element passed in. Let's create a daily sales total function like this:

```
def daily_sales_total(*all_sales):
    total = 0.0
    for each_sale in all_sales:
        total += float(each_sale)
    return total
```

Valid calls to this function include the following:

```
daily_sales_total()            # returns 0.0
daily_sales_total(10.00)       #          10.00
daily_sales_total(5.00, 1.50, '128.75') # Any type is allowed, not just floats!   # sum
```

It doesn't matter how many arguments you pass to this function; it can handle them all. all_sales is simply a tuple that contains all of them (which is why we were able to loop over all_sales within our function definition).

It's possible to mix normal argument definition with varargs, in which case the vararg "argument" acts as a catch-all, such as in this hypothetical definition of a check_web_server that can accept extra arguments.

```
def check_web_server(host, port, path, *args):
```

> **Note**
>
> When using varargs in function definitions, all required parameters must come first, followed by any parameters with default values, with a vararg coming in last.

Similarly, you can use ** in a function signature to accept a variable number of keyword arguments which goes into a dictionary when the function is called.

```
def check_web_server(host, port, path, *args, **kwargs):
```

We've now set up our function such that it must take at least the three initial arguments, but happily accepts any further positional *or* keyword arguments; inside the function we can then inspect the contents of the args tuple or the kwargs dict and either use or discard their contents.

In fact, there's a so-called "universal" Python method signature that consists solely of varargs.

[handwritten: accept any no. of posn args, followed by any no of keywd args]

```
def f(*args, **kwargs):
```

Such a function can be called as `f()`, `f(a, b, c)`, `f(a, b, foo=c, bar=d)` and so on—it accepts any and all input. How such a function handles the contents of args and kwargs of course varies depending on what it's used for.

**kwargs in Django QuerySets: Dynamically Building ORM Queries

Django database API queries often involve keyword arguments. For example:

[handwritten margin: ⓐ] *[handwritten margin: equiv]*

```
bob_stories = Story.objects.filter(title__contains="bob",
subtitle__contains="bob", text__contains="bob",
byline__contains="bob")
```

[handwritten: # filter on 4 conditions]

Clear enough. The following shows how those keyword arguments could also be passed as a dictionary:

[handwritten margin: ⓑ]

```
bobargs = {'title__contains': 'bob', 'subtitle__contains': 'bob',
    'text__contains': 'bob', 'byline__contains': 'bob'}
bob_stories = Story.objects.filter(**bobargs)
```

Having done that, you can see how you would build up the dictionary dynamically:

[handwritten: Create 4 versions of this tuple in dict( )]

```
bobargs = dict((f + '__contains', 'bob') for f in ('title', 'subtitle', 'text',
    'byline'))
bob_stories = Story.objects.filter(**bobargs)
```

[handwritten margin: ✳]

Having done *that*, you can see how this technique could be helpful in streamlining queries with a lot of redundancy—or, even more commonly, helpful in assembling filter arguments whose names are provided dynamically (from options on a search form, for example).

[handwritten margin: @ 239]

Decorators

The last and perhaps most mind-bending concept when learning about Python functions and functional programming is *decorators*. In our context, a Python decorator is a mechanism enabling you to alter or "decorate" the behavior of a function to perform somewhat differently than designed, or to do something in addition to its native task; a decorator is a "function wrapper" if you will. Some of these extra tasks can include logging, timing, filtering, and so forth.

[handwritten margin: ✳]

In Python, a wrapped or decorated function (object) is usually reassigned back to its original name so the wrapped function is compatible with the normal version—because using decorators is analogous to "overlaying" additional functionality on top of what you already had.

The simplest syntax we can present looks something like this:

[handwritten margin: ✳]

```
@deco
def foo():
    pass
```

*[handwritten: Need def deco (func):
    def wrapped func ():
        ...
        return func ()
    return wrapped func]*

In this example, deco is a decorator function that "decorates" the foo function. It takes the foo function, adds some functionality to it and reassigns it back to the foo name. The

`@deco` syntax is equivalent to executing this line of code (given that `foo` is a valid function object):

```
foo = deco(foo)
```

The following is a simple example where we acknowledge or log the calling of a function live as it happens:

```
def log(func):
    def wrappedFunc():
        print "*** %s() called" % func.__name__
        return func()
    return wrappedFunc
```

 # log is a func, decorator: it takes a func as an arg & does something
 # in addn to invoking the func

```
@log
def foo():
    print "inside foo()"
```

⟺

def foo():
* print "inside foo()"*

foo = log (foo)   # foo becomes the name
*   # of the wrapped func*

Now if we execute this code, we get the following output:

```
>>> foo()
*** foo() called
inside foo()
```

Earlier in the chapter, we saw an example of a decorator that took an argument.   *@ 239*

```
@user_passes_test(lambda u: u.is_allowed_to_vote)
```

In this case, we're actually calling a function that then returns the actual decorator—`user_passes_test` is not, itself, a decorator, but a function that takes arguments and uses those arguments to return the decorator to use. The syntax looks something like this:

```
@decomaker(deco_args)
def foo():
    pass
```

This is equivalent to the following snippet, keeping in mind how Python expressions can be chained together:

deco

```
foo = decomaker(deco_args)(foo)
```

Here, the "decorator-maker" (or `decomaker`) takes `deco_args` and returns the decorator that takes `foo` as the function to wrap.

This final example syntax demonstrates applying multiple decorators:

```
@deco1(deco_args)
@deco2
def foo():
    pass
```

 # equiv   foo = deco1(deco_args)(deco2(foo))

We don't discuss this further here, but by the code we have already seen, you can conclude this code is equivalent to

```
foo = deco1(deco_args)(deco2(foo))
```

You may still be wondering, "Why decorators?" In all honesty, wrapping functions is really not new to Python, and neither is taking an object, modifying it, and reassigning it back to the same variable. What is different is that decorators enable you to do this with a simple syntactic notation, the @ character.

For a more complete and user-friendly tutorial on decorators, check out Kent John's "Python Decorators" tutorial at http://personalpages.tds.net/~kent37/kk/00001.html.

Object-Oriented Programming

First of all, this section is not a tutorial on object-oriented programming (OOP). We are just going to dive into creating and using Python classes. If you are new to OOP, doing it in Python is one of the simplest ways to ease into it—it would probably be more beneficial if you read a high-level tutorial first, but it is not a requirement. The main goals of OOP are to provide a logical mapping between code and real-life problems and to promote code reuse and sharing. We also expose you to certain behaviors that are unique to Python.

Class Definitions

In our first example of modeling a real-world problem, we create an address book. To create a class in Python, you need to provide the class keyword, the name of your new class, and one or more *base classes* or classes that your class is based on. For example, if you want to create a Car or Truck class, you can use Vehicle as a base class. If there are no existing classes that you want to derive from, just use Python's root class or type, object, as your base class, like we do here with our address book entry class, AddressBookEntry:

```
class AddressBookEntry(object):
    version = 0.1

    def __init__(self, name, phone):
        self.name = name
        self.phone = phone

    def update_phone(self, phone):
        self.phone = phone
```

Static class members like version can be created as long as the assignment takes place within the class definition—such members are just variables that belong to the class and thus are shared among all instances. Methods are defined just like functions with the addition of a self object as a required first parameter for every method—Python is explicit in this regard.

The variable self refers to a particular instance of a class (other languages use this as the name instead of self). If a class is the blueprint, then an instance is a realization of the class, a real object that you create to manipulate during the course of execution. All variables that begin with `self` and are given in the dotted-attribute notation indicates an instance attribute, meaning an object belonging to a particular instance. If `name` is an instance attribute, you must use `self.name` as a fully qualified reference.

For those coming from other languages with object-oriented features, note Python does not have the concepts of constructors and destructors—there are no keywords `new` nor `free`. We discuss this more in a moment.

Instantiation

In other languages, instances are created with a `new` statement, but in Python, you simply call a class as if it was a function. Rather than a "constructor," Python has an "initializer," thus its name `__init__`. When you instantiate an object, you pass in the parameters that are required by `__init__`. Python creates the object, automatically calls `__init__` with your given arguments, and then finally hands the newly created object back to you.

While we are on the subject of calling methods, we can safely say that it is as simple as a function call. Although you are required to give `self` in method declarations, Python gives you a break in that when you call a method (in the normal *bound* manner), Python automatically passes in `self` *for* you. The following are two examples of creating instances of our `AddressBookEntry` class:

```
john = AddressBookEntry('John Doe', '408-555-1212')
jane = AddressBookEntry('Jane Doe', '650-555-1212')
```

Recall Python creates the instances, calls `__init__` for each, and then returns the objects. Look again; the `self` is not given in the calls, just the name and phone number. Python passes the `self` for you.

Now you can access the attributes directly, such as, `john.name`, `john.phone`, `jane.name`, `jane.phone`. As you can see here via the interactive output, we can access instance attributes quite freely:

```
>>> john = AddressBookEntry('John', '408-555-1212')
>>> john.phone
'408-555-1212'
>>> john.update_phone('510-555-1212')
>>> john.phone
'510-555-1212'
```

Again, notice the `update_phone` method signature has two parameters, `self` and `newphone`, but the only one we need to provide is the new phone number while Python passes in the instance object referred to by `john` as `self`.

Python also supports **dynamic instance attributes**, those that are not declared anywhere in the class definition, yet can be created "on the fly."

```
>>> john.tattoo = 'Mom'
```

This is certainly an advantageous feature, showcasing the flexibility of Python. You can create as many of these attributes as you want any time you want.

Subclassing

Creating a subclass is just like creating a class, only you're going to provide one or more base classes (instead of just `object`). Continuing our previous example, we now create an employer address book entry class.

```
class EmployeeAddressBookEntry(AddressBookEntry):
    def __init__(self, name, phone, id, social):
        AddressBookEntry.__init__(self, name, phone)  # super(self, EmpAddrBkEnt).__init__(...)
        self.empid = id
        self.ssn = social
```

Note we neglected to assign the `name` and `phone` arguments to `self.name` and `self.phone`—this is because our call to `AddressBookEntry.__init__` takes care of that for us. When you override a base class method in this manner, you have to explicitly call it (the original method), which is what we just did. Note we had to pass in the `self` argument this time because we referred to the *class* `AddressBookEntry` instead of an *instance*.

At any rate, aside from potentially overriding the base class's methods, subclasses inherit everything else, so our `EmployeeAddressBookEntry` has `name` and `phone` attributes as well as the `update_phone` method. Django, as well as most other Python programs and frameworks, makes heavy use of subclassing both for its own codebase as well as for features you are concerned with as a Django user.

Inner Classes

Just like the "inner functions" used to create decorators, you are able to create *inner classes*, classes defined inside other classes, as in:

```
class MyClass(object):
    class InnerClass:
        pass
```

This inner class is a real Python class, but is only visible to instances of the `MyClass` class. This is a somewhat esoteric Python feature, but it is used to good effect in Django (see the following sidebar, "Classes and Django Models"). The only inner class you're likely to use in Django—but an important one!—is the `Meta` inner class.

Classes and Django Models

Django data models, the heart of most Django applications, are classes, inheriting from the built-in Django class `django.db.models.Model`. The powerful features that Django's Model class gives you are extensive, and we cover them in depth in Chapter 4. For now, the following is an example from the application we build in Chapter 2, "Django for the Impatient: Building a Blog":

```
from django.db import models
from django.contrib import admin

class BlogPost(models.Model):
    title = models.CharField(max_length=150)
```

```
        body = models.TextField()
        timestamp = models.DateTimeField()

        class Meta:
            ordering = ('-timestamp',)          cf 75, 106
```

This defines a new class called `BlogPost` that inherits from `django.db.models.Model` and has three user-defined fields. The inheritance from `Model` gives `BlogPost` other methods and attributes as well, not least of which are methods that enable you to query the database for `BlogPost` objects, create new such objects, and access related items.

Regular Expressions

Django makes use of a string pattern–matching technique known as **regular expressions** for, among other things, defining your Web site's URLs. Without regular expressions (colloquially known as "regex") we'd have to define each and every possible URL, which would work fine for `/index/` or `/blog/posts/new/`, for example, but quickly breaks down for anything dynamic such as `/blog/posts/2008/05/21/`.

   Many books and online tutorials give introductory coverage of what exactly regular expressions are and how they can be assembled, so we don't spend much time on that here. A good selection of those resources is available at withdjango.com. The rest of this section assumes you're familiar with regex (or have just gone and done some reading on them), so we'll examine how to use them in Python.

The `re` module

Python regular expressions are accessed via the `re` module; one of the more commonly used components of the module is the `search` function. `re.search` returns a match object whose `group` or `groups` method can be used to pull out the matching patterns.

```
>>> import re
>>> m = re.search(r'foo', 'seafood')
>>> print m
<_sre.SRE_Match object at ...>
>>> m.group()
'foo'
>>> m = re.search(r'bar', 'seafood')
>>> print m
None
```

   On success, the `search` function returns a `Match` object that has a `group` method you can call to get the matching string. When it fails, you get `None`. Note the use of the raw string notation, `r''`—as mentioned earlier in the chapter, it's a good habit to use raw strings for regular expressions as they remove much of the need for escaping characters such as backslashes.

Searching Versus Matching

We need to distinguish between a *search*, which looks to match the pattern anywhere in the target string and a *match*, which means the entire string must be described with a single pattern. For example:

```
>>> import re
>>> m = re.match(r'foo', 'seafood')
>>> if m is not None: print m.group()
...
>>> print m
None
>>> m = re.search(r'foo', 'seafood')
>>> if m is not None: print m.group()
...
'foo'
```

In the call to `re.match`, the result was empty, or None because `r'foo'` only matches part of `'seafood'`. `re.search` does get us a result because it's more lenient.

Common Gotchas

In this section, we discuss some of the things that bite newcomers to Python, for example: How *do* you create a single-element tuple? Or, why do I see `self` everywhere in object-oriented Python code?

Single-Item Tuples

While it can be clear to beginners that `()` and `(123, 'xyz', 3.14)` are tuples, it is not so obvious that `(1)` is not. Parentheses are indeed overloaded in Python. When used to enclose an expression, parentheses are used for grouping. If you want a single-element tuple in Python, the not-so-pretty but required idiom is to put a comma after the sole member, as in `(1,)`.

Modules

We have already seen how to import modules and their attributes in two different ways:

```
import random                    # module name is set as a global var
print random.choice(range(10))
```

    AND

```
from random import choice        # function name is defined as a global
print choice(range(10))
```

The namespace implications of the first technique is the module name is set as a global variable, and you access the `choice` function as that global's attribute. In the second example, we are importing the name `choice` directly into our global namespace (and not the module's name). Because of this, there is no need to refer to the attribute as a member of the module anymore. In fact, we only have the attribute name itself.

There is some misconception among new Python programmers that the second way only imports a function but not the entire module. That is not true. The entire module is loaded but only a reference to the one function has been saved. There is no performance difference or memory savings with the `from-import` syntax.

Can I Import a Module More Than Once?

A common newbie worry is that they have module `m.py` and another one `n.py`, both of which import `foo.py`. The question is if `m` imports `n`, is `foo` imported twice? The short answer is yes, but it is not what you think.

Python has the concept of importing a module versus loading a module. A module can be imported many times, but it can only be loaded once. In other words, when Python runs across another `import` statement for a module that has already been loaded, it skips the load process so you don't have to worry about taking up more memory.

Packages

Python packages are a way to distribute a set of Python modules across the filesystem and use the familiar *dotted-attribute* notation to access subpackage modules as if they were merely attributes of another object. In other words, if you were shipping a software product with several hundred modules, it doesn't make too much sense to put them all in the same folder. You *could*, but do you want to? Why not use the filesystem to help organize those modules in a logical and sensible manner?

For example, let's say you had a telephony application. We can organize a directory structure that looks something like this:

```
Phone/
    __init__.py
    util.py
    Voicedata/
        __init__.py
        Pots.py
        Isdn.py
    Fax/
        __init__.py
        G3.py
    Mobile/
        __init__.py
        Analog.py
        Digital.py
```

Phone is the top-level directory or package. Under it are subpackages, but they are really subdirectories containing other Python modules. You immediately notice a file named __init__.py in each subdirectory. That signals to the Python interpreter that files in those folders should be treated as subpackages and not just plain files. They are typically empty, save for the occasional initialization, which can be required before using any code in subpackages.

Let's say we wanted to access the `dial` function for analog cell phones. We could execute:

```
import Phone.Mobile.Analog
Phone.Mobile.Analog.dial()
```

This is a bit cumbersome. In the everyday work world, you would probably take some shortcuts for performance reasons as we briefly described previously, but mostly for your own sanity at not having to type so much! Python and Django are all about simplicity and not repeating yourself. The following shows something more likely to be found in production:

```
import Phone.Mobile.Analog as pma
pma.dial()
```

Mutability

People new to Python often ask if it is "call by reference" or "call by value?" The answer isn't quite that simple and boils down to "it depends"—some objects are passed in to functions as a reference, although others are copied or passed by value. Which behavior is observed depends on the object's **mutability**, which in turn is determined by its type. Because of this dual behavior, Python programmers don't generally use the terms "by reference" or "by value," but instead ask whether an object is **mutable** or **immutable**.

Mutability asks the question of whether an object enables the modification of its value. All Python objects have the following three attributes: type, id, and value. Type and value should hopefully be obvious; the "id" is simply an identification number that uniquely identifies an object from all other objects running in the interpreter.

All three attributes are almost always read-only, meaning they cannot be changed during the lifetime of an object. The only possible exception is the value: If the value can be changed, then it is a mutable object; otherwise it is immutable.

Simple or "scalar" types, including integers and other numeric types, are immutable as are string types like `str` and `unicode`, and finally tuples. Just about everything else—lists, dicts, classes, class instances, and so forth—is mutable.

> **Note**
>
> As you see in this section, mutability is an important aspect of programming Python, This explains why Python offers two "list" types, `list` and `tuple`, where the former is mutable and the latter is not. The capability to specify a list-like object that can be used in situations requiring immutability—such as dictionary keys—can be very useful.

How Mutability Affects Method Calls

One area of caution with mutable objects is in calling their methods. If the method you call modifies a mutable object in any way, then it typically does so "in place," meaning the data structure is modified directly instead of returning a modified copy of the object (in which case the function returns None instead).

A common example of this is list.sort, which sorts the list in place instead of returning it; this tends to trip up many new Python programmers who aren't expecting it! Many other list methods, such as reverse and extend, as well as some dict methods like update (which adds new key-value pairs to the dict) work in place as well.

Thankfully, Python—since 2.4—offers built-in methods such as sorted and reversed, which take an iterable object as input and return a sorted or reversed copy. These are useful in situations where operating in place isn't desirable or you want to save a few extra statements of code. If you're stuck with Python 2.3, to get a modified copy of a list, you'd need to manually copy the list (typically with newlist = list(mylist) or newlist = mylist[:]), and then call the new copy's sort method.

Copying Objects and Mutability

Let's take a look at a common gotcha to new Python programmers, which relates to mutability and the copying of objects. Recall the start of the section, where we mentioned immutable objects are passed by value, but mutable ones are passed by reference. This holds true for both passing arguments into a function or for any other sort of "copying" of an object: Immutable objects, such as ints, become truly copied, but mutable ones only have their *reference* copied over, leaving us with only one object in memory and two references to it.

To illustrate why this is so important, consider the following example of a list with a nested inner list:

```
>>> mylist = [1, 'a', ['foo', 'bar']]
>>> mylist2 = list(mylist)
>>> mylist2[0] = 2          # affects only mylist2
>>> mylist[2][0] = 'biz'    # affects both mylist, mylist2
```

What you can expect is updating the inner list of mylist would only affect mylist, leaving mylist2 alone—but this is not the case! Observe the new values of both lists.

```
>>> print mylist
[1, 'a', ['biz', 'bar']]
>>> print mylist2
[2, 'a', ['biz', 'bar']]
```

The first two objects in mylist are immutable, being an integer and a string, and so mylist2 got its own brand new integer and string objects—thus our replacement of 1 with 2 worked fine. However, the third object in mylist is a list, which is mutable, and thus only a reference to it was copied over into mylist2. Because the third object in both lists is a reference to the single in-memory list object, modification of it in either parent list is reflected in the other.

This sort of copying we have just seen is known as **shallow copying** because of the way it copies over references to mutable objects instead of trying to extract the values within them. If you truly want the latter behavior, known as **deep copying**, then you must import the `copy` module and use `copy.deepcopy`. Please read its documentation carefully—this sort of copying is, naturally, recursive (a problem if you have circular references!) and not all objects are deep-copyable.

Constructor Versus Initializer

Python is object-oriented, but one area where it differs from traditional OOP languages is there is no explicit concept of a constructor. There is no new keyword in Python because you don't really instantiate your classes. Instead, Python creates instances and calls an initializer for you—it is the first method that is called after your object has been created but before Python hands it back to you. Its name is always spelled as __init__.

To instantiate a class, or in other words, to create an object, you call the class as if it were a function.

```
>>> class MyClass(object):
...     pass
...
>>> m = MyClass()
```

Furthermore, because Python automatically calls __init__ for you, if the initializer takes parameters, you pass those into the class "call."

```
>>> from time import ctime
>>> class MyClass(object):
...     def __init__(self, date):
...         print "instance created at:", date
...
>>> m = MyClass(ctime())
instance created at: Wed Aug  1 00:59:14 2007
```

Similarly, Python programmers do not typically implement destructors and destroy their objects, but instead simply enable objects to go out of scope (at which point they are garbage-collected). However, Python objects can define a __del__ method which acts similar to a destructor in other languages, and it's possible to explicitly destroy an object with the del statement (e.g. del my_object).

Dynamic Instance Attributes

Another area of possible confusion to those new to Python (coming from other object-oriented languages) is that instance attributes can be assigned dynamically, after the class is already defined and an instance has been created. For example, take this AddressBook class:

```
>>> class AddressBook(object):
...     def __init__(self, name, phone):
...         self.name = name
...         self.phone = phone
...
>>> john = AddressBook('John Doe', '415-555-1212')
>>> jane = AddressBook('Jane Doe', '408-555-1212')
```

```
>>> print john.name
John Doe
>>> john.tattoo = 'Mom'
>>> print john.tattoo
Mom
```

Notice `self.tattoo` doesn't show up anywhere in the class or method declaration or in any of this class's methods—not even `__init__`! We created that attribute dynamically during runtime. These are called *dynamic instance attributes*.

Coding Style (PEP 8 and Beyond)

Many elements, recommendations, and suggestions for "proper coding style" are in Python, but the overall theme is to keep your code "Pythonic." Programming systems which follow Python's philosophies of keeping things simple, not repeating yourself, creating code that is easy-to-read, promoting elegant solutions and code reuse, and so forth, are tagged with that moniker, and Django is no exception. In our limited amount of space, we can only provide a few basic guidelines. The rest comes with continued experience with Python, Django, and their highly supportive communities. There is an official style guide, and it can be found in PEP 8 (http://www.python.org/dev/peps/pep-0008).

Indent Four Spaces

In a language where block delimitation is done by whitespace and the user base is as diverse as anything, it's a simple fact that editing Python source code is difficult for the eyes if you indent just one or two spaces. It is also true your code wraps too easily if you use eight spaces. The longstanding suggestion from Guido's original essay is four spaces, a perfect medium.

Use Spaces and Not Tabs

Regardless of the platform you develop on, there is always the possibility your code can be moved or copied to another machine of a different architecture or run on a different operating system. Because tabs are treated differently on various platforms, such as, tabs are four spaces on Win32 and eight on POSIX or any Unix-based system, it is wise to avoid using tabs altogether.

If you run into a situation where the Python interpreter is complaining your code has a syntax error but it looks perfect on your screen, there is a good chance a tab has slipped in somewhere because your editor is showing you a "false" view of what your code actually looks like. By explicitly converting all tabs into spaces, you then see where the indentation went wrong in your code.

Don't Write Single-Line Suites on the Same Line as the Header

It's possible to write "one-liners" like this:

```
if is_finished(): return
```

However, we recommend you split it up into multiple lines, like this:

```
if is_finished():
    return
```

The main reason is it makes your code easier to read, plus you don't have to do any extra editing if you ever have to add new lines to your suite.

Create Documentation Strings (aka "docstrings")

Code documentation can be very useful, and Python enables you to not only document your code, but also to make it accessible during runtime. Docstrings can be created for modules, classes, and functions and methods. For example, take this sample script called foo.py:

```
#!/usr/bin/env python
"""foo.py -- sample module demonstrating documentation strings"""

class Foo(object):
    """Foo() - empty class ... to be developed"""

def bar(x):
    """bar(x) - function docstring for bar, prints out its arg 'x'"""
    print x
```

module docstring

class docstring

func docstring

When we say "accessible at runtime," this is what we mean: If you start up the interpreter and import your module, you can access each docstring using the __doc__ attribute for each module, class, and function.

```
>>> import foo
>>> foo.__doc__
'foo.py -- sample module demonstrating documentation strings'
>>> foo.Foo.__doc__
'Foo() - empty class ... to be developed'
>>> foo.bar.__doc__
'bar(x) - function docstring for bar, prints out its arg "x"'
```

Furthermore, you can use the help built-in function to "pretty-print" the docstrings; we'll just give one example here for the module (but you can do the same for the class and the function).

```
>>> help(foo)
Help on module foo:
```

```
NAME
    foo - foo.py -- sample module demonstrating documentation strings

FILE
    c:\python25\lib\site-packages\foo.py

CLASSES
    __builtin__.object
        Foo

    class Foo(__builtin__.object)
     |  Foo() - empty class ... to be developed
     |
     |  Data descriptors defined here:
     |
     |  __dict__
     |      dictionary for instance variables (if defined)
     |
     |  __weakref__
     |      list of weak references to the object (if defined)

FUNCTIONS
    bar(x)
        bar(x) - function docstring for bar, prints out its arg "x"
```

Docstrings for most software available in the Python Standard Library already exist, so if you need help with a built-in function, methods of built-in types, or any module or package attribute, feel free to "ask for `help`," such as `help(open)`, `help(''.strip)`, `help(time.ctime)`, and so forth, assuming you've imported any necessary modules to get access to an attribute.

Summary

In this very large introductory chapter, we attempted to welcome new Django developers to Python. Obviously we cannot be as comprehensive as we would like, but this is really a Django book, not a Python one. With that said, however, we attempted to condense as much relevant Python material as necessary to succeed with Django.

The first three-quarters of the chapter were mostly Python language material along with the appropriate Django relationships spelled out; the final part of the chapter contains more of the "softer skills": the gotchas, style guidelines, and so forth. Hopefully, we've exposed enough of the language to give you the skills to read and write basic Python code, so you can now branch off to the Django world.

In the next section, we're going to immediately get you knee-deep into the Django world by having you build a simple blog application in under 20 minutes. The blog isn't as fully functional as the commercial ones out there, but it should give you an idea of how quickly you can develop and tweak a Django application, and in the process, exercise the newfound Python development skills you picked up in this chapter.

2

Django for the Impatient: Building a Blog

Django bills itself as "the Web framework for perfectionists with deadlines." So let's put ourselves on deadline and see how fast we can produce a simple blog using Django. (We'll address your perfectionist side later.)

> **Note**
>
> This chapter assumes you've already installed Django on your system. If you haven't, consult Appendix B, "Installing and Running Django."

All the work in this chapter is done on the command line in your shell of choice (bash, tcsh, zsh, Cygwin, or what have you). So open your terminal and cd to a directory that is on your PYTHONPATH environment variable. On a Unix-based system such as Linux, Mac OS X, FreeBSD, and so on, you can issue an echo $PYTHONPATH command to see its contents; from a Win32 Command window, type echo %PYTHONPATH%. You can read more about paths in both the installation and Python chapters.

We recommend you try to follow along and actually build the blog as you go. If that's not practical—if you aren't near a computer, or you're just impatient—simply reading it is illuminating too. That's especially true if you have experience with one or more other modern Web frameworks, since many of the basic concepts are familiar.

If you *are* following along on your own computer, and you reach a point where the results you're getting don't match what you see here, stop and re-examine the step you just completed, and then review the two or three steps before that. Look for a spot where you could have skipped over a seemingly unimportant detail or didn't understand a specific instruction. If no light bulbs come on, delete your sample project and start over. The authors used this method when learning Django; in addition to being faster than staring blankly at error messages for hours, the repetition of the steps leading up to your trouble spot really help with your retention!

Creating the Project

The easiest way to organize your Django code when you are starting out is to use what Django calls a **project**: A directory of files that constitute, usually, a single Web site. Django comes with a utility called `django-admin.py` to streamline tasks such as the creation of these project directories. On Unix, it has a default installation into the `/usr/bin` directory, and if you're on Win32, it goes into the `Scripts` folder right in your Python installation, for example, `C:\Python25\Scripts`. In either case, you need to make sure that `django-admin.py` is in your `PATH` so it can be executed from the command line.

To create the project directory for your blog project, issue this `django-admin.py` command:

```
django-admin.py startproject mysite 1
```

On a Win32 box, you need to open a DOS Command window first. It can be accessed via `Start -> Programs -> Accessories -> Command Prompt`. Also, instead of a `$`, you see something like `C:\WINDOWS\system32>` as a shell prompt.

Now take a look at the contents of the directory to see what this command has created for you. It should look something like this on Unix:

```
$ cd mysite
$ ls -l
total 24
-rw-r--r--   1 pbx   pbx      0 Jun 26 18:51 __init__.py
-rwxr-xr-x   1 pbx   pbx    546 Jun 26 18:51 manage.py
-rw-r--r--   1 pbx   pbx   2925 Jun 26 18:51 settings.py
-rw-r--r--   1 pbx   pbx    227 Jun 26 18:51 urls.py
```

If you were developing on a Win32 platform, opening an Explorer window to that folder looks something like Figure 2.1, if we created a folder named `c:\py\django` with the intention of putting our project there.

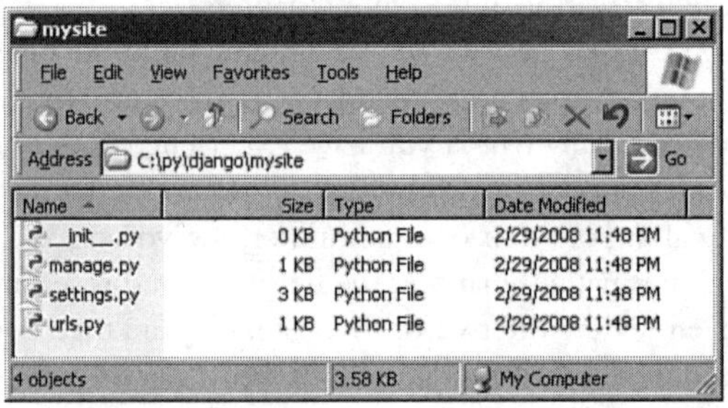

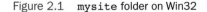

Figure 2.1   `mysite` folder on Win32

--init--.py   manage.py   settings.py   urls.py   myapp1/

Note

models.py   views.py   templates/

As you probably know if you're an advanced Python user, that __init__.py file makes this project directory a Python **package**—a collection of related Python modules. Its status as a package enables us to use Python's dot-notation to address individual pieces of our project, such as mysite.urls. (You can read more about packages in Chapter 1, "Practical Python for Django.")

58

Besides __init__.py, the startproject command has created three other files.

- manage.py is a utility for working with this Django project. You can see from its permissions flags in the directory listing that it is executable. We run it in a moment.

- settings.py is a file containing default settings for your project. These include database information, debugging flags, and other important variables. Any value in this file is available to any of your project's installed apps—we show you the usefulness of that as we progress through this chapter.

- urls.py is what's known in Django as a **URLconf**, a configuration file that maps URL patterns to actions your applications perform. URLconfs are an exciting and powerful feature of Django.

Note

Every file created by the startproject command is Python source code. There's no XML, no .ini files, and no funky configuration syntax. Django pursues a "pure Python" philosophy wherever possible. This gives you a lot of flexibility without adding complexity to the framework. For example, if you want your settings file to import settings from some *other* file or to calculate a value instead of having it hardcoded, there's no barrier—it's just Python.

Running the Development Server

At this point, you haven't built your blog application yet, but nonetheless there are some Django conveniences in place for your use. One of the handiest is Django's built-in Web server. It's a server designed not for deploying public sites, but for quick development. Advantages of using it include

- You don't need to install Apache, Lighttpd, or whatever other Web server software you'd use in actual production—great if you're working on a fresh server or a non-server development machine or just playing around.

- It automatically detects when you make changes to your Python source files and reloads those modules. This is a *huge* time-saver compared to manually restarting your Web server every time you edit your code, which is what's required with most Python Web server setups.

- It knows how to find and display static media files for the admin application, so you can work with it right away.

Running the development (or "dev") server is as simple as issuing a single command. We're going to use our project's `manage.py` utility, a thin wrapper script that saves us the work of telling `django-admin.py` to use our specific project settings file. The command to run the dev server is

```
./manage.py runserver      # or ".\manage.py runserver" on win32
```

You should see something like the following with a slight difference for Win32 platforms where the quit key combination is CTRL-BREAK instead of CONTROL-C:

```
Validating models...
0 errors found.

Django version 1.0, using settings 'mysite.settings'
Development server is running at http://127.0.0.1:8000/
Quit the server with CONTROL-C.
```

Open that link in your browser, and you should see Django's "It Worked!" screen, as shown in Figure 2.2.

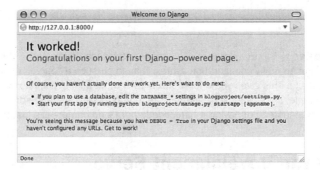

Figure 2.2   Django's initial It worked! screen

Meanwhile, if you look in your terminal session, you see the dev server has logged your GET request.

```
[07/Dec/2007 10:26:37] "GET / HTTP/1.1" 404 2049
```

The four chunks of the log line are from left to right: timestamp, request, HTTP response code, and byte count. (Your byte count is likely to be slightly different.) The response code is 404 ("Not Found") because your project has no URLs defined yet. The It Worked! page is Django's friendly way of telling you that.

> **Tip**
>
> If your server isn't working at this point, retrace your steps. Be ruthless! It's probably easier to delete your whole project and start following this chapter again from the beginning than it is to laboriously check every file and every line of code.

When you've successfully got the server running, we can move on to setting up your first Django application.

Creating the Blog Application

Now that we have a project, we can create applications (or "apps" in Django-speak) within it. To create our blog app, we'll use `manage.py` again.

```
./manage.py startapp blog     # or ".\manage.py startapp blog" on win32
```

[handwritten: Ex: app← blog]

[handwritten: 1] *[handwritten: ✳]*

It's just as simple as starting a project. Now we have a `blog` directory inside our project directory. Here's what's in it, first in Unix format, and then in a screenshot of Windows Explorer (see Figure 2.3).

[handwritten: on PYTHON PATH]

```
$ ls -l blog/
total 16
-rw-r--r--   1 pbx  pbx   0 Jun 26 20:33 __init__.py
-rw-r--r--   1 pbx  pbx  57 Jun 26 20:33 models.py
-rw-r--r--   1 pbx  pbx  26 Jun 26 20:33 views.py
```

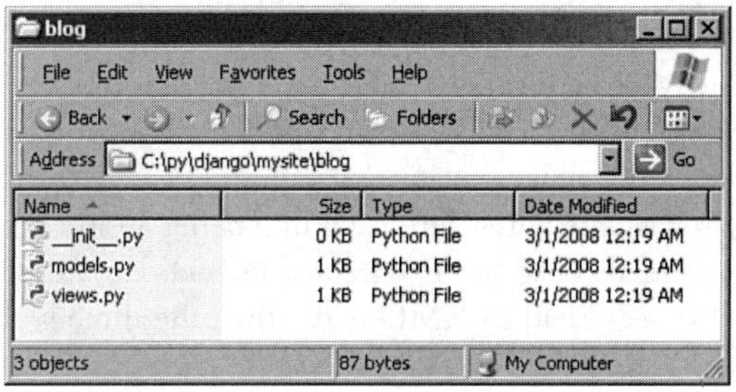

[handwritten: $PROJECT/   (container for projects)]
[handwritten: xyzproj   (a project)]
[handwritten: settings.py urls.py manage.py]
[handwritten: sensor   (an app)]
[handwritten: models.py views.py]

Figure 2.3   `mysite\blog` folder on Win32

Like your project, your app is a package too. The `models.py` and `views.py` files have no real code in them; they're merely placeholders. For our simple blog, in fact, we don't need to touch the dummy `views.py` file at all.

To tell Django this new app is part of your project, you need to edit `settings.py` (which we can also refer to as your "settings file"). Open your settings file in your editor and find the `INSTALLED_APPS` tuple near the bottom. Add your app in dotted module form to that tuple in a line that looks like this (note the trailing comma):   *[handwritten: ✳]*

```
'mysite.blog',
```

[handwritten: eg   docsearch.br-coll]

Django uses `INSTALLED_APPS` to determine the configuration of various parts of the system, including the automatic admin application and the testing framework.

[handwritten: 1 pyex docsearch.manage startapp br-coll]

*[handwritten: Then after runserver, enter urls
127.0.0.1:8000/br-coll
→ 127.0.0.1:8000/docsearch/br-coll]*

Designing Your Model

We've now arrived at the core of your Django-based blog application: the `models.py` file. This is where we'll define the data structures of the blog. Following the principle of Don't Repeat Yourself (DRY), Django gets a lot of mileage out of the model information you provide for your application. Let's create a basic model, and then see all the stuff Django does for us using that information.

Open up `models.py` in your favorite text editor (bonus points if it has a Python mode with syntax coloring). You see this placekeeper text:

```
from django.db import models

# Create your models here.
```

Delete the comment, and then add the following lines:

```
class BlogPost(models.Model):
    title = models.CharField(max_length=150)
    body = models.TextField()
    timestamp = models.DateTimeField()
```

That's a complete model, representing a "BlogPost" object with three fields. (Actually, strictly speaking it has four fields—Django automatically creates an auto-incrementing, unique `id` field for each model by default.)

You can see our newly minted class, BlogPost, is a subclass of `django.db.models.Model`. That's Django's standard base class for data models, which is the core of Django's powerful object-relational mapping system. Also, you notice our fields are defined like regular class attributes with each one being an instance of a particular field class. Those field classes are also defined in `django.db.models`, and there are many more types—ranging from BooleanField to XMLField—than the three we're using here.

Setting Up the Database

If you don't have a database server installed and running, we recommend SQLite as the fastest and easiest way to get going. It's fast, widely available, and stores its database as a single file in the filesystem. Access controls are simply file permissions. For more on how to set up a a database for use with Django, see Appendix B.

If you *do* have a database server—PostgreSQL, MySQL, Oracle, MSSQL—and want to use it rather than SQLite, then use your database's administration tools to create a new database for your Django project. We name this database "djangodb" in our examples, but you can name it whatever you like.

Either way, with your (empty) database in place, all that remains is to tell Django how to use it. This is where your project's `settings.py` file comes in.

Using a Database Server

Many people use Django with a relational database server such as PostgreSQL or MySQL. There are six potentially relevant settings here (though you may need only two): DATABASE_ENGINE, DATABASE_NAME, DATABASE_HOST, DATABASE_PORT, DATABASE_USER, and DATABASE_PASSWORD. Their names make their respective purposes pretty obvious. Just plug in the correct values corresponding to the database server you are using with Django. For example, settings for MySQL look something like this:

```
DATABASE_ENGINE = "mysql"
DATABASE_NAME = "djangodb"
DATABASE_HOST = "localhost"
DATABASE_USER = "paul"
DATABASE_PASSWORD = "pony"   # secret!
```

> **Note**
>
> We haven't specified DATABASE_PORT because that's only needed if your database server is running on a nonstandard port. For example, MySQL's server uses port 3306 by default. Unless you've changed the setup, you don't have to specify DATABASE_PORT at all.

For details on creating a new database and database user (which is required for database servers), see Appendix B.

Using SQLite

SQLite is a popular choice for testing and even for deployment in scenarios where there isn't a great deal of simultaneous writing going on. No host, port, user, or password information is needed because SQLite uses the local filesystem for storage and the native filesystem permissions for access control. So only two settings are needed to tell Django to use your SQLite database.

```
DATABASE_ENGINE = "sqlite3"
DATABASE_NAME = "/var/db/django.db"
```

> **Note**
>
> When using SQLite with a real Web server such as Apache, you need to make sure the account owning the Web server process has write access both for the database file itself and the directory containing that database file. When working with the dev server like we are here, permissions are typically not an issue because the user (you) running the dev server also owns the project files and directories.

SQLite is also one of the most popular choices on Win32 platforms because it comes free with the Python distribution. Given we have already created a c:\py\django directory with our project (and application), let's create a db directory as well.

```
DATABASE_ENGINE = 'sqlite3'
DATABASE_NAME = r'C:\py\django\db\django.db'
```

If you are new to Python, you notice the subtle difference in the first example; we used double quotes around `sqlite3`, whereas in the Win32 version, we used single quotes. Rest assured it has nothing to do with differing platforms—Python does not have a character type, so single quotes and double quotes are treated the same. Just make sure you open and close a string with the same type of quote!

You should also have noticed a small "`r`" in front of the folder name. If you've read Chapter 1, then you know this means to designate the object as a "raw string," or one that takes all characters of a string verbatim, meaning do not translate special character combinations. For example, \n usually means a newline character, but in a raw string, it means (literally) two characters: a backslash followed by an n. So the purpose of a raw string is specifically for DOS file paths, telling Python to not translate special characters (if there are any).

Creating the Tables

Now you tell Django to use the connection information you've given it to connect to the database and set up the tables your application needs. The command to do this is simply:

```
./manage.py syncdb          # or ".\manage.py syncdb" on win32
```

You see some output that starts like this as Django sets up the database:

```
Creating table auth_message
Creating table auth_group
Creating table auth_user
Creating table auth_permission
Creating table django_content_type
Creating table django_session
Creating table django_site
Creating table blog_blogpost
```

When you issue the `syncdb` command, Django looks for a `models.py` file in each of your `INSTALLED_APPS`. For each model it finds, it creates a database table. (There are exceptions to this later when we get into fancy stuff such as many-to-many relations, but it's true for this example. If you are using SQLite, you also notice the `django.db` database file is created exactly where you specified.)

The other items in `INSTALLED_APPS`, the ones that were there by default, all have models too. The output from `manage.py syncdb` confirms this, as you can see Django is creating one or more tables for each of those apps.

That's not all the output you got from the syncdb command, though. You also got some interactive queries related to the `django.contrib.auth` app.

```
You just installed Django's auth system, which means you don't have any superusers
defined.
Would you like to create one now? (yes/no): yes
Username (Leave blank to use 'pbx'):
E-mail address: pb@e-scribe.com
```

```
Password:
Password (again):
Superuser created successfully.
Installing index for auth.Message model
Installing index for auth.Permission model
```

Now you've got one superuser (hopefully yourself) in the auth system. This comes in handy in a moment, when we add in Django's automatic admin application.

Finally, the process wraps up with a couple lines relating to a feature called **fixtures**, which we come back to in Chapter 4, "Defining and Using Models." These enable you to preload data in a freshly created application. For now, we're not using that feature, so Django moves on.

```
Loading 'initial_data' fixtures...
No fixtures found.
```

Your initial database setup is now complete. The next time you run the `syncdb` command on this project (which you do any time you add an application or model), you see a bit less output because it doesn't need to set up any of those tables a second time or prompt you to create a superuser.

Setting Up the Automatic admin Application

The automatic back-end application, or admin, has been described as Django's "crown jewel." For anyone who has tired of creating simple "CRUD" (Create, Read, Update, Delete) interfaces for Web applications, it's a godsend. We get much deeper into the admin in "Customizing the Admin" in Chapter 11, "Advanced Django Programming." For now, let's just turn it on and poke around.

Because it's an optional part of Django, you need to specify in your `settings.py` file you're using it—just like you did with your own blog app. Open `settings.py` and add the following line to the `INSTALLED_APPS` tuple, just underneath `'django.contrib.auth'`.

```
'django.contrib.admin',
```

Every time you add a new application to your project, you should run the `syncdb` command to make sure the tables it needs have been created in your database. Here we can see adding the admin app to `INSTALLED_APPS` and running `syncdb` triggers the creation of one more table in our database:

```
$ ./manage.py syncdb
Creating table django_admin_log
Installing index for admin.LogEntry model
Loading 'initial_data' fixtures...
No fixtures found.
```

Now that the app is set up, all we need to do is give it a URL so we can get to it. You should have noticed these two lines in your automatically generated `urls.py`.

```
# Uncomment this for admin:
#     (r'^admin/', include('django.contrib.admin.urls')),
```

Remove the # character from the second line (and you can remove the first, comment-only line at the same time) and save the file. You've told Django to load up the default admin site, which is a special object used by the contrib admin application.

Finally, your applications need to tell Django which models should show up for editing in the admin screens. To do so, you simply need to define the default admin site mentioned previously and register your `BlogPost` model with it. Open the `mysite/blog/models.py` file, make sure the admin application is imported, and then add a line registering your model at the bottom.

```
from django.db import models
from django.contrib import admin

class BlogPost(models.Model):
    title = models.CharField(max_length=150)
    body = models.TextField()
    timestamp = models.DateTimeField()

admin.site.register(BlogPost)
```

This simple use of the admin is the tip of the iceberg; it's possible to specify many different admin-related options by making a special Admin class for a given model, and then registering the model with that class. We do this shortly, and you also see examples of advanced admin use in later chapters, especially in Parts III, "Django Applications by Example," and IV, "Advanced Django Techniques and Features."

Trying Out the admin

Now that we've set up our Django site with the admin app and registered our model with it, we can take it for a spin. Issue the `manage.py runserver` command again. Now, go to http://127.0.0.1:8000/admin/ in your Web browser. (Don't worry if your dev server address is different; just add an `admin/` onto it, whatever it is.) You should see a login screen, as shown in Figure 2.4.

Type the "superuser" name and password you created earlier. Once you've logged in, you see the admin home page, as shown in Figure 2.5.

We'll tour this interface later in the book; for now, just confirm your application, Blog, is showing up as seen in the screenshot. If it's not, recheck the previous steps.

> **Tip**
>
> The three most common causes for "My app doesn't show up in the admin," problems are 1) forgetting to register your model class with `admin.site.register`, 2) errors in the app's `models.py`, and 3) forgetting to add the app to the `INSTALLED_APPS` tuple in your `settings.py` file.

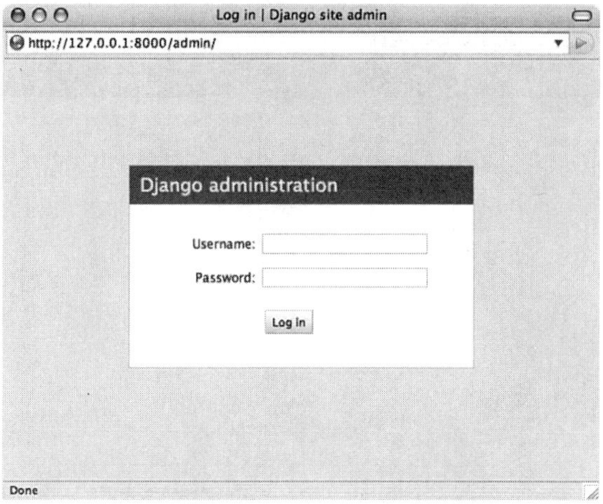

Figure 2.4 The admin login screen

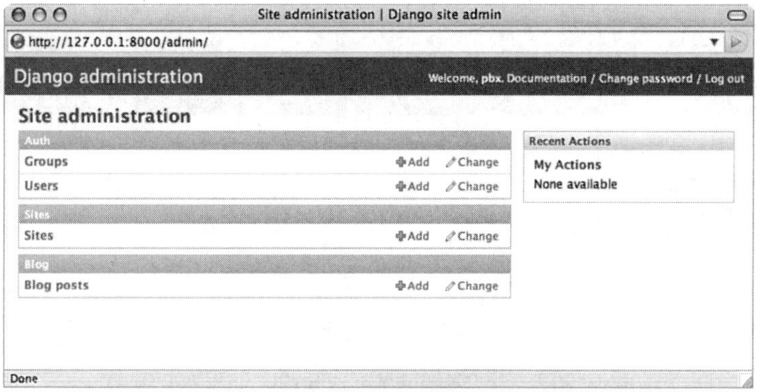

Figure 2.5 The admin home page

What's a blog without content? Click the Add button to the right of Blog Posts. The admin presents a form for adding a new post, as shown in Figure 2.6.

Give your post a title and some scintillating content. For the timestamp, you can click the Today and Now shortcut links to fill in the current date and time. You can also click the calendar or clock icons to pull up handy date and time pickers.

When you're done writing your masterpiece, click the Save button. You see a screen with a confirmation message ("The blog post 'BlogPost object' was added successfully") and a list of all your blog posts—a grand total of one at this point, as shown in Figure 2.7.

Why is the post given the awkward name of "BlogPost object"? Django is designed to flexibly handle an infinite variety of content types, so it doesn't take guesses about what

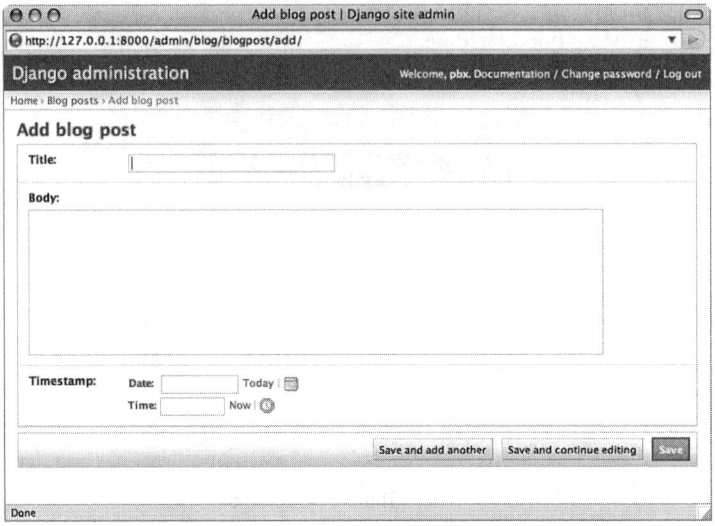

Figure 2.6   Adding new content via the admin

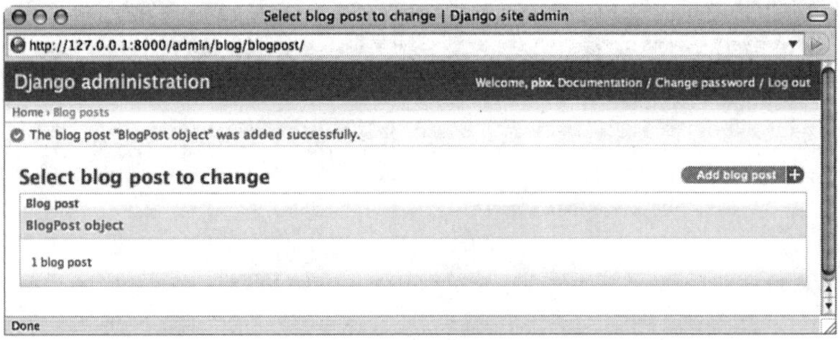

Figure 2.7   Successfully saving your first blog entry

field can be the best handle for a given piece of content. Throughout Part 3's example applications, you see examples of defining how to specify a particular field, or specially constructed string, to be used for your objects' default labels.

Now go ahead and add a second post with different content by clicking on the Add Blog Post + button to the upper-right. When you are returned to the list view, you just see another BlogPost row added to the page. If you refresh the page or go away and come back to your application, the output has not improved any—you just do not feel satisfied with seeing all the entries generically labeled as "BlogPost object," as shown in Figure 2.8. You are not alone if you're thinking, "There has got to be a way to make it look more useful!"

However, we don't have to wait until then to clean up the list display in our admin view. Previously, we enabled the admin tool with the bare minimum of configuration,

Figure 2.8   Not the most useful summary page

namely registering our model with the admin app all by itself. However, with an extra *@66* two lines of code and a modification of the registration call, we can make the presentation of the listing much nicer and more usable. Update your `mysite/blog/models.py` file with a new `BlogPostAdmin` class and add it to the registration line, so your `models.py` looks like this: *compare 66*

```
from django.db import models
from django.contrib import admin
                          Model subclass
class BlogPost(models.Model):
    title = models.CharField(max_length=150)
    body = models.TextField()
    timestamp = models.DateTimeField()
                     ModelAdmin subclass
class BlogPostAdmin(admin.ModelAdmin):
    list_display = ('title', 'timestamp')


admin.site.register(BlogPost, BlogPostAdmin)
```

further info: 102, 160, 164, 186, 193, 223, 227

The development server notices your changes and reloads your models file. If you are monitoring your command shell, you see some output to this effect.

If you refresh the page, you now see much more useful output based on the new `list_display` variable you added to your `BlogPostAdmin` class (see Figure 2.9).

Try clicking on the Title and Timestamp column headers that have appeared—each one affects how your items are sorted. For example, click once on Title to sort in ascending order by title; click the Title header a second time to change to *descending* order.

The admin has many other useful features that can be activated with just a line or two of code: searching, custom ordering, filters, and more. As we've mentioned a few times already, Parts III and IV cover or demonstrate many of these topics in greater detail.

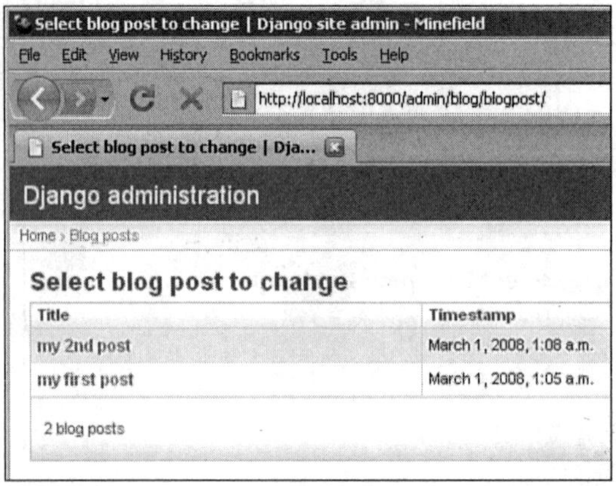

Figure 2.9   Much better

Making Your Blog's Public Side

With the database and admin side of our application taken care of, it's time to turn to the public-facing pages. A page, from Django's perspective, has three typical components:

- A **template** that displays information passed to it (in a Python-dictionary-like object called a `Context`)
- A **view** function that fetches information to be displayed, typically from a database
- A **URL pattern** that matches an incoming request with your view function, optionally passing parameters to the view as well

We'll tackle these three in that order. In a sense this is building from the inside out—when Django processes a request, it starts with the URL patterns, then calls the view, and then returns the data rendered into a template.

Creating a Template

Django's template language is easy enough to read that we can jump right in to example code. This is a simple template for displaying a single blog post:

```
<h2>{{ post.title }}</h2>
<p>{{ post.timestamp }}</p>
<p>{{ post.body }}</p>
```

It's just HTML (though Django templates can be used for any kind of textual output) plus special template tags in curly braces. These are **variable tags**, which display data passed to the template. Inside a variable tag, you can use Python-style dot-notation to access attributes of the objects you pass to your template. For example, this template assumes you have passed it a BlogPost object called "post." The three lines of the template fetch the BlogPost object's `title`, `timestamp`, and `body` fields, respectively.

Let's enhance the template a bit so it can be used to display multiple blog posts, using Django's for template tag.

```
{% for post in posts %}
<h2>{{ post.title }}</h2>
<p>{{ post.timestamp }}</p>
<p>{{ post.body }}</p>
{% endfor %}
```

The original three lines are unchanged; we've simply added a block tag called for that renders a template section once for each of a sequence of items. The syntax is deliberately similar to Python's loop syntax. Note that unlike variable tags, block tags are enclosed in {% ... %} pairs.

Save this simple five-line template in a file called archive.html, and put that file in a directory called templates inside your blog app directory. That is, the path to your template file should be:

```
mysite/blog/templates/archive.html
```

The name of the template itself is arbitrary (we could have called it foo.html), but the templates directory name is mandatory. By default, when searching for templates, Django looks for a templates directory inside each of your installed applications.

Creating a View Function

Now we'll write a simple view function that fetches all our blog posts from the database and displays them using our template. Open up the blog/views.py file and type the following:

```
from django.template import loader, Context
from django.http import HttpResponse
from mysite.blog.models import BlogPost

def archive(request):
    posts = BlogPost.objects.all()
    t = loader.get_template("archive.html")
    c = Context({ 'posts': posts })
    return HttpResponse(t.render(c))
```

Skipping over the import lines for the moment (they just load up the function and classes we need), here's the breakdown of the view function, line by line:

- Line 5: Every Django view function takes a django.http.HttpRequest object as its first argument. It can also take other arguments that get passed in via the URLconf, which is a feature you are using a lot.

- Line 6: When we created our BlogPost class as a subclass of django.db.models.Model, we inherited the full power of Django's object-relational mapper. This line is a simple example of using the ORM (Object-Relational Mapper; see Chapters 3, "Starting Out," and 4 for more) to get all the BlogPost objects in the database.

- Line 7: To create our template object **t**, we only need to tell Django the name of the template. Because we've stored it in the **templates** directory of our app, Django can find it without further instruction.
- Line 8: Django templates render data that is provided to them in a **context**, a dictionary-like object. Our context **c** has only a single key and value.
- Line 9: Every Django view function returns a **django.http.HttpResponse** object. In the simplest case, we pass the constructor a string. The template **render** method returns a string, conveniently.

Creating a URL Pattern

Only one more piece is needed for our page to work—like anything else on the Web, it needs a URL.

We could create the needed URL pattern directly inside **mysite/urls.py**, but that creates a messy coupling between our project and our app. We can use our blog app somewhere else, so it would be nice if it were responsible for its own URLs. We do this in two simple steps.

The first step is much like enabling the admin. In **mysite/urls.py**, there's a commented example line that is almost what we need. Edit it so it looks like this:

```
url(r'^blog/', include('mysite.blog.urls')),
```

This catches any requests that begin with **blog/** and passes them to a new URLconf you're about to create.

The second step is to define URLs inside the blog application package itself. Make a new file, **mysite/blog/urls.py**, containing these lines:

```
from django.conf.urls.defaults import *
from mysite.blog.views import archive

urlpatterns = patterns('',
    url(r'^$', archive),
)
```

It looks a lot like our base URLconf. The action happens in line 5. First, note the **blog/** part of the request URL, which our root URLconf was matching, is stripped—our blog application is reusable and shouldn't care if it's mounted at **blog/** or **news/** [1] or **what/i/had/for/lunch/**. The regular expression in line 5 matches a bare URL, such as **/blog/**.

The view function, **archive**, is provided in the second part of the pattern tuple. (Note we're not passing a string that names the function, but an actual first-class function object. Strings can be used as well, as you see later.)

Let's see it in action! Is the dev server still running? If not, fire it up with **manage.py runserver**, and then go to http://127.0.0.1:8000/blog/ in your browser. You should see a simple, bare-bones rendering of any blog posts you have entered, complete with title, timestamp, and post body.

Finishing Touches

Using the key concepts laid out so far, you could go forward and refine this primitive blog engine in a number of ways. Let's step through a few of them to make this project feel just a little more polished.

Template Niceties

Our template is plain to say the least. Because this is a book on Web programming not Web design, we leave the aesthetic touches to you, but template inheritance is another feature of the template system that can make your life easier, especially as your page styles proliferate.

Our simple template is completely self-contained. But what if our site had a blog, a photo archive, and a links page, and we wanted all these to be based on a common base? Experience tells you the *wrong* way to do this would be to copy and paste your way to three kind-of-identical self-contained templates. The *right* way in Django is to create a base template, and then *extend* this template to generate the other, specific templates. In your `mysite/blog/templates` directory, create a template called `base.html` containing the following:

```
<html>
<style type="text/css">
body { color: #efd; background: #453; padding: 0 5em; margin: 0 }
h1 { padding: 2em 1em; background: #675 }
h2 { color: #bf8; border-top: 1px dotted #fff; margin-top: 2em }
p { margin: 1em 0 }
</style>
<body>
<h1>mysite.example.com</h1>
{% block content %}
{% endblock %}
</body>
</html>
```

"content" hole

because of the {%...%} constructs

Not exactly valid XHTML Strict, but it'll do. The detail to notice is the {% `block` ... %} tag. This defines a named area that subtemplates can change. To make your blog app use this template, change your `archive.html` template so it references this new base template and its "content" block.

```
{% extends "base.html" %}
{% block content %}
{% for post in posts %}
<h2>{{ post.title }}</h2>
<p>{{ post.timestamp }}</p>
<p>{{ post.body }}</p>
{% endfor %}
{% endblock %}
```

 # I will use/fill in the skeleton template 'base.html'

+ My replacement for the 'content' block named "block", here

The `{% extends ... %}` tag tells Django to look for a template named `base.html`, and plug the content of any named blocks in *this* template into the corresponding blocks in *that* template. You should now see something like Figure 2.10 (hopefully your blog posts are more exciting, though).

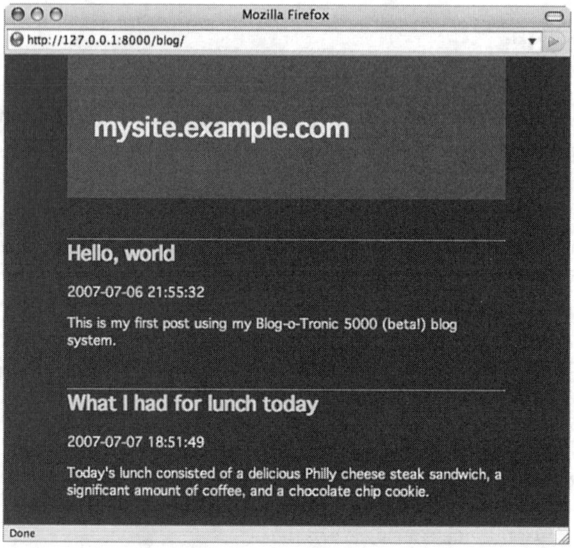

Figure 2.10   The blog, lightly styled

Date-Based Ordering

You should have noticed your blog posts are not being presented in traditional reverse-chronological order. It's easy for us to tell Django to do that; in fact, we have a choice as to where we want to tell it to do so. We can add a default ordering to our model, or we can add it to the `BlogPost.objects.all()` query in our view code. In this case the model is a better location because we most often want posts ordered reverse chronologically. If we set our preferred ordering in the model, any part of Django that accesses our data uses that ordering.

To set default ordering for your model, give it an inner class called `Meta` and set the ordering attribute in that class.

```
class Meta:
    ordering = ('-timestamp',)
```

Take a look at your blog home page (`/blog/`). The newest post should now be on top. The string `-timestamp` is a concise way of telling Django, "order by the 'timestamp' field, and do it in descending order." (If we omitted the "-", they'd be presented in ascending date order instead.)

> **Note**
>
> Don't omit the trailing comma inside the parentheses! It makes this a single-item tuple, rather than just a parenthesized string. Django expects a tuple here; you're allowed to spec- ify as many fields for ordering as you want. If you added `'title'` after the comma, and you had two posts titled "A" and "B" with the same timestamp, post "A" would come first.

Timestamp Formatting Via a Template Filter

That timestamp is handy, but its ISO8601 format is a little nerdy. Let's humanize it a bit by using a cool feature of the Django template system: filters.

Because this is a presentation detail, not a data structure or business logic detail, the appropriate place for it is in the template. Open your `archive.html` file and change the "post.timestamp" line to

```
<p>{{ post.timestamp|date }}</p>
```

To apply a filter to a variable, you simply tack it on to the end of the variable name— inside the curly brackets—using a vertical bar, or "pipe," character. Reload your blog home page. Now your dates appear in a more liberal-arts-friendly form ("July 7 ").

If the default style of the `date` filter isn't to your liking, you can pass it an argument using `strftime`-type formatting. However, rather than using the conversion codes from Python's `time` module, it uses the same formatting directives as PHP's `date` function. For example, if you want to display the day of the week but omit the year, change the line to pass an argument to the date filter.

```
<p>{{ post.timestamp|date:"l, F jS" }}</p>
```

This particular format string gives you dates in the style "Friday, July 6th." Make sure you don't leave any space on either side of that colon—the Django template engine is particular about this.

Summary

Of course, we could continue adding features to our blog engine forever (many people do!), but hopefully you've seen enough to give you a taste of the power of Django. In the course of building this skeletal blog app you've seen a number of Django's elegant, labor- saving features:

- The built-in Web server, which makes your development work more self-contained and automatically reloads your code if you edit it
- The pure-Python approach to data model creation, which saves you from having to write or maintain SQL code or XML description files
- The automatic admin application, which provides full-fledged content-editing fea- tures even for nontechnical users
- The template system, which can be used to produce HTML, CSS, JavaScript, or any textual output format

- Template filters, which can alter the presentation of your data (such as dates) without messing with your application's business logic
- The URLconf system, which gives you great flexibility in URL design while keeping application-specific portions of URLs in the application, where they belong

Just to give you an idea of what's ahead, the following are some things we could proceed to do to our blog using Django's built-in features:

- Publish Atom or RSS feeds of our latest posts (see Chapter 11)
- Add a search feature so that users can locate blog posts containing specific terms (see the CMS example app in Chapter 8, "Content Management System")
- Adopt Django's "generic views" to avoid having to write any code in views.py at all (see the Pastebin example app in Chapter 10, "Pastebin")

You've completed your whirlwind tour of Django basics. Chapter 3, fleshes out with a broad look at Django's key components and the philosophies behind them, as well as provides a recap of some Web development principles central not only to Django itself, but to the lessons we offer in later parts of the book. Chapter 4, takes you down into the details of the framework, where you find answers to the questions of "how, why, and what about ...?" that probably arose as you walked through the previous examples. After Chapter 4, you have a solid enough understanding to follow along and build several example applications: a content management system, a pastebin, a photo gallery, and an Ajax-powered "live blog."

Starting Out

As with any large software project, Django encompasses a large number of concepts, features, and tools, and the set of problems it was designed to solve—namely Web development—also has a large scope. To start learning the details about using Django, you need to understand those problems and the methods frameworks such as Django use to solve them.

This chapter introduces these basic ideas, starting with a tool-agnostic look at the Web, following with explanations of the Web framework model and its constituent parts, and wrapping up with the general development philosophy employed by the creators of Django. The high-level overview in the previous chapter also gives you a bit of context here.

An important note: If you already have a solid background in Web development, some of these concepts should be old hat—but even intermediate and experienced Web developers can benefit from taking a step back and reviewing the fundamentals of the practice. It is all too common to find ourselves mentally constrained by the specific language or toolset at hand, whereas a greater perspective often presents solutions previously hidden from view.

Having a solid handle on these core concepts makes you a better problem solver and allows you to make better choices, both during design and implementation. So please— don't skip ahead!

Dynamic Web Site Basics

At its heart, Web development is conceptually simple. Users request a document from the Web server; the Web server fetches or generates the requested document; the server returns the result to the user's browser; and the browser renders the document. The details tend to vary, but that's really all there is to it. Let's break this down as it applies to Web frameworks such as Django.

Communication: HTTP, URLs, Requests, Responses

HTTP (HyperText Transfer Protocol) encapsulates the entire process of serving Web pages and is the foundation for the Web. Because it's a protocol for client-server communication, it largely consists of **requests** (client to server) and **responses** (server to client). What happens on the server between the two isn't covered by HTTP and is up to the server software (see the following).

The concept of a **request** encapsulates the first part of the process—the client asking the server for a given document. The heart of a request is the **URL**—the "path" to the document being requested—but it can be further parameterized via a number of methods, enabling a single location or URL to exhibit multiple behaviors.

A **response** consists primarily of a **body**—usually the text of a Web page—and accompanying **headers** with extra information about the data in question, such as when it was last updated, how long it should be cached locally, its content type, and so forth. Other, non-HTML content included in a response could be plain text, images, documents (PDF, Word, Excel, and so on), audio clips, and so forth.

Django represents both requests and responses as relatively simple Python objects with attributes for the varying pieces of data and methods for more complex operations.

Data Storage: SQL and Relational Databases

Looked at simply, the Web is about data transfer or the sharing of **content** (meaning, quite literally, anything—blog entries, financial data, ebooks, and so forth). In the Web's early days, content consisted of HTML text files, written by hand, and stored on the server's filesystem. This is known as **static** because requests to the same URL always return the same information. The "path" described previously was more primitive; there were no parameters, as it was merely a path on the server's filesystem where the static content was located. Present day, most content is considered **dynamic** because the data returned by a given URL can vary tremendously depending on factors.

A large part of this dynamic nature is enabled by storing data in a **database**, where instead of a single string of text, one can create multipart pieces of data and link them to one another to represent relationships. To define and query the database, **SQL** (Structured Query Language) is used, often further abstracted by an **ORM** (Object-Relational Mapper), which enables object-oriented programming languages to represent the database as code objects.

SQL databases are organized into **tables**, each consisting of **rows** (for example, entries, items, objects) and **columns** (for example, attributes, fields), similar in overall organization to a spreadsheet. Django provides a powerful ORM, where Python classes represent tables, objects represent individual rows within those tables, and the table's columns are attributes of those objects.

Presentation: Rendering Templates into HTML and Other Formats

The final piece of the Web development puzzle is how to present or format the information requested and/or returned via HTTP and queried from the SQL database. Typically, this is done in **HTML** (HyperText Markup Language) or its newer, more XML-like cousin **XHTML**, along with the sister languages of **JavaScript** for dynamic browser-side functionality and **CSS** (Cascading Style Sheets) for visual styling. Newer applications also use **JSON** (a "light" data format) or **XML** to enable dynamic content.   (AJAX)

To work with data being presented, most Web frameworks provide a **template language**, which blends raw HTML tags with a programming-like syntax for looping over collections of objects, performing logic operations, and other constructs that enable the dynamic behavior desired. A simple example could be an otherwise static HTML document with a piece of logic that says to display the username of the currently logged-in user or to display a "Login" link if the user is not yet logged in.

Some templating systems attempt to be fully XHTML compliant, implementing their programming-like commands as HTML attributes or tags, so the resultant document can be parsed as normal HTML. Others emulate regular programming languages more closely, sometimes with an "alternative tag" syntax where the programming constructs are surrounded with special characters for ease of reading and parsing. Django's template language is one of the latter.

{% ... %}   >   {{ ... }}

prog constr.   var

Putting It All Together

While organizing the Web into the three components outlined previously, one important aspect has been omitted: how they interact with one another. How does a Web application know to execute a SQL query based on a request, and how does it know what template to use when rendering the result?

The answer depends partly on the tools used: Each Web framework or language can approach things in a different way. However, there are generally more similarities than there are differences, and although the next two sections outline Django's own approach, many of these concepts can be found in other frameworks as well.

Understanding Models, Views, and Templates

As you've just seen, dynamic Web development is often broken down into a handful of core components. In this section, we expand further on those concepts, discussing the programming methodologies involved and an overview of how Django implements them (with details and examples in chapters to come).

Separating the Layers (MVC)

The idea of breaking down a dynamic application (Web or otherwise) has been around for some time, usually applied to graphical client-side applications, and is generally known as the **MVC** (Model-View-Controller) paradigm. As you can expect, this means the application is segregated into the **model**, which controls the data, the **view**, which defines how to display data, and a **controller**, which mediates between the two and enables the user to request and manipulate the data.

Compartmentalizing an application in such a manner enables the programmer to be flexible and encourages code reuse among other things. For example, a given view—say, a module that knows how to display graphs of numeric data—could be used on top of various different sets of data, so long as the glue between the two is able to tie them together. Or a specific, single set of data could be displayed in multiple different output formats, such as the aforementioned graph view, a flat text file, or a sortable table. Multiple controllers could enable varying levels of access to the same data model for different users or enable data entry via a GUI application as well as via e-mail or the command line.

The key to successfully leveraging an MVC architecture lies in correctly segregating these different layers of the application. Having one's data model store information about how it should be displayed, although potentially convenient for some setups, means it is much harder to completely swap out one view for another. And having database-specific access codes in one's graphical layout code would cause no end of headaches if you decide to switch database platforms!

Django's Approach

Django adheres to this separation of duties, although it does so in a slightly different manner than the norm. The model aspect stays the same: Django's model layer deals solely with passing data into and out of a database. However, the "view" in Django isn't the final step in displaying the data—Django's views are closer to what are normally considered the "controller" aspects of MVC. They're Python functions which tie together the model layer and the presentation layer (which consists of HTML and Django's template language to be covered later in Chapter 6, "Templates and Form Processing"). To quote the Django development team:

> In our interpretation of MVC, the "view" describes the data that gets presented to the user. It's not necessarily how the data looks, but which data is presented. The view describes which data you see, not how you see it. It's a subtle distinction.

In other words, Django splits the presentation layer in twain with a view method defining what data to display from the model and a template defining the final representation of that information. As for the controller, the framework itself serves as a controller of sorts—it provides mechanisms, which determine what view and template are used to respond to a given request.

Models

The basis for any application, Web or otherwise, is the information it presents, gathers, and modifies. As such, if we examine an application as a set of layers, the model is the bottom layer, the foundation. Views and templates can come and go, changing how data enters and leaves the model and how it is presented, but the model is relatively set in stone.

From the perspective of designing a full-stack Web application, the model is possibly both the easiest to grasp and the hardest to master. Modeling a real-world problem in an object-oriented system is often a comparatively simple task, but for high-traffic Web sites the most realistic model isn't always the most efficient.

The model encompasses a wide range of potential pitfalls, one of which is changing the model code after your application has been deployed. Although you are "just changing code," you have actually altered your database schema under the covers, and this often causes side effects to the preexisting data stored in the database. We go over many of these real-life concerns in the chapters ahead when exploring the design of some example applications.

Views

Views form much (sometimes most or all) of the logic in Django applications. Their definition is deceptively simple: Python functions are linked to one or more defined URLs, which return HTTP response objects. What happens in-between those two endpoints of Django's HTTP mechanisms is entirely up to you. In practice, there are usually a few, similar tasks performed at this stage, such as displaying an object or list of objects from the model or adding new such objects, along with bookkeeping-like tasks such as checking the status of an authenticated application user and either enabling or rejecting access.

Django provides many shortcuts and helper functions for tasks such as these, but you can write everything yourself for full control over the process, for heavy use of the shortcuts for rapid prototyping and development, or for combining the two approaches. Flexibility and power are the name of the game here.

Templates

You should have noticed we just stated the *view* is responsible for displaying objects from the model. That's not 100 percent true. To the extent that view methods just have to return an HTTP response, it's true enough—you could write out a string in Python and return that and be none the worse for wear. However, in the vast majority of cases, it's terribly inefficient to do so, and as mentioned previously, separation of layers is important to adhere to.

Instead, most Django developers use its template language to render the HTML that Web applications so often result in. Templates are essentially HTML text documents with special formatting denoting where to output dynamic values, enabling simple logic constructs such as loops, and so forth. When a view wants to return an HTML document, it usually specifies a template, gives it the information to display, and uses that rendered template in its response.

Although HTML is the most common format, templates don't actually have to contain any—they can be used to create any text format, such as comma-separated values (CSV) or even e-mail message body text. The important thing is they enable a Django project to separate the presentation of its data from the view code which decides what data to present.

Overall Django Architecture

In this chapter thus far, we've covered some of the large architectural components which make up an actual Django system as well as supporting cast just outside its boundaries. Let's put them all together to give you an overall perspective. In Figure 3.1, you can see the HTTP communication protocol is the closest to the user. Using URLs, they can send requests to Django Web applications and can receive responses back to their Web clients, which may also be running JavaScript with Ajax doing any out-of-band server access.

At the opposite end of the spectrum (at the bottom of the figure), you see the database is the persistent storage which is managed under the guidance of your models and the Django ORM, communicating to the database via Python's DB-API as well as the database's client library in the form of an adapter, usually written in C/C++ with a Python interface.

Last but not least, in between we have Django, the heart of the application. Django's MVC paradigm is equivalently spelled out as "MTV"¹ in Django-speak. The views, serving in controller capacity navigate between creating, updating, and deleting the data model through to the database via the ORM while managing the final view to users given its templates.

Connecting the pieces together, the HTTP requests that come in are forwarded by the Web server to Django, which accepts them starting at the request middleware layer. They are then dispatched based on URLconf patterns to the appropriate view, which performs the core part of the work required, using models and/or templates as necessary to create the response. The response then goes through one more layer of middleware that performs any final processing before returning the HTTP response back to the Web server to forward on to the user. Make sense?

Core Philosophies of Django

As a full-stack Web framework initially developed by a small, tightly knit group of programmers, Django has been and continues to be designed with a fairly specific set of philosophies in mind. These ideals reflect the experiences (and to a degree, the personalities) of the core team, but at the same time they tend to line up very well with what any Web developer using any toolkit would agree are "best practices." Understanding these philosophies helps you understand, and make better use of, the framework.

1 Model - Template - View

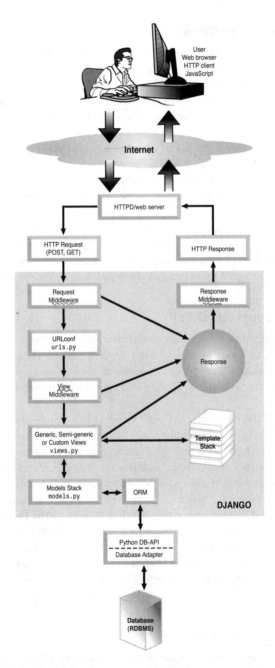

Figure 3.1   A high-level overview of Django's component architechure

Django Tries to Be Pythonic

The programming language used, and that language's community, is often one of the larger influences on any software project's design, and this is no different with Django. Users of Python tend to describe things that mesh well with and generally adhere to the philosophies of the language as being **Pythonic**; although there is no explicit definition of the term, it generally means code exhibits various attributes common to other works in the language.

Among these attributes are the use of terse but powerful syntax (the default syntax of `for` loops or the even-more-concise tool of list comprehensions); the idea there is usually only one *right* way to do any given simple task (such "ways" are often incorporated into the language itself, such as the `get` dictionary method) and favoring the explicit more than the implicit (such as the requirement for a `self` argument in all object methods).

As we see in the example application chapters in Part III, "Django Applications by Example," many Django conventions, methods, and design decisions are Pythonic or strive to be. This makes the framework easier to pick up for programmers with Python experience and also helps to ingrain good programming practices in less experienced developers.

Don't Repeat Yourself (DRY)

One Pythonic attribute that deserves its own section is a principle common to almost all programming: **DRY**, or Don't Repeat Yourself. DRY is perhaps the simplest programming idiom of all because it's just plain old common sense: If you have information in more than one place and it needs to change, you've just made twice as much (or more) work for yourself.

As an example of DRY, consider the need to perform a simple calculation on a few pieces of data, such as the sum of a collection of bank accounts associated with a given individual. In a poorly designed system, this summation can be performed in multiple places throughout the code: pages listing individuals, a page for detailed per-individual information, or a page displaying grand totals for multiple individuals. In a system such as Django's ORM, you can easily honor DRY by creating a `Person` class with a `sum_accounts` method defined only once and then used in all the previous locations.

Although DRY can be easy to apply to simple situations such as the previous example, it's also one of the hardest commandments to adhere to strictly all the time; there are many places where it conflicts with other idioms, Pythonic and otherwise, where trade-offs must be made. However, it is a worthy goal to strive toward and one which becomes easier with experience.

Loose Coupling and Flexibility

Django is a full-stack Web framework in the sense it provides all necessary components for a dynamic Web application: database access, request framework, application logic, templating, and so forth. However, an effort has been made to ensure that users' options are left open: You can use as much or as little of Django as you need and can replace components with other tools as you see fit.

For example, some users dislike Django's template system and prefer alternatives such as Kid or Cheetah. Django view methods don't require that Django's template system be used, so it's entirely possible to have one's views load up Kid or Cheetah, render a template written for those systems, and return the result as part of a Django response object.

The same goes for the database layer. Users who prefer SQLAlchemy or SQLObject, for example, can simply ignore Django's ORM entirely and work with their data via other tools. Conversely, if less common, it's possible to utilize *only* Django's ORM for other projects (even non-Web-oriented ones); it functions with only a minimum of setup.

When all is said and done, however, such modularity comes at a price: Some of Django's nicest shortcuts necessarily encompass the stack as a whole, such as the generic view methods enabling simple display and updating and creating database records. As such, this modular approach to Django is usually best avoided by those new to Python Web development.

Rapid Development

Django was written with rapid, agile development in mind. Working in a fast-paced local newspaper shop, the core team needed a set of tools that would allow them to implement an idea in an extremely short amount of time. The open-sourcing of the framework has not changed the fact that it excels in this area.

Django provides shortcuts at a couple of different levels. The most obvious is the aforementioned generic view collection, which consists of perhaps a dozen or so common tasks. Combined with flexible and powerful parameterization, these generic views can, and often do, make up the entirety of a Web site, enabling creation and modification of database records, display of lists of objects (date-oriented and otherwise) and individual object pages, and more. With only three Python files—site-specific settings, a model declaration, and a map linking URLs to generic views—and some HTML templates, one can create an entire Web site in a matter of minutes or hours.

At a lower level, Django provides many shortcut methods for common tasks at the Python view level itself, so when generic views can't provide what the programmer needs, they can still avoid a lot of boilerplate. Such shortcuts exist for rendering templates with data dictionaries, obtaining a database object, returning an HTTP error if one doesn't exist, processing forms, and so forth.

Combined with the flexibility, terseness, and power of the Python language, these shortcuts enable programmers to focus on getting projects built and out the door quickly, and/or solving domain-specific problems without worrying about grunt work or so-called "glue code."

Summary

We've covered a lot of ground in this chapter: the fundamentals of what Web development is all about, how Django and similar frameworks organize their approach to creating Web sites, and the underlying philosophies driving Django's own development and design decisions. Regardless of what you brought to this chapter, we hope you've gained something from the overview.

At this point in the book, you should now have a decent background in both the basics of developing Web applications as well as the underlying theory and organization of a typical Web framework. In Part II, "Django in Depth," we dive into the details of how to use Django, exploring the various classes, functions, and data structures it uses and showing you more code snippets to help it all make sense.

Django in Depth

II

4

Defining and Using Models

As explained in Chapter 3, "Starting Out," the data model of a Web application is usually its foundation, and at any rate is an excellent place to begin exploring the details of Django development. Although this chapter has two main sections—defining models, and then using them—the two halves are more intertwined than separate. We need to consider how we plan to use our models, while we're defining them, to generate the most effective arrangement of classes and relationships. And, of course, you can't make the best use of a model without understanding the how and the why of its definition.

Defining Models

Django's database model layer makes heavy use of an ORM (Object-Relational Mapper), and it's a good idea to understand the reasoning behind this design decision as well as the pluses and minuses of the approach. Therefore, we start out this section with an explanation of Django's ORM, after which we get into the details of model fields, the possible relationships between model classes, and the use of model class metadata to define specific behaviors of the model or enable and customize the Django admin application.

Why Use an ORM?

Django, along with most other modern Web frameworks (as well as many other application development tools), relies on a rich data access layer that attempts to bridge an underlying relational database with Python's object-oriented nature. These ORMs are still a subject of much debate in the development community with various arguments for and against their use. As Django was designed with the use of an ORM in mind, we present to you four arguments in favor of using them, specifically Django's own implementation.

Encapsulation of Useful Methods

Django model objects, as we cover later in this chapter, are first and foremost a way of defining a collection of fields, which generally map to database columns. This provides the first and primary step in tying the relational database to object-oriented concepts. Instead of a SQL query like `SELECT name FROM authors WHERE id=5`, one can request the

`Author` object whose `id` is 5 and examine `author.name`—this is a much more Pythonic type of interface to the data.

However, model objects can add a lot of extra value to that humble beginning. Django's ORM, like many others, enables you to define arbitrary instance methods, leading to any number of useful things. For example:

- You can define read-only combinations of fields or attributes, sometimes known as **data aggregation** or **calculated attributes**. For example, an `Order` object with `count` and `cost` attributes could expose a `total` that is simply the product of the other two. Common object-oriented design patterns become much easier—façades, delegation, and so forth.

- In Django, the ORM presents the option of overriding built-in database-altering methods such as saving and deleting objects. This enables you to easily define a set of arbitrary operations to be performed on your data before it is saved to the database or to ensure that certain clean-up operations are always called prior to deleting a record, no matter where or how the deletion occurs.

- Integration with the programming language—in Django's case, Python—is generally simple, enabling you to let your database objects conform to specific interfaces or APIs.

Portability

Due to their very nature—being a layer of code between your application and the database itself—ORMs provide excellent portability. Most ORM platforms support multiple database backends, and Django's is no exception. At the time of this writing, code utilizing Django's model layer runs on PostgreSQL, MySQL, SQLite, and Oracle—and this list is likely to grow as more database backend plugins are written.

Safety

Because you are rarely executing your own SQL queries when using an ORM, you don't have to worry as much about the issues caused by malformed or poorly protected query strings, which often lead to problems such as SQL injection attacks. ORMs also provide a central mechanism for intelligent quoting and escaping of input variables, freeing up time otherwise spent dealing with that sort of minutia. This sort of benefit is common with modularized or layered software of which MVC frameworks are a good example. When all the code responsible for a specific problem domain is well-organized and self-contained, it can often be a huge time-saver and increase overall safety.

Expressiveness

Although not directly related to the *definition* of models, one of the greatest benefits of using an ORM (and certainly one of the largest differences, compared to writing raw SQL) is the query syntax used to obtain records from the database. Not only is a higher-level query syntax arguably easier to work with, but the act of bringing the query mechanisms into the realm of Python enables a host of useful tactics and methodologies. For example, it becomes possible to construct otherwise unwieldy queries by looping over data structures, an approach that is generally more compact than the equivalent SQL and can avoid the sometimes tedious string manipulation that can be otherwise required.

Django's Rich Field Types

Django models cover a wide range of field types; some of them are closely tied to their database implementations, although others have been designed with Web form interfaces in mind. Most of them fall between these two extremes. Although an exhaustive list can be found in the official Django documentation, we present a comparison study which covers some of the most commonly used fields. First, we provide a quick introduction to the basics of Django model definition.

```
from django.db import models

class Book(models.Model):
    title = models.CharField(max_length=100)
    author = models.ForeignKey(Author)
    length = models.IntegerField()
```

From the previous, it should be relatively obvious what we've just created: a simplistic model of a book made of up various database-related concepts. It's not much to look at—generally those tasked with cataloging books are interested in much more than just the title, author, and number of pages—but it'll do. It's also perfectly workable. You could throw that example into a Django `models.py` file and be well on your way to a book catalog app with very few modifications.

As you can see, Django uses Python classes to represent objects, which generally map to SQL tables with attributes mapping to columns. These attributes are themselves objects, specifically subclasses of a `Field` parent class; as stated previously, some of them are obvious analogues to SQL column types, although others provide some level of abstraction. Let's examine some specific `Field` subclasses.

- `CharField` and `TextField`: Possibly the most common fields you encounter, these two do much the same thing—they hold text. `CharField`s have a set, finite length, although `TextField`s are essentially infinite; which one you use depends on your needs, including the fulltext search capabilities of your database or your need for efficient storage.

- `EmailField`, `URLField`, and `IPAddressField`: These three fields, among others, are essentially `CharField`s which provide extra validation. Such fields are stored in the database, like a `CharField` but have validation code defined to ensure their values conform to e-mail addresses, URLs, and IP addresses, respectively. It's simple to add your own validation to model fields and thus to create your own "field types" on the same level as Django's built-in ones. (See Chapters 6, "Templates and Form Processing," and 7, "Photo Gallery," for more on validation.)

- `BooleanField` and `NullBooleanField`: `BooleanField` works in most situations where you want to store True or False values, but sometimes you want the capability to store the fact you don't *know* yet if the value is one or the other—in which case the field would be considered empty, or null, and thus `NullBooleanField` was born. This distinction highlights the fact that modeling your data often requires some thought, and decisions sometimes need to be made on a semantic level as well as a technical one—not just how the data is stored, but what it means.

- `FileField`: `FileField` is one of the most complex fields, in no small part because almost all the work involved in its use isn't in the database at all, but in the request part of the framework. `FileField` stores only a file path in the database, similar to its lesser cousin `FilePathField`, but goes the extra mile and provides the capability to upload a file from the user's browser and store it somewhere on the server. It also provides methods on its model object for accessing a Web-based URL for the uploaded file.

These are only a handful of the available field types present in Django model definitions, and as new Django releases come out, new fields are occasionally added or updated. To see the full, up-to-date list of model field classes and what you can do with them, see the official Django documentation. You also see many of these fields throughout this book in example code snippets and example applications in Part III, "Django Applications by Example."

Primary Keys and Uniqueness

A common concept in relational database definition is that of a **primary key**, which is a field guaranteed to be unique across an entire table (or in Django ORM terms across an entire model). These primary keys are typically auto-incrementing integers because such a field is a simple and effective method of ensuring that each row in the table has a unique value.

They're also useful as reference points for relationships between models (which are covered in the next few sections)—if a given `Book` object has an ID number of 5 and is guaranteed to be the *only* `Book` with that ID number, a reference to "book #5" is unambiguous.

Because this type of primary key is fairly ubiquitous, Django automatically makes one for you unless you specify otherwise. All models without an explicit primary key field are given an `id` attribute, which is a Django `AutoField` (an auto-incrementing integer). `AutoField`s behave just as normal integers, and their underlying database column type varies depending on your database backend.

For those wanting more control over primary keys, simply make sure you specify `primary_key=True` for one of your model fields, and that field becomes the primary key for the table in place of `id` (which is omitted in such circumstances). This means the field's values must be completely unique, so specifying it for a string field such as a name or other identifier cannot be a good idea unless you're 110 percent certain you never, ever have duplicates!

Speaking of duplicates, we'll also mention there's a similar argument that can be applied to just about any field in your model: `unique=True`. This enforces uniqueness for the field in question without making that field the primary key.

Relationships Between Models

The capability to define relationships between model objects is, naturally, one of the strongest selling points for using relational databases (as evidenced by the name itself—*relational*) and is also an area where ORMs sometimes tend to differ from one another. Django's current implementation is fairly database-centric, making sure the relations are defined at the database level and not just at the application level. However, because SQL only provides for one explicit form of relation—the foreign key—it is necessary to add some layering to provide more complex relationships. We examine the foreign key first and then move to how it can serve as a building block for the other relationship types.

Foreign Keys

Because foreign keys are fairly simple, Django's implementation of them is similarly straightforward. They're represented as their own `Field` subclass, `ForeignKey`, whose primary argument is simply the model class being referred to, as in the following example:

```
class Author(models.Model):
    name = models.CharField(max_length=100)

class Book(models.Model):
    title = models.CharField(max_length=100)
    author = models.ForeignKey(Author)
```

You should note we need to define classes being referred to at the top because otherwise the `Author` variable name would not be available for use in the `Book` class's `ForeignKey` field. However, you can use a string instead, either the class name if it's defined in the same file, or using dot notation (for example, `'myapp.Author'`) otherwise. Here's the previous example rearranged and rewritten using a string-based `ForeignKey`:

```
class Book(models.Model):
    title = models.CharField(max_length=100)
    author = models.ForeignKey("Author")

class Author(models.Model):
    name = models.CharField(max_length=100)
```

It's also possible to define self-referential `ForeignKey`s by using the string `'self'`. This is commonly used when defining hierarchical structures (for example, a `Container` class defining a `parent` attribute enabling nested `Container`s) or similar situations (such as an `Employee` class with attributes such as `supervisor` or `hired_by`).

Although the `ForeignKey` is only defined on one side of the relationship, the receiving end is able to follow the relationship backward. Foreign keys are technically a *many-to-one* relationship, as multiple "child" objects can refer to the same "parent" object; thus, the child gets a single reference to its parent, but the parent gets access to a *set* of its children. Using the previous example, you could use `Book` and `Author` instances such as:

```
# Pull a book off the shelf - see below in this chapter for details on querying
book = Book.objects.get(title="Moby Dick")       objects is a "manager"
# Get the book's author - very simple
author = Book.author       # simple access to parent " or receiver" of foreign key relationship
# Get a set of the books the author has been credited on
books = author.book_set.all()       book_set is a "manager"
```

As you can see, the "reverse relationship" from `Author` to `Book` is represented by the `Author.book_set` attribute (a **manager** object, outlined later in the chapter), which is automatically added by the ORM. It's possible to override this naming scheme by specifying a `related_name` argument to the `ForeignKey`; in the previous example, we could have defined author as `ForeignKey("Author", related_name="books")` and would then have access to `author.books` instead of `author.book_set`.

> **Note**
>
> The use of `related_name` is optional for simple object hierarchies, but required for more complex ones, such as when you have multiple `ForeignKey`s leading from one object to another. In such situations, the ORM needs you to tell it how to differentiate the two reverse relationship managers on the receiving end of those two `ForeignKey` fields. Django's database management tools lets you know by way of an error message if you forget!

Many-to-Many Relationships

Foreign keys are generally used to define **one-to-many** (or **many-to-one**) relationships—in our previous examples, a `Book` has a single `Author` and an `Author` can have many `Book`s. However, sometimes you need more flexibility. For example, until now we've assumed a `Book` has only one `Author`, but what about books written by more than one person, such as this one?

Such a scenario requires a "many" relationship not only on one side (`Author` having one or more `Book`s) but on both (`Book` also having one or more `Author`s). This is where the concept of **many-to-many** relationships come in; because SQL has no definition for these, we must build them using the foreign keys it does understand.

Django provides a second relationship-oriented model field to handle this situation: `ManyToManyField`. Syntax-wise, they are identical to `ForeignKey`; you define them on one side of the relationship, passing in the class to relate to, and the ORM automatically grants the other side the necessary methods or attributes to use the relationship (typically by creating a _set manager as seen previously with `ForeignKey`s). However, due to the nature of `ManyToManyField`, it doesn't generally matter which side you define it on because the relationship is inherently symmetrical.

> **Note**
>
> If you plan on using Django's admin application, keep in mind the admin forms for objects in
> a many-to-many relationship only display a form field on the *defining* side.

> **Note**
>
> Self-referential `ManyToManyFields` (that is, a `ManyToManyField` on a given model refer-
> encing that same model) are symmetrical by default because it's assumed the relationship
> goes both ways. However, this is not always the case, and so it's possible to change this
> behavior by specifying `symmetrical=False` in the field definition.

Let's update our book example with the newfound realization we must handle
multiple-author books:

```
class Author(models.Model):
    name = models.CharField(max_length=100)


class Book(models.Model):
    title = models.CharField(max_length=100)
    authors = models.ManyToManyField(Author)
```

← authors = models. Foreign key (Author).
↖ note's plural compare p 93

The usage of `ManyToManyField` is similar to the "many" side of a foreign key
relationship:

```
# Pull a book off the shelf
book = Book.objects.get(title="Python Web Development Django")
# Get the books' authors
authors = Book.author_set.all()
# Get all the books the third author has worked on
books = authors[2].book_set.all()
```

with
book
books=
authors[2].book_set.
all()

① book
② authors =
book.author_set.
all()
authors[2]

The secret of the `ManyToManyField` is that underneath, it creates an entirely new table[1]
in order to provide the lookups needed for such a relationship, and it is this table which
uses the foreign key aspects of SQL; each row represents a single relationship between two
objects, containing foreign keys to both.

This lookup table is normally hidden during regular use of Django's ORM and cannot
be queried on its own, only via one of the ends of the relationship. However, it's possible
to specify a special option on a `ManyToManyField`, through, which points to an explicit
intermediate model class. Use of through thus lets you manually manage extra fields on
the intermediate class, while retaining the convenience of managers on the "ends" of the
relationship.

The following is identical to our previous `ManyToManyField` example, but contains
an explicit `Authoring` intermediate table, which adds a `collaboration_type` field to the
relationship, and the through keyword pointing to it.

```
class Author(models.Model):
    name = models.CharField(max_length=100)
```

1 This table would hold
(id, book_id, author_id)
with an uniquely id'd row for
every valid book & author matching

book_id is an FK to book
author_id " " " author

```
class Book(models.Model):
    title = models.CharField(max_length=100)
    authors = models.ManyToManyField(Author, through="Authoring")
class Authoring(models.Model):
    collaboration_type = models.CharField(max_length=100)
    book = models.ForeignKey(Book)
    author = models.ForeignKey(Author)
```

You can query `Author` and `Book` in an identical fashion to our earlier query example and can also construct queries dealing with the type of "authoring" that was involved.

```
# Get all essay compilation books involving Chun
chun_essay_compilations = Book.objects.filter(
    author__name__endswith='Chun',
    authoring__collaboration_type='essays'
)
```

As you can see, this adds significant flexibility to Django's ability to compose relationships meaningfully.

Composition with One-to-One Relationships

In addition to the commonly used many-to-one and many-to-many relationship types you've just seen, relational database development sometimes makes use of a third type, namely **one-to-one** relationships. As with the other two, the name means exactly what it says; both sides of the relationship have only a single-related object.

Django implements this concept as as a `OneToOneField` that is generally identical to `ForeignKey`—it requires a single argument, the class to relate to (or the string "self" to be self-referential). Also like `ForeignKey`, it optionally takes `related_name` so you can differentiate between multiple such relationships between the same two classes. Unlike its cousins, `OneToOneField` does not add a reverse manager for following the reverse relationship—just another normal attribute—because there's always only one object in either direction.

This relationship type is most often used to support object composition or ownership, and so is generally a bit less rooted in the real world than it is in object-oriented design. Before Django supported model inheritance directly (see the following), `OneToOneField` was typically used to implement inheritance-like relationships and now forms the behind-the-scenes basis for that feature.

Constraining Relationships

As a final note regarding the definition of relationships, it's possible—for both `ForeignKeys` and `ManyToManyFields`—to specify a `limit_choices_to` argument. This argument takes a dictionary as its value, whose key/value pairs are query keywords and values (again, see the following for details on what those keywords are). This is a powerful method for specifying the possible values of the relationship you're defining.

For example, the following is a version of the `Book` model class that only works with `Authors` whose name ends in Smith:

```
class Author(models.Model):
    name = models.CharField(max_length=100)


class SmithBook(models.Model):
    title = models.CharField(max_length=100)
    authors = models.ManyToManyField(Author, limit_choices_to={
        'name__endswith': 'Smith'
    })
```

(handwritten annotations: "query keyword", "query value")

> **Note**
>
> It's also possible—and sometimes desirable—to specify this limitation at the form level. See the description of `ModelChoiceField` and `ModelMultipleChoiceField` in Chapter 6.

Model Inheritance

A relatively new feature in Django's ORM at the time of this writing is that of model inheritance. In addition to foreign key and other relationships between otherwise distinct model classes, it's possible to define models which inherit from one another in the same way that normal, non-ORM Python classes do. (Some examples of which can be found in Chapter 1, "Practical Python for Django.")

For example, the previous `SmithBook` class could be defined not as its own stand-alone class that just happens to have the same two fields as the `Book` class, but as an explicit subclass of `Book`. The benefits are hopefully obvious—the subclass can then add or override only the fields that differentiate it from its parent, instead of replicating the entire definition of the other class.

Our simplistic `Book` example doesn't make this sound too exciting, but consider a more realistic model with a dozen or more attributes and a handful of complex methods, and suddenly inheritance becomes a compelling way to adhere to Don't Repeat Yourself (DRY). Do note, however, that composition—the use of `ForeignKey` or `OneToOneField`—is still a viable alternative! Which technique you use is entirely up to you and depends a lot on your planned model setup.

Django currently provides two different approaches to inheritance, each with its own pluses and minuses: **abstract base classes** and **multi-table inheritance**.

Abstract Base Classes

The approach of using abstract base classes is, to put it simply, "Python-only" inheritance—it enables you to refactor your Python model definitions such that common fields and methods are inherited from base classes. However, at a database and query level, the base classes don't exist, and their fields are replicated in the database tables for the children.

This sounds like a violation of DRY, but is actually desirable in scenarios where you don't *want* an extra database table for the base class—such as when your underlying database is legacy or otherwise being used by another application. It's also just a neater way to express refactoring of class definitions without implying an actual object hierarchy.

Let's re-examine (and flesh out) the `Book` and `SmithBook` model hierarchy, using abstract base classes.

```python
class Author(models.Model):
    name = models.CharField(max_length=100)

class Book(models.Model):
    title = models.CharField(max_length=100)
    genre = models.CharField(max_length=100)
    num_pages = models.IntegerField()
    authors = models.ManyToManyField(Author)

    def __unicode__(self):
        return self.title

    class Meta:
        abstract = True

class SmithBook(Book):
    authors = models.ManyToManyField(Author, limit_choices_to={
        'name__endswith': 'Smith'
    })
```

The key is the `abstract = True` setting in the `Meta` inner class of `Book`—it signifies that `Book` is an abstract base class and only exists to provide its attributes to the actual model classes which subclass it. Note `SmithBook` only redefines the `authors` field to provide its `limit_choices_to` option—because it inherits from `Book` instead of the usual `models.Model`, the resulting database layout has columns for `title`, `genre`, and `num_pages`, as well as a many-to-many lookup table for `authors`. The Python-level class also has a `__unicode__` method defined as returning the `title` field, just as `Book` does.

In other words, when created in the database, as well as when utilized for object creation, ORM querying, and so forth, `SmithBook` behaves exactly as if it were the following definition:

```python
class SmithBook(models.Model):
    title = models.CharField(max_length=100)
    genre = models.CharField(max_length=100)
    num_pages = models.IntegerField()
    authors = models.ManyToManyField(Author, limit_choices_to={
        'name__endswith': 'Smith'
    })

    def __unicode__(self):
        return self.title
```

As mentioned, this behavior extends to the query mechanism as well as the attributes of `SmithBook` instances, so the following query would be completely valid:

```
smith_fiction_books = SmithBook.objects.filter(genre='Fiction')
```

Our example isn't fully suited to abstract base classes, however, you'd typically want to create both normal `Books` as well as `SmithBooks`. Abstract base classes are, of course, abstract—they cannot be created on their own, and as stated previously, are mostly useful to provide DRY at the model definition level. Multi-table inheritance, outlined next, is a better approach for our particular scenario.

Some final notes regarding abstract base classes: The inner `Meta` class on subclasses is inherited from, or combined with, that of the parent class (with the natural exception of the `abstract` option itself, which is reset to `False`, as well as some database-specific options such as `db_name`).

In addition, if a base class uses the related_name argument to a relational field such as `ForeignKey`, you need to use some string formatting, so subclasses don't end up clashing. Don't use a normal string, such as `"related_employees"`, but one with `%(class)s` in it, such as `"related_%(class)s"` (refer back to Chapter 1 if you don't recall the details about this type of string replacement). This way, the subclass name is substituted correctly, and collisions are avoided.

Multi-table Inheritance

Multi-table inheritance, at the definition level, appears to be only slightly different from abstract base classes. The use of Python class inheritance is still there, but one simply omits the `abstract = True` `Meta` class option. When examining model instances, or when querying, multi-table inheritance is again the same as what we've seen before; a subclass appears to inherit all the attributes and methods of its parent class (with the exception of the `Meta` class, as we explain in just a moment).

The primary difference is the underlying mechanism. Parent classes in this scenario are full-fledged Django models with their own database tables and can be instantiated normally as well as lending their attributes to subclasses. This is accomplished by automatically setting up a `OneToOneField` between the subclasses and the parent class, and then performing a bit of behind-the-scenes magic to tie the two objects together, so the subclass inherits the parent class's attributes.

In other words, multi-table inheritance is just a convenience wrapper around a normal "has-a" relationship—or what's known as object composition. Because Django tries to be Pythonic, the "hidden" relationship is actually exposed explicitly if you need it, via the `OneToOneField`, which is given the lowercased name of the parent class with a `_ptr` suffix. For example, in the snippet that follows, `SmithBook` gets a `book_ptr` attribute leading to its "parent" `Book` instance.

The following is our `Book` and `SmithBook` example with multi-table inheritance:

```python
class Author(models.Model):
    name = models.CharField(max_length=100)
```

```
class Book(models.Model):
    title = models.CharField(max_length=100)
    genre = models.CharField(max_length=100)
    num_pages = models.IntegerField()
    authors = models.ManyToManyField(Author)

    def __unicode__(self):
        return self.title

class SmithBook(Book):
    authors = models.ManyToManyField(Author, limit_choices_to={
        'name__endswith': 'Smith'
    })
```

As mentioned, the only difference at this point is the lack of the `Meta` class `abstract` option. Running `manage.py syncdb` on an empty database with this `models.py` file would create three main tables—one each for `Author`, `Book`, and `SmithBook`—whereas with abstract base classes we'd only have tables for `Author` and `SmithBook`.

Note `SmithBook` instances get a `book_ptr` attribute leading back to their composed `Book` instance, and `Book` instances that belong to (or that are part of, depending on how you look at it) `SmithBooks` get a `smithbook` (without a `_ptr` suffix) attribute.

Because this form of inheritance enables the parent class to have its own instances, `Meta` inheritance could cause problems or conflicts between the two sides of the relationship. Therefore, you need to redefine most `Meta` options that can otherwise have been shared between both classes (although `ordering` and `get_latest_by` is inherited if not defined on the child). This makes honoring DRY a little bit tougher, but as much as we'd like to achieve 100 percent DRY, it's not always possible.

Finally, we hope it's relatively clear why this approach is better for our book model; we can instantiate both normal `Book` objects as well as `SmithBook` objects. If you're using model inheritance to map out real-world relationships, chances are you prefer multi-table inheritance instead of abstract base classes. Knowing which approach to use—and when to use neither of them—is a skill that comes with experience.

Meta Inner Class

The fields and relationships you define in your models provide the database layout and the variable names you use when querying your model later on—you often find yourself adding model methods such as `__unicode__` and `get_absolute_url` or overriding the built-in `save` or `delete` methods. However, there's a third aspect of model definition and that's the inner class used to inform Django of various metadata concerning the model in question: the `Meta` class.

The `Meta` class, as the name implies, deals with metadata surrounding the model and its use or display: how its name should be displayed when referring to a single object versus multiple objects, what the default sort order should be when querying the database table, the name of that database table (if you have strong opinions on the subject), and so forth.

In addition, the `Meta` class is where you define multi-field uniqueness constraints because it wouldn't make sense to define those inside any single field declaration. Let's add some metadata to our first `Book` example from earlier.

```
class Book(models.Model):
    title = models.CharField(max_length=100)
    authors = models.ManyToManyField(Author)

    class Meta:
        # Alphabetical order
        ordering = ['title']
```

That's it! The `Book` class is so simple it doesn't need to define most of the options the `Meta` inner class provides, and if we didn't really care about a default ordering, it could have been left out entirely. `Meta` and `Admin` are entirely optional, albeit commonly used, aspects of model definition. Let's whip up a more complex example because `Book`'s meta options are fairly boring.

```
class Person(models.Model):
    first = models.CharField(max_length=100)
    last = models.CharField(max_length=100)
    middle = models.CharField(max_length=100, blank=True)

    class Meta:
        # The proper way to order people, assuming a Last, First M. style of
        # display.
        ordering = ['last', 'first', 'middle']
        # Here we encode the fact that we can't have a person with a 100%
        # identical name. Of course, in real life, we could, but we'll pretend
        # this is an ideal world.
        unique_together = ['first', 'last', 'middle']
        # Django's default pluralization is simply to add 's' to the end: that
        # doesn't work here.
        verbose_name_plural = "people"
```

As you can see from the comments, modeling the concept of a person would be rough going without defining some `Meta` options. We have to consider all three fields when ordering records, and to avoid duplication, and having the system refer to more than one person as "persons" can be quaint, but is probably not desired.

For more details on the various `Meta` class options you can define, we defer you to the official Django documentation.

Admin Registration and Options

If you're using the "admin" contrib app that comes with Django, you are making heavy use of admin `site` objects and their `register` function, as well as optional `ModelAdmin` subclasses. These subclasses enable you to define various options concerning how your model is utilized when you're interacting with it in the admin application.

Simply registering your model class with the admin (along with enabling the Admin app itself, covered in Chapter 2, "Django for the Impatient: Building a Blog") is enough to get the admin to pick it up and provide you with basic list and form pages; hooking in a `ModelAdmin` subclass with extra options enables you to hand-pick the fields displayed in list views, the layout of the forms, and more.

In addition, you can specify inline editing options for relational fields such as `ForeignKey`, by creating `Inline` subclasses and referencing them in a `ModelAdmin` subclass. This proliferation of extra classes can seem odd at first, but it's an extremely flexible way of ensuring any given model can be represented in more than one way or in multiple admin sites. Extending the model hierarchy to inline editing also enables you to place an inline form in more than one "parent" model page, if desired.

We leave the detailed explanation of what each option does to the official documentation—and note there are some examples of admin usage in Part 3—but here's a basic outline of what's possible in each of the two main types of `ModelAdmin` options.

- List formatting: `list_display`, `list_display_links`, `list_filter`, and similar options enable you to change the fields shown in list views (the default being simply the string representation of your model instances in a single column) as well as enabling search fields and filter links, so you can quickly navigate your information.

- Form display: `fields`, `js`, `save_on_top`, and others provide a flexible means of overriding the default form representation of your model, as well as adding custom JavaScript includes and CSS classes, which are useful if you want to try your hand at modifying the look and feel of the admin to fit the rest of your Web site.

Finally, realize if you find yourself making *very* heavy use of these options, it can be a sign to consider disregarding the admin and writing your own administrative forms. However, make sure you read the "Customizing the Admin" section of Chapter 11, "Advanced Django Programming," first for tips on just how much you can flex the Django admin before setting out on your own.

Using Models

Now that we've explained how to define and enhance your models, we go over the details of how to create, and then query, a database based on them, finishing up with notes on the raw SQL underpinnings of the overall mechanism.

Creating and Updating Your Database Using `manage.py`

As mentioned previously in Chapter 2, the `manage.py` script created with every Django project includes functionality for working with your database. The most common `manage.py` command is `syncdb`. Don't let the name fool you; it doesn't do a full synchronization of your database with your models as some users can expect. Instead, it makes sure all model classes are represented as database tables, creating new tables as necessary—but *not* altering existing ones.

> ### Database "Synchronization"
>
> The reasoning behind `syncdb`'s behavior is Django's core development team strongly believes one's production data should never be at the mercy of an automated process. Additionally, it is a commonly held belief that changes to database schemas should only be performed when a developer understands SQL well enough to execute those changes by hand. The authors tend to agree with this approach; a better understanding of underlying technology is always preferable when developing with higher-layer tools.
>
> At the same time, an automatic or semi-automatic schema change-set mechanism (such as Rails' migrations) can often speed up the development process. At the time of this writing, there are several non-core Django-related projects in various stages of development attempting to address this perceived deficit in the framework.

Therefore, if you create a model, run `syncdb` to load it into the database, and later make changes to that model, `syncdb` does not attempt to reconcile those changes with the database. It is expected that the developer makes such changes by hand or via scripts or simply dumps the table or database entirely and reruns `syncdb`, which results in a fully up-to-date schema. For now, what's important is that `syncdb` is the primary method for turning a model class into a database table or tables.

In addition to `syncdb`, `manage.py` provides a handful of specific database-related functions which `syncdb` actually builds upon to perform its own work. Table 4.1 shows a few of the more common ones. Among these are commands such as `sql` and `sqlall`, which display the `CREATE TABLE` statements (`sqlall` performs initial data loading as well); `sqlindexes` for creating indexes; `sqlreset` and `sqlclear`, which empty or drop previously created tables; `sqlcustom`, which executes an app's custom initial SQL statements (see the following for more); and so forth.

Table 4.1   **`manage.py` Functions**

`manage.py` Function	Description
`syncdb`	Create necessary tables needed for all apps
`sql`	Display `CREATE TABLE` call(s)
`sqlall`	Same as `sql` plus initial data-loading statements from `.sql` file
`sqlindexes`	Display the call(s) to create indexes for primary key columns

Table 4.1 **manage.py** Functions

manage.py Function	Description
sqlclear	Display the DROP TABLE call(s)
sqlreset	Combination of sqlclear and sql (DROP plus CREATE)
sqlcustom	Display custom SQL statements from .sql file
loaddata	Load initial fixtures (similar to sqlcustom but without raw SQL)
dumpdata	Dump current database contents to JSON, XML, and so on

Unlike syncdb, these sql* commands do not update the database on their own. Instead, they simply print out the SQL statements in question, enabling the developer to read them for verification's sake (ensuring a later syncdb does what the developer intends, for example) or save them to a stand-alone SQL script file.

It's also possible to pipe these commands' output into one's database client for immediate execution, in which case they can act as more granular analogues to syncdb. You can also combine the two approaches by redirecting to a file first, modifying that file, and then redirecting the file into the database for execution (see Appendix A, "Command Line Basics," for more on pipes and redirection).

For more information on how to use these commands and the intricacies of syncdb, see the example application chapters in Part 3 or visit the official Django documentation.

Query Syntax

Querying your model-generated databases requires the use of two distinct, but similar, classes: Managers and QuerySets. Manager objects are always attached to a model class, so unless you specify otherwise, your model classes each exhibit an objects attribute, which forms the basis for all queries in the database concerning that model. Managers are the gateway to obtaining info from your database; they have a trio of methods that enable you to perform typical queries.

- all: Return a QuerySet containing all the database records for the model in question.
- filter: Return a QuerySet containing the model records matching specific criteria.
- exclude: The inverse of filter—find records that *don't* match the criteria.
- get: Obtain a single record matching the given criteria (or raise an error if there are either no matches or more than one).

Of course, we're getting ahead of ourselves—we haven't explained what a QuerySet really is yet. QuerySets can be thought of as simply lists of model class instances (or database rows/records), but they're much more powerful than that. Managers provide a jumping-off point for generating queries, but QuerySets are where most of the action really happens.

QuerySets are multifaceted objects, making good use of Python's dynamic nature, flexibility, and so-called "duck typing" to provide a trio of important and powerful behaviors; they are database queries, containers, and building blocks all rolled into one.

QuerySet as Database Query

As evidenced by the name, a QuerySet can be thought of as a nascent database query. It can be translated into a string of SQL to be executed on the database. Because most common SQL queries are generally a collection of logic statements and parameter matches, it makes sense that QuerySets accept a Python-level version of the same thing. QuerySets accept dynamic keyword arguments or parameters that are translated into the appropriate SQL. This becomes obvious in an example using the Book model class from earlier in this chapter.

```
from myproject.myapp.models import Book

books_about_trees = Book.objects.filter(title__contains="Tree")
```

The keywords accepted are a mix of your model's field names (such as title in the previous example), double underscores for separation, and optional clarification words such as contains, gt for "greater than," gte for "greater than or equal to," in for set membership testing, and so forth. Each maps directly (or nearly so) to SQL operators and keywords. See the official documentation for details on the full scope of these operators.

Going back to our example, Book.objects.filter is a Manager method, as explained previously, and Manager methods always return QuerySet objects. In this case, we've asked the Book default manager for books whose title contains the word "Tree" and have captured the resultant QuerySet in a variable. This QuerySet represents a SQL query that can look like this:

```
SELECT * FROM myapp_book WHERE title LIKE "%Tree%";
```

It's entirely possible to make compound queries, such as one for the Person model also defined previously:

```
from myproject.myapp.models import Person

john_does = Person.objects.filter(last="Doe", first="John")
```

which would result in the following SQL:

```
SELECT * FROM myapp_person WHERE last = "Doe" AND first = "John";
```

Similar results appear when using other previous Manager methods, such as all:

```
everyone = Person.objects.all()
```

which turns into the unsurprising SQL query:

```
SELECT * FROM myapp_person;
```

It should be noted the various query-related options defined in the optional `Meta` model inner class affect the generated SQL, as you can expect; ordering turns into `ORDER BY`, for example. And as we explore later, `QuerySet`'s extra methods and composition capabilities also transmute the SQL, which is eventually executed on the database.

Finally, if you speak SQL yourself and understand the implications of various query mechanisms (both in terms of the result sets and the execution times), you will be better equipped to construct ORM queries, which are faster or more specific than ones you could otherwise have created. In addition, planned and current development work on Django makes it easier to pry open `QuerySet` objects and tweak the resultant SQL—giving you more power than ever.

QuerySet as Container

`QuerySet` is list-like. It implements a partial `list` interface and thus can be iterated over (`for record in queryset:`), indexed (`queryset[0]`), sliced (`queryset[:5]`), and measured (`len(queryset)`). As such, once you're used to working with Python lists, tuples, and/or iterators, you already know how to use a `QuerySet` to access the model objects within. Where possible, these operations are accomplished intelligently. For example, slicing and indexing make use of SQL's `LIMIT` and `OFFSET` keywords.

On occasion, you can find you need to accomplish something with a `QuerySet` that isn't possible or desirable with the existing features Django's ORM provides. In these cases, you can simply turn a `QuerySet` into a list with `list`, after which point it becomes a true list containing the entire result set. Although this is sometimes necessary or useful—such as when you want to do Python-level sorting—keep in mind this can cause a lot of memory or database overhead if your `QuerySet` results in a large number of objects!

Django strives to provide as much power as possible with its ORM, so if you do find yourself thinking about casting to a list, make sure you spend a few minutes skimming this book or the official documentation, or poke around the Django mailing list archives. Chances are good you find a way to solve your problem without pulling the entire `QuerySet` into memory.

QuerySet as Building Block

`QuerySet` is **lazy**; it only executes a database query when it absolutely has to, such as when it is turned into a list or otherwise accessed in ways mentioned in the previous section. This behavior enables one of the most powerful aspects of `QuerySet`s. They do not have to be stand-alone, one-off queries, but can be **composed** into complex or nested queries. This is because `QuerySet` exposes many of the same methods as `Manager`s do, such as `filter` and `exclude`, and more besides. Just like their `Manager` counterparts, these methods return new `QuerySet` objects—but this time they are further limited by the parent `QuerySet`'s own parameters. This is easier to understand with an example.

```
from myproject.myapp.models import Person
doe_family = Person.objects.filter(last="Doe")
john_does = doe_family.filter(first="John")
john_quincy_does = john_does.filter(middle="Quincy")
```

With each step we cut down the query results by an order of magnitude, ending up with one result object, or at least very few, depending on how many John Quincy Does we have in our database. Because this is all just Python, you could use a one-liner.

```
Person.objects.filter(last="Doe").filter(first="John").filter(middle="Quincy")
```

Of course, the astute reader notices this provides nothing we couldn't do with a single call to `Person.objects.filter`. However, what's to say we don't get the earlier `john_does` `QuerySet` in a function call or take it out of a data structure? In that case, we don't know the specific contents of the query we're handling—but we don't always need to.

Imagine we have added a `due_date` field to our `Book` model and are responsible for displaying books that are overdue (defined, naturally, as books whose due date is earlier than today). We could be handed a `QuerySet` containing all the books the library knows about, or all the fiction books, or all the books being returned by a specific individual— the point being that it's some arbitrary collection of books. It's possible to take such a collection and narrow it down to show only the books we're interested in, namely the overdue ones.

```
from myproject.myapp.models import Book
from datetime import datetime
from somewhere import some_function_returning_a_queryset

book_queryset = some_function_returning_a_queryset()
today = datetime.now()
# __lt turns into a less-than operator (<) in SQL
overdue_books = book_queryset.filter(due_date__lt=today)
```

In addition to filtering in this manner, `QuerySet` composition is absolutely required for nonsimple logical constructs, such as finding all the `Book`s written by authors named `Smith` and which are nonfiction.

```
nonfiction_smithBook.objects.filter(author__last="Smith").exclude(genre="Fiction")
```

Although it could have been possible to achieve the same result with query options for negation, such as `__genre__neq` or similar (something Django's ORM used to support in the past), breaking that logic out into extra `QuerySet` methods makes things much more compartmentalized. It's also arguably easier to read this way by breaking the query down into a few discrete "steps."

Sorting Query Results

It should be noted that `QuerySets` have a handful of extra methods that aren't present on `Manager` objects because they only serve to modify a query's results and don't generate new queries on their own. The most commonly used such method is `order_by`, which overrides the default ordering of a `QuerySet`. For example, let's say our previous `Person` class is normally ordered by last name; we can get an individual QuerySet ordered by first name instead, such as:

```
from myproject.myapp.models import Person

all_sorted_first = Person.objects.all().order_by('first')
```

The resulting `QuerySet` is the same as any other, but behind the scenes the SQL-level `ORDER BY` clause was updated as we requested. This means we can continue to layer on more syntax for more complex queries, such as finding the first five people sorted by first name.

```
all_sorted_first_five = Person.objects.all().order_by('first')[:5]
```

You can even sort across model relationships by using the double-underscore syntax you've seen earlier. Let's pretend for a moment our `Person` model has a `ForeignKey` to an `Address` model containing, among other things, a `state` field, and we want to order people first by state and then by last name. We could do the following:

```
sorted_by_state = Person.objects.all().order_by('address__state', 'last')
```

Finally, it's possible to reverse a sort order by prefixing the identifying string with a minus sign, for example, `order_by('-last')`. You can even reverse a whole `QuerySet` (if, for example, your code was passing a `QuerySet` around and you had no direct control over the previous call to `order_by`) by calling a `QuerySet`'s `reverse` method.

Other Ways to Alter Queries

Aside from ordering, there are a few other `QuerySet`-only methods to consider, such as `distinct`, which removes any duplicate entries in a `QuerySet` by using `SELECT DISTINCT` on the SQL side of things. Then there's `values`, which takes a list of field names (including fields on related objects) and returns a `QuerySet` subclass, `ValuesQuerySet`, containing only the requested fields as a list of dictionaries instead of normal model classes. `values` also has a twin method called `values_list`, which returns a list of tuples instead of dictionaries. Here's a quick interactive example of `values` and `values_list`.

```
>>> from myapp.models import Person
>>> Person.objects.values('first')
[{'first' : u'John'}, {'first': u'Jane'}]
>>> Person.objects.values_list('last')
[(u'Doe',), (u'Doe',)]
```

Another useful but often overlooked method is `select_related`, which can sometimes help with a common ORM problem of having an undesirably large number of queries for conceptually simple operations. For example, if one were to loop over a large number of `Person` objects and then display information on their related `Address` objects (considering the scenario in the previous section), your database would be queried once for the list of `Persons`, and then multiple times, one query per `Address`. This would be a lot of queries if your list contained hundreds or thousands of people!

To avoid this, `select_related` automatically performs database joins in the background to "prepopulate" related objects, so you end up with a single, larger query—databases are typically better performers with a few big queries than a ton of small ones. Note, however, `select_related` does not follow relationships where `null=True` is set, so keep that in mind if you're designing a model layout geared for performance.

Some final notes on `select_related`; you can control how "far" it reaches down a chain of relationships with the `depth` argument to prevent a truly gigantic query from happening if you have a deep object hierarchy. Furthermore, you can select only a few specific relationships if you have a wider hierarchy with lots of links between objects by passing their field names as positional arguments.

As an example, the following is how one would use `select_related` to do a simple join of our `Person` with its address and to avoid any other defined `ForeignKey` fields on either `Person` or `Address`:

```
Person.objects.all().select_related('address', depth=1)
```

Not a very exciting example, but that's rather the point; `select_related` and these other methods are only useful when you need to grab more or less than the query engine does by default. If you haven't worked with medium or large Web sites before, these don't seem too useful yet, but they're indispensable once your application is fully developed, and you need to start worrying about performance!

Details on all these functions, as well as `order_by` and `reverse`, can be found on the official Django documentation.

Query Keyword Composition with Q and ~Q

`QuerySet` is further augmented by a keyword-argument-encapsulating class named `Q`, which enables even more complex logic, such as composition of AND and OR using the `&` and `|` operators (which, although similar, should not be confused with their equivalent Python operators, `and` and `or` or the bitwise `&` and `|`). The resulting `Q` objects can be used in place of literal keyword arguments within `filter` or `exclude` methods, such as:

```
from myproject.myapp.models import Person
from django.db.models import Q


specific_does = Person.objects.filter(last="Doe").exclude(
    Q(first="John") | Q(middle="Quincy")
)
```

Although that example is rather contrived—there probably aren't many situations where you'd care about searching for a specific first *or* middle name—it should illustrate how Q is used.

Like QuerySets themselves, Q objects can be composited together over time. The & and | operators, when used on Qs, return new Q objects equivalent to their operands. For example, you can create potentially large queries via looping.

```
first_names = ["John", "Jane", "Jeremy", "Julia"]

first_name_keywords = Q() # Empty "query" to build on
for name in first_names:
    first_name_keywords = first_name_keywords | Q(first=name)

specific_does = Person.objects.filter(last="Doe").filter(first_name_keywords)
```

As you can see, we created a short for loop, primed it with the first item in our list, and then kept "appending" to the resulting Q object by using the | operator. This example actually isn't the best—such a simple scenario would be served better by the __in query operator—but hopefully it illustrates the potential power of composing Q objects together programmatically.

Note

We could have saved a few lines in the previous example by using some functional programming tools Python provides, namely list comprehensions, the built-in method reduce, and the operator module. The operator module provides functional equivalents to operators, such as or_ for | and and_ for &. The three lines surrounding the for loop could have been rewritten as reduce(or_, [Q(first=name) for name in first_names]). As always, because Django is "just Python," this sort of approach can be applied to just about any aspect of the framework.

Finally, you can use the single-operand operator ~ with Q objects to negate their contents. Although the QuerySet exclude method is a more common solution for such queries, ~Q shines when your query logic gets a bit more complex. Take for example this compound one-liner that grabs all the Does, plus anyone named John Smith, but not anyone named John W. Smith.

```
Person.objects.filter(Q(last="Doe") |
    (Q(last="Smith") & Q(first="John") & ~Q(middle__startswith="W"))
)
```

Tacking on exclude(middle_startswith="W") to such a query wouldn't have quite done the trick—it would have excluded any Does with a middle initial of "W," which is not what we want—but we were able to express our specific intentions with ~Q.

Tweaking the SQL with `Extra`

As a final word on what you can accomplish with Django's query mechanisms (and a lead-in to the next section about what they *aren't* currently capable of), we examine the `QuerySet` method `extra`. It's a versatile method, which is used to modify aspects of the raw SQL query that is generated by your `QuerySet`, accepting four keyword arguments that we describe in Table 4.2. Note the examples in this section can make use of attributes that were not defined in earlier model examples, for the sake of being more illustrative.

Table 4.2   **Some of the Parameters that `extra` Accepts**

`extra` Parameters	**Description**
select	Modify parts of SELECT statement
where	Provide additional WHERE clauses
tables	Provide additional tables
params	Safely substitute dynamic parameters

The `select` parameter expects a dictionary of identifiers mapped to SQL strings, which enables you to add custom attributes to the resultant model instances based on SQL SELECT clauses of your choosing. These are handy when you want to define simple additions to the information you pull out of the database and limit those to only a few parts of your code (as opposed to model methods, which execute their contents everywhere). In addition, some operations are simply faster in the database than they would be in Python, which can be useful for optimization purposes.

Here's an example of using `select` to add a simple database-level logic test as an extra attribute:

```
from myproject.myapp.models import Person

# SELECT first, last, age, (age > 18) AS is_adult FROM myapp_person;
the_folks = Person.objects.all().extra(select={'is_adult': "age > 18"})

for person in the_folks:
    if person.is_adult:
        print "%s %s is an adult because they are %d years old." % (person.first,
            person.last, person.age)
```

The `where` parameter takes as input a list of strings containing raw SQL WHERE clauses, which are dropped straight into the final SQL query as-is (or almost as-is; see `params` in the following). `where` is best used in situations when you simply can't make the right query by using attribute-related keyword arguments such as `__gt` or `__icontains`. In the following example, we use the same SQL-level construct to both

search by, and return, a concatenated string using PostgreSQL–style concatenation
with ||:

```
# SELECT first, last, (first||last) AS username FROM myapp_person WHERE
# first||last ILIKE 'jeffreyf%';
matches = Person.objects.all().extra(select={'username': "first||last"},
    where=["first||last ILIKE 'jeffreyf%'"])
```

Possibly the simplest extra parameter is tables, which enables you to specify a list of
extra table names. These names are then slotted into the FROM clause of the query, often
used in tandem with JOIN statements. Remember by default, Django names your tables
as appname_modelname.

Here's an example of tables, which deviates a bit from the rest (and returns to the
Book class with an additional author_last attribute) for brevity's sake:

```
from myproject.myapp.models import Book

# SELECT * FROM myapp_book, myapp_person WHERE last = author_last
joined = Book.objects.all().extra(tables=["myapp_person"], where=["last =
author_last"])
```

Finally, we come to the params argument. One of the "best practices" of performing
database queries from higher-level programming languages is to properly escape or insert
dynamic parameters. A common mistake among beginners is to do simple string concatenation or interpolation to get their variables into the SQL query, but this opens up a
whole host of potential security holes and bugs.

Instead, when using extra, make use of the params keyword, which is simply a list of
the values to use when replacing %s string placeholders in the where strings, such as:

```
from myproject.myapp.models import Person
from somewhere import unknown_input

# Incorrect: will "work", but is open to SQL injection attacks and related problems.
# Note that the '%s' is being replaced through normal Python string interpolation.
matches = Person.objects.all().extra(where=["first = '%s'" % unknown_input()])

# Correct: will escape quotes and other special characters, depending on
# the database backend. Note that the '%s' is not replaced with normal string
# interpolation but is to be filled in with the 'params' argument.
matches = Person.objects.all().extra(where=["first = '%s'"],
    params=[unknown_input()])
```

Utilizing SQL Features Django Doesn't Provide

The final word on Django's model/query framework is that, as an ORM, it simply can't
cover all the possibilities. Few ORMs claim to be a 100 percent complete replacement for
interfacing with one's database via the regular channels; Django is no different, although

the developers are always working to increase its flexibility. Sometimes, especially for those with extensive prior experience with relational databases, it's necessary to step outside the ORM. The following sections are a few thoughts on how this is possible.

Schema Definition and Custom Initial SQL

Aside from standard tables and columns, most RDBMS packages provide additional features such as views or aggregate tables, triggers, the capability to define "cascade" behavior when rows are deleted or updated, and even custom SQL-level functions or datatypes. Django's ORM—like most others—is largely ignorant of such things at the time of this writing, but that doesn't mean you can't use them.

One recently added aspect of Django's model definition framework is the capability to define custom **initial SQL** files, which must be `.sql` files within a `sql` subdirectory of an application, such as `myproject/myapp/sql/triggers.sql`. Any such file is automatically executed on your database whenever you run `manage.py` SQL-related commands such as `reset` or `syncdb` and is included in the output of `sqlall` or `sqlreset`. The feature has its own `manage.py` command, `sqlcustom`, which (such as the other `sql*` commands) prints out the custom SQL it finds.

Through use of initial SQL, you can store schema definition commands within your Django project and know that they are always included when you use Django's tools to build or rebuild the database. Most of the following bullet points can be accomplished by making use of this feature:

- Views: Because SQL views are effectively read-only tables, you can support them by creating Model definitions to mirror their layout, and then use the normal Django query API to interact with them. Note you need to be careful not to execute any `manage.py` SQL-related commands that would attempt to write such a model to the database, or you'd run into problems. As with any SQL library accessing such views, attempts to *write* to the view's table results in errors.

- Triggers and cascades: Both work just fine with inserts or updates generated by normal ORM methods and can be defined via initial SQL files, depending on your database (cascade constraints can be manually added to the output of `manage.py` `sqlall`, if they cannot be created after the fact).

- Custom functions and datatypes: You can define these in initial SQL files, but need to make use of `QuerySet.extra` to reference them from within the ORM.

Fixtures: Loading and Dumping Data

Although not technically a SQL extra *per se*, we'd like to include in this section a look at a Django feature related to working with your database outside the ORM itself: **fixtures**. Fixtures, touched on briefly in Chapter 2, are a name for sets of database data stored in flat files, which are not usually raw SQL dumps, but a database-agnostic (and often human-readable) representation, such as XML, YAML, or JSON.

The most common use for fixtures is as initial data loaded into a database when it is created or re-created, such as "prefilling" database tables used for categorizing user-entered data or loading up test data during application development. Django supports this in a similar fashion to the initial SQL outlined previously; each Django app is searched by a fixtures subdirectory, and within it, a file named initial_data.json (or .xml, .yaml, or another serialization format). These files are then read using Django's serialization module (see Chapter 9, "Liveblog," for more on this topic) and their contents used to create database objects, whenever database create/reset commands are run, such as manage.py syncdb or reset.

Here's a quick example of what a simple JSON fixture file for our Person model class can look like:

```
[
    {
        "pk": "1",
        "model": "myapp.person",
        "fields": {
            "first": "John",
            "middle": "Q",
            "last": "Doe"
        }
    },
    {
        "pk": "2",
        "model": "myapp.person",
        "fields": {
            "first": "Jane",
            "middle": "N",
            "last": "Doe"
        }
    }
]
```

and the output from importing it into our database:

```
user@example:/opt/code/myproject $ ./manage.py syncdb
Installing json fixture 'initial_data' from '/opt/code/myproject/myapp/fixtures'.
Installed 2 object(s) from 1 fixture(s)
```

In addition to initial data, fixtures are also useful as a more 'neutral' (although sometimes less efficient or specific) database dump format than using your database's SQL dump tool—for example, you could dump a Django application's data from a PostgreSQL database and then load it into a MySQL database, something that's not nearly as easy without the intermediate translation step of fixtures. This is accomplished with manage.py dumpdata and/or loaddata.

When using dumpdata and loaddata, the location and name of the fixtures used is more flexible than with initial data. They can have any name (as long as the file extension is still that of a supported format) and can live in the `fixtures` subdirectory, any directory specified in the `FIXTURES_DIRS` setting, or even on an explicit path provided to `loaddata` or `dumpdata`. For example, we can dump out the two `Person` objects imported previously, like so (using the `indent` option to make the output more human-readable).

```
user@example:/opt/code/myproject $ ./manage.py dumpdata  -indent=4 myapp >
➥ /tmp/myapp.json
user@example:/opt/code/myproject $ cat /tmp/myapp.json
[
    {
        "pk": 1,
        "model": "testapp.person",
        "fields": {
            "middle": "Q",
            "last": "Doe",
            "first": "John"
        }
    },
    {
        "pk": 2,
        "model": "testapp.person",
        "fields": {
            "middle": "N",
            "last": "Doe",
            "first": "Jane"
        }
    }
]
```

As you can see, fixtures are a useful way of dealing with your data in a format that's a bit easier to work with than raw SQL.

Custom SQL Queries

Finally, it's important to remember if the ORM (including the flexibility provided by `extra`) doesn't meet your query-related needs, it's always possible to execute fully custom SQL by using a lower-level database adapter. Django's ORM uses these modules to interface to your database as well. These modules are database-specific, depending on your Django database setting, and likely conform to the Python DB-API specification. Simply import the `connection` object defined in `django.db`, obtain a database cursor from it, and query away.

```
from django.db import connection

cursor = connection.cursor()
cursor.execute("SELECT first, last FROM myapp_person WHERE last='Doe'")
doe_rows = cursor.fetchall()
for row in doe_rows:
    print "%s %s" % (row[0], row[1])
```

> **Note**
>
> See the Python DB-API documentation, the "Database" chapter of *Core Python Programming*, and/or the database adapter documentation (see withdjango.com) for details on the syntax and method calls provided by these modules.

Summary

We've covered a lot of ground in this chapter, and with luck, you've come out of it with an appreciation for the amount of thinking that can (and usually should) go into one's data model. You've learned how ORMs can be useful, learned how to define simple Django models as well as more complex ones with various relationships, and seen the special inner classes Django uses to specify model metadata. In addition, we hope you're convinced of the power and flexibility of the QuerySet class as a means of pulling information out of your models and understand how to work with your Django application's data outside the ORM itself.

In the next two chapters, Chapters 5, "URLs, HTTP Mechanisms, and Views" and 6, you learn how to make use of your model in the context of a Web application by setting up queries in your controller logic (views) and then displaying them in your templates.

URLs, HTTP Mechanisms, and Views

In the previous chapter, you learned how to define the data models which form the underpinnings of most Web applications; in the chapter following this one, we show you how to display those models with Django's template language and forms. However, by themselves those two aspects of a Web framework don't do much; you need controller logic deciding what data to render which template with and URL dispatching to determine what logic is performed for a given URL.

This chapter details how Django implements the HTTP request-response architecture introduced in Chapter 3, "Starting Out," followed by an explanation of the simple Python functions that form controller logic, as well as some built-in helper functions that assist with common tasks. *eg, see p 71*

t = loader.get_template ("xyz.html")
c = Context (dict w. key↔val mappings))
return HttpResponse (t.render (c))

URLs

The mechanisms for tying together a request's URL and the resulting response are key to any Web development framework. Django uses a fairly simple, but powerful mechanism which enables you to map regular-expression-based configuration items to Python view methods, as well as link these lists of mappings together by including them within one another. Such a system is easy to use, but enables practically unlimited flexibility.

Introduction to URLconfs

The mappings mentioned previously are stored in Python files called **URLconfs**. These files must expose a `urlpatterns` object, which should be the result of a `patterns` function defined by Django. The `patterns` function, when called, consists of the following: ✳

- A leading prefix string, which can be blank
- One or more Python tuples consisting of a regular expression (regex) string matching a URL or set of URLs; a view function object or string; and, optionally, a dict of arguments for that view function

Here's an example to make sense of this, using an extended version of the URLconf from our blog application in Chapter 2, "Django for the Impatient: Building a Blog":

```
from django.conf.urls.defaults import *

urlpatterns = patterns('myproject.myapp.views',
    (r'^$', 'index'),
    (r'^archives/(?P<year>\d{4})/(?P<month>\d{2})/(?P<day>\d{2})/$', 'archive'),
)
```

[handwritten annotations: "an URLConf", "object", "func call", "prepend to func str", "provided", "func str", "¹"]

Clearly, the regexes (first introduced in Chapter 1, "Practical Python for Django") are the star of the show here. Aside from the lack of leading slashes (which are omitted due to their omnipresence in URLs), the primary thing to look for is the regex characters denoting the beginning and end of a string, ^ and $, respectively.

In practice, the ^ is nearly always required to remove ambiguity about what to match. The URL /foo/bar/ is not the same as /bar/, but the URL-matching regex r'bar/' would match both; r'^bar/' is more specific and matches only the latter.

The $ character is also used more often than not, for the same reason. It ensures the regex only matches the end of a URL and not the middle. However, $ is omitted for URL items designed to include other URLconf files because a URL leading into an include is not the final URL but only part of one.

[handwritten note: "Note; Each tuple may have a 3rd dict arg"]

> **Note**
>
> Examine the first tuple in the previous example. You see it consists solely of r'^$'; that means it matches the root URL of the Web site, /. As mentioned previously, Django strips out the leading slash, and once that's gone, we're left with an empty string with nothing between the beginning (^) and the end ($). You use this a lot in your Django projects to define index or landing pages.

Another aspect of these regexes is they can use a part of regex syntax called **symbolic groups** (the parentheses-clad expressions beginning with ?P<identifier>) to capture parts of the URL that vary. This feature provides the power necessary to define dynamic URLs. In the previous example, we have an archives section of a blog, addressing individual entries based on their date. The fundamental information being accessed by the URL—a blog entry—does not change; only the date being accessed. As we see later, the values captured here are passed to the specified view function, which can use them in a database query or however else it sees fit.

Finally, once you've defined the regex, you simply need to note the function it's linking to and possibly some extra keyword parameters (stored here as a dict). The first argument to patterns, if not empty, is prepended to the function string. Going back to the example for this section, you note the prefix string is 'myproject.myapp.views'; as a result, the full Python module paths go from 'index' and 'archive' to 'myproject.myapp.views.index' and 'myproject.myapp.views.archive', respectively.

[handwritten note at bottom: "¹ leads to view functions: myproject.myapp.views.index( )   myproject.myapp.views.archive (year=<yearval>, month=<monthval>,"]

Replacing Tuples with `url`

A relatively late addition to Django's URL dispatching mechanism is the `url` method, which is designed to replace the tuples outlined previously while remaining nearly identical in structure. It takes the same three "arguments"—a regex, a view string/function, and optional argument dict—and adds another optional, named argument: name. name is simply a string, which should be unique among all your URLs; then, you can use it elsewhere to refer back to this specific URL.

Let's rewrite the previous example using `url`.

```
from django.conf.urls.defaults import *

urlpatterns = patterns('myproject.myapp.views',
    url(r'^$', 'index', name='index'),
    url(r'^archives/(?P<year>\d{4})/(?P<month>\d{2})/(?P<day>\d{2})/$', 'archive',
        name='archive'),
)
```

As you can see, it's a simple drop-in replacement for the older tuple syntax. Because it's an actual function and not just a tuple, it enforces what used to be merely a convention. The first two arguments are required and have no name, although the argument dict is now an optional named argument, `kwargs`, along with the new optional named argument, name.

> **Note**
>
> `kwargs` and name are named arguments instead of positional ones to support the fact they are both optional. You can specify neither of them, either of them, or both without running into problems. Positional arguments (or the use of tuples) would make such a setup far more difficult.

We're presenting this `url` approach after the tuple-based syntax because it's newer; even by the time you read this, there are still likely to be more Django URLconfs out in the wild utilizing tuples than using `url`. However, we strongly encourage you to use `url` in your own code; we have endeavored to set a good example by using it in the rest of this book because it offers more power and flexibility than the tuple approach.

Finally, see the example applications in Part III, "Django Applications by Example," for more information on the name argument and how it can be used to reference back to your URLs from other parts of the code.

Using Multiple `patterns` Objects

One trick commonly used by Django developers is that of refactoring their URLconfs into multiple `patterns` calls per URL file, at least for files which have a nontrivial number of entries. This is possible because the return type of `patterns` is an internal Django object type that can be appended to as if it were a list or other container type. As such, it's easy to concatenate multiple such objects together, and thus it's possible and desirable to segregate them based on the prefix string. Here's a semi-abstract example representing a top-level URL tying together multiple apps.

```
from django.conf.urls.defaults import *
```

Segregating urlpatterns then concatenating them

```
urlpatterns = patterns('myproject.blog.views',
    url(r'^$', 'index'),
    url(r'^blog/new/$', 'new_post'),
    url(r'^blog/topics/(?P<topic_name>\w+)/new/$', 'new_post'),
)

urlpatterns += patterns('myproject.guestbook.views',
    url(r'^guestbook/$', 'index'),
    url(r'^guestbook/add/$', 'new_entry'),
)

urlpatterns += patterns('myproject.catalog.views',
    url(r'^catalog/$', 'index'),
)
```

Note the use of the += operator for the second and third calls to patterns. By the end of the file, urlpatterns contains a conglomerate of all six defined URLs, each with their own distinct mappings thanks to the different prefix arguments. Of course, astute readers notice this still isn't the height of refactoring. The "blog," "guestbook" and "catalog" sections of the URL definitions are themselves slightly repetitive. Next, we cover how to streamline even further by including other URLconfs.

Including Other URL Files with include

The refactoring mindset seen in the previous section can be further applied, by breaking up URLconf files into multiple such files. This is most commonly seen in projects consisting of multiple apps, where there can be a "base" app defining an index page or other site-wide features such as authentication. The base application's URLconf then defines the subsections filled in by other apps and uses a special include function to pass off further URL dispatching to said apps, as seen here in an update to the previous example.

```
## urls.py
```

Concatenation + includes

```
from django.conf.urls.defaults import *

urlpatterns = patterns('myproject.blog.views',
    url(r'^$', 'index'),
    url(r'^blog/', include('myproject.blog.urls')),    @ 121
)
```
↳ NB : no $ but trailing /

```
urlpatterns += patterns('',
    url(r'^guestbook/', include('myproject.guestbook.urls')),   (b) 121
```
↑ note : no $ but trailing /

```
)

urlpatterns += patterns('',
    url(r'^catalog/', include('myproject.catalog.urls')),
)

## blog/urls.py

urlpatterns = patterns('myproject.blog.views',
    url(r'^new/$', 'new_post'),
    url(r'^topics/(?P<topic_name>\w+)/new/$', 'new_post'),
)

## guestbook/urls.py

urlpatterns += patterns('myproject.guestbook.views',
    url(r'^$', 'index'),
    url(r'^add/$', 'new_entry'),
)

## catalog/urls.py

urlpatterns += patterns('myproject.catalog.views',
    url(r'^$', 'index'),
)
```

This example is actually a bit larger than the previous one, but hopefully you can see the benefits for a realistic Web site with dozens of potential URLs for each section; in each scenario, we save a decent amount of typing and repetition of the "blog," "guestbook," and "catalog" parts of the URL definitions. Specifically, we now have a multi-app Web site delegating most URLs to its subapplications, with the exception of the index page, which lives in the blog application (although you can make a base or similar application for such things—it's entirely up to you).

URLconf including can be valuable even within single applications—there's no hard limit on when to use multiple apps versus individual ones, so it's entirely possible to have a Django app with hundreds of URLs. Most developers, in such a situation, would quickly start organizing things into modules, and URLconf including supports this as well. In general, the organization of your site is up to you, and the URLconf mechanisms have been set up to be as flexible as possible, in which includes play a large part.

Function Objects Versus Function-Name Strings

Throughout this section, we've been using strings to denote the Python module path to the view functions to which our URLs link. However, that's not the only way to go about it; Django also enables you to pass in a callable object in place of a string, such as:

```
from django.conf.urls.defaults import *
from myproject.myapp import views

urlpatterns = patterns('', # Don't need the prefix anymore
    url(r'^$', views.index),
    url(r'^blog/', include('myproject.blog.urls')),
)
```

[handwritten: allows]
[handwritten: # callable object now, rather than a string]
[handwritten: 42,239]

This opens up the door to a lot of functionality, such as using decorator functions to wrap generic views or even creating your own callable objects to do more complex delegation to different views. See Chapter 11, "Advanced Django Programming," for more on decorators and other tricks usable with callable views.

> **Note**
>
> It's sometimes tempting to do a blanket `from myproject.myapp.views import *` in your URLconf to use callable views, but this can lead to problems when mixing multiple view modules—imagine two separate view files each defining its own `index` view. Therefore it's probably smart to follow the previous example and import each view module as its own object (using the `from x import y as z` style if necessary), resulting in a cleaner local namespace.

Modeling HTTP: Requests, Responses, and Middleware

You now understand how to set up your URL definitions and associate URLs with view functions; now it's time to detail the ecosystem surrounding those view functions. As discussed in Chapter 3, Django models HTTP in a relatively simple request-response dichotomy with Python objects for requests and responses. Along with the URL dispatching and view functions, a request to your Web application flows such as:

[handwritten: insert optional middleware]
[handwritten: process_request]

- HTTP request occurs to your Web server.
- Web server passes request to Django, which makes a request object.
- Django consults your URLconf to find the right view function.
- That view function is called with the request object and any captured URL arguments.
- The view then creates and returns a response object.

[handwritten: process_view]

- Django turns that response object into a format your Web server understands.
- The Web server then responds to the requesting client.

We first go over the request and response objects and their components, and then get into Django middleware, which provides "hooks" into various stages of the previous process. Afterward, the next major section teaches you what you need to know about the views themselves.

[handwritten: Might have   @ my decorator (arg)   def index (self, req):   ...]
[handwritten: still refer to callable views. index, but it is now decorated]
[handwritten: decorators: 42-44]

[handwritten margin notes: req is a Request obj; Useful: req.GET (dict) req.session (dict) req. req.encoding req.POST (dict) req.method [req.user] req.COOKIES (dict) req.META (dict) req.path req.FILES (dict)]

Request Objects

Once you have your URLconfs set up, you need to define what behavior the URLs exhibit. We go over the details of view methods in a short while, but for now we show you the layout of the HTTP request and response objects, which those views are dealing with. All view functions accept a "request" parameter, which is an `HttpRequest` object, a nicely packaged set of attributes representing the raw HTTP request handed down from the Web server.

GET and POST Dictionaries

The most commonly accessed pieces of request-related data Web developers use are the GET and POST data structures, which are attributes of the `HttpRequest` object (`request.GET` and `request.POST`, as you can expect) and are represented as Python dictionaries. Although identical in structure, they are populated in two different ways, the importance of which is more than you can expect at first. Together, they offer a flexible way to parameterize Web requests.

> **Note** *[handwritten: Query Dict]*
>
> Although closely related to Python's `dict` builtin, `HttpRequest`'s GET and POST attributes are actually instances of a Django-specific `dict` subclass, `QueryDict`, which is designed to mimic the underlying behavior of these data structures in the HTTP CGI specification. All key-value pairs store the value as a list, even in the case of a single value per key to correctly handle the cases where the HTTP server does return multiple values. Typical use of `QueryDict`s as dictionaries returns single items for convenience; you can use `QueryDict` methods, such as `getlist`, when you're interested in multiple values.

GET parameters are passed as part of the URL string, but are not technically part of the URL itself in that they do not define a different resource (or view) but only change the behavior of the resource they're attached to. For example, the URL `/userlist/` can point to a page that lists the users of a community Web site; if the developer wants to break the list so it isn't gigantic, he can decide to note the page number as a GET variable: `/userlist/?page=2`. The view being accessed is still the same, but the developer can look for a `page` key/value pair in the GET dictionary and return the correct page, such as in this abstract example. *[handwritten: better: page = request.GET.get('page', 1)]*

```
def userlist(request):
    return paginated_userlist_page(page=request.GET['page'])
```
[handwritten: just python]

Note with `request.GET`, as with the other dict-like attributes of the request object, it's helpful to make use of dictionary methods such as `get` (see Chapter 1 "Practical Python for Django," for a refresher on dictionaries), so your logic doesn't break down when the parameter you're looking for isn't specified.

POST parameters are not part of the URL but are effectively hidden from the user, often generated by an HTML form within a Web page. One of the attributes of the FORM tag, `action`, denotes which URL the data will be submitted to; if the user submits the form, the URL is called with a POST dict made up of the form fields. This is how most

[handwritten footer: resp is a Response obj: useful: resp.content]

Web forms operate, although they can technically submit their data via the GET method as well. (This is not usually done, as it results in long, messy URLs for no good reason.)

In addition to GET and POST, HttpRequest objects expose a REQUEST dictionary, which searches both of the former in an attempt to return the requested key. This can be convenient in situations where a given key/value pair can be sent to your view via either method, and you're unsure which was used; however, due to the Pythonic philosophy of "explicit is better than implicit," most experienced Django programmers tend not to use this feature.

Cookies and Sessions

Following GET and POST, the next most commonly used aspect of request objects is request.COOKIES, which is yet another dictionary whose key/value pairs expose the HTTP **cookies** stored in the request. Cookies are a simple method by which Web pages can store persistent pieces of information in a user's browser—they power most authentication systems on the Web and are used by some commercial sites to track a user's surfing history.

Most cookies, generally, are used to enable a feature called **sessions**. This means that a Web page can ask the browser for a value identifying the user (which is set when the user first connects to the site or when the user logs in), and then uses this information to customize the behavior of the page for that user. Because cookies are easily manipulated on the client side, thus making it unsafe to store any real data in them, most Web sites store information in a server-side session object (usually via the site's database) and leave only a unique session ID in the cookie itself.

Sessions are often used to implement state, as the HTTP protocol is by nature stateless—each request/response cycle stands by itself and has no knowledge of previous requests nor ways to pass information to later ones. With sessions, Web applications can work around this, storing items of data—such as messages to the user about whether submitting a form successfully saved her changes—on the server and sending them to the user in subsequent responses.

In Django, sessions are presented as yet another dictionary-like attribute of the HttpRequest object, request.session (note the session is lowercase, unlike the others—because sessions are not actually part of the HTTP protocol). Like the COOKIES attribute before it, session can be both read from and written to by one's Python code. When first presented to your code, it contains the session as read from the database based on the user's session cookie. If written to, it saves your changes back to the database, so they can be read later.

Other Server Variables

The previous aspects of the request object are the most often used; however, requests contain a host of other, usually read-only variables, some of which are part of the HTTP specification and others which are convenience attributes specific to Django. The following are all direct attributes of the request object:

- `path`: The portion of the URL after the domain, for example, /blog/2007/11/04/; this is also the string that is handled by the URLconf.
- `method`: One of two strings, `'GET'` or `'POST'`, specifying which HTTP request method was used in this request.
- `encoding`: A string specifying the encoding character set used to decode any form submission data.
- `FILES`: A dict-like object containing any files uploaded via a file input form field, each represented as another dictionary with key/value pairs for the filename, the content type, and the file content itself.
- `META`: Another dictionary, containing the HTTP server/request variables not handled by the other aspects of the request, including `CONTENT_LENGTH`, `HTTP_REFERER`, `REMOTE_ADDR`, `SERVER_NAME`, and so forth.
- `user`: The Django authentication user, which only appears if your site has Django's authentication mechanisms activated.
- `raw_post_data`: The raw, unfiltered version of the POST data contained within this request. The use of `request.POST` is almost always preferable over accessing `request.raw_post_data`, but it's here for examination by those with advanced needs.

[handwritten margin notes: reg. path; NB; Leading "/" always there, so URL conf handler it implicitly; reg. method; reg. encoding; NB @ 127; reg. FILES; name; 160; reg. META; [reg. user]; reg. raw_post_data]

Response Objects

[handwritten: resp is a Response object]

At this point, you've read about the information that is passed into our view function; now we examine what it's responsible for returning, namely a response. From our point of view, responses are simpler than requests—their primary data point is the body text, stored in the `content` attribute. It's usually a large string of HTML, and it's so central to `HttpResponse` objects there are a couple of ways of setting it.

The most common method is via the act of creating the response object—`HttpResponse` takes a string as a constructor argument, which is then stored in `content`.

```
response = HttpResponse("<html>This is a tiny Web page!</html>")
```

[handwritten: eg resp = HttpResponse (html str)]

Just with that, you've got a fully functioning response object, one worthy of being returned farther up the stack to the Web server and forwarded to the user's browser. However, it's sometimes useful to build the response content piece-by-piece; to support this, `HttpResponse` objects implement a partial file-like behavior, notably the `write` method.

```
response = HttpResponse()
response.write("<html>")
response.write("This is a tiny Web page!")
response.write("</html>")
```

[handwritten: resp = HttpResponse (); resp. write (html fragment str)]

Of course, this means you can use an `HttpResponse` for any code that expects a file-like object—for example, the csv module's CSV writing utilities—that adds a lot of flexibility to the process of generating the information your code returns to end users.

Another key aspect of response objects is the capability to set HTTP headers by treating the `HttpResponse` object like a dictionary.

```
response = HttpResponse()
response["Content-Type"] = "text/csv"
response["Content-Length"] = 256
```

response["content"] or response.content ?

Finally, Django provides a number of `HttpRequest` subclasses for many common response types, such as `HttpResponseForbidden` (which uses the HTTP 403 status code) and `HttpResponseServerError` (similar but for HTTP 500 or internal server errors).

Middleware

Although the basic flow of a Django application is fairly simple—take in request, find appropriate view function, return a response—extra layers are available that can be leveraged to add a lot of power and flexibility. One of these extra layers is **middleware**—Python functions executed at various points in the previous process that can alter the effective input (by modifying the request before it reaches the view) or output (modifying the response created by the view) of the *entire* application.

A middleware component in Django is simply a Python class which implements a certain interface, namely it defines one of a number of methods with names such as `process_request` or `process_view`. (We examine the most commonly used ones in the following subsections.) When listed in the `MIDDLEWARE_CLASSES` tuple in your `settings.py` file, Django introspects the middleware class and calls its method at the appropriate time. The order of classes listed in your settings file determines the order in which they are executed.

Django comes with a handful of built-in middleware, some of which are generally useful and others which are required for specific "contrib" applications such as the authentication framework. See the official Django documentation for more on these.

Request Middleware

On the input side sits request middleware, which is defined as a class that implements the `process_request` method, as in the following example:

```
from some_exterior_auth_lib import get_user


class ExteriorAuthMiddleware(object):
    def process_request(self, request):
        token = request.COOKIES.get('auth_token')
        if token is None and not request.path.startswith('/login'):
            return HttpResponseRedirect('/login/')
        request.exterior_user = get_user(token)
```

returns ... COOKIES['auth_token'] if key in dict, else None

 # add new attribute to request obj

 # implicit return of None here ... django continues on

Note the line assigning a value to `request.exterior_user`, which illustrates a common use of request middleware: adding extra attributes to the request object. In the situation where that line is called, `process_request` implicitly returns `None` (Python functions always return `None` if they lack an explicit `return` statement), and in that case Django continues to process other request middleware and eventually the view function itself.

If, however, the test checking for a valid auth token (and making sure the user isn't currently trying to log in!) fails, our middleware redirects the user to the login page. This illustrates the other possible behavior of middleware methods; they can return an `HttpResponse` (or subclass) that is immediately sent off to the requesting client. In this case, because our middleware is a request middleware, everything past that point in the normal flow of things—including the view that would have been called—is skipped.

Response Middleware

As you can expect, response middleware is run on the `HttpResponse` objects returned by view functions. Such middleware must implement the `process_response` method, which accepts `request` and `response` parameters and returns an `HttpResponse` or subclass. Those are the only limitations—your middleware can modify the response it is given or create an entirely new response and return that instead.

One of the most common uses of response middleware is to inject extra headers into the response, either across the board—such as enabling caching-related HTTP features—or conditionally, such as a built-in middleware that sets `Content-Language` equal to the current translation.

Following is a trivial example that does a simple search and replace of "foo" with "bar" on all text output by the Web application:

```python
class TextFilterMiddleware(object):
    def process_response(self, request, response):
        response.content = response.content.replace('foo', 'bar')
```

We could have made this a more realistic example that filters out naughty words (which can be useful for a community Web site, for example), but this is a family book!

Views/Logic

Views (née controllers) form the core of any Django Web application in that they provide nearly all the actual programming logic. When defining and using the models, we're database administrators; when writing the templates, we're interface designers; but when writing views, we're truly *software engineers*.

Although the views themselves can easily account for a large portion of your source code, the Django framework code surrounding views is surprisingly slim. Views represent your business logic and are thus the aspect of a Web application which needs the least glue code and the most custom work. At the same time, built-in *generic* views are one of the most touted time-savers in Web development frameworks such as Django, and we introduce these and methods of using them both on their own and in tandem with custom views.

Just Python Functions

At the heart of it, Django views are Python functions, plain and simple. The only restriction on view functions is they must take an `HttpRequest` object and return an `HttpResponse` object, which is described previously. Also previously mentioned are the regex patterns from the URLconfs, in which you can define named groups. Combined with an optional dictionary parameter, they provide the arguments to the view function, as in the following example (slightly altered from its earlier incarnation):

```
urlpatterns = patterns('myproject.myapp.views',
    url(r'^archives/(?P<year>\d{4})/(?P<month>\d{2})/(?P<day>\d{2})/$', 'archive',
        {'show_private': True}),
)
```

Combined with the `HttpRequest` object, the `archive` view function referenced by the previous URL could have a signature such as:

```
from django.http import HttpResponse


def archive(request, year, month, day, show_private):
    return HttpResponse()
```

As long as it returns an `HttpResponse` of some kind, the inner guts of the method are inconsequential; what we're seeing here is essentially an API. As with any API, you can use prewritten code implementing it or write your own from scratch. We examine your options in that order.

Generic Views

Possibly the most-touted aspect of Django, and Web frameworks in general, is the capability to use predefined code for the so-called **CRUD** operations that make up most of the average Web application. CRUD stands for Create, Read (or Retrieve), Update, and Delete, the most common actions taken in a database-backed application. Showing a list of items or a detail page for a single object? That's Retrieve. Displaying an edit form and altering the database when it's submitted? That's Update or Create, depending on your application and the form in question. Delete should need no explanation.

These tasks and their variants are all provided for by Django's set of **generic views**. As previously shown, they are simply Python functions, but ones that are highly abstracted and parameterized to achieve maximum flexibility in their defined role. Because they handle the logic, framework users simply need to refer to them in their URLconf files, pass the appropriate parameters, and make sure a template exists for the view to render and return.

For example, the `object_detail` generic view is intended to facilitate display of a single object and takes its parameters from both the URL regex and the argument dictionary to do so:

```
from django.views.generic.list_detail import object_detail
from django.conf.urls.defaults import *
```

```
from myproject.myapp.models import Person

urlpatterns = patterns('',
    url(r'^people/(?P<object_id>\d+)/$', object_detail, {
        'queryset': Person.objects.all()
    })
)
```

gen. view — handwritten annotation

URL is like --- /people/123/ — handwritten annotation

In the previous example, we've defined a regex that matches URLs such as /people/25/, where 25 is the database ID of the Person record we want to display. The object_detail generic view needs both an object_id argument and a QuerySet it can filter to find the object identified by that ID. In this case, we provide object_id via the URL and the queryset via the argument dictionary.

Passing Full QuerySets into Generic Views

It can appear inefficient to pass in Person.objects.all() because if executed as-is that QuerySet could be an enormous list of all Person objects! However, remember what you saw in Chapter 4, "Defining and Using Models"—QuerySets can be, and usually are, filtered with filter and/or exclude before they actually turn into a database query. Because of this, you can rest assured the object_detail generic view filters for the specific object in question, resulting in a properly sized query.

Furthermore, by requiring a full-fledged QuerySet instead of, say, the model class (which would be another way of specifying what type of object to look for) Django enables us to do our own filtering if we so choose. For example, an employee-only detail page could pass Person.objects.filter(is_employee=True) into object_detail instead of Person.objects.all().

As always, Django's core team tries to make decisions that give you more flexibility, even if the resulting functionality sometimes appears unintuitive at first glance.

Generic views often expose a handful of options. Some are specific to that view; although others are global, such as a template_name argument enabling the user to override the default location of the view's template or an extra_context dict which enables the user to pass extra information into the template's context. (See Chapter 6, "Templates and Form Processing," for more on templates and contexts.) You can see the official Django documentation for details on all the generic views and their arguments; we go over some of the more commonly used ones next. Note generic views are organized in a two-level module hierarchy for neatness' sake.

django.views.generic . simple. direct_to_template . list_detail, object_list object_detail — handwritten annotation

- simple.direct_to_template: Useful for templates that have some dynamic content (as opposed to *flatpages*, which are static HTML, see Chapter 8, "Content Management System") but require no specific Python-level logic, such as index pages or nonpaginated/mixed list pages.

- list_detail.object_list and list_detail.object_detail: These two provide the primary read-only aspect of most Web apps and are probably the most commonly used generic views, as information display doesn't usually require complex

django.views.generic, create_update, create_object, update_object

logic. However, if you need to perform logic to prepare your template context, you can find yourself wanting custom views instead.

- `create_update.create_object` and `create_update.update_object`: Useful for simple object creation or update, where all you need is the form validation defined in your form or model (see Chapters 6 and 4, respectively) and where no other business logic applies.

- `date_based.*`: A handful of date-based generic views which highlight Django's origin as a publication-oriented framework. They are extremely useful for any date-based data types. Included are date-oriented index and detail pages plus sublist pages ranging from the year down to the day.

Generic views are both a blessing and a curse. The blessing aspect should be obvious; they save a lot of time and can be used to cut out almost all the work involved in simple or moderately complex views. Their usefulness is further expanded by wrapping them within custom views, as we outline next. However, generic views' usefulness can make it difficult to accept that sometimes; you just *have* to write your own completely custom view from scratch, even if the generic view closest to your vision would get you 90 percent of the way there. Knowing when to throw in the towel and go the custom route is a valuable skill, which, like many aspects of software development, can only truly be picked up with experience.

Semi-generic Views

There are times when generic views on their own, called straight from a URLconf file, do not suffice. Often, this requires a completely custom view function to be written, but equally often, a generic view can still be leveraged to do the grunt work depending on the logic required.

The most common use of such "semi-generic" views, in our experience, has been to work around an inherent limitation in the URLconf itself. You can't perform logic with the captured URL parameters until the regex has been parsed. This limitation exists due to the way URLconfs are designed, and it's easy to work around it. Consider the following snippet combining portions of a URLconf file and a view file:

```
## urls.py


from django.conf.urls.defaults import *

urlpatterns = patterns('myproject.myapp.views',
    url(r'^people/by_lastname/(?P<last_name>\w+)/$', 'last_name_search'),
)


## views.py


from django.views.generic.list_detail import object_list
from myproject.myapp.models import Person
```

```
def last_name_search(request, last_name):
    return object_list(request,                    # handoff to generic view
        queryset=Person.objects.filter(last__istartswith=last_name)
    )
```

As you can see, although our function takes the `last_name` argument defined as a named group in the URL regex, we're still delegating 99 percent of the actual work to the generic view. This is possible because generic views are normal Python functions and can be imported and called as such. It's easy to fall into the trap of thinking about the framework as its own language, but as we've emphasized before, it's all just Python, and this sort of trick shows why that's a good thing.

Custom Views

Finally, as mentioned earlier, it's sometimes the case you can't use generic views at all, which brings us back to the beginning of this section; the view functions as a blank slate, conforming only to a simple API, waiting for you, the programmer, to fill it however you want. We share a couple of observations based on our own experience and point out some convenient shortcut functions supplied by the framework; however, in general, this is an area in which your own skills and experiences determine what you do next.

Framework-Provided Shortcuts

As we've stated, once you're in the realm of custom views, Django basically leaves you alone. However, it does provide a handful of shortcuts, most of which are defined in the `django.shortcuts` module.

render_to_response ('.../xyz.html', dict_with_rel)_values) © 132
'xyzdict

- `render_to_response`: A function that replaces the two- or three-step process of creating a `Context` object, rendering a `Template` with it, and then returning an `HttpResponse` containing the result. It takes the template name, an optional context (`Context` object, or dictionary, as usual) and/or MIMEtype, and returns an `HttpResponse` object. Template rendering is covered in Chapter 6.

ⓐ 71
ⓑ 132

- `Http404`: An `Exception` subclass which effectively returns an `HTTP 404` error code and renders a top-level `404.html` template (unless you've overridden this in your `settings.py`). To use it, you `raise` it like you would any other exception, the idea being that when you encounter a 404 condition, it's a full-fledged error, same as if you had tried to add a string to an integer. It is defined in the `django.http` module.

- `get_object_or_404` and `get_list_or_404`: These two functions are simple short-cuts for obtaining an object or list or raising `Http404` if the lookup fails. They take a `klass` argument—which is flexible enough to take a model class, a `Manager`, or a `QuerySet`—and some database query arguments such as those passed to `Managers` and `QuerySets` and attempt to return the object or list in question.

Here are two examples using the previous shortcuts: The first uses `Http404` by itself, and the second shows how to streamline things using `get_object_or_404`—the two

p71   1   t = loader. get_ template ('xyz.html')
               c = Context (dict_with_rel_values)
               return HttpResponse (t. render (c))

functions exhibit identical behavior in practice. Don't worry about the template paths for now; those are explained in more detail in Chapter 6.

Here's the manual method of raising a 404 exception:

```
from django.shortcuts import render_to_response
from django.http import Http404
from myproject.myapp.models import Person


def person_detail(request, id):
    try:
        person = Person.objects.get(pk=id)
    except Person.DoesNotExist:
        raise Http404

    return render_to_response("person/detail.html", {"person": person})
```

And an example of `get_object_or_404`, which you'll usually want to use in place of the preceding method:

```
from django.shortcuts import render_to_response, get_object_or_404
from myproject.myapp.models import Person


def person_detail(request, id):
    person = get_object_or_404(Person, pk=id)

    return render_to_response("person/detail.html", {"person": person})
```

Other Observations

Perhaps a minor point—many Django developers find themselves making use of the "args/kwargs" convention when defining their own view functions. As seen in Chapter 1, Python functions can define `*args` and `**kwargs` to accept arbitrary positional and keyword arguments; although a two-edged sword (concrete function signatures are often a source of excellent documentation, but are lost here), this is often a useful trick to increase flexibility and is also faster to boot. You no longer have to move back to your URLconf file to remember exactly what you named your captured regex parameters or keyword arguments, just define your function as

```
def myview(*args, **kwargs):
    # Here we can refer to e.g. args[0] or kwargs['object_id']
```

and away you go, referring to `kwargs["identifier"]` when necessary. After a while, doing this becomes second nature, and it also makes things easier when you want to pass on a function's arguments to a delegate function—such as in the "semi-generic" views mentioned previously.

Summary

We're now more than halfway done exploring the basics of Django's core components. In addition to the models described in Chapter 4, this chapter has shown you how Django implements URL dispatching and the rest of the HTTP request-response "conversation," including the use of middleware. You've also seen how to put together simple Django view functions, and you've gotten a taste of the included generic views and how they can be utilized.

The next and last chapter in this section of the book, Chapter 6, describes the third major piece of the puzzle, that of rendering Web pages via templates and managing input from users with forms and form validation. Afterward, it's on to Part III where you get to see these concepts put to use in four example applications.

Templates and Form Processing

Now that you've learned about Django's data models and logic processing, it's time for the final piece of the puzzle: how to display information and manage user input. We start with an overview of Django's template language and rendering system with the second half of the chapter covering forms and form processing.

Templates

As touched on in previous chapters, templates are stand-alone text files containing both static content (such as HTML) and dynamic markup specifying logic, looping, and the display of data. The decision of which template to use and what set of data to render it with is made either in the view function itself (via explicit rendering or the use of `render_to_response`) or in the view's arguments (such as the `template_name` argument to generic views).

Django's template language is designed to be used by front-end developers who are not necessarily programmers; because of this and the desire to separate logic from presentation, the template language is emphatically *not* embedded Python. However, the extensible system of **tags** and **filters** (see the following for more) enables the programmers of a Django application to expand the logical constructs available to the template language.

Finally, note that although the template system is generally used to generate HTML (this being the Web and all), it is not married to HTML and can be equally useful in generating log files, e-mail content, CSV files, and any other text-based format. Keeping this in mind allows you to make the fullest use of what Django's templates have to offer.

Understanding Contexts

Templates, being dynamic text documents, wouldn't be very useful if they didn't have any dynamic information to display. The term Django uses for the information passed to a rendered template is **context**—a template's context is essentially a dictionary of key-value pairs, represented as a dict-like `Context` object when rendering takes place.

As seen briefly in Chapters 2, "Django for the Impatient: Building a Blog," and 5, "URLs, HTTP Mechanisms, and Views," every rendering of a template requires a context to be present. Sometimes the context is prepopulated for you, such as in generic views, and you merely append to it with an `extra_context` argument. Other times, as with custom views, you provide the context yourself when calling a template's `render` method, or more commonly as an argument to the helper function `render_to_response`. It's technically possible to render a template with an empty context, but in such situations, you'd be better off using the `flatpages` contrib application—a template with no context is not very dynamic.

The other method for contributing data to template contexts is through **context processors**, a middleware-like aspect of the framework where various functions can be defined to append key-value pairs to *all* contexts just prior to template render time. This is how features such as the authentication framework are able to ensure that certain site-wide pieces of data are always present. Here's a quick example of a context processor.

```
def breadcrumb_processor(request):
    return {
        'breadcrumbs': request.path.split('/')
    }
```

Perhaps not terribly useful—breadcrumbs are rarely that easy in practice—it highlights the simplicity of context processors. You can store your context processor functions anywhere, but as usual, it's probably a good idea to standardize on something, such as a `context_processors.py` file in the root of your project or in an app directory.

Context processors, such as middlewares, are enabled by referring to them in Python module syntax in your `settings.py`, specifically in a tuple named `TEMPLATE_CONTEXT_PROCESSORS`. And in another nod to their similarity to middlewares, order matters; context processors are applied in the order listed within that settings variable.

Template Language Syntax

The syntax of Django's template language is comparable to non-XML-based template languages, such as Smarty or Cheetah, in that it does not attempt to remain XHTML-compliant, but uses special characters to set apart template variable and logic commands from the static content (usually the HTML). As with most other aspects of Django, the template language is only loosely coupled to the rest of the framework, and it is entirely possible to use another template library if desired.

As with most template languages, there are singular commands—such as printing the value of a context variable—and block-level commands, usually logic commands such as "if" or "for." Django's template language uses two conventions, both involving curly braces; variable output is accomplished with double curly braces (`{{ variable }}`), and everything else is accomplished with **tags** (`{% command %}`). Here's a small example, that can render a context similar to the Python dictionary `{ "title_text": "My Webpage", "object_list": ["One", "Two", "Three"] }`.

```
<html>
    <head>
        <title>{{ title_text }}</title>
```

```
    </head>
    <body>
        <ul>
        {% for item in object_list %}
            <li>{{ item }}</li>
        {% endfor %}
        </ul>
    </body>
</html>
```

 # logic tags
 # variable interpolation
row col

It should be noted when you output context variables in your templates, there is an implicit call to unicode, so objects and other nonstring variables are turned into (Unicode) strings as best they can. Be wary—if you're attempting to print objects whose __unicode__ method is not defined, you don't see them in your templates. This is because the default Python representation of an object just happens to be the same format as an HTML tag, specifically text bounded by the < and > characters.

```
>>> print object()
<object object at 0x40448>
```

This is a common pitfall that even experienced Django developers sometimes encounter, so if you're trying to display something and it doesn't show up, make sure you first know what it is and that you know what its string representation is supposed to be!

As you can see, although Django template syntax is not semantically correct HTML, the curly-brace syntax makes it easy to visually distinguish the output and command aspects from the static content. In addition, because Django's development team intended to use the template language for document types other than just HTML, they felt a template system focused on XML output wouldn't make sense.

Template Filters

Although it provides the foundation for building dynamic templates, simple variable output is fairly inflexible. The template framework enables transformation of context variables via mechanisms called **filters**, which are similar to Unix pipes—see Appendix A, "Command Line Basics," if you're not already familiar with pipes. Filters even use the same syntax as Unix pipes, the pipe character: |. They can be chained together, as they always take a single text string as input and return one on output. As you see later in the "Extending the Template" section of Chapter 11, "Advanced Django Programming," filters are simply Python functions. *250*

Django ships with a wide variety of useful filters that encapsulate common Web development and text processing tasks, such as escaping slashes, capitalization, date formatting, obtaining the length of lists or tuples, concatenating strings, and so forth. Here's an example of how filters could be used to transform a list of strings into lowercase.

```
<ul>
{% for string in string_list %}
    <li>{{ string|lower }}</li>
```

1 No. See next page

```
{% endfor %}
</ul>
```

Although most filters take a single string as input, some accept an argument to further parameterize their behavior, such as the `yesno` filter used to take arbitrary (usually boolean) values and print human-useful strings.

```
<table>
    <tr>
        <th>Name</th>
        <th>Available?</th>
    </tr>
    {% for person in person_list %}
    <tr>
        <td>{{ person.name }}</td>
        <td>{{ person.is_available|yesno:"Yes,No" }}</td>
    </tr>
    {% endfor %}
</table>
```

Tags

As you've probably noticed in the previous examples, although variable output and filters are useful, the real power lies in **tags**—thus far we've seen them used to loop over lists of strings or objects, but they're also capable of performing logic (`{% if %}`, `{% ifequal %}`), template inclusion/inheritance (`{% block %}`, `{% include %}` and `{% extends %}`, as seen in the next section), and various other tasks.

Tags are technically free-form and can take any manner of input after the tag name (see the "Extending the Template" section of Chapter 11 for more), but the built-in tags and most user-created tags tend to follow certain conventions, generally a space-delimited list of arguments. Many tag arguments can be context variables, and in fact most of the time, filters can be used as well. For example, the following is how one could check the length of a list before iterating over its contents.

```
{% ifequal object_list|length 10 %}
    <ul>
    {% for item in object_list %}
        <li>{{ item }}</li>
    {% endfor %}
    </ul>
{% endifequal %}
```

Of course, we could have also used the `length_is` filter, which takes a list and argument and returns a boolean value.

```
{% if object_list|length_is:10 %}
    <ul>
    {% for item in object_list %}
```

```
    <li>{{ item }}</li>
  {% endfor %}
  </ul>
{% endif %}
```

As this hopefully illustrates, there's a lot of flexibility in Django's built-in filter and tag library. It's a good idea to become well-acquainted with what's available (the official Django documentation provides an excellent list) to avoid reinventing the wheel.

One final word on tags: The block-level ones such as `{% if %}` and `{% for %}` are capable of altering their local context, which often comes in handy. For example, `{% for %}` provides a local context variable, `{{ forloop }}`, which has a variety of attributes that enable you to take differing actions based on which attributes you use and what loop iteration you are on. Such attributes enable various actions such as what to do at the beginning or end of the loop (`{{ forloop.first }}` or `{{ forloop.last }}`, booleans for whether this is the first or last loop iteration, respectively) or displaying the loop counter (`{{ forloop.counter }}` and `{{ forloop.counter0 }}`, starting at 1 or 0, respectively). Refer to the Django documentation for more information and examples.

Blocks and Extends

One useful set of template tags are those that reach out of the current template and interact with other template files, enabling composition and code reuse via two primary methods: inheritance and inclusion. We go over inheritance first, as it is generally more conducive to logical template organization. Includes, although useful, can easily lead to "include soup," making debugging and development difficult.

Template inheritance is realized via two template tags, `{% extends %}` and `{% block %}`. `{% extends %}` must be called at the top of a template and signals to the rendering engine this template inherits from a higher-level one. For example, you can define a top-level or site-wide template that outlines headers/footers and global navigation; then, a mid-level template for each subsection, which would extend the top-level template (such as adding a second-level nagivation menu); and finally, bottom-level templates for each individual site location, each extending the mid-level template and providing the actual content for the page in question.

`{% block %}` is a block-level tag used to define sections of a template that are intended to be filled in by those extending it. Although blocks are typically used by a template's immediate child, it's not required. Blocks can be ignored (thus displaying whatever is inside them in the parent template) or delegated further to a lower template. Following is a simplistic example using the three-level Web site layout mentioned previously with URLs consisting of `/`, `/section1/`, `/section2/`, `/section1/page1/`, and `/section1/page2/`.

For now, let's omit the index pages for the site root and the sections and focus on the "leaf" pages at the lowest level. As shown next, `base.html` provides the top level wrapping structure with section templates providing the page title (thus denoting which site section users are in) and page templates providing simple content.

[handwritten notes:] parent uses {% block <block-name> %} to specify "holes" in its partial template <parent>.html

Child uses {% extends <parent>.html %} and fills holes

base.html:

```
<html>
    <head>
        <title>{% block title %}My Web site{% endblock %}</title>
    </head>
    <body>
        <div id="header">
            <a href="/section1/">Section 1</a>
            <a href="/section2/">Section 2</a>
        </div>
        <div id="content">
            {% block content %}{% endblock %}
        </div>
        <div id="footer">
            <a href="/about/">About The Site</a>
        </div>
    </body>
</html>
```

section1.html:

```
{% extends "base.html" %}

{% block title %}Section 1{% endblock %}
```

Only fills block title... No fill for block content

section2.html:

```
{% extends "base.html" %}

{% block title %}Section 2{% endblock %}
```

"previous example", from p 141

page1.html:

```
{% extends "section1.html" %}

{% block content %}This is Page 1.{% endblock %}
```

Fill for block content

page2.html:

```
{% extends "section1.html" %}

{% block content %}<p>This is Page 2.</p>{% endblock %}
```

With templates set up per the previous example, the user's browser sees the following when visiting /section1/page2/: 140

```html
<html>
    <head>
        <title>Section 2</title>
    </head>
    <body>
        <div id="header">
            <a href="/section1/">Section 1</a>
            <a href="/section2/">Section 2</a>
        </div>
        <div id="content">
            <p>This is Page 2.</p>
        </div>
        <div id="footer">
            <a href="/about/">About The Site</a>
        </div>
    </body>
</html>
```

The nice thing about template inheritance is it's easy to navigate the template hierarchy and see what template is generating which chunk of HTML on any given page; additionally, compared to an inclusion-based approach that can have code for including headers, footers, sidebars, and so forth on every subpage, inheritance saves a decent amount of typing.

Including Other Templates

Despite the niceties of template inheritance, template inclusion still has its place. Sometimes you need to reuse chunks of HTML or other text that doesn't fit well into the inheritance scheme, such as a commonly used pagination element. Django supports inclusion with {% include %}, which behaves exactly as you can assume, taking the name of the template file to include and replacing itself with the contents of that file. Included files can themselves be fully realized Django templates; their contents are parsed with respect to the context of the including template.

In addition to `{% include %}, Django provides the {% ssi %} tag (where ssi refers to the Apache-ism SSI, or Server Side Includes). {% include %} and {% extends %} refer to template files locally within the defined template directories specified in settings.py; by comparison, {% ssi %} uses an absolute filesystem path. However, in the interests of security, {% ssi %} is limited to a specific set of directories, specified in the settings.py ALLOWED_INCLUDE_ROOTS variable.

Finally, it should be noted both {% extends %} and {% include %} accept context variable names as well as strings, enabling templates to dynamically determine what they are including or inheriting from.

Forms

Templates by themselves are great for displaying information, but entering information *into* one's database is another matter entirely, involving both the creation of HTML forms and the validation and saving of the information submitted. Django provides a **forms** library, which ties together the three main components of the framework: the database fields defined in the model, the HTML form tags displayed in the templates, and the capability to validate user input and display error messages.

As of this writing, Django's form mechanisms are in a transitional state; the library we cover here is currently known as `newforms` and is a modular approach that much improves on its predecessor, referred to as `oldforms` (although at present, `import django.forms` return this older library). We are covering the `newforms` library, referring to (and importing) it in the present tense as `forms`, with the hope that by the time you're actually reading this book, its transition to the forefront of Django's form processing will be complete.

Defining Forms

At the heart of form processing is a class similar to the `Model`: the `Form`. Like models, forms are essentially collections of field objects, except they represent a specific Web input form instead of a database table. Much of the time, what we're interested in is a form that matches 100 percent of a given model; however, having a separate `Form` class creates a useful degree of flexibility.

With a separate form entity, you can hide or otherwise omit specific fields or tie together fields from multiple model classes. Of course, sometimes you want to be able to process forms that have nothing to do with database storage, and that's equally feasible. Let's go over a quick example.

```
from django import newforms as forms
```

```
class PersonForm(forms.Form):
    first = forms.CharField()
    last = forms.CharField()
    middle = forms.CharField()
```

vs   class Person (models.Model):
eg compare p 66

Although this can look suspiciously similar to an earlier model class, it's a completely stand-alone form that just happens to have the same set of fields (except the fact that these are `forms.Field` instances instead of `models.Field` ones). Form fields take arguments, again in similar fashion to how models are defined.

```
class PersonForm(forms.Form):
    first = forms.CharField(max_length=100, required=True)
    last = forms.CharField(max_length=100, required=True)
    middle = forms.CharField(max_length=100)
```

The previous example now defines a form made up of three text fields; when validation occurs (see the following), it generates errors unless the `first` and `last` fields are filled in. Furthermore it ensures they are no larger than 100 characters in length. There's a lot of overlap between database field types and form field types—check the official documentation for a detailed list of form `Field` classes if you're curious about what's available outside the examples in this chapter.

Model-Based Forms

In the interests of preserving DRY, Django makes it possible to obtain a `Form` subclass for any model class or instance, using a special variation called `ModelForm`. A `ModelForm` is basically identical to a regular `Form`, but has a `Meta` inner class (similar to that of model classes), which has one required attribute, `model`, whose value is the `Model` class in question. The following is functionally identical to the regular `Form` defined previously:

```
from django import newforms as forms
from myproject.myapp.models import Person

class PersonForm(forms.ModelForm):
    class Meta:
        model = Person
```

 # Obtain a Form class
 # directly from a Model class

In general, you need to define at least one such `ModelForm` for every model class you create, even if it's just this simple base case. This approach highlights the separation of the data definition (the model) from the data entry and validation (the form) and provides a lot of flexibility.

The use of `ModelForm` "copies" your `Model` class's fields into `Form` fields. This is generally straightforward—a model `CharField` becomes a form `TextField` or a `ChoiceField` if it defines `choices`—although there are a few caveats well-documented on the official Django site in a table. The main thing to keep in mind is fields are considered to be `required=True` unless the model has set them to be `blank=True`, in which case they become optional (`required=False`).

Saving `ModelForms`

Forms generated in this way have one important difference from those generated manually; they have a save method, which, if validation succeeds, saves their information as a database row and then returns the resulting `Model` object. The implications of this become more obvious once you've read about how to get that information into the form and how it's validated, but know that `save` makes it easy to go from a POST dict to a database create (or update) in a few steps. Continuing the previous example (details on this process appear later in the chapter):

```
from myproject.myapp.forms import PersonForm

form = PersonForm({'first': 'John', 'middle': 'Quincy', 'last': 'Doe'})
```

```
new_person = form.save()     # save to db + return models.Model instance
```

```
# Will result in the __unicode__() output for the new Person
print new_person
```

* There are often situations where you want to modify input data between the time a form is submitted and the time it hits the database. Sometimes this can be done by updating the POST dict before handing it to the form, but other times it's easier to do it after the form is done validating (but still before it arrives at the model layer). The latter approach usually makes the most sense because it takes place after the raw POST data has been turned into Python values.

* For this sort of flexibility to exist, the save method takes an optional commit argument (defaulting to True), which controls whether it actually updates the database. Setting it to False still gives you the model object, but leaves you responsible for calling that object's save method. This example only hits the database once, rather than twice, which is what would happen without commit=False.

```
form = PersonForm({'first': 'John', 'middle': 'Quincy', 'last': 'Doe'})
```
↖ a subclass of forms. ModelForm

```
# We get a Person object, but the database is untouched.
new_person = form.save(commit=False)     # create instance of model but
                                         # do not create row in db
```

```
# Update an attribute on our un-saved Person.
new_person.middle = 'Danger'
```

```
# Now we can update the database for real.
new_person.save()
```

Another common scenario concerning commit=False is when you're using inline editing of related objects. In such cases, a single ModelForm is validating and saving data for both the primary object and its related objects. Because relational databases naturally need target rows to exist before they can be referenced, it's not possible to save the related objects while delaying the saving of your primary object.

Save-m2m

? only for many-to-many

Therefore, when a ModelForm contains related object information and you use commit=False, Django adds an extra method to the form (not the resulting Model object!) called save_m2m, which enables you to correctly stagger the chain of events. In this example, let's say the Person model has a self-referential many-to-many relationship. 1

```
# This input to PersonForm would contain "sub-forms" for additional Person
# objects related to the primary one via the ManyToManyField.
form = PersonForm(input_including_related_objects)
```

```
# Those related objects can't be saved at this point, so they are
# deferred till later.
new_person = form.save(commit=False)
```

```
# Update an attribute on our un-saved Person.
```

1 E.g. "guardian" relationship
   A person may have many guardians (also persons)
   A guardian may have many wards (also persons)

```
new_person.middle = 'Danger'

# After we save to the DB, our Person exists and can be referenced by
# the related objects.
new_person.save()
```
 # results in new db row   new_person is a model instance

```
# So now we save them as well. Don't forget to call this, or your related objects
# will mysteriously disappear!
form.save_m2m()
```
 # results in [model +] db updates (?) for related objects

As you can see, the need to consider immediate saving versus deferred saving adds some complexity to the use of the `save` method; thankfully, that complexity is optional, and most of the time you are happily `save`-ing without worry.

Differing from the Model

Sometimes, you want to modify your form so it's not an exact replica of your model. Hiding certain fields is a common requirement, and only slightly less common is the need for wholesale exclusion or inclusion of fields. Creating a regular `Form` subclass from scratch isn't usually necessary, as there are a few different ways to accomplish the task with `ModelForms`.

The `Meta` inner class of `ModelForms` enables you to define a couple of optional attributes, `fields`, and `excludes`, which are simply lists or tuples of field names to either include or exclude (naturally, you can only use one of these at a time!). For example, the following gives you a `Person` form that omits the middle name:

```
from django import newforms as forms
from myproject.myapp.models import Person

class PersonForm(forms.ModelForm):
    class Meta:
        model = Person
        exclude = ('middle',)
```

Given a `Person` that only has `first`, `middle`, and `last` model fields, the following use of `fields` is exactly equivalent to the previous:

```
class PersonForm(forms.ModelForm):
    class Meta:
        model = Person
        fields = ('first', 'last')
```

An important note to keep in mind is when calling such a form's `save` method, it only attempts to save the fields it knows about. This can cause problems if you omit fields that the model considers to be required! Make sure such fields are either marked as optional with `null=True` or have default values defined with the `default` argument.

Aside from determining which fields from the model are displayed, you can also override the `forms`-level `Field` subclasses used in validating/displaying specific fields. Just define them explicitly, as seen toward the beginning of this part of the chapter, and that definition overrides whatever would have been taken from the model. This is useful both for changing the arguments passed to the form-level `Field`—such as `max_length` or, `required`—or for altering the class itself (perhaps making a `TextField` display as a `CharField` or adding choices to a `CharField` by making it a `ChoiceField`). For example, the following simply tightens validation on the first-name field to be shorter than usual:

```
class PersonForm(forms.ModelForm):
    first = forms.CharField(max_length=10)

    class Meta:
        model = Person
```

Deserving special mention here are the relationship form fields, `ModelChoiceField` and `ModelMultipleChoiceField`, which correspond to `ForeignKey` and `ManyToManyField`, respectively. Although it's possible to specify the `limit_choices_to` argument to the model-level fields, you can also specify a `queryset` argument to the form-level fields, which naturally expect a specific `QuerySet` object. In this way, you can override any such limitations (or lack thereof) at the model level and customize your `ModelForm` instead, as in the following where we assume a `Person` model with a non-limited `parent` `ForeignKey` to other `Person` objects:

```
# A normal, non-limited form (since the Model places no limits on 'parent')
class PersonForm(forms.ModelForm):
    class Meta:
        model = Person

# A form for people in the Smith family (whose parents are Smiths)
class SmithChildForm(forms.ModelForm):
    parent = forms.ModelChoiceField(queryset=Person.objects.filter(last='Smith'))

    class Meta:
        model = Person
```

Form Subclassing

In many scenarios, both with normal `Forms` and `ModelForms`, it's possible to take advantage of the object-oriented nature of Python to avoid repeating yourself. `Form` subclasses can themselves be subclassed, and the resultant classes contain all the fields of their predecessors. For example:

```
from django import newforms as forms


class PersonForm(forms.Form):
    first = forms.CharField(max_length=100, required=True)
    last = forms.CharField(max_length=100, required=True)
    middle = forms.CharField(max_length=100)
```

[handwritten: Person Form ↑ Aged Person Form]

```
class AgedPersonForm(PersonForm):
    # first, last, middle all inherited
    age = forms.IntegerField()

class EmployeeForm(PersonForm):
    # first, last, middle all inherited
    department = forms.CharField()

class SystemUserForm(EmployeeForm):
    # first, last, middle and department all inherited
    username = forms.CharField(maxlength=8, required=True)
```

It's also possible to perform so-called "mix-ins," which make use of multiple inheritance.

```
class BookForm(forms.Form):
    title = forms.CharField(max_length=100, required=True)
    author = forms.CharField(max_length=100, required=True)

class InventoryForm(forms.Form):
    location = forms.CharField()
    quantity = forms.IntegerField()

class BookstoreBookForm(BookForm, InventoryForm):
    # Has title, author, location and quantity
    pass
```

[handwritten: Can have a mixin w ModelForm and Form(s) ?]

When applying this approach to `ModelForm` subclasses, note you can alter `Meta` attributes as well, typically updating or adding `fields` or `excluding` values to further limit the available fields.

Filling Out Forms

In Django's forms library, any given form instance is either **bound**, meaning it has some data associated with it, or it is **unbound**, meaning it's effectively empty. Unbound, empty forms are used primarily for generating an empty HTML form for users to fill out because you can't validate them (unless a completely empty form is a desired input, which is rather unlikely), and you probably wouldn't want to save their contents to a database either. Bound forms are where most of the action lies.

Binding data to a form is done at instantiation time, and once instantiated, a form is effectively immutable. This can sound inflexible, but it makes the process of using and applying forms more explicit and orthogonal than it can otherwise be; it also removes any ambiguity about the validation state of a form whose data has been altered (as was possible in the `oldforms` library).

Let's generate a bound form based on our earlier `Person`-related `ModelForm` subclass, embedded in the beginnings of what could become a form-processing view function. The use of `request.POST.copy()` is not explicitly required, but it's a good idea. You can

[handwritten: 143ff]

modify your copy of the dict while preserving the original contents of the request, in case it's needed farther down the line.

```
from myproject.myapp.forms import PersonForm


def process_form(request):
    post = request.POST.copy() # e.g. {'last': 'Doe', 'first': 'John'}
    form = PersonForm(post)
```

It should be noted that adding extraneous key/value pairs to a form's data dict is not a problem; forms simply ignore any input that does not correspond to their defined set of fields. This means you can take a POST dict from a large form and use it to fill a `Form` object representing a subset of those fields, for example.

It's also possible to create forms that, although unbound, are loaded with initial values displayed when the form is printed in a template. The aptly named `initial` constructor argument is a dict, just as the positional argument used for binding. Individual form fields have a similar parameter, enabling them to specify their own default value, but the form-level dict overrides these if there's a conflict.

Here's an example of creating a form, modifying our custom `PersonForm` from earlier to prefill the last name field with "Smith" (via the form definition) and the first name field with "John" (at runtime when creating the form instance). Users can, of course, override either of these when they fill out the form.

```
from django import newforms as forms
from django.shortcuts import render_to_response


class PersonForm(forms.Form):
    first = forms.CharField(max_length=100, required=True)
    last = forms.CharField(max_length=100, required=True, initial='Smith')
    middle = forms.CharField(max_length=100)


def process_form(request):
    if not request.POST: # Display the form, nothing was submitted.
        form = PersonForm(initial={'first': 'John'})
        return render_to_response('myapp/form.html', {'form': form})
```

> **Note**
>
> If our `initial` argument to the instantiation of `PersonForm` had instead been something such as `{'first': 'John', 'last': 'Doe'}`, the instance-level "Doe" value (for the `'last'` key) would have overwritten the class-level "Smith" value from the form definition.

A major benefit of using the instance-level `initial` argument is that its values can be constructed at the time of the form's creation. For example, this allows you to reference information not available at the time the form or model is defined, typically info in the request object.

Observe how we can make use of this in a view function that deals with adding new `Person` records, relative to another such record. Pretend for now we have a new "parent" self-referential `ForeignKey` on the `Person` model and that we have a simple `ModelForm` defined for `Person`.

```python
from django.shortcuts import get_object_or_404, render_to_response
from myproject.myapp.models import Person, PersonForm
```

```python
# View's URL: /person/<id>/children/add/
def add_relative(request, **kwargs):
    # Display the form if nothing was POSTed
    if not request.POST:
        relative = get_object_or_404(Person, pk=kwargs['id'])
        form = PersonForm(initial={'last': relative.last})
        return render_to_response('person/form.html', {'form': form})
```

[handwritten annotations: Person model has Field (p93); relative = models.ForeignKey (Person); model class (could be Manager or queryset); [3]; # Display initial version # of form, w. last filled # in]

For brevity's sake, we've omitted the handling of a submitted form, something a real view function would probably be concerned about! Note how we obtained the `relative` object based values in the URL, and then passed that relative's last name as the initial value of `last` in our form. In other words, we've set things up so children automatically get their parents' last name filled in—something that could come in handy if your users are doing a lot of data entry.

Validation and Cleaning

Although forms are generally stateless, they do require some sort of trigger to perform validation on the data they've been bound to, if they've been bound at all (validation and cleaning do not apply to unbound forms). To cause a form to run its validation routines, you can explicitly call its `is_valid` Boolean method, or you can call one of its display methods (see the following), all which implicitly perform validation as well.

[handwritten annotation: is_valid()]

Let's rejigger our previous `add_relative` form processing view, so it handles form input as well as empty form display. This involves changing the logic around to be a bit more flexible, with a common Django idiom that checks for the existence of the POST dict and handles validation (or generates an empty form), and then "falls through" to displaying the form. The form then displays either for non-POST requests or for POST requests that failed to validate.

[handwritten annotation: Some HTML in app has a link with this URL to "add children". The HTML form's ACTION also specifies this URL]

```python
# View's URL: /person/<id>/children/add/
def add_relative(request, **kwargs):
    # Get the parent relative

    # Validate if the form was POSTed
    if request.POST:
        form = PersonForm(request.POST)
        if form.is_valid:
            new_person = form.save()
            return HttpResponseRedirect(new_person.get_absolute_url())
```

[handwritten annotations: # Instantiate a PersonForm instance; # Check if form is valid; # Maybe form.save(commit=True) 144]

```
# Otherwise, prep an empty form with the relative pre-filled
else:
    relative = get_object_or_404(Person, pk=kwargs['id'])
    form = PersonForm(initial={'last': relative.last})
# Display the form for non POST requests or failed validations.
# Our template will display errors if they exist.
return render_to_response('person/form.html', {'form': form})
```

Once validation has been triggered, the form object gains one of two new attributes: errors, a dictionary of error messages, or cleaned_data, a dictionary containing the "clean" versions of the values originally bound to the form. You never find both at once, as cleaned_data is only generated when the form validates, and of course errors only applies if the validation failed.

myform.errors
or
myform.cleaned_data

The format of the errors dictionary is simple; the keys are the field names, and the values are lists of strings (each string being a message about why the form's validation failed). errors, naturally, only contain key/value pairs for fields with errors to display. Later in the chapter, we explore some helper methods that Form objects provide for easy display of these error messages.

Behind the concept of "clean" data is the need for input data to be **normalized**—translated from one or more potential input formats into a consistent output format appropriate for validation and database storage. For example, forms whose bound data comes straight from a request.POST dictionary generally contains strings, and thus any numeric fields' cleansing process casts those strings to ints or longs, date-related fields parse strings such as "2007-10-29" into datetime objects, and so forth.

forms.date

Although normalization is required for the automatic validation and saving methods to work correctly, it also means any Python code interacting with the form's contents has access to the correct data types. If you find the need to examine the original prenormalized data, it is still available as the form's data attribute.

Form Display

Form objects have a handful of helpful methods that enable you to display them in various predefined HTML formats; these methods print out the entire innards of the form, sans the <form> tags and submit buttons, and include <label> tags as well. It's also possible to display each form field individually, if you need finer-grained control over the output. Finally, it should be noted that although you generally use these display methods in templates, it's not required—you can call any and all such methods at the Python level if you should find the need.

Each Django form field knows how to display itself as an HTML tag or tags, and this behavior can be modified via **widgets**, covered at the end of the chapter. Additionally, the name and id attributes for these tags, as well as the for attribute in their corresponding <label> tags, are all drawn from the field's attribute name on the Form class you defined in the beginning. The text inside the <label> tags are, by default, generated by taking the field names, capitalizing, changing underscores to spaces, and appending a trailing : character if the field name didn't end in punctuation to begin with.

Here's an example to help you make sense of these various options and how they affect the HTML output. First, a recap of a manually created `PersonForm`:

```
from django import newforms as forms

class PersonForm(forms.Form):
    first = forms.CharField(max_length=100, required=True)
    last = forms.CharField(max_length=100, required=True, initial='Smith')
    middle = forms.CharField(max_length=100)
```

and a sample of how this translates into HTML for the `first` field when displayed as part of a table:

```
<tr><th><label for="id_first">First:</label></th><td><input id="id_first"
type="text" name="first" maxlength="100" /></td></tr>
```

It's possible to change the behavior of the `id` attributes and `<label>` tags by way of the form's `auto_id` constructor argument: `False` prevents the display of ids and labels entirely; `True` uses the fields' attribute names, as shown previously; and strings containing the string format character, such as `'id_%s'`, replaces the format character with the attribute name. In addition, the trailing `:` character in labels can be overridden by the `label_suffix` argument, which is simply a string.

The following is how one would create an instance of `PersonForm` with `auto_id` turned off and `label_suffix` also turned "off" by setting it to the empty string:

```
pf = PersonForm(auto_id=False, label_suffix='')
```

and what the `first` field would look like when that form is displayed:

```
<tr><th>First</th><td><input type="text" name="first" maxlength="100" /></td></tr>
```

Finally, the same setup, but with custom string values for `auto_id` and `label_suffix`:

```
pf = PersonForm(auto_id='%s_id, label_suffix='?')
```

which would output the following:

```
<tr><th><label for="first_id">First?</label></th><td><input id="first_id"
type="text" name="first" maxlength="100" /></td></tr>
```

As you can see, the auto-generated form output Django provides is fairly flexible. We show you how to actually obtain this sort of output from a form object in this next section.

Displaying Forms Wholesale

By default, printing a form uses its `as_table` method, wherein the form is printed out two fields per row, using `<tr>` and `<td>` tags, although it omits the `<table>` tags to be more flexible. `as_table` is accompanied by its brethren `as_p`, which uses paragraph tags, and `as_ul`, which uses list-item tags (but, as usual, omits the wrapping `<ul>` tags themselves).

> **Note**
>
> Forms omit the "outside" wrapping tags, such as `<table></table>` because including
> them would make it much more difficult to integrate wholesale form display with the rest of
> your template's HTML. The same holds true for submit buttons—many template designs
> require the use of different methods for form submission, such as `<input type="button"
> />` or `<input type="submit" />`, and so Django leaves that decision entirely up to you.

When displayed wholesale in this manner, validation errors are also automatically
printed, if they exist: A `<ul>` tag with one or more `<li>` tags is displayed near the appropriate field, depending on the output method used. `as_table` and `as_ul` print error lists
within the same tag as the field itself (the `<td>` and `<li>` tags, respectively) and `as_p` creates new paragraphs to hold the error lists. In each case the errors are printed as shown
previously, or before, the form elements.

It's possible to customize the way error lists are displayed by subclassing
`django.forms.util.ErrorList` and passing your subclass as the `error_class` argument
to the form in question. And if you want to change the order of the fields/error lists,
simply rearrange the order they appear in on your `Form` class—it's that simple.

Displaying Forms Piecemeal

In addition to the convenience methods outlined previously, it's possible to exert finer
control over how your form is arranged. The individual `Field` objects are available
through dictionary keys on the form itself, enabling you to display them whenever and
wherever you want. You can also iterate over the form itself, thanks to Python's duck typing capabilities. Regardless of how you obtain them, each field has its own `errors` attribute, a list-like object whose string representation is the same unordered list previously
displayed in the wholesale methods (and overridden the same way).

In `oldforms`, the simplest way to override the default HTML representation of a form
field was to access the field's `data` attribute and wrap it with custom HTML—a trick that
is still possible with `newforms`. However, the power of `Widgets` hopefully makes that
approach less necessary than it was in the past.

Widgets

A **widget**, in Django forms parlance, is an object that knows how to display an HTML
form element. In similar fashion to model `Field` subclasses and form `Field` subclasses,
Django provides a decently sized default library of `Widget` subclasses. Every form field is
paired with a specific `Widget` so its data can be displayed when it comes time to render
the form in a template. `CharFields` use by default a `Widget` subclass named `TextInput`,
for example, which just renders `<input type="text" />`.

The default field-widget pairings often suffice, in which case you don't even notice
the widgets themselves. However, there are scenarios where you find yourself needing to
modify attributes of a field's widget or replacing the widget with an entirely different one.
The former is more common as it provides a way for you to change HTML attributes of

the field in question. The following is an example of changing the "size" attribute of an otherwise normal text field:

```
from django import newforms as forms


class PersonForm(forms.Form):
    first = forms.CharField(max_length=100, required=True)
    last = forms.CharField(max_length=100, required=True)
    middle = forms.CharField(max_length=100,
        widget=forms.TextInput(attrs={'size': 3}
    )
```

Use of that form would result in a `middle` field such as:

```
<input id="id_middle" maxlength="100" type="text" name="middle" size="3" />
```

As you can see, this type of modification is possible because `Widget` subclasses (such as `TextInput`) accept an `attrs` dict, which maps directly to HTML tag attributes. In this case, we don't want to limit the actual input size of the middle name (users can still type up to 100 characters), but we do want its display size to be smaller than the default.

Overriding a Field's Default Widget

The `widget` parameter for `Field` subclasses can also be used to replace the default widget entirely, by passing in a different `Widget` subclass; for example, one could use a `Textarea` to replace a `TextInput`. Utilizing this aspect of form fields enables a clean separation of a field's display qualities (the widget) from its validation behavior (the form field). It also means you can define your own `Widget` subclasses if the built-in ones don't fulfill your needs.

Although the details of defining from-scratch widgets is outside the scope of this chapter, we can share a quick and easy way to use `Widget` subclassing to save time. If you find yourself often making use of the `attrs` dict for a specific widget, you can subclass the `Widget` in question and give it a default `attrs` dict.

```
from django import newforms as forms


class LargeTextareaWidget(forms.Textarea):
    def __init__(self, *args, **kwargs):
        kwargs.setdefault('attrs', {}).update({'rows': 40, 'cols': 100})
        super(LargeTextareaWidget, self).__init__(*args, **kwargs)
```

The previous example uses a little bit of dictionary cleverness; `setdefault` acts like `get` in that it returns an existing value for the given key or the supplied value if that key isn't already set. However, it also alters the dictionary in question to store that value permanently. It's used here to ensure that the `kwargs` keyword-argument dictionary has an `attrs` dict, regardless of the original arguments to the constructor. We then `update` the resulting `attrs` dict with our intended defaults.

The end result is our new `LargeTextarea` widget behaves exactly like a normal `Textarea`, but always has 40 rows and 100 columns by default. It's then possible to use our new widget for all the fields that we want displayed as a larger-than-normal text area. For the next example, let's say we store our custom form-related classes in an app-local `forms.py`.

```
from django import newforms as forms
from myproject.myapp.forms import LargeTextareaWidget

class ContentForm(forms.Form):
    name = forms.CharField()
    markup = forms.ChoiceField(choices=[
        ('markdown', 'Markdown'),
        ('textile', 'Textile')
    ])
    text = forms.Textarea(widget=LargeTextareaWidget)
```

ChoiceField in form

Of course, it's possible to go one step further. Because the `widget` argument in a `Field` subclass simply sets its `widget` attribute, we can subclass the field itself to always use our custom widget.

```
class LargeTextareaWidget(forms.Textarea):
    def __init__(self, *args, **kwargs):
        kwargs.setdefault('attrs', {}).update({'rows': 40, 'cols': 100})
        super(LargeTextareaWidget, self).__init__(*args, **kwargs)

class LargeTextarea(forms.Field):
    widget = LargeTextareaWidget
```

as before

Now we can change the previous form-creating example to use the custom field.

```
class ContentForm(forms.Form):
    name = forms.CharField()
    markup = forms.ChoiceField(choices=[
        ('markdown', 'Markdown'),
        ('textile', 'Textile')
    ])
    text = LargeTextarea()
```

cf p 96~7

As usual, the fact that Django is pure Python means it's easy to swap out various classes and objects like this when the need arises. Keeping this in mind helps you spot other areas where customization can be utilized.

Summary

In this chapter, you've learned about Django's template syntax and how templates are rendered against context dictionaries, including more complex subjects such as template inheritance and inclusion. In addition, you know how to generate forms—both stand-alone and ones representing specific model classes—and cause them to validate data and display themselves as HTML. Finally, we exposed some of the customization possible with the power of widgets.

This chapter marks the end of Part II, "Django in Depth," and you now have a decent background in what Django has to offer; everything from model definition, URLs and request handling, and now templates and forms. The next four chapters in Part III, "Django Applications by Example," contain example applications making use of the material you've already seen and also introduces a handful of new or expanded concepts as they go along.

widgets   forms. Text Input   forms. Text Area
                                                        ↑
derived widget   Large Text Area Widget

form   forms. Form
                        ↑
derived form   Content Form

field   forms, Field
                        ↑
derived Field   Large Text Area

Django Applications by Example

7

Photo Gallery

project ← gallery
app ← items   (~ photo album)

A common feature of many content-driven Web sites is the capability for users to add not only text, but also files—office documents, videos, PDFs, and of course the ubiquitous image. In this example application, we show you a working example of Django's image upload field—ImageField—as used in a simple gallery-type application. In addition, we make our own custom ImageField subclass capable of automatically generating thumbnails. Finally, we are designing the app with a dynamic root URL to maximize ease of deployment.

The application we are building is simplistic—a collection of generic Items, each of *✗* which can have multiple Photo associations, with this small hierarchy represented by a gallery Django project and an items app within (for lack of a better name).

One could expand on this application to build a more typical gallery site, where our Item becomes more like a container or folder solely used for organizing photos. Or you could make it into a sort of showroom application, where each Item has additional attributes (such as a car's model, make, and year) enabling for more sophistication. For our example, you can think of each Item as a stand-alone photo album.

We don't want to do any more work than is necessary, so our app makes use of generic views where possible, and we do all its data entry via Django's built-in admin. As such, its layout is pretty small:

- Static in-template welcome message on landing (index) page.
- Landing page features a "showcase" (small subset of thumbnails). *landing page*
- Listing page shows all Items on the site.   *items list*
- Detail views for each Item with list of all its Photos (thumbnails again). *item detail*
- Detail views for each Photo displaying image at full resolution.   *photo detail*

We start off by defining the model, and then walk through the steps necessary to get file uploads working via the admin application. This is followed by detaied creation of our custom model field. Finally, we go over applying DRY to our URLs and create the front-end templates used to display our thumbnails and images to the rest of the world.

> **Note**
>
> This example application assumes an Apache + `mod_python` setup, although it can, of course, be modified to work with other deployment strategies. Because a gallery involves serving lots of static media—such as images—Django's development server doesn't really cut it. You can find out more about Apache configuration in Appendix B, "Installing and Running Django." *295*

The Model

Following is this application's `models.py`, and aside from a single change we are making later on, it's complete. Note the `get_absolute_url` methods are using the `@permalink` decorator, which is covered toward the end of the chapter. 173

```python
class Item(models.Model):
    name = models.CharField(max_length=250)
    description = models.TextField()

    class Meta:
        ordering = ['name']

    def __unicode__(self):
        return self.name
```

173

```python
    @permalink        # to reconstruct the URL
    def get_absolute_url(self):
        return ('item_detail', None, {'object_id': self.id})
```
172: Url patterns   name value,   list,   dict,   "parent"
                          in url(...)   posh args   keyword args   Photo → Item

```python
class Photo(models.Model):
    item = models.ForeignKey(Item)
    title = models.CharField(max_length=100)
    image = models.ImageField(upload_to='photos')     dir rel. to MEDIA-ROOT
    caption = models.CharField(max_length=250, blank=True)

    class Meta:
        ordering = ['title']

    def __unicode__(self):
        return self.title
```

173
```python
    @permalink  1
    def get_absolute_url(self):
        return ('photo_detail', None, {'object_id': self.id})
```

102
```python
class PhotoInline(admin.StackedInline):       # the inline subclass
    model = Photo
```

---

1 Expects its wrapped func (here, got-absolute-url) to return a 3-tuple: (URL-name, list of posh args, dict of keyword args) which is used to reconstruct the URL

```
class ItemAdmin(admin.ModelAdmin):
    inlines = [PhotoInline]

admin.site.register(Item, ItemAdmin)
admin.site.register(Photo)
```

Reference inline subclass in this ModelAdmin subclass

102, 69

As you can see, the `Item` is simple with the `Photo` being more the star of the show—it not only has the relation to its parent `Item`, but a title, the image itself, and an optional caption. Both objects are registered with the admin application; they also both have a `Meta.ordering` attribute set.

Our main focus is the `ImageField` in the `Photo` model, as that's the field we are eventually customizing and also takes a bit of setup compared to most other model fields. Let's explore how to get that working.

Preparing for File Uploads

Before we can upload files to our gallery site, we need to be specific about where we want Django to put them. `FileFields` and `ImageFields` store uploaded data to a subdirectory of one's `settings.py`-defined `MEDIA_ROOT`, which is specified in the `upload_to` field argument. In our model code, we've set this to `'photos,'` so if our `settings.py` contained the following:

MEDIA-ROOT

```
MEDIA_ROOT = '/var/www/gallery/media/'
```

our photos would necessarily end up in `/var/www/gallery/media/photos/`. If that directory doesn't exist, it needs to be created, and it also needs to be writable by whatever user or group your Web server is running as. On our Debian-based system, we're running Apache as the `www-data` user, so we can have a short shell session that looks like this (see Appendix A, "Command Line Basics," for details on using the command line):

```
user@example:~ $ cd /var/www/gallery/media
user@example:/var/www/gallery/media $ ls
admin
user@example:/var/www/gallery/media $ mkdir photos
user@example:/var/www/gallery/media $ ls -l
total 4
lrwxrwxrwx 1 root  root    59 2008-03-26 21:41 admin ->
/usr/lib/python2.4/site-packages/django/contrib/admin/media
drwxrwxr-x 2 user user 4096 2008-03-26 21:44 photos
user@example:/var/www/gallery/media $ chgrp www-data photos
user@example:/var/www/gallery/media $ chmod g+w photos
user@example:/var/www/gallery/media $ ls -l
total 4
lrwxrwxrwx 1 root  root    59 2008-03-26 21:41 admin ->
/usr/lib/python2.4/site-packages/django/contrib/admin/media
drwxrwxr-x 2 user www-data 4096 2008-03-26 21:44 photos
```

/usr/lib/python2.4/site-packages/ — *django/contrib/admin/media* } symlink

MEDIA-ROOT
var
www
gallery
media
admin   photos

./photos [755, user, user]

[775, user, www-data]

symlink

@ 162

(Make photos grp-writable, with grp = www-data)

@161
ⓑ 208

The previous is only possible if your normal user is also in the `www-data` group—depending on your system setup you can find yourself having to use `sudo` or similar approaches, which is fine. We've found that when doing lots of system tasks that intersect with our Web server's domain, it's very useful to make ourselves part of its group; then as long as directories or files are group-writable (as previously shown) both the Web server and our user can interact with them.

Finally, note that a more fleshed-out application would probably have another symlink or two in the `media` directory—you need your CSS and JavaScript, after all—and your Web server needs to be configured to serve it up normally. If you use `mod_python` with Apache, for example, you need a short config block to "punch through" the Django-handled URL space so Apache serves your media files directly. See Appendix B for more on `mod_python` configuration.   *295,*

Installing PIL

At this point—once we've added our custom app to our `settings.py` and have run `syncdb`—we're almost ready to upload some images. However, as we see in a moment, there's one final task remaining. If we were to load up our admin site as things currently stand (with our Django project installed and the photos upload folder set up), chances are good we'd see a screen similar to that in Figure 7.1.

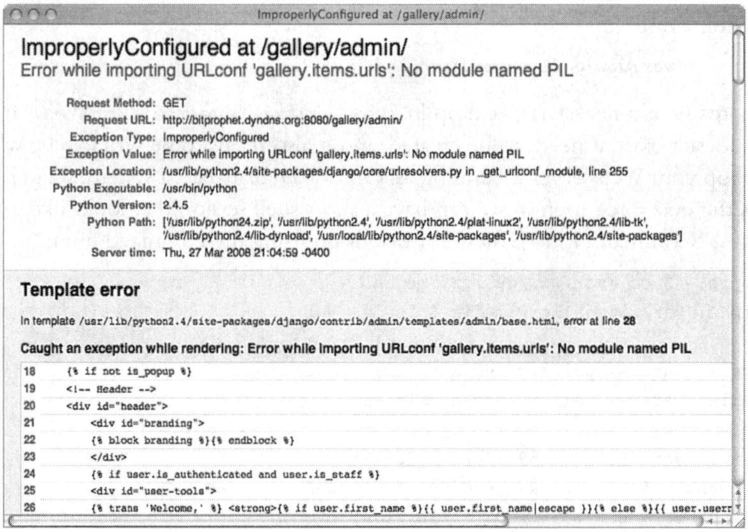

Figure 7.1   What happens when you don't have PIL installed

In other words—we need a special Python library to use `ImageField`, specifically **PIL**, or the Python Imaging Library. PIL is a commonly used Python library that can handle all sorts of image manipulation. `ImageField` uses it *PIL* to verify that uploaded files are images and to store their height and width if you use the optional `height_field` and `width_field` options; we use it further to do our thumbnail resizing.

To install PIL for Unix-based systems, such as Linux or Mac, download the Source Kit from http://www.pythonware.com/products/pil/ and run `setup.py install` in its install directory once you've unpacked it. For Win32, you would download the appropriate `.exe` installation binary for your version of Python and install it.

A simpler way to install third-party Python packages on any platform is Easy Install. It knows about dependencies and makes download plus installation a complete one-step solution. You simply run `easy_install pil` to accomplish the same thing as all the steps previously described. To find out more information about obtaining and using the Easy Install tool, visit the PEAK Developers' Center at http://peak.telecommunity.com/DevCenter/EasyInstall.

Testing `ImageField`

Regardless of how you did it, once PIL is installed and we've restarted and/or reloaded our Web server, the PIL-related errors should go away, and we can move onward and do a simple test of our `ImageField`.

Because of the way the gallery's model is constructed, *160* we can't just upload a random image not associated with an `Item`. A careful look at the model definition shows we've set up admin and inline classes, so our `Photo` objects can be edited as part of their parent `Item`. This enables us to easily add images at the same time as we define our items, and you can see this in Figure 7.2.

cf 160–161

"parent"

"children"

cf p 160–1

Item fields
photos store
or FK for photo

photo fields

Figure 7.2   The ImageField

After saving our new Item, the selected image (in our case, a picture of one of the authors' pet rabbit) is uploaded and stored. We can verify this via the admin, as seen in Figure 7.3.

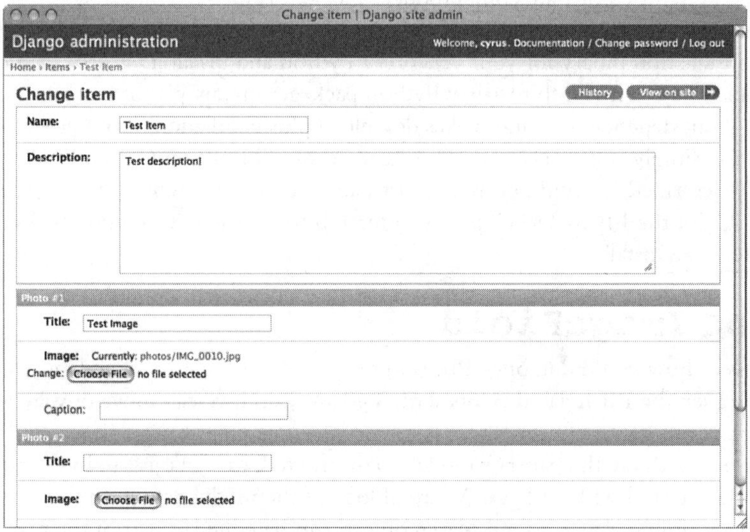

existing file

Figure 7.3   The admin interface, post-upload

Note the Currently: link above the file selector for the first Photo—clicking it shows the uploaded image, as shown in Figure 7.4.

We can also verify the file upload via the command line.

```
user@example:/var/www/gallery/media/photos $ ls -l
total 144
-rw-r--r-- 1 www-data www-data 140910 2008-03-27 21:26 IMG_0010.jpg
```

It's taken a bit of explanation, but as you can see, getting up and running with image uploads is pretty painless—up till now all we've really done is define a model, create a folder to hold the images, and install the imaging library. Now we can finally show you the interesting stuff, namely how to extend ImageField to perform thumbnailing.

Building Our Custom File Field

Because Django provides no thumbnailing capabilities out of the box, we write our own model field, which is capable of transparently handling thumbnail creation, deletion, and display by subclassing ImageField. The official Django documentation has excellent information on writing entirely new model fields from scratch—here, we just want to tweak existing behavior, which is a bit simpler and probably more common.

Figure 7.4   Checking the current value of an ImageField

Don't Fear the Source

It's all too common for programmers to treat the libraries they work with—even fully open source ones—as black boxes with defined input and output behavior, but which are otherwise mysterious. Although this can be appropriate in some cases, such as in verbose or low-level languages where these libraries can get truly gigantic or byzantine, it's often not the case with Python source code.

Pythonic, well-written libraries are generally pretty easy to crack open and comprehend, and Django is no exception. We don't pretend the entire codebase is perfectly refactored and commented, but much of it is in great shape, and developers—even intermediate ones—can get a lot of benefit out of diving into code to figure out what makes Django tick. What we do in this chapter is not fully documented—but it is relatively easy to figure out just by reading the source for `django.db.models.ImageField` and its parent classes.

To accomplish this, we needed to override four methods of our parent `ImageField` class, and in the process added one simple, private method as a refactoring aid. The source code that directly inspired this chapter is heavily commented—documentation greatly helps with the process of understanding new territory—but we've removed most of that here to make it easier to read.

Our thumbnailing `ImageField`, called—naturally—`ThumbnailImageField`, is stored in `gallery.items.fields`. It consists solely of some imports, a refactoring-based utility function, and a couple of subclasses that modify some built-in Django classes. If you're unfamiliar with Python's approach to object-oriented subclassing, see Chapter 1, "Practical Python for Django," for details.

Let's step through our file top-to-bottom.

1 Create gallery/items/fields.py

Initialization

Every Python file, except for some rare cases, begins with imports, and this one's no different.

fields.py:

```python
from django.db.models.fields.files import ImageField, ImageFieldFile
from PIL import Image
import os
```

Imports are simple; all we need for this task are the parent classes of `ImageField` and `ImageFieldFile`, PIL's `Image` class, which does the thumbnailing for us, and the built-in `os` module for handling the thumbnail files themselves.

private method: refactoring aid

```python
def _add_thumb(s):
    """
    Modifies a string (filename, URL) containing an image filename, to insert
    '.thumb' before the file extension (which is changed to be '.jpg').
    """
    parts = s.split(".")
    parts.insert(-1, "thumb")
    if parts[-1].lower() not in ['jpeg', 'jpg']:
        parts[-1] = 'jpg'
    return ".".join(parts)
```

or √

is format of s

`_add_thumb` is a utility function that, as the docstring says—always use good docstrings—takes the original image's file path and inserts the string ".thumb." So an uploaded image named `rabbit.jpg` would result in a thumbnail of `rabbit.thumb.jpg`; because our code can only generate JPEG thumbnails, it also changes the extension if necessary. *(PIL converts to JPEG if neccessary)*

```python
class ThumbnailImageField(ImageField):
    """
    Behaves like a regular ImageField, but stores an extra (JPEG) thumbnail
    image, providing get_FIELD_thumb_url() and get_FIELD_thumb_filename().

    Accepts two additional, optional arguments: thumb_width and thumb_height,
    both defaulting to 128 (pixels). Resizing will preserve aspect ratio while
    staying inside the requested dimensions; see PIL's Image.thumbnail()
    method documentation for details.
    """
    attr_class = ThumbnailImageFieldFile
```

@167

Not much to say here—we're defining our new subclass, having it inherit from `ImageField`, and putting in a nice big docstring. This way, anyone using Python's help system, or automated documentation tools, gets a decent idea of what our code does.

The single line of actual code here, concerning `attr_class`, is used to update a special *@ 166* class our field uses as a delegate for attribute access. We go into detail about this class in the next section. The last piece of this introduction is __init__:

```
def __init__(self, thumb_width=128, thumb_height=128, *args, **kwargs):
    self.thumb_width = thumb_width
    self.thumb_height = thumb_height
    super(ThumbnailImageField, self).__init__(*args, **kwargs)
```

Our overridden __init__ is also fairly simple—we're just storing the desired max width and height of our thumbnail for use during the resize operation. This enables easy reuse of the field with varying thumbnail sizes.

Adding Attributes to the Field

Many fields are relatively low-key and don't modify their containing model objects, but in our case, we want to make it easy to get to the extra information we provide (our thumbnails' filenames and URLs). The solution is to subclass a special class that `ImageField` uses to manage its attributes, `ImageFieldFile`, which is used when one performs attribute lookups on the field itself.   *@ 166*

For example, to obtain the filesystem path for an `ImageField` called image, you use `myobject.image.path`; in such a scenario, `.path` is an attribute on `ImageFieldFile`. Because Django caches the file data when possible and delegates the file to a lower layer, this is done via Python properties. (See Chapter 1 for a refresher on the `property` built-in   *?* function.)

The following code snippet illustrates how the default Django codebase implements `ImageFieldFile.path`:

```
def _get_path(self):                              name of the image attr class
    self._require_file()
    return self.storage.path(self.name)          read func
path = property(_get_path)      # property : "Attach result to desired attribute name"  (b)
```

This snippet is taken from the `FieldFile` class (which is the parent of `ImageFieldFile`, used — as you can guess — by `ImageField`). Recall our previous utility function _add_thumb, and how it transforms a given file path, and you can guess what we'll do to add the `.thumb_path` and `.thumb_url` attributes to our field:

```
class ThumbnailImageFieldFile(ImageFieldFile):
    def _get_thumb_path(self):        retrieves (via property above) the path to the image
        return _add_thumb(self.path)  , uses  property  (b)
    thumb_path = property(_get_thumb_path)

    def _get_thumb_url(self):         retrieves (via property, not shown) the url of the image
        return _add_thumb(self.url)
    thumb_url = property(_get_thumb_url)
```

Because the `.path` and `.url` getters are already defined, and they take care of the minute boilerplate required for safe operation (the call to `self._require_file`, seen in the previous snippet concerning _get_path), we are free to omit that extra code. We simply perform our `_add_thumb` transformation and attach the result to the desired attribute names, with `property`.

With `ThumbnailImageFieldFile` defined above our `ThumbnailImageField` and referenced in the `attr_class` line at the top of `ThumbnailImageField`, we have added two new attributes to our field, which you can use in Python code or templates: `myobject.image.thumb_path` and `myobject.image.thumb_url` (given, of course, that `myobject` is a Django model instance and `image` is a `ThumbnailImageField` on that model).

Subclassing `ImageFieldFile` and tying that subclass to our `ImageField` subclass is probably not an obvious action to take; most custom model fields won't need to go this far. In fact, as a user of Django, you'll likely never see this particular aspect of the model (although it's more accessible now than it used to be—the previous version of this section was a little more complex). However, it highlights the fact that the Django core team tries to apply extensible design to the internals of the framework and not just its public API.

Now that we have access to our desired thumbnail's URL and filesystem path, we move on to actually creating (and removing) that thumbnail file.

Saving and Deleting the Thumbnail

The crux of the matter, creation of the thumbnail file itself, is an overridden `save` method on `ThumbnailImageFieldFile` (not `ThumbnailImageField`!) that looks like this:

```
def save(self, name, content, save=True):
    super(ThumbnailImageFieldFile, self).save(name, content, save)
    img = Image.open(self.path)      # open orig image
    img.thumbnail(                    # create thumbnail via PIL
        (self.field.thumb_width, self.field.thumb_height),
        Image.ANTIALIAS
    )
    img.save(self.thumb_path, 'JPEG')  # save the thumbnail
```

The call to the superclass's save takes care of normal saving operations for the primary image file, so all our method has to do is the three-step sequence of opening that original image, creating the thumbnail, and saving that thumbnail to our thumbnail filename. Note the use of `self.field` that lets us access the `Field` that this `File` object belongs to, which is where we've stored the desired thumbnail dimensions. Leveraging the PIL `Image` class, which we imported at the beginning, enables our code to be very simple indeed.

As a final step, we need to make sure our thumbnails are cleaned up when their "parent" images are deleted:

```
def delete(self, save=True):
    if os.path.exists(self.thumb_path):
        os.remove(self.thumb_path)
    super(ThumbnailImageFieldFile, self).delete(save)
```

Thanks to Python's syntax, this excerpt almost describes itself. We obtain the filename of our thumbnail, delete it (if it exists, of course—no point inviting an error if the file's not there), and tell our superclass to do its own file deletion (which removes the original image). If it wasn't obvious, the `delete` method, like `save`, is triggered by `ImageField` when its container model object is deleted.

> ### Order of Operations
>
> The order of operations in our `delete` method matters and is something to be considered whenever you subclass. If we had called `super` first, the call to `self.thumb_path` would have generated an error because it in turn calls `self.path`, which—if you recall the previous code snippet—tries to ensure the field's main file exists! Therefore, we need to wait until the last possible minute to remove that file, lest our class break down.

Using `ThumbnailImageField`

Now that we've defined our subclass of `ImageField`, it's time to put it to work. All that's needed is to add a new import to our `models.py`:

```
from gallery.items.fields import ThumbnailImageField
```
in file: gallery/items/fields.py

and to replace `models.ImageField` with the thumbnail version in our `Photo` model:

```
class Photo(models.Model):
    item = models.ForeignKey(Item)
    title = models.CharField(max_length=100)
    image = ThumbnailImageField(upload_to='photos')
    caption = models.CharField(max_length=250, blank=True)
```

After a reload of our Web server, there's no noticeable change in the admin because we didn't modify anything that has to do with the form aspect of the field, as seen in Figure 7.5.

Post-upload, things also look identical to the earlier example, as shown in Figure 7.6. However, checking our upload directory, we see the fruits of our labor.

```
user@example:/var/www/gallery/media/photos $ ls -l
total 148
-rw-r -r - 1 www-data www-data 140910 2008-03-30 22:15 IMG_0010.jpg
-rw-r -r - 1 www-data www-data   1823 2008-03-30 22:15 IMG_0010.thumb.jpg
```

Success! Unfortunately, it takes a bit of time to get to the point where we can view the thumbnail, as we've yet to show you the templates our application uses to display them. Before we do so, it's time to quickly explore the secondary aspect of this application: how we've set up a fairly simple approach to preserving DRY in our URLs.

Setting Up DRY URLs

Until now, we've focused solely on the model aspects of the gallery app. It's time to go over our URL structure, which provides the context necessary to understand the templates in the next section. First, though, we need a bit of background to explain a rather

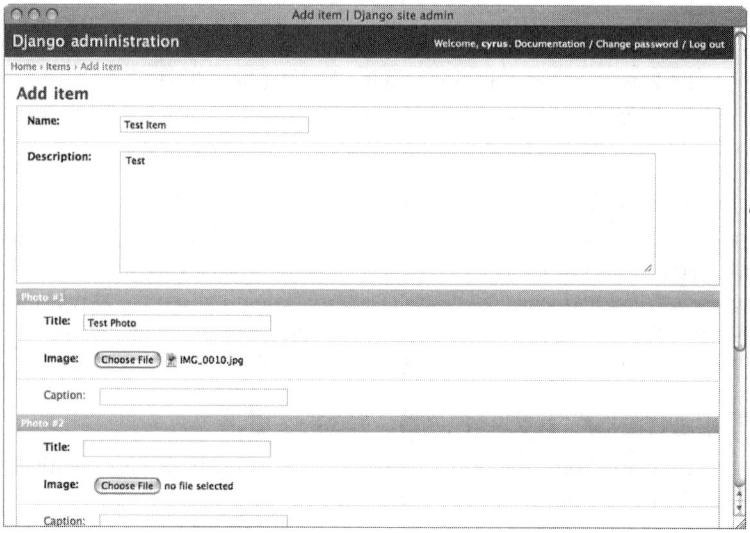

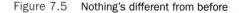

Figure 7.5   Nothing's different from before

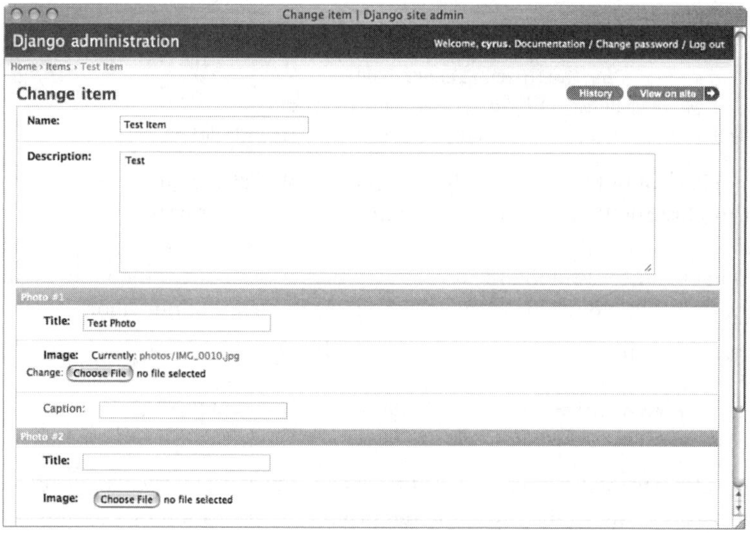

Figure 7.6   Still nothing new from a visual perspective

unusual setup. Because of how this application was developed, it was desirable to have it work equally well at the top level of a domain (such as http://www.example.com/) or as a subsection (for example, http://www.example.com/gallery/).

By default, a Django site is assumed to be in the former situation—URLs are parsed from the root of the domain, even if one's Web server handler is hooked in higher up.

Because of this, one's URLs must include the entire URL path, so a site at /gallery/ needs all its URLs prefixed with that string.[1] We've simply done the obvious thing and stored that value as a settings.py variable and referenced it where necessary.

```
ROOT_URL = '/gallery/'
```
 # So URLs like http://www.example.com/gallery/... work

A better name might be URL-PREFIX (?)

Because a couple of other settings.py variables rely on URL paths, we can put it to use right away for our authentication login URL, the media URL, and the admin's media prefix.

```
LOGIN_URL = ROOT_URL + 'login/'
MEDIA_URL = ROOT_URL + 'media/'
ADMIN_MEDIA_PREFIX = MEDIA_URL + 'admin/'
```

Next, because of how Django's URL include system works, we have to use a two-file root URLconf setup, where the "normal" top-level urls.py simply uses ROOT_URL, and then calls the "real" urls.py, which is blissfully ignorant of ROOT_URL and its implications. Here's the root urls.py: *in .../gallery, the project dir.*

```
from django.conf.urls.defaults import *
from gallery.settings import ROOT_URL

urlpatterns = patterns('',
    url(r'^%s' % ROOT_URL[1:], include('gallery.real_urls')),
```
) here: r'^gallery/' : pluck off the leading "/"

> **Note**
>
> We needed to slice ROOT_URL to chop off the leading slash because settings.py variables that use it—such as LOGIN_URL—require that leading slash in order to be correct absolute URLs. However, because Django's URL parsing omits that leading slash character, we have to get rid of it for our URLs to parse correctly.

Here's our "real" root URLconf, which we've called real_urls.py due to a lack of imagination:

```
from django.conf.urls.defaults import *
from django.contrib import admin

urlpatterns = patterns('',
    url(r'^admin/(.*)', admin.site.root),
    url(r'^', include('gallery.items.urls')),
)
```

---

[1] Django 1.0 introduced a new Apache configuration directive, PythonOption django.root <root>, which takes the place of much of the ROOT_URL functionality we outline here. However, we're leaving this part of the chapter intact, as an example of how Django's "just Python" approach enables you to alter its behavior in various ways.

Finally, it's useful for templates to have access to ROOT_URL to construct similarly DRY-compatible include URLs, such as those needed for CSS or JavaScript includes. This can be accomplished with a simple context processor (covered previously in Chapter 6, "Templates and Form Processing").

135-6 [handwritten]

```
from gallery.settings import ROOT_URL

def root_url_processor(request):
    return {'ROOT_URL': ROOT_URL}
```

access ... /gallery/settings.py [handwritten]

And that's it! After applying those handful of tweaks to a normal Django project, everything now hinges on the value of ROOT_URL—it's currently set to '/gallery/', meaning the application should live at http://www.example.com/gallery/, as mentioned previously. If we wanted to deploy the application to just http://www.example.com/, all we need to do is change ROOT_URL to '/' (and update our Web server config so Django is hooked in at the root level), and we're done.

The `Item` App's URL Layout

To complete the DRY-ness of our URL structure, we're going to apply a three-part approach for our objects' get_absolute_url methods. The first and most important part, you've already seen throughout the book—the use of the url function for defining our URLconfs, which enables us to give our URLs unique names. Following is the urls.py contained within the items app itself:

```
from django.conf.urls.defaults import *
from gallery.items.models import Item, Photo

urlpatterns = patterns('django.views.generic',
    url(r'^$', 'simple.direct_to_template',
        kwargs={
            'template': 'index.html',
            'extra_context': {'item_list': lambda: Item.objects.all()}
        },
        name='index'
    ),
    url(r'^items/$', 'list_detail.object_list',
        kwargs={
            'queryset': Item.objects.all(),
            'template_name': 'items_list.html',
            'allow_empty': True
        },
        name='item_list'
    ),
    url(r'^items/(?P<object_id>\d+)/$', 'list_detail.object_detail',
        kwargs={
            'queryset': Item.objects.all(),
```

[handwritten annotations: "lambda?", "or template-name ?", "items_listing.html", "(1) 175,173", "url path", "view", "dict"]

```
            'template_name': 'items_detail.html'
        },
        name='item_detail'
    ),
    url(r'^photos/(?P<object_id>\d+)/$', 'list_detail.object_detail',
        kwargs={
            'queryset': Photo.objects.all(),
            'template_name': 'photos_detail.html'
        },
        name='photo_detail'
    ),
)
```

As you can see, the application consists of an index page, a list of items, per-item pages, and per-photo pages, each with the obvious name defined. These names can be referenced with the {% url %} templatetag, as we see next in the templates section, as well as with the permalink decorator that wraps get_absolute_url, such as:

```
class Item(models.Model):
    name = models.CharField(max_length=250)
    description = models.TextField()

    class Meta:
        ordering = ['name']

    def __unicode__(self):
        return self.name

    @permalink
    def get_absolute_url(self):
        return ('item_detail', None, {'object_id': self.id})
```

The permalink decorator expects its wrapped function to return a three-tuple consisting of the URL name, a list of positional arguments, and a dictionary of named arguments, which are used to reconstruct the URL. As you can see from the previous example, the item detail view takes no positional arguments and one named argument, and that's what we've provided in our get_absolute_url.

When set up in this way, Item.get_absolute_url returns the appropriate URL, even if our URL structure changes, thus preserving DRY (albeit at the cost of making get_absolute_url behave rather oddly if the decorator is ever removed).

Tying It All Together with Templates

Finally, after making our custom model field and tweaking our URL setup, all that's left—because we're using entirely generic views—are the templates. We use a simple inheritance setup to maximize DRY, starting with our base template for structure and a dash of CSS.

(0) *(base.html)*

```html
<html>
    <head>
        <title>Gallery - {% block title %}{% endblock %}</title>
        <style type="text/css">
            body { margin: 30px; font-family: sans-serif; background: #fff; }
            h1 { background: #ccf; padding: 20px; }
            h2 { background: #ddf; padding: 10px 20px; }
            h3 { background: #eef; padding: 5px 20px; }
            table { width: 100%; }
            table th { text-align: left; }
        </style>
    </head>
    <body>
        <h1>Gallery</h1>
        {% block content %}{% endblock %}
    </body>
</html>
```

① *(next to title block)*

② *(next to block content)*

Next up is the index page. In the application that inspired this chapter, it was fleshed out a bit more with some light CMS-like functionality to enable the "welcome" blurb to be edited in the admin; we've omitted that here in the interest of brevity. Instead, we've just got a static welcome paragraph and a short list of three highlighted Items, which is controlled in the URLconf. (It's currently a list of all items, but could easily be changed to meet some other criteria.)

(index.html)

```django
{% extends "base.html" %}


{% block title %}Home{% endblock %}
{% block content %}


<h2>Welcome to the Gallery!</h3>
<p>Here you find pictures of various items. Below are some highlighted
items; use the link at the bottom to see the full listing.</p>

<h3>Showcase</h3>
<table>
    <tr>
    {% for item in item_list|slice:":3" %}
        <td>
            <a href="{{ item.get_absolute_url }}"><b>{{ item.name }}</b><br />
            {% if item.photo_set.count %}
                <img src="{{ item.photo_set.all.0.image.thumb_url }}" />
            {% else %}
                <span>No photos (yet)</span>
            {% endif %}
            </a>
        </td>
```

(0) *(before extends line)*

(1) *(before block title line)*

(2) *(before block content line)*

via extra-context — *filter* *(handwritten note pointing to the for/slice line)*

count of items in photo_set != 0 *(handwritten note pointing to the if line)*

© 173

```
        {% endfor %}                                          >>
    </tr>
</table>
<p><a href="{% url item_list %}">View the full list &raquo;</a></p>

{% endblock %}
```

The previous template code renders the page view as seen in Figure 7.7.

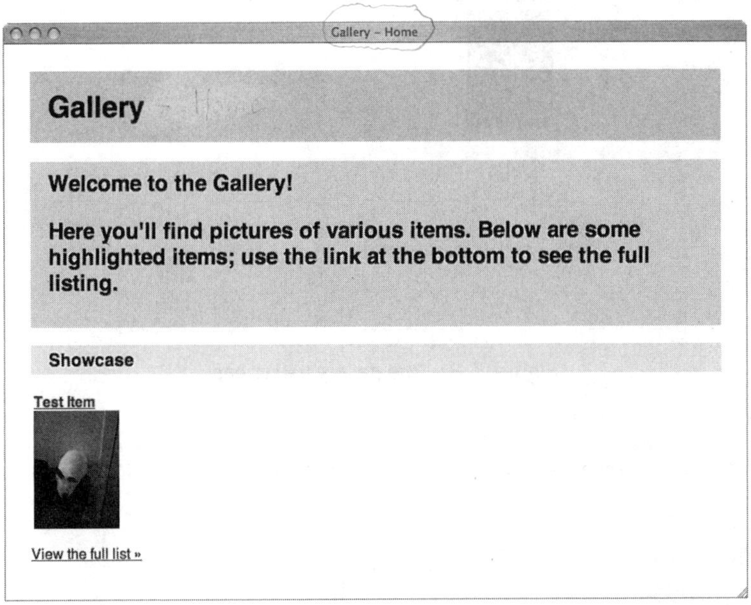

Figure 7.7   The gallery index page

Note the use of both `get_absolute_url` and `{% url %}` for linking to item detail pages and the item list, respectively; and, most importantly, the use of `image.thumb_url` on the first image in each item's list of photos. An improvement on how we approach the "which thumbnail to use for an item" problem could be to update the `Photo` model to mark a specific image as the "representative" one—which is just one of many ways this application could be extended.

The item listing (`items_listing.html`) is just a more complete version of the highlight list on the index page, using the same tricks, as shown in Figure 7.8.

```
{% extends "base.html" %}

{% block title %}Item List{% endblock %}

{% block content %}
```

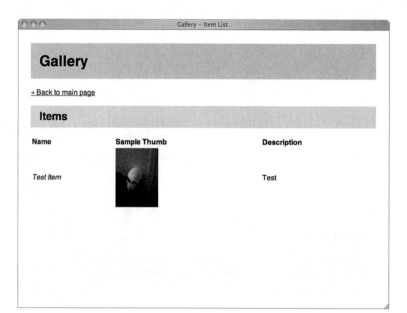

Figure 7.8   The gallery listing page

172

```
<p><a href="{% url index %}">&laquo; Back to main page</a></p>

<h2>Items</h2>
{% if object_list %}
<table>
    <tr>
        <th>Name</th>
        <th>Sample Thumb</th>
        <th>Description</th>
    </tr>
    {% for item in object_list %}
    <tr>
        <td><i>{{ item.name }}</i></td>
        <td>
            {% if item.photo_set.count %}
            <a href="{{ item.get_absolute_url }}">
                <img src="{{ item.photo_set.all.0.image.thumb_url }}" />
            </a>
            {% else %}
            (No photos currently uploaded)
            {% endif %}
        </td>
        <td>{{ item.description }}</td>
```

queryset

- Count > 0?

```
    </tr>
    {% endfor %}
</table>
{% else %}
<p>There are currently no items to display.</p>
{% endif %}

{% endblock %}
```

Similarly, the item detail view (`items_detail.html`), is like the item listing view except that it lists all the photos instead of just using the first one as a representative, as shown in Figure 7.9.

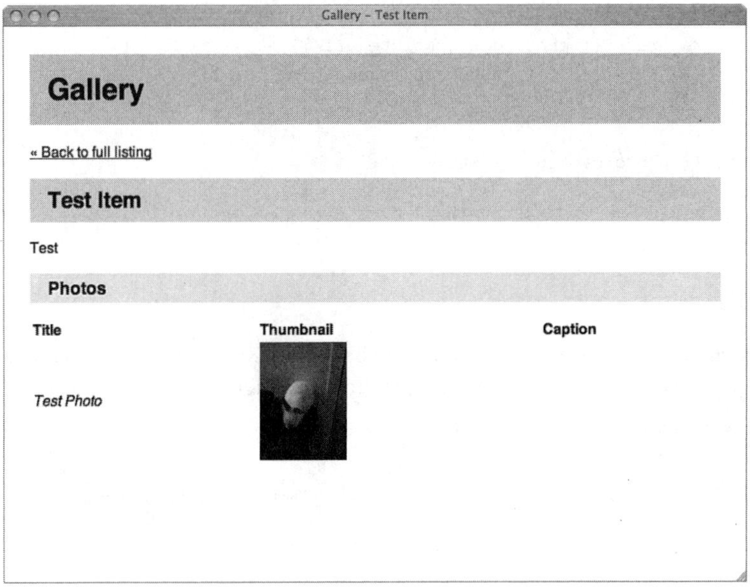

Figure 7.9   An item detail page

```
{% extends "base.html" %}

{% block title %}{{ object.name }}{% endblock %}

{% block content %}                              ≪

<p><a href="{% url item_list %}">&laquo; Back to full listing</a></p>
```

(items_detail.html)

```
<h2>{{ object.name }}</h2>
<p>{{ object.description }}</p>

<h3>Photos</h3>
<table>
    <tr>
        <th>Title</th>
        <th>Thumbnail</th>
        <th>Caption</th>
    </tr>
    {% for photo in object.photo_set.all %}
    <tr>
        <td><i>{{ photo.title }}</i></td>
        <td>
            <a href="{{ photo.get_absolute_url }}">
                <img src="{{ photo.get_image_thumb_url }}" />
            </a>
        </td>
        <td>{{ photo.caption }}</td>
    </tr>
    {% endfor %}
</table>

{% endblock %}
```

Finally, the following shows the photo detail view (photos_detail.html), which is the only place we actually use image.url, as shown in Figure 7.10.

```
{% extends "base.html" %}

{% block title %}{{ object.item.name }} - {{ object.title }}{% endblock %}

{% block content %}

<a href="{{ object.item.get_absolute_url }}">&laquo; Back to {{
object.item.name }} detail page</a>

<h2>{{ object.item.name }} - {{ object.title }}</h2>
<img src="{{ object.get_image_url }}" />
{% if object.caption %}<p>{{ object.caption }}</p>{% endif %}

{% endblock %}
```

Summary

It's been a bit of a whirlwind tour, but hopefully at this point you've got a fairly complete picture of how this application has come together.

- We defined our models and used the admin to demonstrate how image uploading works, including the necessary system-level setup.
- The desire for thumbnails drove us to define a new subclass of Django's image field and its related file class, during which we simply overrode a few methods to perform the resize and provide access to the thumbnail file.
- We made full use of Django's DRY URL features, including implementing a "root URL" setting (similar to one added to Django core just prior to 1.0) to help us maintain flexible URLs.
- Finally, we created simple templates to enable users to navigate and view our photos.

Figure 7.10   The photo detail view

8

Content Management System

Acommon question from new Django users is, "Is there an open source CMS (Content Management System) written in Django?" Our typical answer is not always what people want to hear—that you should build your own. This chapter explores a couple of ways to do this with Django; first, by leveraging a contrib app that makes it easy to create and publish "flat" HTML pages, and then by making a more in-depth, but still simple, content creation system.

What's a CMS?

People mean many different things by "CMS." It can be easier to build one using the tools Django provides than to try adapting someone else's solution, unless that solution is already nearly identical to what you want.

The "CMS" label is used to refer to many different application types. To one person it can mean a basic interface for editing Web page content displayed in templates, such as a blog. To another it can encompass complicated permissions and workflow rules, generation of multiple output formats from a single source, multiple versions and editions, and all sorts of non-Web content (and the indexing, archiving, and managing thereof).

In other words, nearly everyone's CMS application is custom to some extent. And Django's sole purpose is to make it easier for you to develop custom Web applications. Practical-minded developers are rightfully cautious about reinventing the wheel, but it can be that your specific wheel hasn't been invented yet.

As the ecosystem of open source Django applications matures, we will likely see a few CMS-type apps become mature enough to be recommended frequently, accumulating their own communities of users and maintainers. The perfect one for your needs might even be out there already. So do look around (see Appendix D, "Finding, Evaluating, and Using Django Applications," for some pointers), but don't feel shy about implementing your own solution.

The Un-CMS: Flatpages

The simplest Django-powered CMS doesn't require writing any code at all. Django ships with an application called "Flatpages" that is suitable for simple cases. What's most appealing about the Flatpages app is that, if it works for you, there's very little setup to be done and no code of your own to maintain.

Another convenience is that the URLs pointing to your Flatpages-based pages are specified via the admin; you don't have to edit a URLconf file to add a new page. Before you get too excited, though, here are some of its limitations.

- All pages can be edited by all administrative users who have access to the Flatpages application; users can't "own" individual pages.

- Aside from title and content attributes and a few special-purpose fields we discuss, there's not much to a Flatpages object; there's no creation date or other bits of data you can have associated with a particular page.

- Because it's a provided ("contrib") app, you can't easily change its admin options, add new fields, or model methods.

Assuming those aren't showstoppers for you, however, Flatpages can be useful. We explore how to set up and use Flatpages in the next few sections, followed by a look at setting up a more robust, custom CMS application.

Enabling the Flatpages App

Here's a quick overview of the steps necessary to get Flatpages up and running.

1. Create a new Django project with django-admin.py.

2. Open your project's settings.py and update your MIDDLEWARE_CLASSES setting to include django.contrib.flatpages.middleware.
   FlatpageFallbackMiddleware.

3. Add django.contrib.flatpages and django.contrib.admin to your INSTALLED_APPS settings.py variable.

4. Run manage.py syncdb to get Django to create the necessary tables.

5. Update your urls.py, uncommenting the default admin-related line to activate it.

6. (Re)start your Web server of choice.

Once you've followed the previous steps, log in to the admin site, and you should see what looks like Figure 8.1.

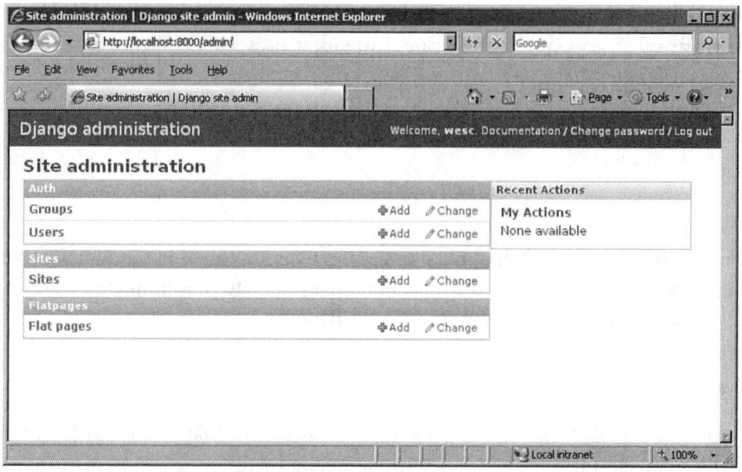

Figure 8.1   The admin page after logging in with the Flatpages app available

Click Add to create a new Flatpage object (see Figure 8.2). Only the url, title, and content fields are required. Make sure the URL includes leading and trailing slashes, as indicated.

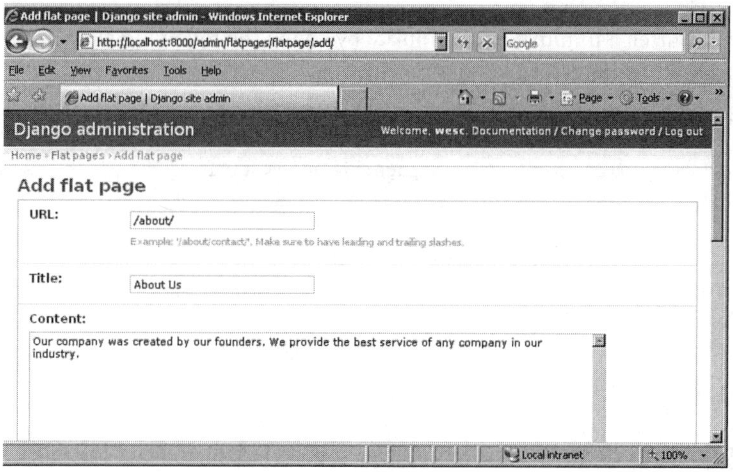

Figure 8.2   The Flatpage Add screen

Create one or two pages now, so you have something to look at when you get to the testing step!

We go straight into the templates next because Flatpages requires no URL management aside from what you've already done. Instead, it uses a special piece of Django middleware that intercepts 404 errors and looks up the requested URL in the list of Flatpage objects. If it finds a match, the Flatpages app takes over. If it doesn't, the 404 is passed through for normal error handling.

Note

The 404-handling aspect of Flatpages also means it can be used in tandem with a regular Django application, enabling you to simply and easily specify your flatpages ("About Us" or "Legal") without having to constantly update a URLconf.

Flatpage Templates

Individual Flatpage objects have a `template_name` attribute that can be customized, but by default the Flatpages app looks for a template called `flatpages/default.html` among the templates available. That means you need to create a "flatpages" template directory in one of the locations listed in your project's `TEMPLATE_DIRS` setting or inside a "templates" folder inside one of the applications listed in your `INSTALLED_APPS` setting if you're using the `app_directories` template loader. Either way, create that directory now.

Your template is passed an object called `flatpage` that you can use as you'd expect. For example:

```
<h1>{{ flatpage.title }}</h1>
<p>{{ flatpage.content }}</p>
```

So, make yourself a minimal page template by saving the following code as `default.html` in the directory you just created. *All flatpage objects display w. this template*

```
<html>
    <head>
        <title>My Dummy Site: {{ flatpage.title }}</title>
    </head>
    <body>
        <h1>{{ flatpage.title }}</h1>
        <p>{{ flatpage.content }}</p>
    </body>
</html>
```

Testing It Out

At this point, try to load up your flatpage(s). For example, if your server is running on your workstation, and you created a Flatpage object via the admin whose URL value is `/about/`, you would load up http://localhost:8000/about/ in your browser. It should display the `title` and `content` fields' values using your `default.html` template, as shown in Figure 8.3.

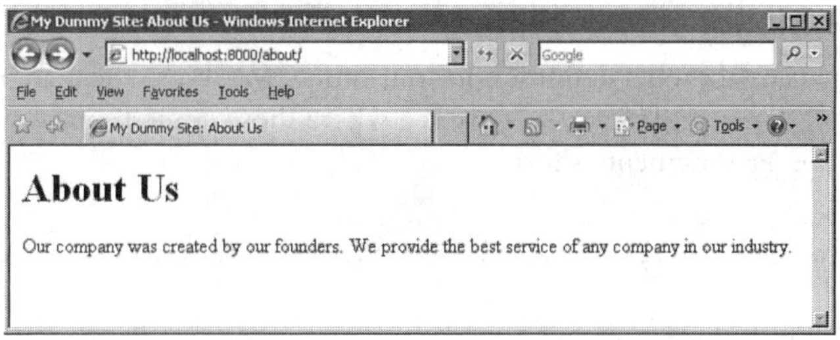

Figure 8.3   An example of an "About Us" Flatpage

Hopefully you've seen enough to get a taste of how Flatpages is intended to be used and how well it fills its particular niche. We now focus on the meat of the chapter—an example of a more robust CMS application.

Beyond Flatpages: A Simple Custom CMS

Flatpages are fine, but as outlined previously, they have many limitations. Getting beyond them is as simple or as complex as the needs of your site. Let's walk through the process of using Django to build a custom CMS that goes beyond Flatpages. Specifically, we want our solution to

- Enable users to enter text in a convenient non-HTML format that is automatically converted to HTML
- Create page URLs based on human-friendly text rather than database-friendly integer primary keys
- Provide pieces of a basic workflow—associating a staff user with each story and enabling each story to be marked as belonging to one of several production stages
- Maintain creation and modification dates
- Provide for categorization of stories with the capability to view stories by category
- Offer a simple search function available on all pages

These are all things that Django facilitates. Most of them involve features you have already seen; part of learning how to build Django applications is learning how to effectively combine these features to get your results with as little unneccessary work as possible.

To begin with, you need to have another Django project set up (as usual, refer to Chapter 2, "Django for the Impatient: Building a Blog," for a refresher on how to create a project, its database, and so forth). We refer to our project as cmsproject with a single application named cms.

Let's start with the model.

Making the Model

Following is the central model definition for our little CMS. Note there are references to two other models (User and Category); we see where those come from, as well as add a few necessary import statements, shortly.

cmsproject/cms/models.py

```
class Story(models.Model):
    """A hunk of content for our site, generally corresponding to a page"""

    STATUS_CHOICES = (
        (1, "Needs Edit"),
        (2, "Needs Approval"),
        (3, "Published"),
        (4, "Archived"),
    )

    title = models.CharField(max_length=100)
    slug = models.SlugField()
    category = models.ForeignKey(Category)
    markdown_content = models.TextField()
    html_content = models.TextField(editable=False)
    owner = models.ForeignKey(User)
    status = models.IntegerField(choices=STATUS_CHOICES, default=1)
    created = models.DateTimeField(default=datetime.datetime.now)
    modified = models.DateTimeField(default=datetime.datetime.now)

    class Meta:
        ordering = ['modified']
        verbose_name_plural = "stories"

    @permalink
    def get_absolute_url(self):
        return ("cms-story", (), {'slug': self.slug})

class StoryAdmin(admin.ModelAdmin):
    list_display = ('title', 'owner', 'status', 'created', 'modified')
    search_fields = ('title', 'content')
    list_filter = ('status', 'owner', 'created', 'modified')
    prepopulated_fields = {'slug': ('title',)}


admin.site.register(Story, StoryAdmin)
```

(handwritten annotations:)
© 187 — should specify unique = True
@ 192 — # used to reconstitute url 1) > p 192 ¹
URL name — positional args — keyword args
ⓑ 195

Inside the model class definition itself, the first bit of code defines four stages of a simplified workflow. Your process can have other steps, of course.

Although using Django's mapping approach for field choices, as demonstrated here with STATUS_CHOICES, has many conveniences, in this case it does still boil down to integers in the database. You are not easily able to redefine what "1" means later, so it's worth

(handwritten note at bottom:)
get-absolute-url (+ permalink decorator) is used to build the url that points to self, a particular story object
Use is like that on p 197! `<a href="{{ story.get-absolute-url }}">...</a>`

pausing a moment to be reasonably sure you've got a comprehensive list. This is true especially if you are going to be ordering your model instances based on the value of the field, as we have reason to do so here.

We also are able to use these values in our public views to determine what can be seen by our site visitors, that is, we want them to see "Published" and "Archived" stories but not those that "Needs Edit" or "Needs Approval." This is just the logic that is determined by the business, project, and/or appplication requirements.

If you find yourself with a list of choices like this that just don't settle down into a simple hardcoded list, what you probably want instead is a `ManyToManyField`, which can serve the same purpose but whose choices can be edited in the admin just like your other data.

After the `STATUS_CHOICES` definition come the field definitions.

- `title`: The title we display, both in the browser's title bar and in a heading on the rendered page.
- `slug`: The unique name for the page that is used in its URL. This is nicer than a plain integer primary key.
- `category`: The category for this item. This is a foreign key to another model we define in a moment.
- `markdown_content`: The page content in Markdown format (more on Markdown next).
- `html_content`: The page text as HTML. We automatically render this at edit time, so when pages are displayed there is no markup translation overhead. To reduce possible confusion, this field is not directly editable (and thus does not show up in editing forms in the Django admin app).
- `owner`: An admin user (or, as Django sees it, a foreign key reference to a `User` object) who "owns" this piece of content.
- `status`: The item's place in the editorial workflow.
- `created`: The item's creation time, automatically set to the current time (courtesy of Python's `datetime` module).
- `modified`: The item's modification time, initially set to the current time. We need to take special steps to make sure this gets updated when the item is edited. This timestamp is displayed on the story detail pages.

One cosmetic touch we make in this model, purely for users of the admin, is to specify a `verbose_name_plural` attribute in the `Meta` inner class. This keeps our model from showing up in the admin app with the incorrect name of "Storys." Finally, we have a permalinked `get_absolute_url` method, first mentioned in Chapter 7, "Photo Gallery."

Imports

All we need to import, besides the usual `django.db.models` (and an associated `permalink` decorator function we explain next), is the `datetime` module (which we use for our `created` and `modified` fields) and the `User` model that comes with Django's `contrib.auth` app. Last is the Django admin module, used to register our models with the admin app.

```
import datetime                                   # For   cmsproject/cms/models.py
from django.db import models
from django.db.models import permalink
from django.contrib.auth.models import User
from django.contrib import admin
```

Like the `Flatpages` app, you might find the `User` model lacking in certain respects once you get into building advanced Django applications. For example, its idea of what constitutes a user name can clash with your requirements. However, `User` is a significant convenience, an adequate and complete solution, and extremely useful as-is in many real-world applications.

Completing the Model

So our `User` object is coming straight from Django's contributed "auth" app. But what about `Category`? That's ours; here is its model definition, which should appear in the `models.py` file directly above the `Story` model definition.

```
class Category(models.Model):                           .../cms/models.py
    """A content category"""
    label = models.CharField(blank=True, max_length=50)
    slug = models.SlugField()

    class Meta:
        verbose_name_plural = "categories"

    def __unicode__(self):
        return self.label

class CategoryAdmin(admin.ModelAdmin):
    prepopulated_fields = {'slug': ('label',)}

admin.site.register(Category, CategoryAdmin)
```

The `Category` model is simple, almost trivial. You often see models this simple—sometimes simpler with just a single specified field—in Django applications. We could hack up a similar effect by having a "category" field on our `Story` model, but that would make some things difficult (renaming categories) and others impossible (adding attributes to categories, for example, descriptions). Django makes it so easy to build a proper relational model that it almost always makes sense to do so.

doc ➤ ● doc category   seq-year, seq-key, ...
pg ➤ ● pg category

As with `Story`, we also set a `verbose_name_plural` attribute here so we don't appear illiterate to users of the admin.

Controlling Which Stories Are Viewed

Our database contains both publishable (3 and 4 from `STATUS_CHOICES` previously shown) and not-yet-publishable (statuses 1 and 2) stories. We want a convenient way to have only the former viewable on the site's public pages, although of course making sure the full set is editable in the admin. Because this is a matter of business logic rather than presentation style, it should be implemented in our model.

We *could* make it happen via `{% if...%}` tags in our templates, but that solution would end up being needlessly brittle, verbose, and repetitive. (If you don't believe this, we encourage you to try it—the negatives become apparent before you're through!) Based on your authors' collective experience, it's *always* a good idea to keep business logic out of your templates because over time they turn into spaghetti!

We add this capability to our `Story` model via a custom `Manager`. For more on this technique, see the "Custom Managers" section of Chapter 4, "Defining and Using Models." Add the following code to your `models.py` file, just following the `import` statements:

```
VIEWABLE_STATUS = [3, 4]

class ViewableManager(models.Manager):
    def get_query_set(self):
        default_queryset = super(ViewableManager, self).get_query_set()
        return default_queryset.filter(status__in=VIEWABLE_STATUS)
```

We first define `VIEWABLE_STATUS` as a simple list of integers corresponding to the statuses that merit a story being "viewable" by the general public. This is a module-level attribute, meaning it is available to other methods we can add in the future.

Next, we instantiate the manager objects within our model. At the bottom of your `models.py`, following the field and `Meta` inner class definitions, add the following two lines, remembering to indent them properly so they belong to the `Story` class:

```
admin_objects = models.Manager()
objects = ViewableManager()
```

As mentioned in Part 4, because the `admin_objects` manager is defined first, it becomes our model's default manager and is used by the admin—ensuring stories at all stages are editable by staff. The name is not special, except as a reminder to us about what its purpose is.

Then we create an instance of our custom manager using the conventional `objects` name. Because we use this name in our URLconf and views, all our public pages automatically receive the special, filtered queryset of stories provided by the custom `ViewableManager`.

Working with Markdown

As a finishing touch on our models, we overwrite the built-in `save` function to apply a light markup language, called Markdown, to the text users enter via the admin. Somewhat similar to Wiki-style syntax, Markdown offers an simpler alternative to creating Web content. Editing Markdown is much more pleasant than raw HTML and is familiar to anyone who has composed a plaintext e-mail or edited a Wiki page.

You could easily use Textile, ReStructuredText, or other light markup languages as well. The key trick we are employing here is to override the model's `save` method to "automagically" turn the Markdown into HTML right away, so the translation doesn't have to be made on every page request—we mentioned this earlier when describing the pair of `markdown_content` and `html_content` fields.

Why Not WYSIWYG?

Presuming that a Web-based content management system is aimed at relatively nontechnical users, some might find our use of Markdown here a bit nerdy. Fair enough. It is indeed possible to integrate various WYSIWYG (What You See Is What You Get) HTML editors with the Django admin, giving users what is hopefully a more familiar experience.

The downside of this approach, besides the extra initial effort of implementation, is a WYSIWYG text area *still* doesn't turn a Web browser into Microsoft Word, and you can bump up against browser incompatibilities. That said, such tools can increase the appeal and adoption of tools such as this CMS among nontechnical users. For recommended WYSIWYG plugins and other advice, visit withdjango.com.

To use Markdown with Python, you have to first download the Python–Markdown module as it is not part of the standard library. You can find it at http://www.freewisdom. org/projects/python-markdown/. Once it's installed, import the `markdown` function from the `markdown` module with the following statement:

```
from markdown import markdown
```
10/2/11   not on cypress

This import might look circular, but in fact, it's a common Python idiom when a module and the attribute you're importing from that module share the same name.

Not knowing Markdown doesn't impair your ability to understand this application, but for the uninitiated, following are a few examples. You can try them out in the Python interpreter if you like. For this demo, we define a helper function, `tidy_markdown`, that makes things print a little cleaner by removing the newlines (\n) that Markdown inserts in its output. (When we're using Markdown for more extended pieces of HTML, those newlines prevent the output from being a single extremely long line.)

```
>>> from markdown import markdown
>>> def tidy_markdown(text):
...     return markdown(text).replace('\n', '')
>>>
>>> tidy_markdown("Hello")
'<p>Hello</p>'
>>> tidy_markdown("# Heading Level One")
```

import markdown
markdown.markdown(III
first | second
:--- | ---:
a. | b
III ,['tables'])

10/2/11   – sudo easy-install markdown   2.0.3
– synaptic: install python-markdown   2.0.3-1   ← using

```
'<h1>Heading Level One</h1>'
>>> tidy_markdown("Click here to buy my book (<http://withdjango.com/)">)
'<p><a href="http://withdjango.com/">Click here to buy my book</a></p>'
>>> tidy_markdown("""
... An alternate H1 style
... =====================
... > A blockquote              will be indented
... * Bulleted item one
... * Bulleted item two
... """)
'<h1>An alternate H1 style</h1><blockquote><p>A blockquote</p></blockquote><ul>
<li>    Bulleted item one </li>
<li>    Bulleted item two </li></ul>'
```

As you can see, the input is plain text in Markdown syntax, and the function output is valid HTML.

So back to our Django application: To have our Markdown content automatically converted to HTML as we save it, we make an addition to our model code. It's a simple three-line function, placed just above the assignment to `admin_objects` (but at the same indent level as the rest of the model class).

```
def save(self):
    self.html_content = markdown(self.markdown_content)
    self.modified = datetime.datetime.now()
    super(Story, self).save()
```

When our code (or any application that works with our model, such as the Django admin) attempts to save an object to the database, our model's `save` method is called first, translating the user-entered Markdown content into HTML. (If you need a review of the syntax of the `super` call, see Chapter 1, "Practical Python for Django".)

Database purists can cringe at the presence of a field whose contents can be easily computed from those of another field. If the conversion had no computational cost, we wouldn't need to store the rendered HTML. It's also a common trade-off that is different for every project. We're assuming computing power is the limiting factor here, such as for a site that gets lots of traffic but doesn't necessarily have a lot of content. For a site where database size is the greater concern—such as a community forum with thousands or millions of database entries—computing on every page view can be a more viable choice.

Because the model field storing our HTML is marked `editable=False`, it is not displayed in the admin interface. This keeps the user's interactions cleaner and eliminates the frustrating possibility that someone can edit the rendered HTML then overwrite those changes by clicking Save. All changes get made to the Markdown source, converted to HTML, and saved to the `html_content` field without requiring any explicit attention. At save-time we also update the `modified` field with a current timestamp.

For more on Markdown and its syntax, see the official site at http://daringfireball.net/projects/markdown/. You should also know Python-Markdown also comes with some useful contributed extensions. In fact, this book was *written* in Markdown with the help of the Wrapped Tables "`wtables`" extension (see http://brian–jaress.livejournal.com/5978. html)! There is also a second Markdown project in Python should you want to investigate *that*; see http://code.google.com/p/python-markdown2/.

URL Patterns in `urls.py`

With the overridden `save` function out of the way, our models are finally all fleshed out. Before we move on to the views and templates, let's ensure our URLs are in place. Here's our project-level `urls.py`.

```
urlpatterns = patterns('',
    url(r'^admin/(.*)', admin.site.root),
    url(r'^cms/', include('cmsproject.cms.urls')),
)
```

The admin line is the same as always; the other URL pattern prefixes all URLs to the CMS app with "cms/." If you want another prefix, such as "stories" or "pages," you can, of course, specify that here. See Chapter 7 for an alternate approach for flexible root URLs.

Next, the file mentioned in the previous call to `include` is our app-level `urls.py`, which looks like this:

```
from django.conf.urls.defaults import *
from cms.models import Story

info_dict = { 'queryset': Story.objects.all(), 'template_object_name': 'story' }

urlpatterns = patterns('django.views.generic.list_detail',
    url(r'^(?P<slug>[-\w]+)/$', 'object_detail', info_dict, name="cms-story"),
    url(r'^$', 'object_list', info_dict, name="cms-home"),
)

urlpatterns += patterns('cmsproject.cms.views',
    url(r'^category/(?P<slug>[-\w]+)/$', 'category', name="cms-category"),
    url(r'^search/$', 'search', name="cms-search"),
)
```

In order, our URLs provide for the display of individual stories, the full list of stories, lists of stories by category, and lists of stories matching a search request.

Because we're again taking advantage of Django's generic views, this is where much of the action is in our application. We have four URL patterns, split into two `patterns` objects due to the differing view prefixes; however, we could also have directly imported and used the view functions themselves.

> **Note**
>
> We chose to use strings here because we'd like to start using the admin and the generic views before fully fleshing out our custom views; trying to import not-yet-defined functions wouldn't work too well in that scenario. The use of strings and/or function objects in URLs is often relatively arbitrary—use whatever works best for you.

As you've seen in many of the previous chapters, generic views have many optional arguments to control their behavior. We're using just one of those arguments here; `template_object_name`, which enables our story object to be referred to as `story` in the template rather than the default name of `object`.

Admin Views

You should now have a functioning admin site for the CMS app. (Make sure you run `manage.py syncdb` at some point, so your database tables are created.) Connect to it now. Figure 8.4 is what you should expect to see from the admin page once you log in. Figure 8.5 shows the Add Story page, which shows up after clicking on Add.

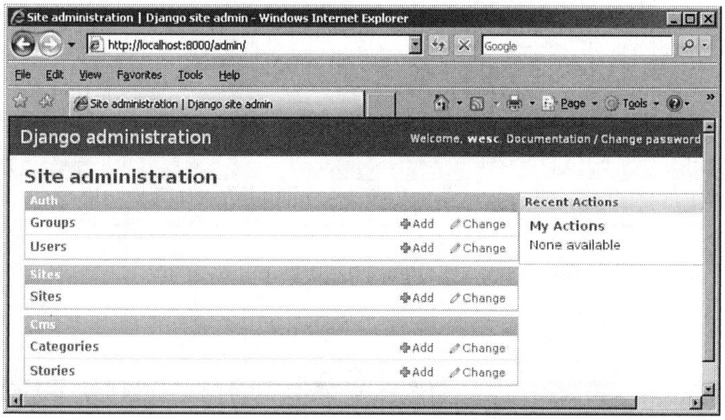

Figure 8.4   The admin page

You can also choose to create a category. If you do and click the "+" on the Add Story page, you see a small popup as in Figure 8.6.

For example, enter "Site News" in the Label field. You see a Web-friendly string appearing in the Slug field at the same time (see Figure 8.7).

Now we can continue and finish adding our story. In our example, we set the status to Published (see Figure 8.8).

Once you save it, you should be redirected to the CMS Story page (see Figure 8.9) where your story should show up now.

Now you are welcome to add more and/or to edit stories, making sure at least one of them has Published or Archived status so there is something to see on the live site!

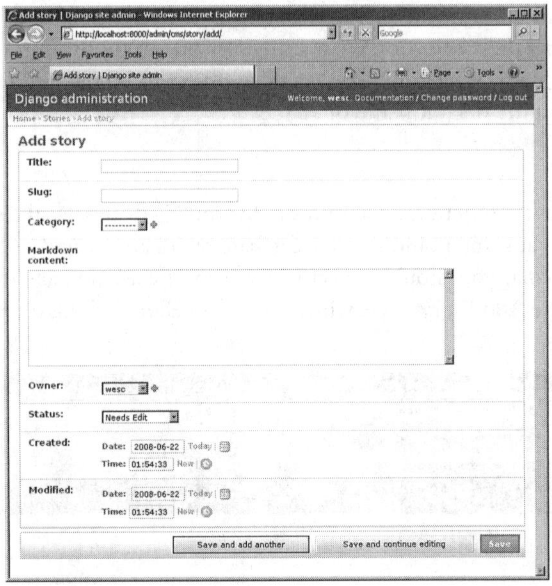

Figure 8.5   Adding a story in the admin

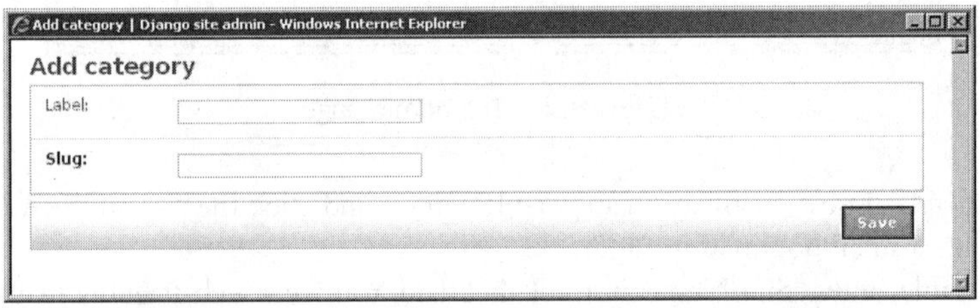

Figure 8.6   Adding a category while adding a story

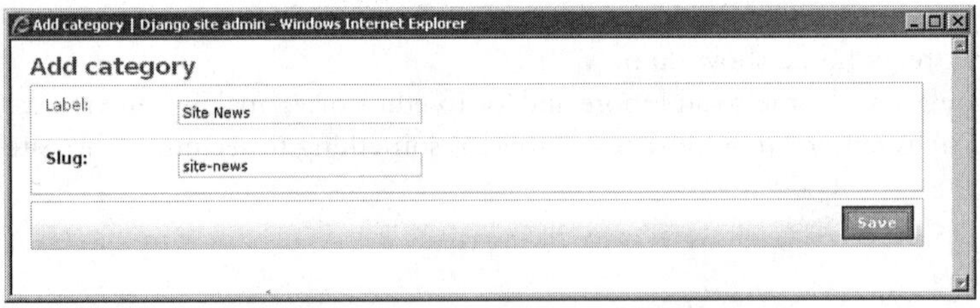

Figure 8.7   Adding the "Site News" category

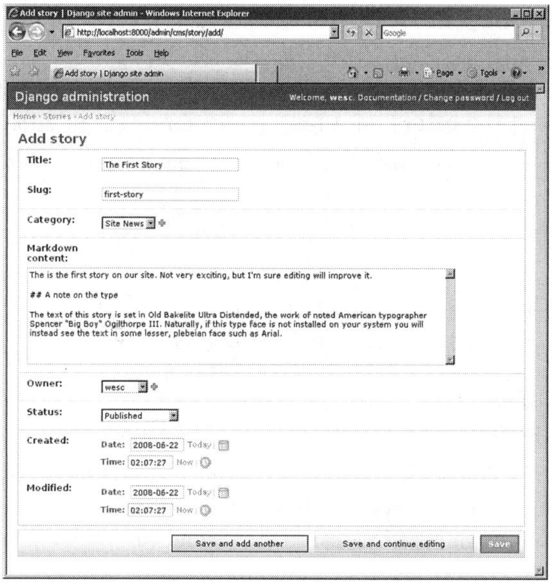

Figure 8.8   Completing our first story

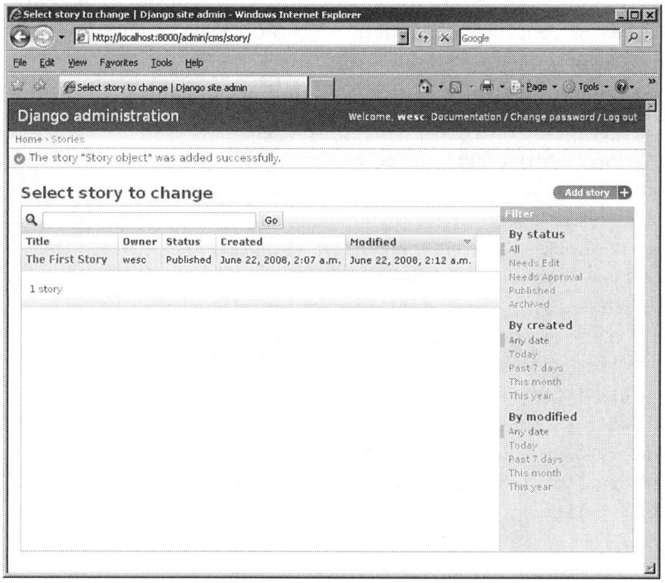

Figure 8.9   Viewing the list of stories in the admin;
note the available filters

Displaying Content Via Generic Views

As seen earlier in the URLconf, we're using generic views for most of our front-end display purposes. However, we need a couple lines of custom view code for our per-category listings. Here's the start of our `views.py` file for this application.

```
from django.shortcuts import render_to_response, get_object_or_404
from django.db.models import Q
from cms.models import Story, Category


def category(request, slug):
    """Given a category slug, display all items in a category."""
    category = get_object_or_404(Category, slug=slug)      Get category obj. identified by slug
    story_list = Story.objects.filter(category=category)
    heading = "Category: %s" % category.label
    return render_to_response("cms/story_list.html", locals())
```

As you can see, it's a simple view function, but one that isn't quite able to be handled by one of the existing generic views, which is why we needed to write it directly. We move on to our templates now and return to the second custom view, one providing a search interface, afterward.

Template Layout

As with most Django projects, there is a `base.html` template that is extended by all others. In this case, we only have two more: `story_detail.html` and `story_list.html`. Create all three files in your `cms` folder, and set `TEMPLATE_DIRS` with the full directory path to your project in your `settings.py` file.

Let's start with the simple base template, which looks like this:

```
<!DOCTYPE html PUBLIC "-//W3C//DTD HTML 4.01//EN"
"http://www.w3.org/TR/html4/strict.dtd">
<html lang="en">
    <head>
        <title>{% block title %}{% endblock %}</title>
        <style type="text/css" media="screen">
            body { margin: 15px; font-family: Arial; }
            h1, h2 { background: #aaa; padding: 1% 2%; margin: 0; }
            a { text-decoration: none; color: #444; }
            .small { font-size: 75%; color: #777; }
            #header { font-weight: bold; background: #ccc; padding: 1% 2%; }
            #story-body { background: #ccc; padding: 2%; }
            #story-list { background: #ccc; padding: 1% 1% 1% 4%; }
            #story-list li { margin: .5em 0; }
        </style>
    </head>
    <body>
        <div id="header">
            <form action="{% url cms-search %}" method="get">
```

enclose search form {

url 4), p 192

```
            <a href="{% url cms-home %}">Home</a> &bull;
            <label for="q">Search:</label> <input type="text" name="q">
        </form>
    </div>
    {% block content %}
    {% endblock %}
  </body>
</html>
```

We explain the various Django-specific pieces of this template later in the chapter. Now we need a template for displaying an individual story (`story_detail.html`), which, as we've said before, extends the base template.

visual: p 198

```
{% extends "cms/base.html" %}
```
(Story is object renamed)
```
{% block title %}{{ story.title }}{% endblock %}
{% block content %}
    <h1>{{ story.title }}</h1>
    <h2><a href="{% url cms-category story.category.slug %}">{{ story.category
}}</a></h2>
    <div id="story-body">
        {{ story.html_content|safe }}         ⓐ
    <p class="small">Updated {{ story.modified }}</p>
    </div>
{% endblock %}
```
192: url 3)

This is almost the simplest possible useful template—it expects only a single template variable, `story`. As long as this template is passed an object with `title` and `html_content` attributes, it should be happy.

One important item in the template is the `safe` filter that is applied to our `html_content` field. By default, Django auto-escapes all HTML in templates to protect against malicious user-entered content (a growing and serious security concern among Web applications). Because our Markdown source originates from trusted users, we feel justified in marking the content as "safe" and letting the browser treat the HTML literally, rather than escaping `<em>` to `&lt;em&gt;` and so on.   ⓐ

Our list template, `story_list.html`, is used by several different views that need to display multiple stories—category listings, search results, and the home page.

visual   p 197

```
{% extends "cms/base.html" %}
{% block content %}
    {% if heading %}
        <h1>{{ heading }}</h1>
    {% endif %}
    <ul id="story-list">
    {% for story in story_list %}                    1
        <li><a href="{{ story.get_absolute_url }}">{{ story.title }}</a></li>
    {% endfor %}                           p186
    </ul>
{% endblock %}
```

1 Could do this, less efficiently, with
{% url cms-story story.slug %}

This is only slightly more complex than our detail template. It loops through the items in `story_list`, creating an `<li>` element for each where the title is used as link text for a link to the story's detail page.

Displaying Stories

Because we are using story slugs, the URLs display our stories on our dev server with http://localhost:8000/cms/first-story/. Make sure your runserver has been restarted, load the URL into your browser, and you should see something like Figure 8.10.

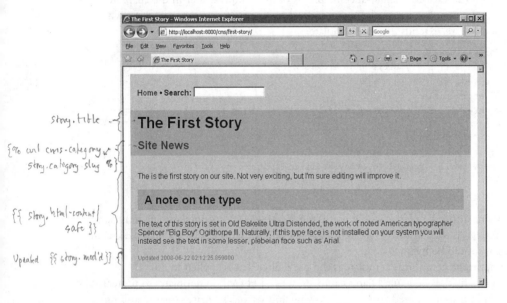

Figure 8.10   The "detail page" for our first story

Next, we test out the `object_list` view that is displayed when we visit our site's home page. This URL is http://localhost:8000/cms/, and when you visit the home page, you should see something like Figure 8.11.

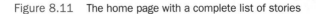

Figure 8.11   The home page with a complete list of stories

The titles of the stories are links, generated by the `get_absolute_url` method we created previously.   ⟋ 186

Note our page has a search box on it! Read on to understand how we make it work.

Adding Search

Being able to search textual content is a must. For a public site, just adding a Google Site-Search box is always an option (http://www.google.com/coop/cse/), but it's nice to have a bit more control over the search process and the presentation of results.

Let's add a simple search function to our site. Only a few pieces are needed to make this happen.

- An HTML form containing a search field added to our `base.html` template so it appears on every page
- A view function that accepts input from this form and finds matching articles
- The `story_list.html` template we have already created, which we use to display those results

If you recall our earlier look at the `base.html` template, it includes a search box in the header. For that box to *do* something, we need a view that processes the form when it is submitted.

This task can't be handled via a generic view, so we need another small custom view function. Add this code to your `views.py` right after the definition for the `category` method:

```python
def search(request):
    """
    Return a list of stories that match the provided search term
    in either the title or the main content.
    """
    if 'q' in request.GET:
        term = request.GET['q']
        story_list = Story.objects.filter(Q(title__contains=term) |
            (markdown_content__contains=term))
        heading = "Search results"
    return render_to_response("cms/story_list.html", locals())
```

This is a custom view, but it doesn't really need its own template. We're able to reuse our `story_list.html` template as long as we provide it with what it expects—a `QuerySet` of `Story` model objects in a context variable named `story_list`. The search algorithm is simpleminded; a `Story` matches if the complete literal text submitted via the form is found in either the title or the Markdown content.

Let's add a few more "stories." In our example, we add an "About Us" page (just like in our Flatpages example) and mark it as Archived. We then add a Contact Us page but leave it in a Needs Edit state. Our admin screen should now show all three and their statuses, as seen in Figure 8.12.

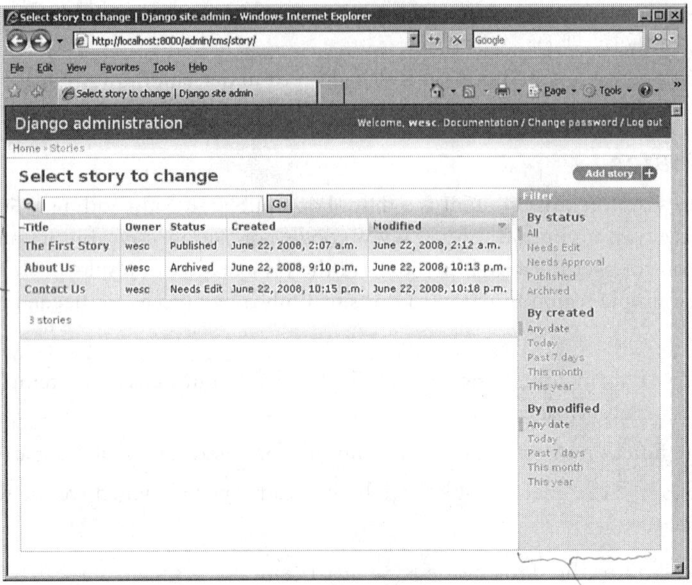

list-display p 186

Figure 8.12   The Admin page with a complete list of stories

via list-filter, p 186

In the main home page, however, we should only show the pages and provide the links of pages that we've enabled public access to (Published or Archived as controlled by VIEWABLE_STATUS). On visiting the home page as we do in Figure 8.13, you can see the Contact Us page does *not* show up!

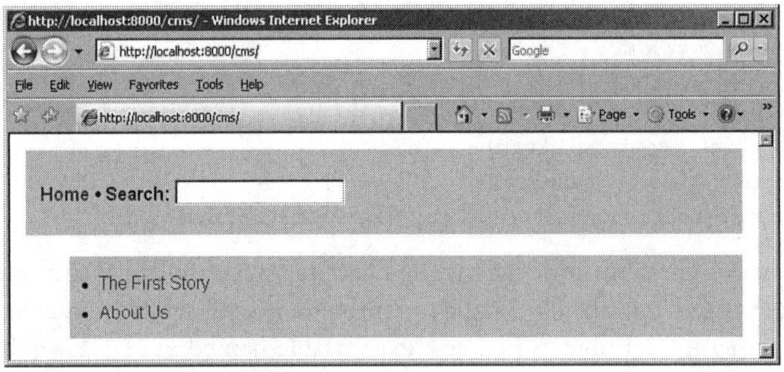

Figure 8.13   The Home page with a list of publically
viewable stories

Now, let's try out the search feature. On searching for the word, "typographer," we see the only matching document is our first story, as shown in Figure 8.14.

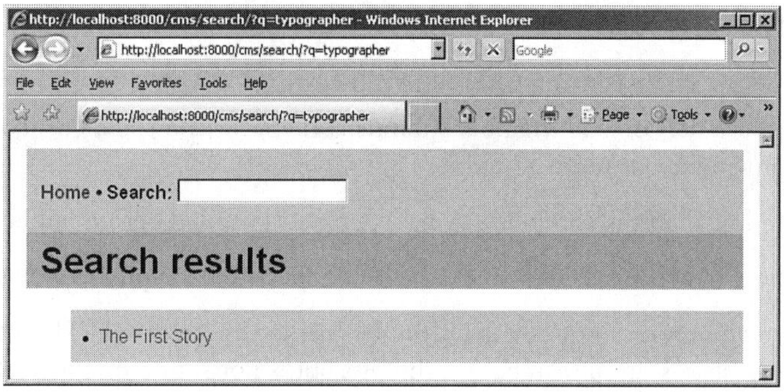

Figure 8.14   The Search Results page (also a list of publically viewable stories)

This concludes the core functionality that we're implementing for our CMS. Let's discuss the final behavioral aspects of our application: managing users and permissions and a workflow as dictated by business logic.

Managing Users

Our system features a concept of ownership; each story is associated with a specific Django user object. There is no technical obstacle to a user editing or deleting content not marked as theirs—and no obstacle to their changing the ownership field, in fact. The presence of this field doesn't create any per-object access control that did not exist before.

> **Note**
>
> In the near future, it will be possible to implement a more granular "per-object permissions" system in Django, using new admin-related features that were still in development at the time of writing. For more on this, see withdjango.com.

Nonetheless, this kind of informal or loosely enforced ownership can still be quite useful inside an organization where mutual trust exists. This is really not much different from an office environment where you trust that others don't steal your special red stapler or shred documents in your filing cabinet. The convenient thing about the way we've implemented ownership here is we're leveraging Django's built-in user model. We don't have to add any model code at all. Therefore we manage users using the Django admin.

As a superuser in the admin, you can use the admin to control who has the capability to edit users and groups and which of them have the right to access your `Story` model. You can also make it possible for users to edit `Story` objects but not `Category` objects. This would be a reasonable restriction, as most content editors are not reorganizing the information architecture of the site, but merely adding or updating existing content items.

[handwritten margin note: ✱ but, how? cf 193: Can add users, groups]

Supporting Workflow

Here's the simple content workflow that motivates our status field and its choices:

1. An outside writer or staff member submits content for the page. This content is in draft form and needs to be edited.

2. After the initial edit is complete, a final approval is needed before publication.

3. Once the article is marked as "published," it appears on the public Web site.

4. If the article becomes out of date, it can be marked as "archived." This can mean, for example, it shows up in searches on the site, but is not featured in a "Recent articles" list on the home page.

This chapter's example doesn't involve any customization of the admin. If it did, this field would be used heavily by custom views that can do things such as color code items by their stage or present users with lists of action items when they logged in to the admin.

> **Note**
>
> You can find out more about customizing the admin in Chapter 11, "Advanced Django Programming."

Note our `models.py` uses the the `list_filter` feature of the Django admin to offer convenient selection of stories at any one of the four stages. For example, an editor can use these to select all stories at the Needs Edit stage or an intern charged with culling old material can look just at the items with Archived status.

Possible Enhancements

As suggested at the beginning of this chapter, there are as many different CMS architectures as there are users. The example application you've built in this chapter could be taken in several different directions, depending on what features are desired. Here are a few ideas.

Pagination. With only a few or a few dozen stories, our list pages remain manageable. But once you get into the realm of hundreds of items, displaying them all on a single page can be daunting to the user and potentially detrimental to the performance of your site as well. Likewise, if a search returns hundreds of results it's unlikely that the user wants to see them all at once. Luckily, Django offers some built-in support for pagination, mostly in the form of the `django.core.paginator` module. For more, see the official Django documentation.

More powerful search. Our search function is handy, but doesn't offer the power that something as familiar as a Web search engine does; a multiword phrase, for example, should ideally be treated as a collection of independent search terms unless otherwise specified. The implementation here could be made more sophisticated, but if you are doing full-text searching over large numbers of records you probably would benefit from something such as Sphinx, a search engine with available Django integration. For more, see withdjango.com.

Status change notifications. We've already got a custom `save` method that handles our Markdown rendering. We could easily extend this to improve our workflow system by detecting when a story's status has been changed and sending a notification e-mail to the person responsible for handling stories at that stage. A key piece of implementing this would be to replace our status field with a `ForeignKey` to a full-fledged Status model, which in addition to the numerical value and label fields implied of our `STATUS_CHOICES` list would have a `status_owner` field, a `ForeignKey` field to the `User` model. Our `save` method would compare the recorded `status` value with the one about to be saved; if they differed, it would use Django's `send_mail` function to notify the associated user.

Dynamically generated navigation. Our app doesn't address the issue of site navigation, except to present a full list of all stories by default. For a real site, we'd need something better. One option would be to add some navigation-related fields to our `Story` model. A more flexible solution would be a separate `Navigation` model, which could be as simple as three fields: position in the overall sequence of navigation items, label to be displayed to the user, and a `ForeignKey` to the story that navigation item should link to.

User comments. Our CMS works well for publishing content, but doesn't offer end users any way to contribute. A natural addition along these lines would be to enable comments to be posted on individual stories. Fortunately, Django has an excellent built-in commenting system that can work with both registered and anonymous users. Unfortunately, when we went to press, this system was pending a major rewrite, so we aren't able to document it in this edition. However, if this functionality is of interest, check out the official documentation, which will be updated as soon as the feature is available.

Static files. Many marketing and public relations organizations desire the capability to upload content to distribute to customers, existing and potential, as well as providing presentations, reports, technical white papers, and so on, all in the form of PDF files, Word documents, Excel spreadsheets, ZIP archive files, and so forth.

Summary

It's been a long chapter, but you should have gotten a good overview of how to leverage many of Django's core components and contrib applications, both for a simple flatpages-based site and a more complex attempt at building a CMS.

By now, we hope you're becoming familiar with the way Django apps are made: creating a project and applications with the command-line tools, thinking up a model definition (including how to leverage the admin), defining URLs, using both generic and custom views, and creating a template hierarchy.

There are two more example applications left in this part of the book: one using Ajax to create a liveblog and a look at a Django-based pastebin.

9

Liveblog

This book is about writing Web applications with Django, and as you've seen so far, the framework has sufficient built-in functionality, so you can accomplish a lot without straying outside of what it offers. However, like all tools, Django does have limits, and one popular piece of Web functionality that it explicitly omits is the integration of **Ajax**, or Asynchronous JavaScript And **XML**.

Thankfully, all this really means is Django doesn't tie you to a *single* Ajax library, of which there are many, but simply leaves the door open for you to use one of your choosing.

In this chapter, we show you a relatively simple use of Ajax, the so-called "liveblog." A **liveblog** is a Web page listing a number of short, timestamped entries capable of refreshing itself with new content without any user interaction. Those familiar with Apple's media events in recent years have seen this sort of application on various Mac news and rumor sites such as macrumorslive.com. The same concept is used to a lesser extent on normal, static blogs, which cover live events in the same format, but usually without the dynamic updating.

Our example application goes over everything you need to know to integrate Ajax with a Django Web application without going too deep into the specifics of complex client-server interaction or animation. We also point out in a few places how Django works well with Ajax while remaining toolkit-agnostic.

> **Note**
> As with some of the other example applications, we're going to use Apache here to make it easier to serve our static files (in this case, our JavaScript).

What Exactly Is Ajax?

When someone mentions the term "Ajax" with relation to Web development, as opposed to the house-cleaning product, they are typically talking about two distinct but often intertwined behaviors.

- Web pages pulling in extra information without requiring the user to reload or navigate elsewhere—think GMail and how it displays various e-mails, inboxes, and forms without your browser reloading and/or redrawing the entire page.

- Advanced "dynamic" user interface behavior—think Google Maps' map scrolling and zooming, or the drag-and-drop interfaces featured on various "widget"-based personal portal sites.

In terms of implementation, the "extra information" aspect of Ajax can be thought of as mini-requests where the browser and server engage in a normal HTTP conversation behind the scenes without a full page reload. We get into the details of how that's accomplished later in the chapter; for now, just note the response part of these conversations is typically in XHTML or XML (thus the "X" in Ajax) or in a light data format known as JSON.

The UI aspect of Ajax is just fancy client-side Javascript and DOM manipulation, made recently accessible due to more powerful browsers and client computers. If you consider the display possibilities of correctly styled Web markup elements and the fact that Javascript is a full-fledged programming language, this means a Web page now resembles a canvas for traditional GUI animation techniques.

Why Ajax Is Useful

From a developer's perspective, the capability to have a Web page engage in mini-requests is useful for a couple of reasons. It saves bandwidth in high-traffic situations, as the client browsers are only requesting specific chunks of data instead of an entire page, and it creates a more responsive user experience because the browser window isn't constantly redrawing everything. This makes Web applications feel much more like desktop apps.

Although they are sometimes considered "eye candy," advanced animations, drag-and-drop, and other "Web 2.0" features can also greatly enhance the user experience, as long as they're done unobtrusively and in moderation. Coupled with the reduced amount of page reloading enabled by mini-requests, well-integrated animation and special effects further blur the line between the Web and the traditional GUI.

Planning the Application

Before we get into the code, let's lay out a simple specification for what features our application has and decide what tools (specifically, which Ajax library) we use to build it. First, let's nail down some requirements, defining exactly what the application is supposed to do.

- Our application consists of a single Web page. No need for anything fancy—we're just setting up a site capable of liveblogging a single event at a time.

- It tracks a single, sequential stream of information. Again, just keeping it simple.

- The "stream" consists of timestamped text paragraphs. Therefore, we only need two fields in our model.

- This stream is displayed in reverse chronological order with the most recent first. So the most recent info is always at the top of the page.

- An initial page load displays the current state of the stream. Users visiting an in-progress liveblogging see all entries up through the present without any Ajax necessary.

- The page asks the server for new entries once a minute. Here's where the Ajax comes in.

- Entries are submitted via the Django admin. However, it would be easy to make a custom form for this purpose as well, if desired—you could even use Ajax on the back end for submissions for responsiveness' sake.

Choosing an Ajax Library

A number of Ajax JavaScript libraries are available at the time of writing, each with various strengths and weaknesses and with differing focus. Some of them attempt to deliver a large number of UI widgets, whereas others stay largely within the domain of making JavaScript an easier language to work with. They also differ in their approaches to updating JavaScript with their own syntax for manipulating and navigating the HTML structure of a Web page.

Many of these libraries have multiple components available for download, focusing on "core" elements such as the JavaScript language updates, "network" elements for the mini-request aspect, "widget" elements for the UI widgets, and of course a "full" version with the entire package. So in addition to choosing a toolkit, you also need to figure out what you want to do with that toolkit and download the correct version.

This seems like a lot of effort to go through, but it's necessary. A large, bulky JavaScript library that needs to be downloaded with every page view can require a decidedly non-trivial amount of resources on the hosting Web server. Therefore, enabling developers to pick and choose components lets them only include what they need for their application.

Without further ado, here's a quick rundown of the best-known Ajax toolkits and where to get them.

- Dojo: (dojotoolkit.org) One of the larger Ajax libraries, Dojo has absorbed a few smaller libraries and offers multiple download options.
- jQuery: (jquery.com) A newer library that provides a powerful "chaining" syntax for selecting and operating on multiple page elements at the same time.
- MochiKit: (mochikit.com) One of the more "Pythonic" JavaScript libraries, which has taken inspiration from sources such as Python and Objective-C.
- MooTools: (mootools.net) MooTools has an extremely modular download system, enabling for a very customizable library setup.
- Prototype: (prototypejs.org) Originated from the Ruby on Rails Web framework, but has since branched out to be a stand-alone library.

- Yahoo! User Interface (YUI): (developer.yahoo.com/yui) The best of Yahoo!'s recent and ongoing JavaScript UI work, packaged for community use.

In our example application, we are using jQuery, although this is largely an arbitrary choice on the part of the authors. The simple Ajax functionality we use here would be possible in any of the previous frameworks.

Laying Out the Application

Time to roll up our sleeves and get started! This example application, which we call liveupdate, lives inside a generic Django project named liveproject. In addition to the app itself, we have the standard projectwide templates folder and a projectwide media folder (to house our JavaScript), so our initial setup can look something like the following output (from the Unix tree command):

tree cmd

```
liveproject/            project
|-- __init__.py
|-- liveupdate/         app
|   |-- __init__.py
|   |-- models.py
|   |-- urls.py         app level urls
|   `-- views.py
|-- manage.py
|-- media               # symlinked into document root ala p 161
|   `-- js
|-- settings.py
|-- templates/
|   `-- liveupdate
`-- urls.py             project level urls ... include app level urls
```

Note the structure of the media folder is solely our own convention—nothing in Django forces you to organize your media files in any specific manner or even to have it hosted within your project folder. In our case, we're going by habits borne of developing larger sites with many different JavaScript, CSS files, and images, where a separate js subfolder makes a lot of sense. We're not using external CSS or images for this particular example, but if we were, we'd have sibling img and css folders accompanying it.

Placing our media inside our Django project folder makes managing it on the server and in our source control a lot simpler. Symlinking the media folder into our Apache document root (and making sure Apache is configured to AllowSymlinks there) ensures the media files within are also served up correctly. [4]

For our liveupdate app, we've got the generic package of one file each for models, urls, and views. Right now, given the previous requirements, our urls and models are extremely simple, and there aren't any nongeneric views yet. Following are the contents of the app-level URLconf file liveupdate/urls.py (which should be included in the project-level urls.py as usual), which just lists our Update objects:

1 *We are doing the Django work on the web-server machine*

```
from django.conf.urls.defaults import *
from liveproject.liveupdate.models import Update

urlpatterns = patterns('django.views.generic',
    url(r'^$', 'list_detail.object_list', {
        'queryset': Update.objects.all()
    }),
)
```

 # liveproject/liveupdate/urls.py

urls also on ⓑ 216

{ patt, view [, kwargs] [, name] }

The model

Now let's show you the `models.py` file, which defines the `Update` model class (including the default ordering) as well as setting it up for admin use:

```
from django.db import models
from django.contrib import admin


class Update(models.Model):
    timestamp = models.DateTimeField(auto_now_add=True)
    text = models.TextField()

    class Meta:
        ordering = ['-id']

    def __unicode__(self):
        return "[%s] %s" % (
            self.timestamp.strftime("%Y-%m-%d %H:%M:%S"),
            self.text
        )


admin.site.register(Update)
```

@ 210

For reverse ordering by id (⇒ by time, also)

5
4
3

admin 102

Finally, here's our first stab at the template (`templates/update_list.html`), which is the initial "static" view of the current state of our updates list users see when they first load the site:

```
<html>
    <head>
        <title>Live Update</title>
        <style type="text/css">
            body {
                margin: 30px;
                font-family: sans-serif;
                background: #fff;
            }
            h1 { background: #ccf; padding: 20px; }
            div.update { width: 100%; padding: 5px; }
            div.even { background: #ddd; }
            div.timestamp { float: left; font-weight: bold; }
            div.text { float: left; padding-left: 10px; }
```

white

← no div.odd (?)

*Float el. to the left
of the one following it*

```
            div.clear { clear: both; height: 1px; }
        </style>

    </head>
    <body>
        <h1>Welcome to the Live Update!</h1>
        <p>This site will automatically refresh itself every minute with new
        content -- please <b>do not</b> reload the page!</p>

        {% if object_list %}
            <div id="update-holder">
                {% for object in object_list %}
                <div class="update {% cycle even,odd %}"id="{{ object.id }}">
                    <div class="timestamp">
                        {{ object.timestamp|date:"Y-m-d H:i:s" }}
                    </div>
                    <div class="text">
                        {{ object.text|linebreaksbr }}
                    </div>
                    <div class="clear"></div>
                </div>
                {% endfor %}
            </div>
        {% else %}
            <p>No updates yet -- please check back later!</p>
        {% endif %}
    </body>
</html>
```

(handwritten margin notes: cycle: dj24 151 ; class= "update even" / "update odd" ; This code constructed by Callbacks p 217)

As you can see, the template is fairly plain from a logic standpoint and lacks any JavaScript or JavaScript includes. In the next section, we flesh out the template's dynamic aspects by leveraging jQuery.

Before we do this, let's try giving our app a quick test drive to get a feel for it before *(handwritten: 65)* we add in the core functionality. Enable the Admin (referring to earlier chapters if you need to remember the specifics), run manage.py syncdb, start or reload Apache, and navigate to the admin.

You should see the usual admin controls for our Update model class, so click the Add link and fill out the text area as in Figure 9.1. Note that because we specified *(handwritten: @ 209)* auto_now_add in our timestamp field, all we need to do is enter the text—all the better for quick updates to our liveblog.

Once you've added an entry, the admin shows your newly added Update, such as in Figure 9.2 .

You can also see the "static" version of the liveblog by hitting the root front-end URL, as in Figure 9.3. *(handwritten: ···/liveupdate/)*

The base of our application is in place—it's now time to apply the Ajax.

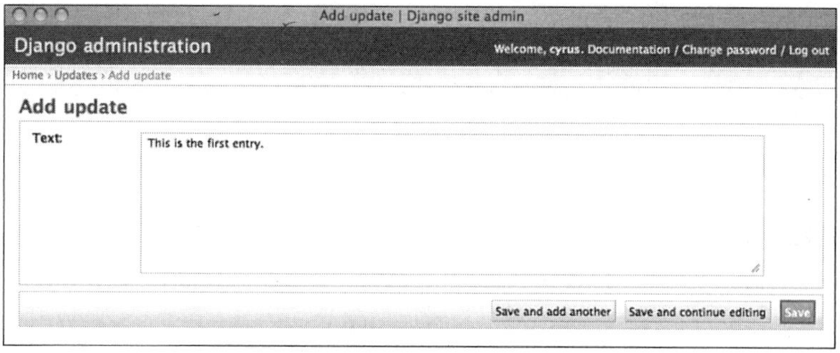

Figure 9.1   Adding a new `Update` entry

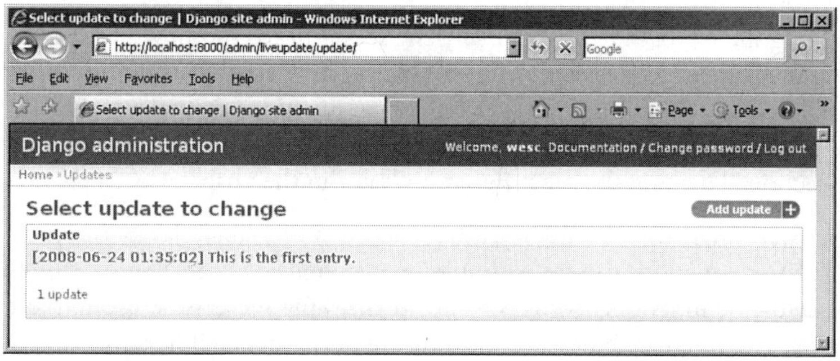

Figure 9.2   The Admin page after logging in with Liveupdate app available

[handwritten note in right margin]
Note:
If change an
update, app (as is)
will not show
changes. This an
arg for using
date time rather than
id...

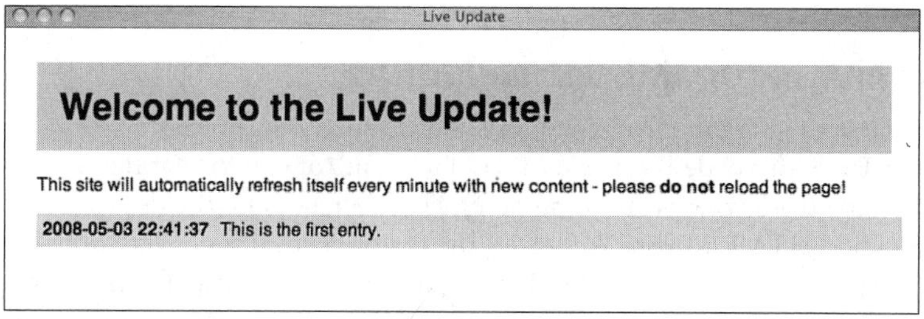

Figure 9.3   The liveblog with one lonely entry

Putting the Ajax In

This section takes up most of the rest of the chapter, but don't be discouraged! You need a lot of background to fully understand what's going on when using Ajax, and as usual we want to make sure we give you the chance to learn something instead of simply finding out what to copy and paste.

We start with a quick overview of what's required to use Ajax and what format it uses to transmit information, followed by installation and testing of an Ajax-capable JavaScript library, and finally show you the actual code that performs the magic, both on the server side and in the browser.

The Basics

Practically speaking, "implementing Ajax" for a Web site consists of three primary tasks.

- Importing the library: Because we're using a third-party library to do the heavy lifting, we must include it in our template before it can be used.
- Defining the client-side callback function: We use the library to write a function that makes a mini-request to the server and updates the Web page with the result.
- Defining the server-side logic: Finally, the server needs to know how to respond to the mini-request, so we must define a Django view capable of doing so; Ajax-capable views are normal views (that is to say, functions that take an HTTP request and return an HTTP response), which occasionally have an extra header or two (see the section "Creating the View Function" later in the chapter).

The first step, importing the library, usually consists of a single JavaScript include, although the two functions can be as simple or as complex as your logic requires. Typically, the client-side functionality takes more work, as the server-side is often just a bridge between your JavaScript and the database; but this varies depending on your specific needs and those of your users. In addition, if you're interested in using the UI aspects of your Ajax library, that code also lives at the template level, whether or not it executes concurrently with the mini-requests.

The "X" in Ajax (Or XML Versus JSON)

The dialogue between your client- and server-side functions can technically consist of any format your JavaScript code is capable of handling (and/or any format that HTTP can transmit because that's what we're using here). However, because the desired result is to transform or add HTML to your Web page, the majority of Ajax conversations—as noted earlier—utilize XML (of which XHTML is a variant) or a text data format called JSON (JavaScript Object Notation), which is simply text that can be evaluated as a JavaScript variable.

XML is arguably more commonly used, and of course lent its first initial to the name of the technology due to its popularity as an intersystem data transfer language. Given the intimate relationship between XML and (X)HTML, it's also well-suited to the task because JavaScript and various Web development tools are already designed for manipulating its hierarchical data structure. In addition, it's entirely possible to format your HTML on the server-side (with, say, a Django template and the rendering engine), thus simplifying your client-side code to a function that just drops it in place, ready-made.

JSON has recently risen in popularity due to its terse, readable syntax, and the fact it can be less bandwidth-intensive than XML. As a plus, its syntax is strikingly similar to that of Python's data structures (strings, dicts, and lists). You can find out more about the JSON syntax at http://json.org.

Here's a quick example of a simple JSON data structure.

```
{"first": "Bob", "last": "Smith", "favorite_numbers": [3,7,15]}
```

Even if you don't know any JavaScript, your Python background should make it obvious this is a dictionary with a couple string values and a third value that is a list of integers. Such a string evaluates to a working data structure in JavaScript and can then be utilized by client-side code.

JSON as Python

In many cases, JSON can be directly evaluated as a Python data structure, which would be useful when sending data from the client JavaScript back to the server. However, there are a few incompatibilities with Python, such as the JSON `true` and `false` Booleans versus Python's (which are title-cased) and JSON's `null` and Python's `None`. In such cases, an actual Python/JSON parser must be employed. To learn more about JSON and Python interoperability, see the previously listed JSON Web site as well as articles found at http://deron.meranda.us/python/comparing_json_modules/ and http://blog.hill-street.net/?p=7.

We are using JSON in our application, but XML is still a popular choice; there is no shortage of examples, how-to documents, and tutorials for both formats in print and online.

Installing the JavaScript Library

Because we've settled on using jQuery for this example, we need to download it via the Download link at http://jquery.com. jQuery comes as a single library and is not compartmentalized like some of the others, but it does offer multiple downloads—minified, packed, and uncompressed. All three are functionally equivalent but have different file sizes and require different amounts of client CPU time to decompress.

We are using the minified variant of the current version of jQuery, which at press time was 1.2.6, but any version 1.2.x works for our code here. (Versions older than 1.2.x also work but lack the getJSON function and thus require an extra statement to evaluate JSON strings.)   10/4/11   jquery is vers 1.6.4

jQuery needs to be included in our templates, and as such should live alongside our custom JavaScript in `liveproject/media/js/`. From a Win32 machine, just use a Web browser to download the file into that folder. On Unix-based hosts, such as Mac OS X and Linux, we like to use the `wget` or `curl` command line tools to download files directly, such as (using our browser's Copy function to grab the final download URL):

```
user@example:/opt/code/liveproject $ cd media/js/
user@example:/opt/code/liveproject/media/js $ wget
http://jqueryjs.googlecode.com/files/jquery-1.2.6.min.js
```

```
 -2008-05-01 21:52:15 -  http://jqueryjs.googlecode.com/files/jquery-1.2.6.min.js
Resolving jqueryjs.googlecode.com... 64.233.187.82
Connecting to jqueryjs.googlecode.com|64.233.187.82|:80... connected.
HTTP request sent, awaiting response... 200 OK
Length: 54075 (53K) [text/x-c]
Saving to: `jquery-1.2.6.min.js'

100%[=====================================================>] 54,075
227K/s    in 0.2s

2008-05-01 21:52:16 (227 KB/s) - `jquery-1.2.6.min.js' saved [54075/54075]
```

Now that we've got the library in our media directory, we need to add it to our template by adding this line in our <head> tag (note /media/custom is a symlink in our Apache docroot pointing to our liveproject/media directory).

```
<script type="text/javascript" language="javascript"
    src="/media/custom/js/jquery-1.2.6.min.js"></script>
```

We're all set to start using jQuery now, so we first do a simple setup and test, and then move on to the real functionality.

Setting Up and Testing jQuery

Ajax libraries typically provide an easy way to access the library's code, the current browser document, or the current DOM object. jQuery uses a somewhat unique syntax for almost all its functionality; the variable name $ is bound to a special callable object, which is either called as a function (for example $(argument)) or used to hold special methods (such as $.get(argument)).

For example, $(document) returns an object that's generally comparable to the normal JavaScript document variable, but with jQuery magic added to it. One such extra method is ready, used to execute a JavaScript function when the page loads (while avoiding problems with JavaScript's built-in onLoad).

As an example of this (and to set the stage for our eventual functionality) add the following, just after the include of jQuery itself, inside the <head> tag of your template:

```
<script type="text/javascript" language="javascript">
    $(document).ready(function() {
        alert("Hello world!");
    })
</script>
```

JavaScript is similar to Python in that functions are "first-class" or regular objects; advanced JavaScript development makes heavy use of modifying objects and passing functions around. In this case, $(document).ready takes a function to execute when the page is ready, and we're just defining that function anonymously—similar to how Python's lambda would work if it could span multiple lines. If all went well, and the template is able to include jQuery, our JS snippet just pops open a dialog window with "Hello World!" when you refresh the page, which is a nice proof-of-concept, but isn't very exciting.

Embedding JavaScript Actions in Our Template

Let's make things a bit more interesting and change it to dynamically add a `<div>` (one representing an `Update` object, albeit a hardcoded one) to our list when the page loads. This is, of course, the same action our live update code is doing later on with live data.

```
<script type="text/javascript" language="javascript">
    $(document).ready(function() {
        $("#update-holder").prepend('<div class="update">\
            <div class="timestamp">2008-05-03 22:41:40</div>\
            <div class="text">Testing!</div>\
            <div class="clear"></div>\
        </div>');
    })
</script>
```

Source p 210

loads in a hard-coded `<div class: "update"> ... </div>`

What's going on here is we're using jQuery's selector syntax, which enables you to pass a CSS-like string to the `$()` query function and whose result is then a `Query` representing all matching objects. In this case, we're looking for the `<div id="update-holder">` tag defined in our previous template, and so we use the `#` character, which is CSS parlance for selecting an object ID.

Once selected, we use the `prepend` method, which prepends an object or HTML string to the contents of the selection—so here, it tacks on another `<div class="update">` to the beginning of our list. Not bad for a single line of JavaScript! Let's see the result when we load the page, as shown in Figure 9.4.

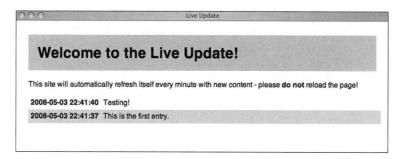

Figure 9.4   Testing our live updating JavaScript

We're all set now—we know jQuery is installed and working. It's time to go back to the server-side and create our Django view. We are implementing a tiny data-serving API, which we can then hook into with jQuery's request mechanism for the final step.

Creating the View Function

The quickest and easiest way to implement our stated requirement for this feature—the capability for our JavaScript to ask for all updates newer than the latest one it currently has—is to set up a normal URL. If we needed to send more than one piece of info in our request, we'd probably want to use a POST-based API, but here we can get away with something simple.

Let's say our Ajax-capable view lives at the URL /updates-after/<id>/, where <id> is the latest ID the requesting JavaScript has seen. Our view can do a simple query based off that ID number and return all newer Update objects. The return format is a JSON-encoded version of those model objects that our client-side JS can easily parse and wrap in HTML.

> ### Timestamps Versus IDs
>
> There are actually two ways we could have gone about ordering our Update objects here: the ID approach and a timestamp string approach. Using IDs, as we did, is a bit simpler (no parsing of timestamp strings into Python datetime objects at query time) and more granular (depending on how often Updates are entered into the database—you could have more than one for the same timestamp!). However, the ID approach makes the assumption that IDs are always autoincrementing, as Django's automatic ones typically are—but this is not always the case in the real world.
>
> Of course, technical know-how is only part of a developer's job—knowing how to correctly translate requirements into a live and working solution can be more tricky than it sounds.

To do this, we need to add one line to our app-level URLconf file, liveupdate/urls.py.

```
url(r'^updates-after/(?P<id>\d+)/$',
    'liveproject.liveupdate.views.updates_after'),
```

Here is the corresponding view function in liveupdate/views.py.

```
from django.http import HttpResponse
from django.core import serializers

from liveproject.liveupdate.models import Update

def updates_after(request, id):
    response = HttpResponse()
    response['Content-Type'] = "text/javascript"
    response.write(serializers.serialize("json",
        Update.objects.filter(pk__gt=id)))
    return response
```

We save a lot of time here by leveraging a built-in Django serializing library, which translates model objects into arbitrary text formats, including XML, JSON, and YAML. The serializers.serialize function does its work on a QuerySet, selecting the objects based on primary key (pk)—in our case, we are asking only for the objects whose ID is greater than the value of the id passed in.

The function then returns the resulting string in the format of our choice—here, it's JSON—which we write into our response using HttpResponse's file-like behavior. Finally, setting the Content-Type header of our response is necessary for JavaScript to ✳ correctly parse and use the body of the response.

The nice thing about using human-readable serialized text formats is we can debug them easily. Figure 9.5 shows what happens if we manually visit the URL http://localhost:8000/updates-after/0/ in our browser with a single test Update in our database.

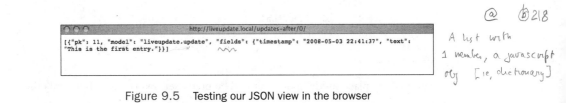

*@ (b) 218
A list with
1 member, a javascript
obj [ie, dictionary]*

Figure 9.5   Testing our JSON view in the browser

We're almost done—the final step is to write the keystone of the whole thing, the JavaScript to interface with this API view, and update the page with its response.

Using the View Function Via JavaScript

JavaScript provides a built-in timer function that is capable of evaluating arbitrary code at ✳ certain intervals, called setInterval, which takes a string to evaluate and an interval period in milliseconds, such as:

```
setInterval("update()", 60000);
```

This makes an update() call every 60,000 milliseconds or 60 seconds. Paired with a useful jQuery method called getJSON—which performs a mini-request to a URL and ✳ parses the result as JSON—we've got our Ajax at last. Here's the end result:

```
<script type="text/javascript" language="javascript">
    function update() {
        update_holder = $("#update-holder");
        most_recent = update_holder.find("div:first");
        $.getJSON("/updates-after/" + most_recent.attr('id') + "/",
            function(data) {
                cycle_class = most_recent.hasClass("odd")
                    ? "even" : "odd";
                jQuery.each(data, function() {
                    update_holder.prepend('<div id="' + this.pk
                        + '" class="update ' + cycle_class
                        + '"><div class="timestamp">'
```

select & hold onto the containing div
Select first child div
 # request
process returned json, referenced as data: list of json dicts
ref to a dict in the JSON list ... like 9.5 above. Construct code as per p 210

Construct the $.getJSON() call,
Including the treatment of each item (dict) in the list like @

jQuery 1.3
<sel>.each(<callback>) p 93
$.each(<dict or map>, <callback>) p 122

<div id="ddd" class="update even"><div class="timestamp"> ts </div>
<div class="text"> txt </div><div class="clear"></div></div>
Learning jQuery 1.3: could use $.each(data, function(entry index, entry){...
here, then entry['pk'] rather than this.pk   (p 123)

```
                                          ⓑ 217
                                         ⌒
                      + this.fields.timestamp
     Code             + '</div><div class="text">'
        constructor   + this.fields.text
                   ⌠  + '</div><div class="clear"></div></div>'
                   ⌡ );
                      cycle_class = (cycle_class == "odd")
            ed            ? "even" : "odd";
          c      });
        b    }
            );
      a
      }
ⓐ 214  $(document).ready(function() {
            setInterval("update()", 60000);
        })
    </script>
```

The action taking place inside update should be pretty self-explanatory, but here's the rundown:

1. We grab the container object (update_holder) and the most recent existing update item (most_recent) via jQuery's various selection methods.

2. most_recent's HTML ID attribute (which we've filled in with the server-side database ID number for convenience purposes) is used to construct the URL, which is getJSON's first argument.   210

3. The second argument is the usual anonymous function, encompassing the following remaining points.

4. The first line in the function initializes the "even/odd" CSS class variable.

5. We then use jQuery's each function to iterate over the JSON data from our view, which is giving us a list of serialized Update objects.

6. Those Update objects are used to construct new HTML snippets, prepended to the container <div>.

7. Finally, the CSS class is cycled at the end of each loop iteration to alternate the row colors.

Once update has been so defined, the actual "action" code executed within ready is simply our previously mentioned call to setInterval. After posting additional blog entries, you should see them automatically loaded onto the Web page within a minute of saving them. Although we can't actually show you this code in action—animated GIFs or videos don't display well in book form—Figure 9.6 is a screenshot of what the site looks like after a handful of updates have been entered.

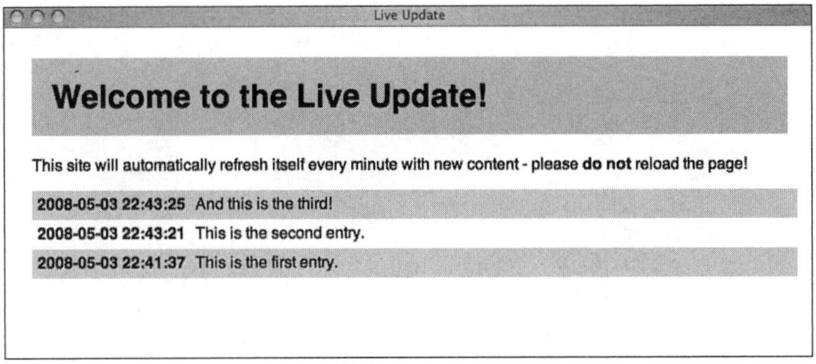

Figure 9.6   The final look of the liveblog with multiple entries

Summary

Although we've made good use of jQuery's powerful selection syntax and its getJSON function to provide the client-side functionality, neither of them was absolutely required to use the server-side functionality we've set up here. Not only do most of the other Ajax libraries have similar tools handy, but it's actually fairly easy to work with our small API view without any special libraries whatsoever.

The key here is everything involved speaks HTTP—our view expects the usual GET HTTP request, and similar views can use POST as well—and the return value (sent via HTTP) is also an open format, JSON. Just as Django's internal components strive to be flexible and compartmentalized, the use of Ajax with Django relies on being similarly open and well-defined.

This chapter has focused more on the mini-request aspect of Ajax, but there's plenty of reading material regarding many amazing things you can do with JavaScript on the UI front. We recommend you check out Appendix D, "Finding, Evaluating, and Using Django Applications," for some places to start looking, and remember—it's tempting to put a lot of graphical bells and whistles in your application, but your users will thank you for only doing so in moderation!

10

Pastebin

A major part of Django's appeal for many developers is the fact it allows you to write Web applications using Python. Paradoxically, another major part of Django's appeal is its generic views feature, enables you to create Web applications without writing much Python code at all. (You learned about generic views in Chapter 5, "URLs, HTTP Mechanisms, and Views.")

Django's generic views can be a powerful tool for rapid development and prototyping. Don't be fooled by the name though. Generic views are not just temporary scaffolding. Newcomers to Django can be forgiven for thinking the name must refer to some sort of default template for displaying your data, but the reality is quite different. Remember, a Django **view** is Python code that accepts an `HttpRequest` and returns an `HttpResponse`. The design of the data objects passed to that view, and the template used to render that response, are completely up to you.

In this section, we walk through a simple pastebin application that relies on generic views. Here are the features our application has

- A form for submitting new items with one mandatory field (the content) and two optional ones (the poster's name and a title)
- A clickable list of recent items
- A detail view for each item
- An administrative interface that allows us (as site owners) to edit or delete existing entries
- Syntax colorizing
- Periodic cleanup of outdated items

To achieve all this, we write approximately zero lines of imperative Python code. We create a model file that describes our data and its attributes and templates to display it, but nearly every other aspect of our application is handled by Django itself.

> **Note**
>
> The code for this example application is functionally similar to the first version of dpaste.com, the Django community pastebin. The present-day dpaste.com no longer is a pure-generic-views application, but the heart of its simplicity and utility is present in this chapter's code.

One note on approach before we dive in: The essence of this example is seeing how much work we can hand off to the framework. Some might call this approach lazy, but every line of code you don't write is one you don't have to debug. So in this example, where there's a choice between writing a little more code to get some custom behavior or enabling Django to do it for us, we're going to allow Django to do it.

Defining the Model

Here's the complete `models.py` for our pastebin application. It defines a simple five-field data structure, some `Meta` options, and a couple methods that are leveraged by the generic view code and our templates. It also registers our model with the admin and sets some list-related admin options.

```python
import datetime
from django.db import models
from django.db.models import permalink
from django.contrib import admin

class Paste(models.Model):
    """A single pastebin item"""

    SYNTAX_CHOICES = (
        (0, "Plain"),
        (1, "Python"),
        (2, "HTML"),
        (3, "SQL"),
        (4, "Javascript"),
        (5, "CSS"),
    )

    content = models.TextField()
    title = models.CharField(blank=True, max_length=30)
    syntax = models.IntegerField(max_length=30, choices=SYNTAX_CHOICES, default=0)
    poster = models.CharField(blank=True, max_length=30)
    timestamp = models.DateTimeField(default=datetime.datetime.now, blank=True)

    class Meta:
        ordering = ('-timestamp',)
```

```
    def __unicode__(self):
        return "%s (%s)" % (self.title or "#%s" % self.id,
        ➥self.get_syntax_display())

    @permalink
    def get_absolute_url(self):
        return ('django.views.generic.list_detail.object_detail',
            None, {'object_id': self.id})

class PasteAdmin(admin.ModelAdmin):
    list_display = ('__unicode__', 'title', 'poster', 'syntax', 'timestamp')
    list_filter = ('timestamp', 'syntax')

admin.site.register(Paste, PasteAdmin)
```

[handwritten margin note:]
```
def get_syntax_display (self):
    d = dict (self. SYNTAX_CHOICES)
    return d [self, syntax]
        cf p 231
```

Most of these elements you have seen before. What's unusual here is these lines constitute the bulk of the custom Python code for your pastebin application. Except for some
simple rules in our application's `urls.py`, the heavy lifting is done by the framework itself.

Applications based on generic views, such as this one, really show off the power that
Django's DRY (Don't Repeat Yourself) philosophy yields. In the example we're about to
build, the five field definitions at the core of our previous model (`content`, `title`, `syntax`,
`poster`, and `timestamp`) are used by:

- The `manage.py syncdb` command, which creates a table in the database
- The admin app, which generates an editing interface for our data
- The `object_detail` generic view, which fetches instances of our model and sends
  them to the template system for display
- The `create_update` generic view, which generates and processes a submission form
  for adding new paste items

The model methods are also used in multiple places. The admin app uses the
`__unicode__` object when it needs to refer to the object by name (for example, in
deletion-confirmation messages), and the `get_absolute_url` method for generating "View
on site" links. Our template uses `__unicode__` implicitly anywhere it needs to display the
name of an item and `get_absolute_url` to generate links in the list of recent items.

Creating the Templates

Now let's create some basic templates that are used to render our content to the user. First
we need a base template, a technique you've seen in earlier chapters such as Chapter 7,
"Photo Gallery." Save this in `pastebin/templates`.

[handwritten margin note: base template]

```
<html>
<head>
<title>{% block title %}{% endblock %}</title>
<style type="text/css">
    body { margin: 30px; font-family: sans-serif; background: #fff; }
```

```
    h1 { background: #ccf; padding: 20px; }
    pre { padding: 20px; background: #ddd; }
</style>
</head>
<body>
    <p><a href="/paste/add/">Add one</a> &bull; <a href="/paste/">List all</a></p>
    {% block content %}{% endblock %}
</body>
</html>
```

Once our base template is set up, let's create a form for users to paste their code to our application. Save the following in `pastebin/templates/pastebin/paste_form.html`. (Keep reading for an explanation of the seeming redundancy in the path name.)

form template

```
{% extends "base.html" %}
{% block title %}Add{% endblock %}
{% block content %}
<h1>Paste something</h1>
<form action="" method="POST">
Title: {{ form.title }}<br>
Poster: {{ form.poster }}<br>
Syntax: {{ form.syntax }}<br>
{{ form.content }}<br>
<input type="submit" name="submit" value="Paste" id="submit">
</form>
{% endblock %}
```

Next, we make a template for our list view. This shows all the recently pasted items and enables the user to select one with a click. Save this to `pastebin/templates/pastebin/paste_list.html`.

list view template

```
{% extends "base.html" %}
{% block title %}Recently Pasted{% endblock %}
{% block content %}
<h1>Recently Pasted</h1>
<ul>
    {% for object in object_list %}
    <li><a href="{{ object.get_absolute_url }}">{{ object }}</a></li>
    {% endfor %}
</ul>
{% endblock %}
```

displays object. -- unicode --()

Finally, we make a detail page template. This is the one people spend the most time looking at. Save this as `pastebin/templates/pastebin/paste_detail.html`.

detail template

```
{% extends "base.html" %}
{% block title %}{{ object }}{% endblock %}
{% block content %}
<h1>{{ object }}</h1>
```

```
<p>Syntax: {{ object.get_syntax_display }}<br>
Date: {{ object.timestamp|date:"r" }}</p>
<code><pre>{{ object.content }}</pre></code>
{% endblock %}
```

Designing the URLs

Because the structure of our application is so clear, creating our URLs is fairly easy. The only tricky part here is the apparatus needed to take advantage of generic views. We need to design three URL patterns—one for listing all items, one for showing individual items, and one for adding new items.

```
from django.conf.urls.defaults import *
from django.views.generic.list_detail import object_list, object_detail
from django.views.generic.create_update import create_object
from pastebin.models import Paste
                                          model class
display_info = {'queryset': Paste.objects.all()}
create_info = {'model': Paste}
                                          create new dict from existing dict +
                                                       keyword arg (s)
urlpatterns = patterns('',
    url(r'^$', object_list, dict(display_info, allow_empty=True)),
    url(r'^(?P<object_id>\d+)/$', object_detail, display_info),
    url(r'^add/$', create_object, create_info),       dict
)
```

This is really the heart of our application. We import three function objects, view functions, from django.views.generic:

- django.views.generic.list_detail.object_list
- django.views.generic.list_detail.object_detail
- django.views.generic.create_update.create_object

In addition to the HttpRequest that all Django views, generic or otherwise, take as their first argument, these views also get passed a dictionary of additional values; we define two different ones in our previous URLconf. The names, display_info and create_info, are arbitrary (although _info is a conventional suffix for these dictionaries), but their contents are structured specifically for the generic views we are using. The list_detail views expect a queryset containing all eligible objects with a key of queryset. The create_update views expect the model class (not an instance) with a key of model. In the case of object_list, we add allow_empty=True to the dictionary to tell the view we want to see the page even if there are no objects in the database.

There are many other possible values you can include in these dictionaries. Because they are the primary method for customizing the behavior of generic views they can get quite crowded. For a full list of the options in these views, see the official Django documentation. For now we're keeping it simple.

> **Note**
>
> There's a special rule at play here that is worth knowing about when you begin expanding your use of these `_info` dictionaries. The code in your URLconf is not evaluated fresh on every request. This means that, if nothing special were done, the `Paste.objects.all` queryset we set up here could actually get stale as new objects were added, edited, or removed by users or site admins. Luckily, Django knows this and is explicitly instructed not to cache the data with the key `queryset`.

Trying It Out

Even though we haven't written much in the way of imperative code, we now have a functional application. Let's try it out. When we launch the app, we see a screen as shown in Figure 10.1—an empty pastebin.

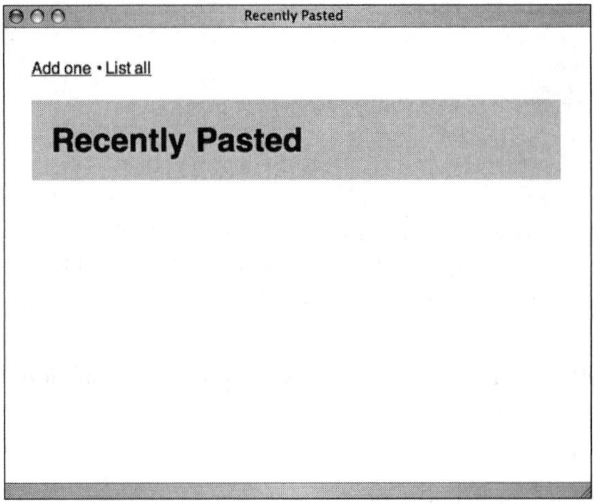

enter
... /paste

Figure 10.1   The empty pastebin

Let's think for a moment about all the things Django has done to get this page to us; it parsed our requested URL, determined which view needs to be called, passed an (empty) queryset derived from our model, found our template file, rendered the template using the appropriate context, and returned the resulting HTML content to the browser.

Now let's add some content. If we click the Add One link, we should see our blank form. This form is a collaboration between Django's view and our template. The generic `create_update` view introspects our model, generates HTML form elements, and passes them to our template in the `{{ form }}` template variable. Our template unpacks these elements and displays a form to the user. Note the `<form>` tags and the submit button were our responsibility.

The resulting form should look something like Figure 10.2.

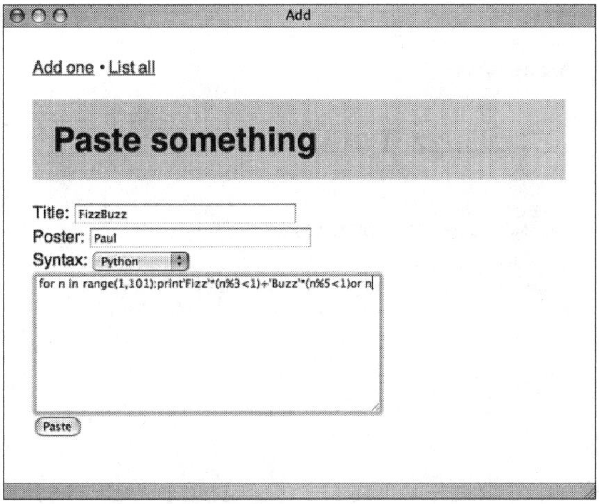

Figure 10.2   The Add One form

Our friendly pastebin doesn't force the user to do much. Only the Code field is required, in fact. Pastebins are only useful if they are convenient, and long lists of required fields are not convenient.

By filling in the form and clicking the Paste button, we are calling Django's `create_update` generic view again. Because the data is being sent via HTTP POST instead of GET, the view knows that instead of displaying our blank form, it needs to process the user's input and (if possible) store it in the database.

One aspect of the `create_update` view we don't illustrate here is validation. What happens if the user omits a required field? In this case, the form is simply displayed again. Our extremely simple template does not include code that looks for or displays validation error messages, but in fact Django *is* passing them along in the `{{ form.errors }}` template variable. A more robust implementation would look for those errors and display them as helpful messages to the user.

Assuming the user has managed to fill in the one required field and click Paste Django processes the form input (again, via the `create_update` generic view) and stores it in the database. It then redirects to the newly created object's `get_absolute_url` and presents us with our submission rendered via the `pastebin_detail.html` template, as shown in Figure 10.3.

This is the most likely thing that a user wants after submitting an item—a view of that item and a URL that can be sent to others.

If the user wants to see what other items are in the pastebin, the List All link takes him there. Via Django's `object_list` generic view and our `paste_list.html` template, a simple bulleted list of pasted items is displayed, as shown in Figure 10.4.

This list illustrates the working of the `object_list` generic view nicely. The `display_info` dictionary in our URLconf passes the queryset representing all our Paste

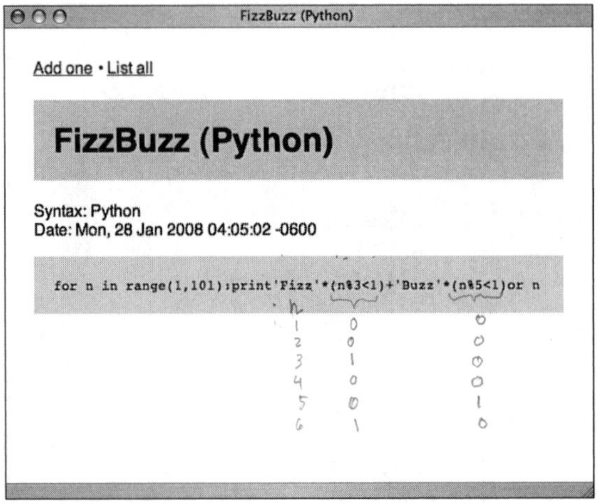

Figure 10.3   The newly pasted item

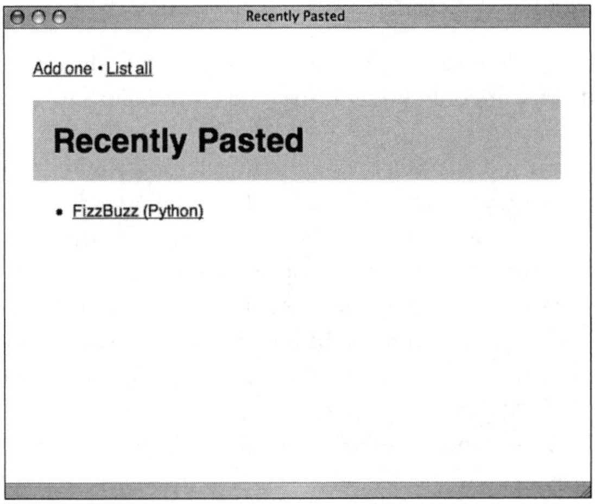

Figure 10.4   The list of submitted items

objects to the `object_list` view. That view passes the objects along to our template, where our concise `{% for object in object_list %}` loop generates the clickable list.

Note

In practice, a list of submitted items is not necessarily a great feature for this type of site. Pastebin users typically care only about their own submissions. Pastebin operators have been known to muse, "Why do spammers keep pasting stuff into my pastebin?" The answer, of course, is spammers "care" about any mechanism by which their content can be placed in front of unsuspecting users. A pastebin's list of recent items serves this purpose handily, despite being an incongruous venue for commercial messages.

Finally, don't forget on top of all the parts of our application that we more or less explicitly designed, we also get the admin app. Given the options we specified in our `PasteAdmin` class, our admin looks something like Figure 10.5.

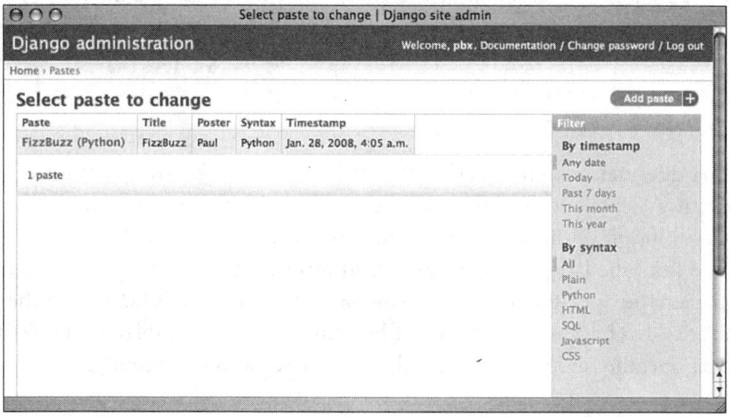

Figure 10.5   The admin screen

Note by using our model's `__unicode__` method as the first argument to the admin's `list_display`, rather than a particular model field, the clickable name for each item can be adjusted depending on what information is available.

What you have at this point is a useful, usable application powered entirely by Django's generic views. Although a perfectly reasonable strategy for enhancing the application would be to begin adding your own custom view code, there are actually many more improvements you could make while sticking to generic views. We tackle three: keeping the list of recent pastes manageable, adding syntax highlighting to our entries, and scheduling cleanup of old entries.

Limiting Number of Recent Pastes Displayed

That Recently Pasted list is cool when you have only a few items, but if you were running a busy public site, the list could quickly grow unwieldy. There are ways we could limit the number of items in this list. Given our focus on generic views, the best place to take care of it here is in the template.

This just takes one change to line 6 of our `paste_list.html` template, applying a slice filter to `object_list`.

```
{% for object in object_list|slice:":10" %}
```

Here's how this works: The URLconf passes the template a queryset representing all the pastes in the database. They're sorted in descending order by timestamp, thanks to the `ordering = ('-timestamp')` line in our `models.py`. The for-loop in the template then takes the top ten items and iterates over them.

The value passed to the `slice` filter is exactly what we'd pass to a normal Python object, minus the brackets. An equivalent example in Python would be something such as:

```
>>> number_list = [15, 14, 13, 12, 11, 10, 9, 8, 7, 6, 5, 4, 3, 2, 1]
>>> print number_list[:10]
[15, 14, 13, 12, 11, 10, 9, 8, 7, 6]
```

If Django's querysets weren't "lazy"—that is, if we passed the complete list of objects just to throw away all but ten—this would be madness. If we had thousands of items, the memory consumption of our Web server processes would skyrocket. Because the queryset isn't evaluated until the last possible moment (in this case, the `for` loop in our template), there's no penalty for specifying `Paste.objects.all()` in the URLconf and then slicing in the template. Also, because the choice of how many items to display in the list is really a presentational one, the template is an excellent place to do the trimming.

Syntax Highlighting

A pastebin is a lot more useful (and attractive) if it knows how to properly apply colored syntax highlighting to the submitted snippets. There are various ways to do this (including the excellent Python-based library **Pygments**, which dpaste.com uses), but the easiest path to implementation here is to make the highlighting happen on the client side in Javascript.

Pygments

A programmer named Alex Gorbatchev created an excellent and widely used high-lighting utility in Javascript. Called simply Syntax Highlighter, it can be fetched from Google Code (http://code.google.com/p/syntaxhighlighter/).

Syntax Highlighter

A full set of instructions and examples on using Syntax Highlighter can be found on the project's Web site, but here's a run-through of how we'd get syntax highlighting for our Python code samples.

First, we update our `paste_detail.html` template to look like this.

```
{% extends "base.html" %}
{% block title %}{{ object }}{% endblock %}
{% block content %}
<h1>{{ object }}</h1>
<p>Syntax: {{ object.get_syntax_display }}<br>
Date: {{ object.timestamp|date:"r" }}</p>
<code><pre name="code" class="{{ object.get_syntax_display|lower }}">
    {{ object.content }}</pre></code>
<link type="text/css" rel="stylesheet"
    href="/static/css/SyntaxHighlighter.css"></link>
<script language="javascript" src="/static/js/shCore.js"></script>
<script language="javascript" src="/static/js/shBrushPython.js"></script>
```

```
<script language="javascript" src="/static/js/shBrushXml.js"></script>
<script language="javascript" src="/static/js/shBrushJscript.js"></script>
<script language="javascript" src="/static/js/shBrushSql.js"></script>
<script language="javascript" src="/static/js/shBrushCss.js"></script>
<script language="javascript">
dp.SyntaxHighlighter.HighlightAll('code');
</script>
{% endblock %}
```

We added `name` and `class` attributes to our `<pre>` tag. This enables our code block to be located by the Javascript when it runs.   *missing p 222-3*

```
<pre name="code" class="{{ object.get_syntax_display|lower }}">
```

That's all it takes. When the browser renders the page, the syntax highlighter JavaScript code runs, transforming the bland monochromatic code sample before the user even sees it. The output should look something like Figure 10.6.

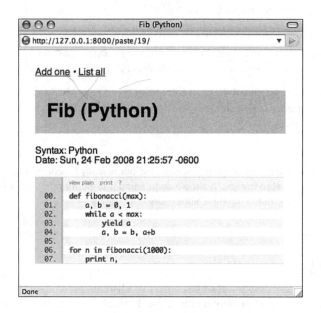

Figure 10.6   Syntax coloring applied to a Python source snippet

Cleanup Via Cron Job

Items posted on pastebin sites tend to be ephemeral, so it's nice to perform some periodic automated cleanup of older items. The best way to do this is with a nightly **cron job** running on your server.

Cron jobs and other Django scripts that are designed to run outside the Web server environment are another testament to the power of Django's "it's just Python" approach. Writing a script that does stuff with your Django app's objects involves very little that is specific to Django. The following simple script depends on the following assumptions:

- The environment variable DJANGO_SETTINGS_MODULE has been set to a string containing the Python pathname of your project's settings file (for example, "pastesite.settings").
- You have a setting named EXPIRY_DAYS in your project's settings module.
- Your project's name is "pastesite."

Assuming those are taken care of, there's little else for you to do other than test and deploy.

```python
#!/usr/bin/env python
import datetime
from django.conf import settings
from pastesite.pastebin.models import Paste

today = datetime.date.today()
cutoff = (today - datetime.timedelta(days=settings.EXPIRY_DAYS))
Paste.objects.filter(timestamp__lt=cutoff).delete()
```

older than cutoff date

The last line of the script is where all the action is—it uses Django's ORM to select all objects in the database whose timestamp is older than the calculated cutoff, and then deletes them en masse.

> **Note**
>
> Depending on your database engine, you can also periodically "vacuum" or reclaim the space left by the deleted entries. A simple code snippet to perform this on a SQLite database can be found at http://djangosnippets.org.

Summary

Hopefully you are now convinced of the power of Django's generic views. Our example pastebin site is simple in its implementation, but think of all the features it has: input validation, redirect-on-post, detail and list views, and so on. But perhaps even better than having these is knowing that with Django we have a solid base for expansion. If we want to localize our app, or fortify it against Digg-level traffic by adding caching, Django is ready for us.

IV

Advanced Django Techniques and Features

11

Advanced Django Programming

In this chapter, we explore a number of different advanced techniques that can be applied to your Django code, such as the generation of RSS and other formats, customizing the behavior of the admin application, and advanced use of the templating system.

The next chapter, Chapter 12, "Advanced Django Deployment," consists of a similar group of topics, such as testing, data imports, and scripting—things that are more tangential to your core application logic. In both chapters, order doesn't really matter—feel free to skip around as you see fit.

Customizing the Admin

Django's admin app is, in some ways, its crown jewel. This can seem odd to say about a component that lives in the "contrib" directory—those that inhabitant these confines are usually optional add-ons not core components. However, Django's developers have labeled it that way because it's the right thing to do—you don't *have* to use the admin when you use Django, so it shouldn't be required. But make no mistake: The admin app is a powerful and compelling application. If your project requires you to quickly create a polished, usable interface for adding and editing data, the admin is your friend.

Throughout the rest of the book, you've seen some of the customizations possible via `ModelAdmin` subclasses. For instance, just setting the `list_display`, `list_filter`, and `search_fields` options gives you much of the basic customization that you need.

It's also been mentioned that the admin site used in our examples is the "default" admin site—and that's because it's possible to set up multiple different admin sites for extra flexibility. This enables you to go a ways toward having different admin views for different groups of users, for example.

However, inevitably you want the admin to do more. It's not uncommon for new Django developers, after playing with the admin for a while, to say something such as, "I've been reading the documentation, and there's this one thing I can't figure out how to make it do. But if it *just did this one additional thing*, it would be the perfect tool!"

In the following, we show you some ways you can customize and extend the admin app to do some things people commonly request. However, as you read this section, keep in mind *the admin is just another Django app*. It's an incredibly useful one with a lovely interface and a lot of configurability, but in the end it if doesn't do what you want, you have the power to replace it with something else.

Depending on the depth of the customizations you find yourself contemplating, it could be wiser in the end to develop your own custom admin rather than trying to twist the existing one into doing things it wasn't really designed for. If the well-established techniques outlined here don't go far enough for you, it's probably time to consider creating your own admin. With this cautionary note out of the way, following are some of the more advanced admin customizations available.

Changing Layout and Style Using `Fieldsets`

The admin app's `fieldsets` setting gives you some very granular control over how data is displayed. For example, it's probably what you want to use if you want to add some custom CSS styles to particular elements, group fields in a certain way, add Javascript input helpers to selected fields, or initially have certain fields display in a hidden state.

Here's a trivial example model with display customization done using `fieldsets`.

```
class Person(models.Model):
    firstname = models.CharField(max_length=50)
    lastname = models.CharField(max_length=50)
    city = models.CharField(max_length=50)
    state = models.CharField(max_length=2)


class PersonAdmin(admin.ModelAdmin):
    fieldsets = [
        ("Name", {"fields": ("firstname", "lastname")}),
        ("Location", {"fields": ("city", "state")})
    ]


admin.site.register(Person, PersonAdmin)
```

In Python-speak, the `fieldsets` setting is a list of **two-tuples**. The first item of each tuple is a string label for the group of fields, and the second item is a dictionary of settings for that group. Inside the dictionary, the keys are the names of particular options (we list them next); the associated values can be of various types depending on the particular option. In our minimal previous example, the `fields` option is being set to a tuple of field names.

The result is the fields grouped via our use of the `fieldsets` option are displayed together in the admin, as seen in Figure 11.1.

Here are the options you can use (as dictionary keys per the previous example) under the `fieldsets` setting.

- classes: This option specifies a tuple of strings, which are the names of CSS classes (ones available in your rendered template) that should be applied to this field group. The admin predefines a few classes that can be handy here: "collapsed," which

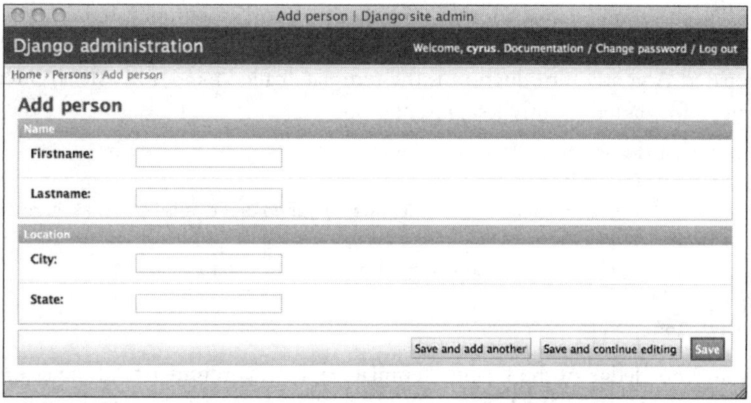

Figure 11.1   New fields in our admin

causes the fieldset to be collapsed under its header with a JavaScript-based toggle for expansion; "monospace," which can be used for HTML `textarea` fields that are intended to contain code; and "wide," which gives the fieldset a wider (though fixed) width in the admin. Look in the "media" directory inside django.contrib. admin to find the default stylesheets if you're curious about what other classes you can use.

Note

If you are a practitioner of the "progressive enhancement" style of JavaScript development, the CSS classes you add via this option can serve as hooks for your custom JavaScript code—for example, if you want to add a WYSIWYG editor to a textarea.

- description: This option specifies a string that is used as a description of the field group. Think of it as group-level `help_text`. Django's default admin CSS styles are carefully written to display text such as this in a readable, unobtrusive way. These nice design touches add even more value to simple labeling features such as this.

- fields: As explained previously, this option specifies a tuple of field names that should be grouped together visually in the admin. If the dictionary in which this option is set is prefaced by a string (for example, "Name" in our previous example), that label is used for the group. Otherwise, it appears without a textual header.

Extending the Base Templates

Going beyond simple settings changes, you can also make some significant adjustments to the appearance of your admin app by replacing one or more of the base templates with your own version. Of course, you're not actually *replacing* per sé, but overriding the original templates with your own files, as we explain next.

Technically, the admin is just another Django app, but it's a complicated one on all levels. The twisty maze of templates that it uses is not something a beginner should dive into unprepared. A gentle introduction is the template called `base_site.html`. Here's the whole thing, reformatted slightly for presentation.

```
{% extends "admin/base.html" %}
{% load i18n %}
{% block title %}{{ title|escape }}|{% trans 'Django site admin' %}{% endblock %}
{% block branding %}
<h1 id="site-name">{% trans 'Django administration' %}</h1>
{% endblock %}
{% block nav-global %}{% endblock %}
```

With your knowledge of the Django template system, you understand the `extends` tag at the top is probably doing the heavy lifting here. You're correct. A more complicated template called `base.html` is the true underlying template for all the admin pages. However, the two things in it you'd likely want to customize—the page's `<title>` and the `<h1>` header block—have been tidily abstracted into `base_site.html`.

As for the customization, simply change the strings "Django site admin" and "Django administration" to whatever values are appropriate for your application and save the template. But where to save it?

To override the contents of this template, you need to create your own customized copy, and then help the Django template loader find it before the default one. You can place your copy either inside one of your applications' template directories (if you're using the `app_directories` template loader) or in one of your `TEMPLATE_DIRS` locations.

In either case, you need to place it inside a subdirectory labeled `admin`, so the `extends` tags in the other admin templates can locate it correctly.

If you're placing it inside one of your applications (for example, `myproject/myapp/templates/admin/base_site.html`), make sure your application comes before the `django.contrib.admin` in your `INSTALLED_APPS` setting. Because the template loader searches those apps' template directories in order, if the admin is listed before your app, the Django template loader ceases its search when it finds the original template.

If you'd like to delve a little deeper into customizing the admin templates, the next one to look at is `index.html`. It's a bit more complex than `base_site.html`, but it is worth looking at if you want to significantly rearrange the main admin page.

Adding New Views

Short of writing an entire custom admin app, the ultimate step in admin customization is writing your own admin views. This is far preferable to hacking up the Django admin app's code directly.

At the very least, such hacks place an onerous maintenance burden on you, their creator, every time the main Django codebase is updated. If changes in upstream that conflict with your customizations have been made, you have to constantly deal with merging the two together. Additionally, if you make your customizations as stand-alone admin views, they are much easier to share with other Django developers, who can in turn contribute fixes and improvements back to you.

Writing new admin views is "just Django" in the sense there is very little about it specific to the admin. There are three basic requirements:

- Your view should ideally be mapped to a URL that is "inside" the admin app's URL space. This is more for user comfort than anything, but Django's URLconf system makes it easy, so there's little reason not to do it.

- Your view should look like the rest of the admin; in other words, it should render its responses using the admin site templates.

- Your view should use Django's authentication decorators—explained in the next section—to enforce access.

Authentication Decorators

Before you go any further in this section, if you're new to Python and need a refresher on the concept of decorators, read this paragraph and then flip back to the section on decorators in Chapter 1, "Practical Python for Django." Decorators are functions that change *@ 42* other functions. Your Django views are functions. You want to change them in a specific way—to restrict access so that only certain users can call them—and this is a natural fit for decorators.

You can think of the decorator as a guard for your view function. If the user passes your test, they're in—the view runs and the page displays. If the user fails the test, she is redirected elsewhere. (By default, users are redirected to /accounts/login/ plus a parameter that says where users should be redirected after they've successfully logged in, for example, /accounts/login/?next=/jobs/101/. You can set LOGIN_URL in your settings.py to customize this URL if needed.)

For enforcing authentication, a single decorator does most of the heavy lifting for you, called user_passes_test.

To use this decorator, in addition to the view that you are guarding you also need to *✗* provide a utility function that actually applies the test in question. This function must take a User object and return a boolean (True or False). Such a function can be simple, even *@43* trivial:

```
def user_is_staff(user):          or     user_is_staff = lambda u: u.is_staff
    return user.is_staff
```

Having defined that function, your use of the decorator would be something such as this:

```
@user_passes_test(user_is_staff)       # the decorator  (w. an arg)
def for_staff_eyes_only(request):      # the view                    ←
    print "Next secret staff meeting date: November 14th"
```

funct (view) being wrapped
↓
user_passes_test (lambda u: u, is_staff) (for_staff_eyes_only)

That definition of `user_is_staff` almost feels like a waste of a function, doesn't it? This is where `lambda` comes in (for an introduction to `lambda`, refer back to Chapter 1). With `lambda` we can define an ad-hoc, "anonymous" function right in the decorator line itself.

```
@user_passes_test(lambda u: u.is_staff)
def for_staff_eyes_only(request):
    ...
```

Moving on with our example, let's say you need to slice it finer than staff-or-not-staff. One of the handy things about Django's admin and auth apps is they offer a convenient permissions system for managing your users. You already know that each model gets its own set of create/update/delete permissions in the admin, but these permissions are also accessible in your Python code. If you had a `SecretMeeting` model and accompanying privileges listed in the auth system, and you were creating a view that allowed certain people to add new secret meetings, your decorated function could look like this:

```
@user_passes_test(lambda u: u.can_create_secretmeeting)
def secret_meeting_create(request):
    ...
```

With a mix of Django's predefined permissions and your own application-specific ones, you should be able to control access in whatever way you like.

Using Syndication

Django provides a convenient facility, the Syndication app (`django.contrib.syndication`), for generating RSS or Atom feeds from any collection of model objects. This makes it incredibly easy to add feeds to your Django project.

The Syndication app is highly configurable, but it is easy to get started with thanks to its sensible defaults. There are only two essential steps: first, a special class that produces feed objects; second, a rule in your URLconf that passes these objects to the Syndication app. The easiest way to understand how this all works is to jump right into the code. We base this example on the Blog application developed back in Chapter 2, "Django for the Impatient: Building a Blog."

The Feed Class

To configure your feeds, you define a separate module containing special feed classes, which are then imported directly into your URLconf. Django doesn't place any restrictions on where you place this file (or even what its name is), but a sensible location is inside your app directory, and the usual name is `feeds.py`. So, inside your `mysite/blog` directory, you would create a file called `feeds.py` containing the following code:

```
from django.contrib.syndication.feeds import Feed
from mysite.blog.models import BlogPost
```

```
class RSSFeed(Feed):
    title = "My awesome blog feed"
    description = "The latest from my awesome blog"
    link = "/blog/"
    item_link = link

    def items(self):
        return BlogPost.objects.all()[:10]
```

The `title` and `description` attributes are used by the consumer of the feed (for example, a desktop RSS reader) to label the feed. The `link` attribute specifies what page is associated with your feed. Your site's domain name is prepended to whatever partial URL you provide.

The `item_link` attribute is used to determine what page to load if the reader wants to see the Web page associated with an individual feed item. By setting `item_link` to `/blog/`, we're saying that a click on any individual feed item sends the user to the front page of our blog—and if you're thinking that seems kind of inflexible, you're right. A better technique is to extend your BlogPost model with a `get_absolute_url` method. The Syndication app automatically uses it if it's present.

The `items` method is the heart of this class—it decides what objects are returned to the Syndication app. The code here returns the first ten objects in our list of blog posts; because our `BlogPost` model has its `Meta.ordering` attribute set to `"-timestamp"` (reverse-chronological order), we get them in reverse-chronological order.

This class we've created is just about the simplest thing that works. It contains only the items that the Syndication app absolutely requires. There are many optional attributes and more flexible ways specifying some of the required ones. In learning the possible customizations, it's useful to understand that many attributes in a feed class can actually be one of three things:

- A hardcoded value (as with the previous `title`, `description`, and `link`)
- A method that takes no explicit arguments (the implicit `self` referring to the feed is required of course)
- A method that takes one explicit argument (an individual feed item)

The Syndication app figures out which one you're doing by taking intelligent advantage of Python's "duck typing." The Syndication app looks for these three options (where applicable) in reverse order from how they're listed here: If it finds a one-argument method with the appropriate name, it uses that, passing in the current feed object; next, it looks for a no-argument method and calls that if found; failing those two, it looks for a hardcoded value. Failing all three, it throws a `FeedDoesNotExist` exception (because in that case your feed is broken).

Giving the Feed a URL

Having created the class that handles the actual generation of the feed, all that's left is to give your feed a working URL. Continuing with our blog example, we would update our app's URLconf file (`mysite/blog/urls.py`) so it looks like this:

```
from django.conf.urls.defaults import *
from django.contrib.syndication.views import feed
from mysite.blog.views import archive
from mysite.blog.feeds import RSSFeed

urlpatterns = patterns('',
    url(r'^$', archive),
    url(r'^feeds/(?P<url>.*)/$', feed, {'feed_dict': {'rss': RSSFeed}}),
)
```

We've added just three lines. Two are imports; we bring in the `feed` view object from the Syndication app, and we bring in our new `RSSFeed` class from our blog app.

We've also added a fairly complicated-looking URL pattern. Breaking it down into its three components, we have:

- `r'^feeds/(?P<url>.*)/$'`: Our URL regex. Because we're inside the "blog" app, which currently lives at the URL `/blog/`, this means URLs of the form `/blog/feeds/FOO/` are captured with "FOO" being passed along to our view function.

- `feed`: The view function we've imported from `django.contrib.syndication.views`.

- `{'feed_dict': {'rss': RSSFeed}}`: In any `urlpatterns` tuple, we can provide a third item such as this, a dictionary that is used to pass additional arguments to the view function. We're passing one argument, called `feed_dict`, which is a one-item dictionary mapping the string "rss" to our RSSFeed class. We could add other types of feeds simply by creating the needed classes and referring to them in this dictionary.

Though the key we use in our context dict ("rss") happens to be the type of feed, it could be anything—"latest" for the latest posts, for example. The Syndication app doesn't restrict us there. It just wants to know how to connect requests to Feed classes that it can use.

Doing More with Feeds

Offering RSS or Atom feeds can be a great improvement to a regularly (or irregularly) updated site. Although these formats are ostensibly simple, rolling your own code for feed output is tedious and error-prone. The well-known Universal Feed Parser (http://feedparser.org/) ships with more than *three thousand tests* to make sure it robustly handles the huge range (some would say "mess" rather than "range") of published feeds. By using

Django's Syndication app, you produce clean, valid output with a very small investment of code and configuration.

If you require more customization than we've covered here, see the official Django documentation. It's unlikely that you ever have to take the roll-your-own approach again.

Generating Downloadable Files

Because Django is a Web framework, naturally we think of it mostly as a tool for generating HTML and sending it via HTTP. But Django is perfectly adaptable to other types of content and other modes of delivery.

Two factors make this true. The first is that Django's template language is text-based, not XML-based. A Web framework that can only do XML templating doesn't help you much when you also need to generate plain text reports or e-mail.

The second factor is simply that Django's exposure of the HTTP mechanisms driving your Web site enables you to tweak the various HTTP headers involved. Therefore, you're able to set the Content-Type to a non-HTML value, such as JavaScript (as with the JSON view in Chapter 9, "Liveblog") or add a Content-Disposition header to force downloading instead of browser rendering.

Here are a few short examples of using Django to generate non-Web-page output. Some of them use the template system, as we've just mentioned; others don't because there are times when *any* template system is just unnecessary overhead. As always, use the right tool for the job.

Nagios Configuration Files

One real-life example that we share briefly with you here hinges on a well-known open source monitoring system, Nagios (http://nagios.org/). Like many similar projects, it embraces the Unix convention of plain-text configuration files with a published format; such config files are an excellent target for Django's template system.

One of the authors is, at the time of writing, producing a small, highly customized internal application to (among other things) generate a partial Nagios configuration setup. It's based on a Django app that serves as a central database of information on systems and services; this catalog is then exported to a format Nagios can understand, enabling the user to keep track of systems in one place and have Nagios monitor them.

Here's a simplified example of the system-service hierarchy model (in the real application, this information is spread among a number of models).

```
class System(models.Model):
    name = models.CharField(max_length=100)
    ip = models.IPAddressField()


class Service(models.Model):
    name = models.CharField(max_length=100)
    system = models.ForeignKey(System)
    port = models.IntegerField()
```

Next is a template that can generate a per-host Nagios service-check file, again greatly simplified from the real thing. Its intended context is a single System object, system.

```
define host {
    use             generic-host
    host_name       {{ system.name }}
    address         {{ system.ip }}
}
```

should be single curly braces

```
{% for service in system.service_set.all %}
define service {
    use                  generic-service
    host_name            {{ system.name }}
    service_description  {{ service.name }}
    check_command        check_tcp!{{ service.port }}
}
```

> **Note**
>
> Don't be confused by the single curly-braces; they're part of the Nagios file format and aren't parsed by Django's template system. The template system only cares about double curly-braces or curly-braces paired with percent signs.

{{ var }} , {% tag... %}

When rendered, the previous template gives us a working Nagios file that defines the system as a Nagios host record and writes out any services associated with it, using a network check command that makes sure the recorded TCP port is up and running.

vCard

The Vcard format is a text-based format for contact information. It is a supported import and export format for many popular address book, e-mail, and PIM (Personal Information Manager) products, including Evolution, the OS X Address Book, and Microsoft Outlook.

If you have contact information in a Django app, you can want to be able generate vCards so that users can import that contact information into their local address book or PIM application.

This sample code uses the vObject module (available from http://vobject.skyhouseconsulting.com/), which makes generating vCard data a bit easier.

```
import vobject


def vcard(request, person):
    v = vobject.vCard()
    v.add('n')
    v.n.value = vobject.vcard.Name(family=person.lastname, given=person.firstname)
    v.add('fn')
    v.fn.value = "%s %s" % (person.firstname, person.lastname)
```

```
    v.add('email')
    v.email.value = person.email
    output = v.serialize()          # Output is a string
    filename = "%s%s.vcf" % (person.firstname, person.lastname)
    response = HttpResponse(output, mimetype="text/x-vCard")
    response['Content-Disposition'] = 'attachment; filename=%s' % filename
    return response
```

[Handwritten margin notes:]
Review Response Objects 125-6
Review JSON handling 216
create obj
Set content, mimetype
set header

The most significant bit here is the manipulation of the `HttpResponse` object to provide a non-HTML MIME type and a filename for the download. Rather than returning an `HttpResponse` directly, we first create the object, setting the content and MIME type. Then we set the response's `Content-Disposition` header to specify an attachment. Returning that response object at the end of our view sets the transaction in motion, and the user receives the generated file.

This technique shows off Django's excellent mix of high-level and low-level tools. The `HttpResponse` object makes it easy for us to leverage our knowledge of browsers, servers, and HTTP to customize the response we return—yet we don't need to think about any of the other parts of the response unless we want to.

This method can be used with any non-HTML file type you want to generate and deliver, as seen in the following examples.

Comma-Separated Value (CSV)

When it's time to get tabular data out of your application, nothing beats the CSV (comma-separated value) format as a lowest common denominator. Every programming language under the sun can deal with it, and virtually any application designed to work with structured data (Microsoft Excel, Filemaker Pro) can import and export it. Python's handy `csv` module is there to help you.

The first thing many programmers try to do when confronted with a CSV-related task is to write their own parser or generator. CSV is simple, after all, right? Just some commas and some numbers. Oh, and maybe some other characters. And maybe some quotation marks if there are commas in those characters. And maybe some escaping if there are quotation marks inside those quotation marks. This is getting complicated! Good thing somebody wrote a module to take care of it for us.

Let's say we have been charged with turning the `person` data from the previous vCard example into a simple spreadsheet with columns for first name, last name, and e-mail address. First, let's try it out in the interpreter to make sure we are using the `csv` module correctly. We use Python's handy `stringIO` module to capture the output because the `csv` module is designed to work with file-like objects. (`StringIO` provides a file-like interface to strings.)

```
>>> import csv, StringIO
>>> output = StringIO.StringIO()
>>> output_writer = csv.writer(output)
>>> people = [("Bob", "Dobbs", "bob@example.edu"),
```

[Handwritten margin notes:]
@ 246
"Dry run" using StringIO rather than file-like response obj

```
... ("Pat", "Patson", "pat@example.org"),
... ("O,RLY", "O'Reilly", "orly@example.com")]
>>> for p in people:
...     output_writer.writerow(p)
...
>>> print output.getvalue()          # retreive value written to stringID object
Bob,Dobbs,bob@example.edu
Pat,Patson,pat@example.org
"O,RLY",O'Reilly,orly@example.com
```

Looks good—it quoted the troublesome item that contained a comma. So, what does this look like as a Django view function? Very similar, thanks to the fact that Django's `HttpResponse` objects, like `StringIO` objects, are "file-like"—that is, they have the write method that `csv.writer` is looking for.

list of tuples : [(first, last, email), ...] (1)

```
def csv_file(request, people):
    import csv
    response = HttpResponse(mimetype="text/csv")
    response_writer = csv.writer(response)
    for p in people:
        response_writer.writerow(p)        wrch csv to response
    response['Content-Disposition'] = 'attachment; filename=everybody.csv'
    return response
```

(1) create python obj and a writer if necc
(2) set content type / mime type
(3) write response
(4) set header

@ 245

When a user makes a request that hits this view, an `HttpResponse` object is still returned—that's a requirement of all Django views, you recall—but instead of containing `text/html` content, it contains `text/csv` content, as well as a `Content-Disposition` header that, for most browsers, triggers a download rather than an attempt at in-browser display.

CSV is a handy answer to those inevitable "can we get our data out of Django and into application X" questions. Almost any program that works with structured data can read CSV.

Charts and Graphs Using PyCha

PyCha (http://www.lorenzogil.com/projects/pycha/) is a simple, elegant charting and graphing library for Python, based on the Cairo graphics system. PyCha doesn't try to accommodate every output format or configuration option under the sun, but it does have two strong points: a relatively Pythonic syntax and default output that actually looks quite pleasant.

As in the previous CSV example, the major tricks specific to Django are getting our output into a string so we can return it and setting the proper mime-type on our response.

```
def pie_chart(request):
    import sys, cairo, pycha.pie
    data = (
        ('Io on Eyedrops', 61),
```

```
        ('Haskell on Hovercrafts', 276),
        ('Lua on Linseed Oil', 99),
        ('Django', 1000),
        )
    dataset = [(item[0], [[0, item[1]]]) for item in data]
    surface = cairo.ImageSurface(cairo.FORMAT_ARGB32, 750, 450)
    ticks = [dict(v=i, label=d[0]) for i, d in enumerate(data)]
    options = {
        'axis': {'x': {'ticks': ticks}},
        'legend': {'hide': True}
    }
    chart = pycha.pie.PieChart(surface, options)
    chart.addDataset(dataset)
    chart.render()
    response = HttpResponse(mimetime="image/png")
    surface.write_to_png(response)
    response['Content-Disposition'] = 'attachment; filename=pie.png'
    return response
```

 # chart is drawn on the surface object (handwritten)

Write surface as png to response (handwritten)

The basic gist here is we've obtained a `surface` object, which is the primary drawing element in Cairo, and drawn our chart on it by passing it into the `pycha.pie.PieChart` constructor, and then calling the resulting chart's `render` function. Once this drawing has been taken care of, we use the surface's `write_to_png` method—which expects to write binary PNG data to a file-like object—and give it our response.

Therefore, at the end of the view function, our response is a PNG image, and we simply set its headers accordingly and return it so it gets sent to the browser, which downloads it.

Figure 11.2 is the resulting image.

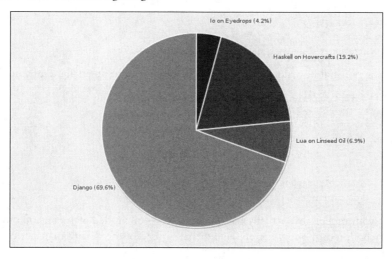

Figure 11.2   PyCha example chart

In a real view, of course, rather than hard-coding our data inside the view function, we would fetch it from our database using a Django ORM query. Depending on your application, you can even consider writing a custom template tag that took data from a certain QuerySet and rendered it into a PNG chart. This would also be an excellent place to use caching because generating graphics files on the fly is a bit resource-intensive.

also,
p 189

Enhancing Django's ORM with Custom Managers

Though Django's ORM system is not designed as a complete replacement for SQL, it's more than sufficient to power many Web applications. You've already learned how to supplement Django ORM queries by passing raw SQL commands via the extra method. However, custom **managers** give you another way. You've already used managers, even if you didn't know it, as in this code example:

model

```
really_good_posts = Post.objects.filter(gemlike=True)
```

Post.objects is a manager object. It's an instance of a class that inherits from models.Manager, and the methods of this class determine what you can do with a query-set—filtering, in the case of this example.

A custom manager is simply a class *you* define that also inherits from models.Manager. It can be useful in two distinct ways: changing the set of objects returned by default (normally all objects in the table) and adding new methods to manipulate that set of objects.

Changing the Default Set of Objects

Let's say instead of writing the previous query over and over, you would like to have a more concise way to tell Django you only want the "gem-like" posts from your database. Easy. Write a manager like this:

```
class GemManager(models.Manager):
    def get_query_set(self):
        superclass = super(GemManager, self)
        return superclass.get_query_set().filter(gemlike=True)
```

So far so good, but how do you use it? Simply assign it to be an attribute of your model.

```
class Post(models.Model):
    """My example Post class"""
    title = CharField(max_length=100)
    content = TextField()
    gemlike = BooleanField(default=False)

    objects = models.Manager()          # default manager
    gems = GemManager()                 # our new manager
```

@ 249

Notice your model now actually has *two* managers—one called objects and one called gems. They both return querysets; objects behaves just like the default manager of the same name.

@ 248

> **Note**
>
> Our definition of the `objects` manager here is exactly equivalent to the one Django normally creates for us automatically. We have to define it explicitly on this model because of the way Django behaves in the presence of additional managers—the first one it sees on the model becomes the default manager, which is used by the admin when selecting objects. If we omitted the `objects = models.Manager()` line, the admin wouldn't be able to show us the "non-gem-like" posts.

Having seen the code for the new manager `gems`, it's probably pretty apparent what it does. Via Python's `super` function, it calls the `get_query_set` method of the parent class (`models.Manager`), and then filters the result just like we were already doing before the custom manager.

How do we use it? Just as you'd expect—in the same way you use the default `objects` manager.

```
really_good_posts = Post.gems.all()
```

And of course, because your new custom manager returns a queryset, you can do further operations on it with `filter`, `exclude`, and other queryset methods.

Adding New Manager Methods

The custom manager we defined previously is useful syntactic sugar. That is, it makes what would otherwise be a fairly verbose query:

```
really_good_posts = Post.objects.filter(gemlike=True)
```

into something much more compact:

```
really_good_posts = Post.gems()
```

If we are working a lot with this set of objects, this would certainly make our code read better, but it isn't the whole story on custom managers. We can get even more power by adding custom methods to our custom manager class, enabling us to pass arguments for more flexibility.

Continuing our contrived example, let's imagine we want to be able to compactly specify a queryset containing only posts that mention a certain word in both the title and the content. We could specify this with normal Django syntax as follows:

```
cat_posts = Post.objects.filter(gemlike=True, title__contains="cats",
    content__contains="cats")
```

That's getting a little long, and if it's a type of query that we use repeatedly, we find ourselves wanting something a bit more compact, such as:

```
cat_posts = Post.objects.all_about("cats")
```

> **Note**
>
> One of the interesting challenges posed by creating custom classes and methods such as these is clear naming. Finding a good method name that reads well in the `Post.objects.foo` sort of chain is worth some effort; you (and anyone else who uses your

code) look at it often. As a rule of thumb, managers should be nouns ("objects," "gems"); manager methods should be verbs ("exclude," "filter") or adjectives ("all," "latest," "blessed").

Here's what the code behind such a manager method looks like:

```
class AllAboutManager(models.Manager):
    """Only return posts that are really good and all about X"""
    def all_about(self, text):
        posts = super(AllAboutManager, self).get_query_set().filter(
            gemlike=True,
            title__contains=text,
            content__contains=text)
        return posts
```

Strictly speaking, custom `Managers` don't give you any power you don't have without them. However, the clearer and less cluttered you can make the API of your model, the easier it is to write and maintain all the other code in your project that makes use of it.

Extending the Template System

Django's templates, which you learned about in Chapter 6, "Templates and Form Processing," embody a couple of deliberate design decisions that are not shared by all such systems. As we've mentioned, it's designed to produce all sorts of text, not just XML variants such as XHTML. This makes it useful for producing JavaScript, CSS, plain-text e-mail, and other text-based output.

Django templating also differs from some other systems in that it is not a reinvention of, or a wrapper around, a full-fledged programming language. This increases the speed of template processing, reduces the overall complexity of the framework, and keeps things simpler and cleaner for nonprogrammers who are designing pages.

For many projects, the built-in capabilities of the template system are fine. However, there can be times when you need or want it to do more. In this section, you learn how to create custom template tags and filters and even use third-party template systems in place of Django's provided one.

Simple Custom Template Tags

Let's say you want to display a randomly selected image on the front page of your site. With what you know already, you could do this fairly easily. In your view code, you build a list of image files. Then, using Python's `random.choice` function, you select one, and you pass that value to your template. The code for your view function can look something like this:

```
def home_view(request):
    img_files = os.listdir(settings.RANDOM_IMG_DIR)
    img_name = random.choice(img_files)
    img_src = os.path.join(settings.RANDOM_IMG_DIR, img_name)
```

```
    # ... other view processing goes here ...
    render_to_response("home.html", {'img_src': img_src})
```

(This code follows general good Django practice of keeping configuration values, such as RANDOM_IMG_DIR in your settings.py file, where they can be accessed by all your project's apps and changed easily if needed.)

Finally, in your template you have an image tag that used the value you had passed:

```
<img src="{{ img_src }}" />
```

That's all fine as far as it goes. But suppose you decide to include that random image on a *different* page, driven by a *different* view. Or your designer says, "Hey, I have five other places I could use that random image thing... except three of them would have to pull images from a different directory.... Can you do that?" Yes, you can!

The key is a feature called **custom template tags**. The same mechanisms Django uses to define its own template tags are also available to you as a programmer. That means you can create a simple tag that your designer can use. Even better, the tag can be made to take a path argument, so your designer can have his/her "special" cases, too.

The code for a tag like this is fairly simple, so we start with the implementation, and then work backward, explaining the details. The tag we end up with looks like this in use:

```
<img src="{% random_image "faces/thumbnails" %}" />
```

The name of the tag is random_image; the quoted string after the colon is a path name. We use a partial path that is assumed to be relative to MEDIA_ROOT. The Django template system takes care of parsing the argument and passing its value to your function (as template tags are just that—functions).

Here's the complete code that defines the tag. As always, it's up to us to import whatever modules we need to do our work. Most of this code is plain old Python; we focus our explanation on the Django-specific parts.

```
import os
import random
import posixpath
from django import template
from django.conf import settings

register = template.Library()

def files(path, types=[".jpg", ".jpeg", ".png", ".gif"]):
    fullpath = os.path.join(settings.MEDIA_ROOT, path)
    return [f for f in os.listdir(fullpath) if os.path.splitext(f)[1] in types]


@register.simple_tag
def random_image(path):
    pick = random.choice(files(path))
    return posixpath.join(settings.MEDIA_URL, path, pick)
```

The first new thing you have noticed is the `register = template.Library()` line. The `template.Library` instance gives us access to decorators that turn our simple functions into tags and filters that can be used by the template system. Although the name of the instance is arbitrary in the sense it could be called something else and still work, calling it `register` is a strongly encouraged and accepted Django convention which makes it easier for others to understand your code.

The `files` function is a simple helper that gives us a list of filenames whose extensions indicate they are images.

The `random_image` function is executed when our tag is used in a template, passing the path from the template tag. It gets a list of image filenames in the provided directory via `files`, chooses one, prepends your `MEDIA_URL` to make a path suitable for use in an img tag, and returns that path. (The use of `posixpath.join` here has nothing to do with POSIX paths; it's just a good function for joining URL pieces, making sure that we only end up with a single slash between them, and unlike `os.path.join`, it uses forward slashes even on Windows.)

If there's a magic line in this code, it's the `@register.simple_tag` decorator on the `random_image` function. This turns our simple function into something that can be used by the template engine.

Though we've only defined one tag here, the file we've created is actually a Django **tag library**, which can hold many tags. So save the file with a name that suits the library; for example, imagine we are going to add other random-content tags to this library, called `randomizers.py`.

The file needs to be saved in a directory called `templatetags` that is somewhere on the template system's search path. That is, either inside one of your INSTALLED_APPS (if you have `django.template.loaders.app_directories.load_template_source` listed in your `settings.TEMPLATE_LOADERS`), or inside one of the directories listed in your TEMPLATE_DIRS setting (if you have `django.template.loaders.filesystem.load_template_source` listed in your `settings.TEMPLATE_LOADERS`).

The `templatetags` directory is expected to be a Python package, which means you need to create an `__init__.py` file inside it—an empty one will do. If you forget to create that `__init__.py` file in your `templatetags` directory, you get an error, but not one that makes the problem obvious.

```
TemplateSyntaxError at /yourproject/
'randomizers' is not a valid tag library: Could not load template library
from django.templatetags.randomizers, No module named randomizers
```

So, if you get that error, create an empty `__init__.py` file in your `templatetags` directory. (If you want a refresher on why Python wants that file there, see the section on modules and packages in Chapter 1.)

With all that taken care of, your new tag is now ready for use by any applications in your project.

To make the new tag available for use in a given template, you use the template system's `load` tag at the top of the template where you are using the tag. The `load` tag takes
one argument, the module name of the library (no ".py").

```
{% load randomizers %}
```

Once the tag library is loaded into a template, the tags it defines are available in that
template as if they were a built-in part of Django. Your new `random_image` tag can take as
an argument either a literal string or a template variable. So, for example, you could determine in your view at runtime the specific directory from which random images are
drawn, and pass that to your template as `image_dir`. Then, your use of the `random_image`
tag can look like this:

```
<img src="{% random_image image_dir %}" />
```

It's also easy to define tags that take multiple arguments. The `simple_tag` decorator
and Django's template system take care of checking to see the number of arguments
passed is the same as the number expected.

Let's make a new random-image tag, based on the old one, which takes a second argument. Let's say we want to be able to specify exactly what file type (extension) is used. For
example, if our image directory has PNG, GIF, and JPEG images, we can specify we only
want to select from the PNGs.

Here's the new function to add to your `randomizers.py` file.

```
@register.simple_tag
def random_file(path, ext):
    pick = random.choice(files(path, ["." + ext]))
    return posixpath.join(settings.MEDIA_URL, path, pick)
```

The new tag is called `random_file`, and leverages the `files` function from the previous version. This new version simply adds a second argument, `ext`, and provides that (as a
one-item list and with the needed "." prepended) to the `files` function as its optional
second argument.

Our new template tag looks like this in use.

```
<img src="{% random_file "special/icons" "png" %}" />
```

For cases such as these where you want to provide template authors (including yourself) with a compact and readable way to generate values that would otherwise require
custom code in multiple view functions, simple custom template tags can be just what you
need. If you're already wanting something more complex, read on.

Inclusion Tags

Our previous example tags return simple strings. If you want a custom tag that returns
more complex content—a dynamic snippet of HTML for example—you can be tempted
to have your template tag function build and return that HTML. Don't do that. The principle of MVC (see Chapter 3, "Starting Out") means you should keep HTML in your

templates, not in your view functions; likewise, you should keep hardcoded HTML out of your template tag functions if possible.

To address this, you could write a `simple_tag` that used the template engine, but Django provides a more convenient and flexible option: **inclusion tags**.

Inclusion tags are most useful when you want to render a piece of content with some values from the current template context. For example, let's say your template has a variable called `{{ date }}` that contains the current date, and you'd like to have a template tag that renders a simple calendar for the current month.

Let's build that tag now. Our tag is based on Python's `calendar` module, which can give us the month as a list containing lists of day numbers (spots that lie before the beginning or after the month contain a 0).

```
>>> import calendar
>>> calendar.monthcalendar(2010, 7)
[[0, 0, 0, 1, 2, 3, 4], [5, 6, 7, 8, 9, 10, 11], [12, 13, 14, 15...
```

Now we just need a transformation that gives us a list where those zeroes have been turned into blanks—because we don't want the days before the beginning of the month or the days after the end of the month showing up as zeroes. We do this using a list comprehension on the values returned by `calendar.monthcalendar`.

```
>>> import calendar
>>> month = calendar.monthcalendar(2010, 7)
>>> [[day or '' for day in week] for week in month]
[['', '', '', 1, 2, 3, 4], [5, 6, 7, 8, 9, 10, 11], [12, 13, 14...
```

The slightly tricky list comprehension says go through every week in the month; for each week, go through every day; for each day, if it has a nonzero (Boolean `True`) value, use *that*; otherwise use the empty string.

Because Django's template engine doesn't care whether we pass it integers or strings, the motley assortment of data types doesn't cause us a problem. If we are passing this data to a Python function for further processing, the mix can give us pause.

The `calendar` module even provides us the names of the days and months.

```
>>> list(calendar.day_abbr)
['Mon', 'Tue', 'Wed', 'Thu', 'Fri', 'Sat', 'Sun']
>>> list(calendar.month_name)
['', 'January', 'February', 'March', 'April', 'May', 'June', 'July'...
```

In this age of CSS layouts, calendars are still tabular data, and so we generate the calendar HTML with table tags. Let's create a small template just for our calendar; we presume that the full list is passed in as `weeks`:

```
<table>
<tr><th colspan='7'>{{ month }} {{ year }}</th></tr>
<tr>{% for dayname in daynames %}<th>{{ dayname }}</th>{% endfor %}</tr>
{% for week in weeks %}
    <tr>
```

```
    {% for day in week %}
        <td>{{ day }}</td>
    {% endfor %}
    </tr>
{% endfor %}
</table>
```

Our preferred naming convention for partial templates, including templates such as this one that are used by inclusion tags, is to start their names with an underscore. This serves as a visual reminder that they are not intended to be full-fledged document skeletons. Call your template fragment _calendar.html and save it somewhere that the template system can find it, whether that's in your application's templates directory or in one of your TEMPLATE_DIRS.

Now for the actual inclusion tag function. Create this as a new file in your templatetags directory, calling it inclusion_tags.py.

```
@register.inclusion_tag("_calendar.html")
def calendar_table():
    import calendar
    import datetime
    date = datetime.date.today()
    month = calendar.monthcalendar(date.year, date.month)
    weeks = [[day or '' for day in week] for week in month]
    return {
        'month': calendar.month_name[date.month],
        'year': date.year,
        'weeks': weeks,
        'daynames': calendar.day_abbr,
    }
```

Notice our function returns a dictionary; this is provided as the context dict when rendering the template we provided in the call to @register.inclusion_tag. In other words, any key in this dictionary becomes a variable in the template that can be used to display the corresponding value.

Other than what we've described previously, there's nothing magical about inclusion tags. They exist to help you keep presentation separate from logic and to do so in a convenient way. You could create a tag via simple_tag that builds up and returns a big hunk of HTML, but that would be ugly to maintain. You could create a tag that made its own calls to the template engine, but that would be extra boilerplate. Inclusion tags enable you to write more compact code and keep template content in templates—where it belongs.

We add a quick-and-dirty stylesheet to our page just to dress up the calendar a bit. Place this code at the top of _calendar.html.

```
<style type="text/css">
td, th { padding: 4px; width: 30px; background: #bbb; }
td { text-align: right; }
</style>
```

When you want to use this tag, simply type {% load inclusion_tags %} at the top of the template in which you want to use it; when we use the tag, we just type a simple {% calendar_table %} at the spot where we want the calendar grid to appear.

The calendar grid, depending on our browser looks something like Figure 11.3.

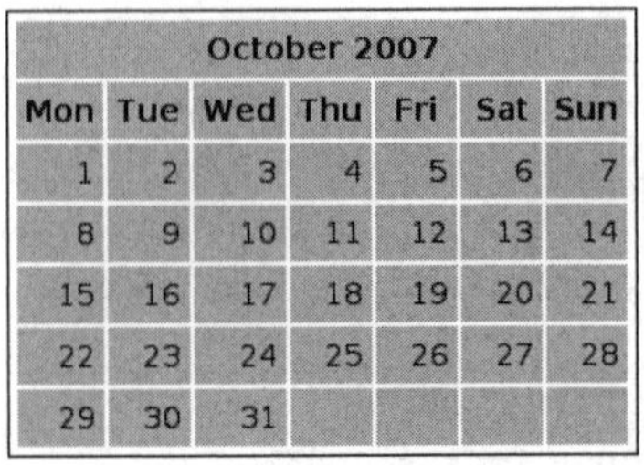

October 2007						
Mon	Tue	Wed	Thu	Fri	Sat	Sun
1	2	3	4	5	6	7
8	9	10	11	12	13	14
15	16	17	18	19	20	21
22	23	24	25	26	27	28
29	30	31				

Figure 11.3   Our calendar

Not bad! Because of the tidy separation of business logic from presentation, your designer can easily tweak the tag's template file. Meanwhile, you or other developers can make content changes, such as localizing the month and day names without having to touch the template (or any templates that include it) at all.

Custom Filters

Django's template system comes with a large number of very useful filters, but once in a while, there is reason to add your own. Filters are easy to use, and in fact, they're easy to write as well. Like the other tags you've seen so far, there's a convenient decorator syntax.

Filters are just functions—functions that, in most cases, accept strings and return strings. A fun example that isn't very complicated (or at least not very long—it can look a little hairy depending how you feel about regular expressions) is a wikify filter that turns words in **CamelCase** into HTML links suitable for use on a wiki. Here's the whole thing:

```
import re
from django.template import Library
from django.conf import settings

register = Library()
wikifier = re.compile(r'\b(([A-Z]+[a-z]+){2,})\b')

@register.filter
def wikify(text):
    return wikifier.sub(r'<a href="/wiki/\1/">\1</a>', text)
```

This tag expects a string; all occurrences of CamelCase words inside the string are replaced with links to /wiki/CamelCasedWord/. It can be used in a template such as this (presuming variables called `title` and `content` holding the page's title and wiki-markup content, respectively).

```
{% load wikitags %}
<h1>My Amazing Wiki Page: {{ title }}</h1>
<div class="wikicontent">
{{ content|wikify }}
</div>
```

Filters with an Extra Argument

The previous `wikify` function takes one argument; its value is the value of whatever expression appears in your template to the left of the " | " (pipe) character that precedes your filter name. But what if you also want the user of the filter to be able to adjust the action of that filter by passing an additional argument?

Filters can be written to take a second argument as well. Often this second argument is used to adjust the action of the filter. For example, let's say you want a function that displays a string only if that string contains a certain sequence of characters (think of this like the Unix command `grep`). You could accomplish this with `if/then` template tags, of course, but a filter would be much more compact.

```
{{ my_string|grep:"magic" }}
```

The definition of the filter looks like this:

```
@register.filter
def grep(text, term):
    if text.contains(term):
        return text
```

Arguments to filters are always quoted and separated from the filter name with a colon. Even when you are using it as a number or other nonstring data type, Django's template syntax requires that it be quoted. So if you made a filter designed only to print input text when it was longer than a certain number of letters, it can look like this in use.

```
{{ bla_bla_bla|hide_if_shorter_than:"100" }}
```

The implementation of a tag such as this needs to account for the type conversion to get its work done. So inside our filter we use the `int` function to do our conversion.

```
@register.filter
def hide_if_shorter_than(text, min_len):
    if len(text) >= int(min_len):
        return text
```

We convert the `min_len` argument to an `int` explicitly because it is passed to us as a string for the reason described previously.

Perhaps confusingly, the first argument that is passed to filter functions—the actual value that is being "filtered" or modified—is not restricted to being a string. You realize this must be true just from looking at the date- and time-related filters, which operate on

Python `datetime` objects. Along these lines, this means you can also make filters that operate on nonstring objects. It's unusually simple because so much of Web development is manipulation of string data, but it's possible.

If you know that your filter function can get passed some nonstring data, but you *want* to treat it as a string, there's a `stringvalue` decorator that you can add to your function. Multiple decorators can be applied to a single function, so if we decided to add this decorator to our `hide_if_shorter_than` function, we'd simply add `@stringvalue` on its own line underneath the `@register.filter` line.

> **Note**
>
> Order matters when applying decorators to a function. The order we mention previously—`@register.filter`, followed by `@stringvalue`, followed by the function itself—makes the input to the filter a string. Reversing that order to be `@stringvalue` followed by `@register.filter` would only ensure that the *output* of our filter is a string. A subtle, but important, distinction.

More Complex Custom Template Tags

More complex custom template tags are possible—for example, paired block-style tags that perform some transformation on the content they enclose. Creating tags such as these are complex, involving fairly direct manipulation of the internal machinery of the Django template engine. It's a lot more work than the previous simple decorators and not often needed. For details on advanced custom template tags, see the online Django documentation at www.djangoproject.com/documentation/templates_python.

Alternative Templating

The template engine's job in Django is to prepare strings that serve as the content of `HttpResponse` objects. Once you understand this, it's clear that if, for some reason, you decided you couldn't accomplish your goals using Django's provided template language, using a different template engine would not be major surgery.

Plain Text

Here's the simplest possible alternative templating mechanism for Django.

```
def simple_template_view(request, name):
    template = "Hello, your IP address is %s."
    return HttpResponse(template % request.META['REMOTE_ADDR'])
```

No third-party modules necessary—this view just uses Python's built-in string templating syntax.

Choosing an Alternative Templating Mechanism

Django gains a lot of strength from being a fairly integrated stack. However, it's not intended to be a monolith—if you want to replace a component of Django with a third-party package you like better, in most cases you can.

The template system is an especially handy place to be able to do this. Why would you want a different template system?

- You have come to Django from another system whose template syntax you prefer.
- You run other projects written in other Python Web frameworks, and you'd like to settle on a common templating language.
- You are converting a project from another Python Web framework and have existing templates you don't have time to translate.
- Your presentational logic requires features that can't easily be added to Django's template language.

Using Other Template Engines: Mako

One popular third-party template engine, and the one we use in this section, is **Mako**. It is quite different from the Django template language in appearance and design, but it does share some common virtues: It's extremely fast, it's not bound to XML-like languages, and it has a similar inheritance mechanism.

Mako replaces the Python templating framework called **Myghty**, which in turn was based on an influential system written in Perl called HTML::Mason. Mako has been used by sites such as reddit.com and python.org and is currently the default template engine of another Python web framework, Pylons. So if you're looking at alternative templating systems, Mako is a good place to start. Among its cited influences are the Django template system itself, so despite the syntactic differences, there is some conceptual overlap that makes going back and forth between the two systems easier than it could be otherwise.

Unlike Django templates, Mako's syntax is Python-based. This is a significant departure from the Django template philosophy, which strives to limit the amount of programming logic that makes its way into templates. Both approaches have their merits. The idea behind the Mako approach is that it is simple for Python programmers, while Python's clear syntax helps keep it accessible to template designers.

Before we build a Django view that uses Mako, here's a simple example in the interpreter to give you a feel for how Mako works.

```
>>> from mako.template import Template
>>> t = Template("My favorite ice cream is ${name}")
>>> t.render(name="Herrell's")
"My favorite ice cream is Herrell's"
>>> context = {'name': "Herrell's"}
>>> t.render(**context)
"My favorite ice cream is Herrell's"
```

In the first example, we explicity pass in the actual variable name, and in the second, we use a context as we have been doing throughout. Recall that context is simply a dictionary that we are passing to the render method. It should look very familiar—at this simple level, it's nearly identical to the way Django's template engine works.

Mako also has a filtering syntax that is much like Django's.

```
>>> from mako.template import Template
>>> t = Template("My favorite ice cream is ${name | entity}")
>>> t.render(name="Emack & Bolio's")
"My favorite ice cream is Emack & Bolio's"
```

Now let's wire up a Django view to use a Mako template.

```
from mako.template import Template


def mako_view(request):
    t = Template("Your IP address is ${REMOTE_ADDR}")
    output = t.render(**request.META)
    return HttpResponse(output)
```

In this view, we're doing the same thing we did in the previous interactive example—creating a new Mako template and rendering it with a context coming from the request's META object we saw briefly in Chapter 5, "URLs, HTTP Mechanisms, and Views."

If you are really going to use Mako, of course, you want to store your templates in the filesystem (or possibly in the database), have Django be able to find them just like it finds its own templates (without having to specify full paths), create a Mako-friendly render_to_response method, and so on. Luckily, much of this work has been done for you by other Django/Mako pioneers. There's some very helpful code posted on Django Snippets (http://www.djangosnippets.org/snippets/97/) and with the accompanying blog post linked from that page you should be off and running.

Summary

As mentioned in the introduction, this chapter has been all over the map, but we hope that we've opened some doors for you as a Django developer and made it more obvious how flexible and extensible the framework really is. The next chapter, Chapter 12, concludes Part IV of the book with another assortment of sections on advanced topics.

Advanced Django Deployment

As with Chapter 11, "Advanced Django Programming," this chapter consists of a handful of mostly unrelated sections on varied topics. Chapter 11 dealt with topics relating to your own application code; here, we go over topics that are a little more tangential and have to do with deploying your applications, updating the environment they run in, or modifying Django itself.

Writing Utility Scripts

Django is a Web framework, but that doesn't mean you can't interact with it outside of a browser. In fact, one of the great things about Django being written in Python, as opposed to a Web-specific language, such as ColdFusion or PHP, is that it's designed for use in a command-line environment. You can have periodic or ad-hoc operations you need to perform on the data managed by your Django application yet not have the need to create a full Web interface.

Some common use cases for Django-powered utility scripts include

- Creating cached values or documents that you rebuild every night (or every hour)
- Importing data into your Django models
- Sending out scheduled e-mail notifications
- Generating reports
- Performing cleanup tasks (for example, deleting stale sessions)

This is an aspect of using Django where solid Python skills are especially valuable. When you write a Django utility script, you're just writing Python with a small amount of environment setup required by Django.

The following are a few examples of Django utility scripts. We explain each one after showing the code, so you can determine what approach works best for your project.

Cronjobs for Cleanup

In SQLite (and some PostgreSQL) databases with significant churn—deletion of old records and adding of new records—a periodic "vacuum" operation is useful to reclaim unused space. On dpaste.com, for example, most entries stay in the database for a month and are then purged. This means that every week there is about 25 percent churn.

Without periodic vacuuming, the database would become gigantic. Even though SQLite claims to support database files up to 4GB in size, we'd rather not test that limit. The following is what the vacuuming script on dpaste.com looks like. It runs nightly under the control of cron. (If running on Windows-based systems, you have to create its automation as a "service.")

```python
import os
import sys
os.environ['DJANGO_SETTINGS_MODULE'] = "dpaste.settings"
from django.conf import settings

def vacuum_db():
    from django.db import connection
    cursor = connection.cursor()
    cursor.execute("VACUUM")
    connection.close()

if __name__ == "__main__":
    print "Vacuuming database..."
    before = os.stat(settings.DATABASE_NAME).st_size
    print "Size before: %s bytes" % before
    vacuum_db()
    after = os.stat(settings.DATABASE_NAME).st_size
    print "Size after: %s bytes" % after
    print "Reclaimed: %s bytes" % (before - after)
```

At the top of this script, after the first two imports, we do some manual setup of our environment—specifically, we set the all-important DJANGO_SETTINGS_MODULE environment variable so that Django knows which project we are working with.

This script assumes both Django itself and the parent directory of your project are on your Python path. They can be symlinked from site-packages, installed as Python eggs, or included in a PYTHONPATH environment variable. If you need to set them manually inside your script, you have extra lines such as these after the initial two import statements:

```python
sys.path.append('/YOUR/DJANGO/CODEBASE')
sys.path.append('/YOUR/DJANGO/PROJECTS')
```

Substitute your own paths, of course—the first one points to the directory where the Django source code lives on our system (like all Django pioneers we are of course running it from a fresh Subversion checkout); the second adds our project directory to `sys.path` so all our projects can be found by the various `import` statements that reference them.

The key thing to remember about writing Django-based utility scripts is that in the end it's just a Python script. As long as Python knows where to find Django and your project, and Django knows where to find your settings file, you're all set.

Data Import/Export

The command line is also a good place for tools that are used infrequently and not by end users. For example, if you periodically receive data that needs to be inserted into your database, you can write a Django utility script to handle that task.

Now, if your Django project is sitting on top of a SQL database, you can wonder why you would go through the seemingly indirect route of creating a Python/Django script to handle the import when you could instead just use SQL.

The answer is typically that your data needs to be converted or massaged in some way before being converted to SQL. The fact is, if you're going to import some foreign data format more than once or twice, it is less work to write a tool that works directly with the provided data format (CSV, XML, JSON, plain text, or what have you) instead of doing one-off search and replace operations in your text editor in an attempt to wrangle that data into a sequence of SQL `INSERT` statements.

This is an area where the "batteries included" aspect of Python—specifically the fact that it has libraries for parsing an incredibly wide variety of file formats—really pays off. For example, if you were building an e-mail archive and wanted to import a Unix-style "mbox" file, you could leverage Python's `email` module in the standard library rather than writing your own clever, but inevitably either labor-intensive or flawed (or both) parser.

The following is a simple model that can be used to store e-mail messages—in fact, it is very much like the model used on purportal.com for the "spammy scam" message archive.

```
class Message(models.Model):
    subject = models.CharField(max_length=250)
    date = models.DateField()
    body = models.TextField()
```

Assuming the presence of such a module and the presence of an mbox file whose path is given in your project's `settings.MAILBOX` setting, you can import mail into the model like this:

```
import os, mailbox, email, datetime
try:
    from email.utils import parsedate  # Python >= 2.5
except ImportError:
    from email.Utils import parsedate  # Python < 2.5

os.environ['DJANGO_SETTINGS_MODULE'] = "YOURPROJECT.settings"
from django.conf import settings
```

or YOURPROJECT.YOURAPP

```
from YOURAPP.models import Message

mbox = open(settings.MAILBOX, 'rb')
for message in mailbox.PortableUnixMailbox(mbox, email.message_from_file):
    date = datetime.datetime(*parsedate(message['date'])[:6])
    msg = Message(
        subject=message['subject'],
        date=date,
        body=message.get_payload(decode=False),
    )
    msg.save()

print "Archive now contains %s messages" % Message.objects.count()
# Depending on your application, you might clear the mbox now:
# open(MAILBOX, "w").write("")
```

As mentioned, this is only one small example of how to write scripts concerning your Django projects. Python's standard library—to say nothing of the collection of third-party libraries available—covers an enormous amount of ground. If you plan to become a serious Django developer, it is definitely worth your time to skim the Python "stdlib" (http://docs.python.org/lib/), so you have an idea of what's out there.

Customizing the Django Codebase Itself

Customizing the internal code of Django is a measure of last resort. Not because it's difficult—it's Python, after all, and it's a clean codebase with significant amounts of internal documentation in docstrings and comments. No, the reason we discourage you from leaping into Django internals to "fix" some problem you are having is that it's often not worth the effort.

Django is a project under active development. Because stability is prized, keeping up with the main line or "trunk" version of Django is a pretty safe prospect. As new features get added and old bugs get fixed, you can follow the reports on code.djangoproject.com and upgrade any time you're comfortable. However, if you've got your own customized version, you are effectively locking yourself out of upgrades to the trunk. Or, at best, you are setting yourself up for a great deal of work as you try to merge the new updates with your old changes. Distributed version control systems can make this easier if you must do it. (See Appendix C, "Tools for Practical Django Development," for more on that approach.)

Finally, if you find yourself irresistably drawn to hacking on the Django codebase itself, think about whether the change you are making for your own purposes can be effectively generalized so it would make a useful addition to the framework for others. If you think this is true, be sure to read "Contributing to the Django Project" in Appendix F, "Getting Involved in the Django Project."

Caching

High-traffic sites are rarely limited in their performance by how fast the Web server can send data. The bottleneck is almost always in the generation of that data; the database is not able to answer queries quickly enough, or the server's CPU can be bogged down executing the same code over and over for every request. The answer to this problem is caching—saving a copy of the generated data, so the relatively "expensive" database or computation steps don't have to be performed every time.

For high-traffic sites, caching is a must, no matter what back-end technology you use. Django has fairly extensive support for caching with three different levels of control depending on what works for your site architecture. It also provides a handy template tag that enables you to identify particular sections of rendered pages that should be cached.

A Basic Caching Recipe

Django's cache framework presents the first-time user with a potentially confusing number of possible configurations. Although the needs of every site (and the capabilities of every server) are different, you have a better handle on how to use this tool if we begin with a concrete example. As a bonus, it happens to be a configuration that's suitable for a large number of sites—so this can be all you need to know about caching in Django.

Get a Baseline

The entire point of caching is improving site performance, so it makes sense to make some measurements beforehand. Every site is different, and the only way you know the effect of caching on *your* site is to test it.

One widely available tool for doing basic server benchmarking is `ab`, the Apache benchmarking tool. If you have Apache installed, you have `ab` as well. On any POSIX-based system such as Linux or Mac OS X, it should already be available due to being on one of your paths. On a Windows-based system, it can be found where you've installed Apache, for example, `C:\Program Files\Apache Software Foundation\Apache2.2\bin`. (For more usage information, see its manual page at http://httpd.apache.org/docs/2.2/programs/ab.html.)

The way it works is you give it a URL and a number of requests to make, and it gives you performance statistics. Here's the output of running `ab` on our example blog app from Chapter 2, "Django for the Impatient: Building a Blog." The bottom line here, literally and figuratively, is the relative change in "requests per second." Don't think too much about the absolute numbers in our example because they're tied to the the particular three-year-old laptop we used to run this test—hopefully your server performance is better!

```
$ ab -n 1000 http://127.0.0.1:8000/blog/
...
Benchmarking 127.0.0.1 (be patient)
...
Finished 1000 requests
...
```

```
Time taken for tests:    27.724 seconds
...
Requests per second:    36.07 [#/sec] (mean)
```

So, about 36 requests per second. Now let's turn on caching and see what kind of difference it makes.

Add the Middleware

Django's caching features happen via a piece of middleware that is not active by default. To use it, open your `settings.py` file and add `django.middleware.cache.` `CacheMiddleware` to your `MIDDLEWARE_CLASSES` setting. In general, you want to add it at the end because certain other middleware (notably `SessionMiddleware` and `GZipMiddleware`) has the potential to interfere with the HTTP `Vary` header on which the caching framework depends.

Set the Cache Type

The caching framework offers no less than *four* cache data storage mechanisms or backends. To keep things simple for now we use Django's default cache backend, a local-memory cache called `locmem`. It stores cached data in RAM, which makes retrieval instantaneous. Though many caching solutions store the cache on disk, an in-memory cache can give great performance benefits. (If you're skeptical, see the following for discussion of Memcached, an extremely high-performance cache originally designed to support LiveJournal.com.)

Add this line to your `settings.py`:

```
CACHE_BACKEND = "locmem://"
```

(The peculiar, pseudo-URL style of this setting makes more sense when you've seen some of the other backends, which use the URL format to encapsulate configuration arguments. Because it's the default backend, strictly speaking we don't need to set it unless we want something different. However, as Python lore says, "Explicit is better than implicit," and switching backends or adding some of the configuration parameters outlined next is simpler if you have this setting in place.)

Try It Out

That's all it takes to turn on basic, site-wide caching in Django. Now let's see how our new, cache-enabled site performs.

```
$ ab -n 1000 http://127.0.0.1:8000/blog/
...
Benchmarking 127.0.0.1 (be patient)
...
Finished 1000 requests
...
Time taken for tests:    8.750 seconds
```

```
. . .
Requests per second:     114.29 [#/sec] (mean)
```

That's more than *three times* faster, and all it took was two lines of code in our
settings.py. Also, keep in mind that our blog app is very lightweight in terms of database queries and business logic; you can generally expect the improvement to be much
greater for more complicated apps.

Caching Strategies

Though the results we got with the previous simplest possible cache implementation are
impressive, they aren't suitable for all situations. We haven't addressed specifying how *long*
cached items should live, the caching of content that is not a full Web page (for example,
complex sidebars or widgets), what to do about pages that need to be exempt from
caching (admin pages, for example), or what arguments are available for performance tun-
ing. Let's talk about some of them now.

Site-wide

What we enabled previously is known as the **site-wide** caching feature. Django simply
caches the result of all requests that don't involve GET or POST arguments. We've gone
through the simplest possible usage, but there are a few other settings.py settings to
help you tune it.

- CACHE_MIDDLEWARE_SECONDS: The number of seconds that a cached page should be
  used before being replaced by a fresh copy. The default value for this setting is 600
  (ten minutes).

- CACHE_MIDDLEWARE_KEY_PREFIX: A string that is used to prefix keys to items in the
  cache. If you are sharing a cache across several Django sites, whether in memory,
  files, or a database, this ensures no key collisions occur across site boundaries. You
  can use any unique string for these settings—the site's domain name or
  str(settings.SITE_ID) are both sensible choices.

- CACHE_MIDDLEWARE_ANONYMOUS_ONLY: Simple URL-based caching doesn't always
  play nicely with interactive Web applications, where the content at a given URL
  can change frequently in response to user input. Even if the public side of your site
  doesn't involve user-created content—if you're using the Django admin app—you
  want to set this setting to True to make sure that your changes (additions, deletions,
  edits) are instantly reflected in the pages of the admin site.

If Django's page caching works for your needs, then the previous information is as
much as you need to know. However, it's not suitable for all situations. Let's see what
other, more granular options Django offers for caching and when you can take advantage
of them.

The Per-view Cache

The site-wide cache assumes every part of your site should be cached for the same amount of time. However, you can have other ideas. For instance, let's say you run a news site and track the popularity of individual stories, aggregating those statistics to generate lists of the most popular pages. A "Yesterday's Top Stories" list can clearly be cached for 24 hours. "Today's Top Stories," on the other hand, changes over the course of the day. To strike a balance between keeping the content fresh and the server load reasonable, we might want that page to be cached for only five minutes.

Presuming those two lists are generated by two separate views, turning on caching is as simple as applying a decorator.

```
from django.views.decorators.cache import cache_page
```

```
@cache_page(24 * 60 * 60)
def top_stories_yesterday(request):
    # ... retrieve stories and return HttpResponse
```

```
@cache_page(5 * 60)
def top_stories_today(request):
    # ... retrieve stories and return HttpResponse
```

The cache_page decorator takes a single argument, the number of seconds that the page should be cached. That's it; there's nothing else you have to do to make this work.

The per-view decorators depend on the fact that all Django views accept an HttpRequest object and return an HttpResponse object. They use the former to learn what URL was requested; the cached data is stored key-value style with the URL as the key. They use the latter to set appropriate cache-related headers on the HTTP response.

Controlling Cache-Related Headers

Up until this point in our coverage of caching, we've focused on what *you* do on *your* server to determine how often cached content is regenerated. In practice, caching is a conversation between your server and the clients that connect to it (including external cache servers that you might not have control over). This conversation is shaped by special headers, called "cache-control" headers, that you can pass along in your HTTP responses.

The most basic form of additional cache control Django gives you is a "never cache" decorator.

```
from django.views.decorators.cache import never_cache
```

```
@never_cache
def top_stories_this_second(request):
    # ... we don't want anybody caching this
```

This instructs downstream recipients of your page that it is not to be cached. As long as they abide by that standard (RFC 2616), it won't be. The never_cache decorator is actually a wrapper around a more powerful and flexible caching-related tool that Django offers: `django.views.decorators.cache.cache_control`.

The `cache_control` decorator modifies the `Cache-control` header of your `HttpResponse` to communicate your caching policies to Web clients and downstream caches. You can pass the decorator any of six boolean settings (`public`, `private`, `no_cache`, `no_transform`, `must_revalidate`, `proxy_revalidate`) and two integer settings (`max_age`, `s_maxage`).

For example, if you want to force clients and downstream caches to "revalidate" your page—to check whether it has been modified, even if the cached version they are holding has not yet expired—you can decorate your view function such as:

```
from django.views.decorators.cache import cache_control


@cache_control(must_revalidate=True)
def revalidate_me(request):
    # ...
```

Most sites are unlikely to need many, if any, of the fine-grained options provided by the `cache_control` decorator. But if you do need them, it's nice to have this functionality available rather than having to manually alter the headers of the `HttpResponse` object yourself.

Django also gives you control over the `Vary` HTTP header. Normally, content is cached using just the URL as the key. However, you can have other factors that affect what content is returned for a specific URL—logged-in users, for example, can see a different page than anonymous ones, or the response can be customized based on the user's browser type or language setting. All those factors are communicated to your server via HTTP headers in the page request. The "Vary" response header lets you specify exactly which of those headers have an effect on the content.

For example, if you are sending different content from the same URL depending on what the request's `Accept-Language` header says, you can tell Django's caching mechanism to consider that header as well.

```
from django.views.decorators.vary import vary_on_headers


@vary_on_headers("Accept-Language")
def localized_view(request):
    # ...
```

Because varying on the "Cookie" header is a common case, there's also a simple `vary_on_cookie` decorator for convenience.

The Object Cache

The previous caching options focus on caching *pages*—every page on your site in the case of the site-wide cache and individual pages (views) in the case of the per-view cache.

These solutions are extremely simple to implement. However, in some situations you can leverage this caching infrastructure directly to store individual chunks of data.

Let's say you're running a busy site and have an information box on many pages as the result of some expensive process—for example, it can be the result of processing a large file that is periodically updated. Your pages are otherwise relatively quick to generate, and this generated information is displayed on many pages, and then it makes sense to use object caching.

Django's object cache—really just a simple key/value store in which you can assign expiration times—enables you to save and retrieve arbitrary objects, so you can focus on the ones you know to be resource-intensive. Here's some code based on our imaginary example with no caching yet.

```
def stats_from_log(request, stat_name):
    logfile = file("/var/log/imaginary.log")
    stat_list = [line for line in logfile if line.startswith(stat_name)]
    # ... go on to render a template which  display stat_list
```

Now, although that list comprehension in line 3 might be slick, it's not going to be particularly speedy on a large log file. What we want to do is insulate ourselves from having to assemble `stat_list` on every request. Our primary tools for solving this is the `cache.get` and `cache.set` methods from `django.core.cache`.

```
from django.core.cache import cache
```

```
def stats_from_log(request, stat_name):
    stat_list = cache.get(stat_name)
    if stat_list == None:
        logfile = file("/var/log/imaginary.log")
        stat_list = [line for line in logfile if line.startswith(stat_name)]
        cache.set(stat_name, stat_list, 60)
    # ... go on to render a template which  display stat_list
```

The `cache.get` call returns any cached value (object) for the given key—until that object expires at which point `cache.get` returns `None`, and the item is deleted from the cache.

The `cache.set` method takes a key (a string), a value (any value that Python's `pickle` module can handle), and an optional time to expiration (in seconds). If you omit the expiration argument, the timeout value from the CACHE_BACKEND setting is used. See the following for details on CACHE_BACKEND.

There's also a `get_many` method, which takes a list of keys and returns a dictionary mapping of those keys to their (possibly still-cached) values. One final note in case you didn't notice: The object cache does *not* depend on Django's caching middleware—we merely imported `django.core.cache` and didn't ask you to change any settings or add any middleware.

The cache Template Tag

Django provides one final caching option: the `cache` template tag. It provides a way to use the object cache from the template side without having to alter your view code. Although some developers do not like the idea of an optimization artifact such as caching appearing in the presentation layer, others find it expedient.

For the sake of example, let's say we have a template that displays information on a long list of items and that the process of generating that information is somewhat resource-intensive. Let's also say the page as a whole, outside this list, changes on every page load, so simple caching of the entire thing is of no benefit, and that the long list only needs to be updated every five minutes at most. Because the "expensiveness" of the list output is a combination of our display loop and the expensive method call inside the loop, there is not a single point of attack in our view or model code where we can solve this. With the `cache` template tag, though, we can apply caching right where we need it.

```
{% load cache %}
... Various uncached parts of the page ...
{% cache 300 list_of_stuff %}
    {% for item in really_long_list_of_items %}
        {{ item.do_expensive_rendering_step }}
    {% endfor %}
{% endcache %}
... Other uncached parts ...
```

The entire previous output of the `for` loop is cached. The cache tag takes two arguments: the length of time the content should be cached, in seconds, and a cache key for the content.

In certain cases, a static key for the content isn't sufficient. For example, if your site is localized and the rendered data is specific to a the current user's language preference, you want the cache key to reflect that fact. Luckily, the `cache` tag has an optional third parameter designed for this sort of situation. This parameter is the name of a template variable to be combined with the static key name (`list_of_stuff` in the previous example) to create the key.

To accommodate the fact that the contents of `list_of_stuff` is different for each language, your `cache` tag can look like this:

```
{% cache 300 list_of_stuff LANGUAGE_CODE %}
```

> **Note**
>
> This last example assumes you are passing `RequestContext` to your templates, which adds extra variables to your template context based on your context processor settings. The `django.core.context_processors.i18n` internationalization is activated by default and provides the `LANGUAGE_CODE` variable. See Chapter 6, "Templates and Form Processing," for more on context processors.

Caching Backend Types

In your previous introduction to Django caching, you were introduced to the "locmem" cache type. Here is the full list:

- `dummy`: For development only; actually performs no caching, but enables you to leave your other cache settings intact, so they work correctly with the cache on your live site (which uses one of the following nondevelopment backend types).
- `locmem`: A reliable in-memory cache that is multiprocess safe. This is the default.
- `file`: A filesystem cache.
- `db`: A database cache (requires creating a special table in your database).
- `memcached`: A high performance, distributed, in-memory cache; the most powerful option.

The `CACHE_BACKEND` setting takes a URL-style argument, beginning with the cache type followed by a colon and two slashes (three in the case of `file`). The development backends, `dummy` and `locmem`, take no further arguments. Configuration of the `file`, `db`, and `memcached` backends is described next.

The `CACHE_BACKEND` setting also takes three optional arguments.

- `max_entries`: The maximum number of unique entries the cache stores; the default is 300. Remember, it's likely that a relatively small number of items account for the bulk of the load of the server, so the cache doesn't have to store *everything* to make an improvement. And because of the way expiry works, the cache tends to be dominated by frequently used items. If you have very little RAM or very large objects in the cache, reduce this value; if you have lots of RAM or are storing tiny objects, you can increase it.
- `cull_percentage`: Poorly named, this argument is not a percentage; it specifies what portion of the entries in the cache are removed when the `max_entries` limit is reached. It defaults to 3, meaning the oldest 1/3 of the cache's entries is deleted each time the cache becomes full.
- `timeout`: The length of time cached content should live, in seconds; the default is 300 (five minutes). This number is used not only in determining when something should be deleted from the cache, but also in creating the various headers that tell Web clients about the cache-ability of the content you are sending.

These arguments are specified URL-argument style, such as this:

```
CACHE_BACKEND = "locmem://?max_entries=1000&cull_percentage=4&timeout=60"
```

That tells Django to use the local-memory cache, to keep 1000 entries, remove 1/4 of them when the cache becomes full, and set the expiry of cached items to 60 seconds after their creation time.

File

All that the `file` backend requires is a directory that is writable by the Web server process. Remember to use three slashes after the colon; the first two mark the end of the URL's "scheme" portion, although the third indicates the path is absolute (that is it starts at the root of the filesystem). Like other file settings in Django, use forward slashes here, even on Windows.

```
CACHE_BACKEND = "file:///var/cache/django/mysite"
```

Of course, on a Windows-based system, it looks more like this:

```
CACHE_BACKEND = "file:///C:/py/django/mysite/cache"
```

Database

To use the database cache backend, you need to make sure you have the cache table set up in your database. The command to do this is

```
$ python manage.py createcachetable cache
```

The last argument is the table name; we recommend simply calling it `cache` as we have next, but you can call it whatever you like. Once you've set up the table, your `CACHE_BACKEND` setting becomes

```
CACHE_BACKEND = "db://cache/"
```

This is a very simple table with only three columns: `cache_key` (the table's primary key), `value` (the actual data being cached), and `expires` (a `datetime` field; Django sets an index on this column for speed).

Memcached

Memcached is the most powerful caching option that Django provides. Not surprisingly, it is also more complicated to set up than the others. But if you need it, it's worth it. It was originally created at Livejournal.com to ease the load that 20 million page views per day were putting on their database servers. It has since been adopted at Wikipedia.org, Fotolog.com, Slashdot.org, and other busy sites. Memcached's home page is located at http://danga.com/memcached.

The major advantage Memcached offers over the other options listed here is easy distribution across multiple servers. Memcached is a "giant hash table in the sky"; you use it like a key-value mapping such as a Python dictionary, but it transparently spreads the data across as many servers as you give it.

Even though Memcached is much more heavy-duty than the other caching options presented here, it's still just a cache and a memory-based one at that. It's not an object database. One Memcached FAQ answers questions like "How is memcached redundant?" and "How does memcached handle failover?" and "How can you dump data from or load data into memcached?" with the answers "It's not, it doesn't. and you don't!" Your reliable, persistent store of data is your database; Memcached just makes it fast. (For a great deal of

fascinating detail about the creation and architecture of Memcached, see this article at
http://www.linuxjournal.com/article/7451.)

You need two things to run Memcached: the software itself and the Python bindings
that Django uses to talk to Memcached. You should be able to easily find a package for your
Linux distribution or check Darwin Ports or Macports for your Mac OS X system. A
Windows-based memcached can be found at http://splinedancer.com/memcached-win32.

Next, on the server where your Django app is running, you need to give Python the
capability to talk to memcached. You can do this either with the pure-Python client
`python-memcached` (http://tummy.com/Community/software/python-memcached) or a
faster version called `cmemcache` that relies on a C library (http://gijsbert.org/
cmemcache/). `python-memcached` is also available via Easy Install for mindless installation
and setup.

Set up your server so it automatically starts the memcached daemon on bootup. The
daemon has no configuration file. The following line tells memcached to start up in daemon mode, using 2GB of RAM, listening on IP address 10.0.1.1:

```
$ memcached -d -m 2048 -l 10.0.1.1
```

If you're curious about the full spate of command line options for memcached, check
its manual page or other documentation. On POSIX-based systems, you put this command in the operating system startup scripts, while on Windows-based systems, you have
to set it up as a service.

Now that you have your memcached daemon running, tell Django to use it via the
`CACHE_BACKEND` setting.

```
CACHE_BACKEND = "memcached://10.0.1.1:11211"
```

Django requires us to specify a port; by default, Memcached uses port 11211, and
because we didn't specify a port on our previous command line, that's the port our
Memcached server is listening on. If you're using multiple servers, separate them by
semicolons.

```
CACHE_BACKEND = "memcached://10.0.1.1:11211;10.0.5.5:11211"
```

Finally, although Memcached takes a bit more setup than the other backends, it is still
just that—a backend—and thus it behaves identically to the rest once it's installed properly.

Testing Django Applications

It has become an uncontested point that having an automated test suite for your application is a good thing. This is especially true in dynamically typed languages, such as Python,
which don't offer the safety net of compile-time type checking.

> **Note**
>
> This chapter presumes you already have caught the testing religion and focuses on the *how*
> rather than the *why*. If you feel like you could use more convincing, though, please see our
> additional reading and resources at withdjango.com.

Python is blessed with excellent testing support in the form of two complementary modules—doctest and unittest—as well as a number of popular independent tools. This chapter, like Django itself, focuses on the two built-in systems, but if you are curious about the wider world of Python testing you can learn more at the previous URL.

The bad news is testing Web applications is hard. They are inherently untidy with all kinds of real-world interactions such as database connections, HTTP requests and responses, e-mail generation, and so on. The *good* news is Django's testing support makes it relatively easy to incorporate testing into your project. Before getting into the specifics of Django's testing support, let's review the Python foundations on which it's built.

Doctest Basics

A doctest is simply a copy of an interactive Python session included in the **docstring** of a module, class, or function. We then use the doctest module's test runner to discover, execute, and verify these tests. For a review of docstrings and their uses, see Chapter 1, "Practical Python for Django."

For example, here's a simplistic function we can easily write a test for.

```
def double(x):
    return x * 2
```

If we were testing this function manually in the interpreter, we can type something such as this:

```
>>> double(2)
4
```

We get the expected result, and declare the function has passed. To add the doctest to the function, we copy the literal text of that interactive session into the function's docstring.

```
def double(x):
    """
    >>> double(2)
    4
    """
    return x * 2
```

When this function is tested by the doctest module's test runner, the command double(2) is executed. If its output is "4," all is well. If it's not, a report is issued.

The test runner is smart enough to skip over nontest text, too (such as regular old documentation text not prefixed by or immediately following >>>), so we can add a more human-readable introduction.

```
def double(x):
    """
    This function should double the provided number. We hope.
    >>> double(2)
    4
    """
    return x * 2
```

Unittest Basics

The `unittest` module complements `doctest` with a different approach. It is an adaptation of the JUnit testing framework for Java, which in turn took its inspiration from the original unit testing work done in Smalltalk. Typical use of plain old `unittest` tests in Python looks something like this:

```
import unittest

class IntegerArithmeticTestCase(unittest.TestCase):
    def testAdd(self):
        self.assertEquals(1 + 2, 3)
    def testMultiply(self):
        self.assertEquals(5 * 8, 40)

if __name__ == '__main__':
    unittest.main()
```

This example is a complete script; when executed on its own, it runs its test suite. This happens via the `unittest.main()` call, which searches for all subclasses of `unittest.TestCase` and calls any methods beginning with `test`.

Running Tests

Django tests can be run with the following command:

```
./manage.py test
```

Django automatically detects tests (of either kind) in the `models.py` files of all applications listed in your `INSTALLED_APPS` setting. You have the option of narrowing these choices with additional arguments to the `test` command specifying an individual app or even a specific model within an app, for example, `manage.py test blog` or `manage.py test blog.Post`.

Additionally, the `test` command looks for unit tests in any files named `test.py` that live within app subdirectories (at the same level as your `models.py`). Therefore, you can keep your unit tests in either or both locations—whatever suits you best.

Testing Models

Models are typically tested with doctests because Django looks for these in each of your installed apps' models when you run the `manage.py test` command. If you have a basic model that consists solely of data fields, you don't have much to test. Your model in this case is a simple declarative representation of your data with the actual logic being handled by Django's well-tested internals. As soon as you begin adding model methods, however, you are introducing logic that needs testing.

For example, let's say you have a `Person` model that includes a birthdate field, and you have a model method to calculate the person's age as of a certain date. That code can look something like this:

```
from django.db import models

class Person(models.Model):
    first = models.CharField(max_length=100)
    last = models.CharField(max_length=100)
    birthdate = models.DateField()

    def __unicode__(self):
        return "%s %s" % (self.first, self.last)

    def age_on_date(self, date):
        if date < self.birthdate:
            return 0
        return (date - self.birthdate).days / 365
```

Code, such as our `age_on_date` method, is notorious for susceptibility to "fencepost" errors, where boundary conditions (for example, testing on the person's birthday) can yield incorrect results. Using doctests, we can guard against these and other errors.

If we were going to manually test our age method, we would run the Python interpreter, creating example objects and performing method calls, such as:

```
>>> from datetime import date
>>> p = Person(firstname="Jeff", lastname="Forcier", city="Jersey City",
... state="NJ", birthdate=date(1982, 7, 15))
>>> p.age_on_date(date(2008, 8, 10))
26
>>> p.age_on_date(date(1950, 1, 1))
0
>>> p.age_on_date(p.birthdate)
0
```

Of course, as you can surmise from what you already know about doctests, we can simply lift this straight out of the interactive session and place it into the docstring for the `age_on_date` method, so the method looks like this:

```
def age_on_date(self, date):
    """
    Returns integer specifying person's age in years on date given.

    >>> from datetime import date
    >>> p = Person(firstname="Jeff", lastname="Forcier",
    ... city="Jersey City", state="NJ", birthdate=date(1982, 7, 15))
    >>> p.age_on_date(date(2008, 8, 10))
    26
```

```
>>> p.age_on_date(date(1950, 1, 1))
0
>>> p.age_on_date(p.birthdate)
0
"""
if date < self.birthdate:
    return 0
return (date - self.birthdate).days / 365
```

Finally, we can use the aforementioned `manage.py` command to execute our test:

```
user/opt/code/myproject $ ./manage.py test myapp
Creating test database...
Creating table auth_permission
Creating table auth_group
Creating table auth_user
Creating table auth_message
Creating table django_content_type
Creating table django_session
Creating table django_site
Creating table django_admin_log
Creating table myapp_person
Installing index for auth.Permission model
Installing index for auth.Message model
Installing index for admin.LogEntry model
.
- - - - - - - - - - - - - - - - - - - - - - - - - - - - - - - - - - - - -
Ran 1 test in 0.003s

OK
Destroying test database...
```

A lot of output for one little test, of course, but once your entire model hierarchy is fully tested, you get a nice line or two of periods with the occasional E or F when unexpected errors or test failures occur.

Finally, note that although doctests probably fulfill your needs most of the time, don't hesitate to set up model-related unit tests when more complex business logic or inter-model relationships come into the picture. If you're new to the world of testing, it takes time to figure out what to use when—but don't give up!

Testing Your Entire Web App

Testing your web application from top to bottom is by no means an easy task and cannot be 100 percent automated using the same test scripts as every Web app is surely different. However, there are several tools out there that have proven quite useful.

The first one you should check out is built into Django itself and at the time of writing was quite new. It's simply referred to as "the Django test client" and is documented on

the official Django Web site http://www.djangoproject.com/documentation/testing/
#testing-tools. The test client offers an easy way to mock up a typical request-response
cycle and tests certain conditions throughout.

When you find you need more control than the built-in test client gives you, it can be
time to move up to an older and more featureful tool called Twill, found at http://twill.
idyll.org/. Like Django's test client, it's fully command-line based and is designed to be
easy-to-use but still powerful—your typical Pythonic library.

Another test tool, one making waves more recently, is Selenium (see http://selenium.
openqa.org/). Unlike the other two, it's an HTML/JavaScript-based test tool created
specifically for testing Web applications from a truly browser-based perspective. It supports
most major browsers on most platforms, and because it's JavaScript-based, can test Ajax
functionality as well. The application codebase is compartmentalized into 2.5 to 3 distinct
modes of operation: Selenium Core, Selenium RC (Remote Control), and Selenium IDE
(Integrated Development Environment).

Selenium Core (http://selenium-core.openqa.org/) represents the heart of the (manual and automated) testing of Web applications. Some people refer to it as running Selenium in "bot mode." It's the workhorse. The core can also perform browser compatibility
tests in addition to your Web app's system functional testing.

Selenium RC (http://selenium-rc.openqa.org/) gives its users the ability to create
full-fledged automated tests in a variety of programming languages. You write your test
apps; they are run by Selenium Core—you can think of it as a scripting layer that sits on
top of the Core, a "code mode" if you will.

A great tool to get started with Selenium is the IDE (see http://selenium-ide.openqa.
org/). It's written as a Firefox extension and is a full IDE that enables you to record and
play back Web sessions as tests. It can also output tests in any of the languages supported
by Selenium RC, so you can further enhance or modify those tests. You can set break-
points as well as single-step through tests. Because it's written on Firefox, one common
FAQ is whether it exists for Internet Explorer (IE). The answer is no; however, the
"record mode" of the IDE enables you to run them on IE via Selenium Core.

Aside from these three tools—the Django test client, Twill, and Selenium, you can find
more reading on Web application testing at http://www.awaretek.com/tutorials.
html#test and by following links found therein.

Testing the Django Codebase Itself

The Django framework itself has an extensive test suite. Every bugfix is generally accompanied by a **regression test** that ensures the bug doesn't resurface unnoticed. New functionality is also typically accompanied by tests that ensure it works as intended.

You can run these tests yourself. This can be especially useful if you are having trouble
running Django on a little-used platform or in an unusual configuration. Although it's
always wise to check your own code first, it's possible you have uncovered an unusual bug

that hasn't been seen before. A failing test or tests in the built-in suite enables you to create a bug report that is taken much more seriously.

Running Django's test suite is easy with one minor hurdle: It needs to be pointed to a settings file, so it knows how to create its test database. This can be the settings file of any active project, or you can create a dummy project (that is one with no apps) and fill out only the DATABASE_* settings in the settings.py file.

The test runner is at the top level of the installed Django directory in a directory called tests. (This is not to be confused with the test package that is part of the overall Django package.) Invoking the command looks like this:

```
$ tests/runtests.py  -settings=mydummyproject.settings
```

This is a pretty quiet process because tests are only supposed to produce output if they fail. Because the test suite can take a while to run, you can see more feedback about the tests in progress. The runtests.py command takes a -v verbosity argument. At -v1 the process begins with output such as this:

```
.................................................E...EE...
```

The E characters indicate tests producing an error; this summary is followed by output that details the nature of those failures, so you can determine if it's an artifact of your setup or an actual problem in Django.

At verbosity -v2 the output begins with a long list of imports, followed by messages detailing the creation of the test database and its tables (the "..." in the following example represent lines removed from the actual output for brevity).

```
Importing model basic
Importing model choices
Importing model custom_columns
Importing model custom_managers
Importing model custom_methods
Importing model custom_pk
Importing model empty
...
Creating test database...
Processing contenttypes.ContentType model
Creating table django_content_type
Processing auth.Message model
Creating table auth_message
Processing auth.Group model
Creating table auth_group
Processing auth.User model
Creating table auth_user
...
```

Seeing an indicated failure when running the test suite doesn't necessarily mean you have found something wrong with Django—if you're unsure, a good first step is to post to the Django-users mailing list with your configuration details and failed test output.

Summary

This chapter covered a number of advanced topics, and together with Chapter 11, we hope it's given you a good overview of the kind of depth you can go into when it comes to Django development. These topics are only a sample of what's possible, of course: Web application development, like most other computer-based disciplines, is not self-contained but branches out into many other general areas, much like Python itself, which is capable of handling a wide variety of situations and technologies.

At this point, you're just about done with our book—congratulations! The appendices are all that's left, although they—like these last two chapters—are still important parts of the book, covering a number of different subjects from command-line usage and installing and deploying Django to a list of external resources and development tools.

Finally, you might find it useful to go back and reread (or at least skim) the earlier parts of the book; now that you've seen just about all the topics we've wanted to cover, the earlier code examples and explanations can give you additional insight. This is true of any technical book, of course, not just this one.

V

Appendices

Appendix A
Command Line Basics

The vast majority of Web servers (not to mention e-mail servers, file servers, and so forth) run on POSIX-compliant operating systems such as Linux, FreeBSD, or other Unix variants, and Django-based Web servers are no exception; most of the core Django team and a large portion of the community run the framework on such machines. If you haven't previously been exposed to the command-line interfaces common in such environments, this appendix gives you a basic overview, so the examples in the rest of the book make more sense.

For those of you in the Windows world, this appendix may not have a lot of immediately applicable knowledge, but we suggest you give it a read (or at least a skim) anyway—chances are very good that you find yourself in a position to make use of it in the future. In addition, it's a general consensus that the more programming languages, platforms, and techniques programmers are exposed to, the better they are able to utilize both the new tools and the tools they're currently familiar with.

If you want to practice any of these commands in a Windows-based system, we would suggest Cygwin, a Linux-like environment for Windows. It consists of an emulation layer as well as a set of command-line tools familiar to Unix users, some of which are featured throughout this appendix. What it *isn't* meant to do, however, is to turn your PC into a server. You can find out more information about Cygwin as well as download it at http://cygwin.com.

If you are a Mac user, you are in luck. Mac OS X is derived from one of the offshoots of BSD (Berkeley Software Distribution) Unix, giving your computer much of the functionality of a full-fledged server. To play with the command line, just open the Terminal application (found in `/Applications/Utilities`). From here on out, we assume you have access to some Unix "shell" with which to issue command-line requests.

Putting the "Command" in "Command Line"

Instead of using a mouse-driven interface to press buttons and fill out text fields, Unix-like server operating systems are driven by **command interpreter**s or **shell**s, text prompts that accept commands and execute them one at a time. As a programmer, you're likely familiar with programming language expressions: print a string, call a function with some parameters, and so on. The command line is much the same.

Following shortly is a simple example wherein we list the contents of our current directory (Windows calls these "folders"), list the contents of a subdirectory, and remove a file in that subdirectory. Note the $ character is the **prompt**, and featured in the following examples is a simple prompt denoting which lines are commands being entered and which lines are output from those commands.

Other shells can use different characters—besides $, you can also see > or %. (The Python interpreter shell has a prompt of >>>.) In addition to the character(s) appearing immediately before the user input, many prompts have extra info such as your current username, host, or directory (as do some examples in this book, which utilize user@example $).

Here's a quick example where we list the contents of the current directory, and then remove a file in a subdirectory.

```
$ ls
documents   code   temp
$ ls documents
test.py
$ rm documents/test.py
$
```

Both commands used previously are programs, or binaries, located somewhere in the current executable path. (See the next section for details on paths.) Although programs can theoretically exhibit any behavior, there are established standards for how to specify arguments and options. Traditionally, a Unix command consists of up to three parts: the command's name, options controlling how the command behaves, and arguments, which specify the subcommands to run, files to operate on, and so forth.

Taking the last command from the previous example, rm is the program name (rm standing for "remove"), and documents/test.py is an argument, specifically the file to remove. If we want to remove an entire directory, we can pass options to rm to control its behavior, like we do here:

```
$ ls temp
tempfile1   tempfile2
$ rm temp
rm: cannot remove 'temp': Is a directory
$ rm —help
Usage: /bin/rm [OPTION]... FILE...
Remove (unlink) the FILE(s).

  -d, —directory      unlink FILE, even if it is a non-empty directory
  -f, —force          ignore nonexistent files, never prompt
  -i, —interactive    prompt before any removal
      —no-preserve-root do not treat '/' specially (the default)
      —preserve-root    fail to operate recursively on '/'
```

```
    -r, -R, --recursive   remove the contents of directories recursively
    -v, --verbose         explain what is being done
        --help      display this help and exit
        --version   output version information and exit
$ rm -rf temp
$
```

As a general rule, rm cannot remove directories, so that's why we weren't able to use it in this situation. However, passing the -r and -f options—combined into a single option string for convenience (see the following "Options and Arguments" section for more)—enables rm to recursively remove directories, no questions asked, and so it removes the temp directory without further trouble.

As you can see from the previous example, programs usually contain built-in help information about what their options and arguments are. Almost every program on a Unix system accepts the --help or -h options, which results in some sort of help message. These generally contain enough info for anyone, novice or expert, to get some use out of the program.

Note

If you're following along, your output can differ from ours due to the variety of Unix systems out there—programs often have slightly different implementations from platform to platform. Core utilities, such as rm and ls, are not immune to this, although there is usually at least a small set of options common to every system.

If the built-in help isn't good enough, or you need more details on a given option, there's the man system (short for "[user] manual"), which provides a full set of information about each command, often explaining its arguments in greater detail and/or giving usage examples. man itself is, of course, a program like all the others, and it generally takes a single argument—the name of the program whose "man page" (short for "manual page") you want to read. One command often thrown at novice Unix users is man man, which of course is the man page for the man command itself.

For better or worse, Unix-based systems are often geared toward the self-learner; because you're obviously not averse to reading, however, the authors are sure you'll do fine! And in all seriousness, you'll do yourself a favor if you form such a habit: Those with experience are known to be rather rude to newer folks who ask questions without looking for the answer first.

Unix Program Names

Many, if not most, Unix programs have odd-looking names such as rm, ls, sed, and so on. Such names exist partly due to computing history (the keyboards and displays we take for granted nowadays used to be much slower) and partly because they simply save typing; in environments that are largely or entirely keyboard-based, one obviously gets more done if the commands take less time to type.

The shortened names are sometimes obvious, such as with `rm` ("**rem**ove") and `ls` ("**l**i**s**t"), and other times less so—`sed` is short for "**s**tream **ed**itor." Many names, especially for comparatively newer programs, are made up of various acronyms built on other acronyms; the popular `gcc` is short for "**G**NU **C** **c**ompiler," wherein GNU is a reference to the GNU project, or "**G**NU's **N**ot **U**nix."

In general, Unix command names often end up like regular acronyms—once you know what they're used for, the actual meaning ceases to matter quite so much, as the shortened form takes on the meaning all by itself.

Options and Arguments

We presented previous program options and arguments as being two distinct aspects of the program's specification, but this is not entirely true. At their core, options and arguments are simply a long string presented to the program, which it can interpret any way it pleases. Because of this, the standards presented here are simply that—standards—and variations on them are commonly found, depending on how strictly the program's author wants to adhere to the norm.

In general, all arguments or options to a program are delimited by spaces with options usually being prefixed by a hyphen or dash character, -, and appearing before arguments, which have no prefix. Some programs also accept a so-called "long option" format, which typically uses two dashes and more than one character for the option name—such as the `--help` option we mentioned previously.

```
$ rm --help
Usage: rm [OPTION]... FILE...
```

This is the standard: utility/program name, followed by zero or more options of either type, followed by zero or more arguments (as some commands can sometimes take no arguments at all). Options can be specified one at a time separated by spaces:

```
$ rm -r -f temp
```

but they can also be combined into a single option string to save typing, as we did in the earlier example:

```
$ rm -rf temp
```

Note you cannot combine long and short options in this way, as that wouldn't make much sense, but they can be otherwise interleaved:

```
$ rm -rf --verbose temp
```

Options can themselves be parameterized with arguments, depending on the option involved. For example, the `head` program is intended to return only the top few lines of a given file or chunk of text; how many lines it returns is controlled with the -n argument, such as the following example, which returns the top five lines of the file `myfile.txt`:

```
$ head -n 5 myfile.txt
```

By default (with any `-n` option), `head` displays the first ten lines. Note that, as with the combination of multiple options into one string, option arguments do not have to be separated from their option with a space, but can be combined as one string.

```
$ head -n5 myfile.txt
```

Finally, although traditional Unix programs tend to accept a strict ordering of `<program> <options> <arguments>`, many Linux applications are more lenient and enable options to be specified at any point, such as:

```
$ head myfile.txt -n5
```

Or:

```
$ rm -rf temp --verbose
```

Although this tendency of Linux applications is very convenient (such as when one types a command and only at the end remembers an option he forgot), the authors recommend you try to become used to the more strict form found on true Unix systems. Otherwise you find yourself on a FreeBSD or Mac OS X machine, constantly tripped up by the programs' complaints about your argument order. Trust us, we've been there!

The examples here have been kept simple for purposes of illustration, but if you look at examples of command-line program usage found all over the Web (or check out various `man` pages and `--help` outputs), you see that command-line programs provide an astounding amount of power and flexibility in terms of altering their behavior. And we're not done yet—the next section introduces a whole new dimension of how the Unix command line works.

Pipes and Redirection

By their nature, command lines deal almost exclusively with text, both for input and output. However, in addition to the input and output from and to the user, Unix programs also communicate between themselves and files on disk via an input/output abstraction known as **pipes**. As implied by their name, pipes are a mechanism for directing the flow of text between various combinations of the terminal a user is interacting with, programs, and files.

Every Unix program deals with three potential types of output and input: input, regular output, and error-related output. When nothing special is going on, programs interface with the so-called "standard" pipes, which end up pointing to the text terminal the user is viewing. For example, when you use the `cat` command (short for "concatenate") to spit out the contents of a file, what happens is that `cat` opens the file or files in its arguments and puts their contents into the `stdout` stream, such as in this example where we `cat` the contents of a grocery list.

```
$ cat groceries.txt
Milk
Canned corn
Peanut butter
```

```
Can of soup
Powdered milk
```

Here, because we are just running `cat` by itself, `stdout` dumps the text of the grocery list to our terminal. If `cat` ran into an error condition, such as being given the name of a file that didn't exist, it would print out an error message to the `stderr` stream, which also goes directly to the user by default.

```
$ cat foo.txt
cat: foo.txt: No such file or directory
```

The neat thing about the abstraction of pipes is when we depart from the normal scheme of things and use what's known as the **pipe operator**, |, to tell the command shell to *redirect* the `stdout` of one program into the `stdin` stream of another. `stdin`, the third type of program I/O, is of course short for "standard input." Many programs accept text from `stdin` in addition to, or instead of, expecting the user to give them the names of files to read.

By way of example, let's revisit the use of `head` with relation to our grocery list and ascertain what the first item on our list is.

```
$ cat groceries.txt | head -n1
Milk
```

Notice how we're not telling `head` what file to deal with and instead use the pipe character to redirect the output of the `cat` command into the `head` command. The result is the same as if we had passed the filename to `head` directly.

```
$ head -n1 groceries.txt
Milk
```

A more realistic example can use the `grep` utility, which among other things can be used to return only lines matching a given regular expression (see Chapter 1, "Practical Python for Django," for information on those). Let's use pipes to take the output of a `grep` command, which filters (in a case-insensitive fashion) our grocery list for items with the word "can" in their name:

```
$ grep -i "can" groceries.txt
Canned corn
Can of soup
```

and then use `head` to pare the results down to just the first item.

```
$ grep -i "can" groceries.txt | head -n1
Canned corn
```

As mentioned previously, we can use more than one pipe in a single command. Let's use `grep`'s sister command, `sed`, to do a replacement of the word "corn" with the more generic "veggies."

```
$ grep -i "can" groceries.txt | head -n1 | sed -e "s/corn/veggies/"
Canned veggies
```

Finally, as mentioned, you can redirect these text streams to and from files using the > and < characters. Keeping with the pipe notation of operating from left to right, > is used for directing `stdout` to a file, and < for redirecting a file to `stdin`. For example, in the previous example we've done a search and replace, albeit a not terribly useful one, but once displayed on the terminal, our hard work is gone (short of copying and pasting, of course). Let's redirect it to a new file.

```
$ grep -i "can" groceries.txt | head -n1 | sed -e "s/corn/veggies/" > filtered.txt
```

This command creates a new file (or overwrites an existing file—so be careful!) named `filtered.txt`, and it contains the line "Canned veggies." Note the command produces no output to the terminal—that's because we *redirected* `stdout` to the file, and because it's been redirected, we don't get to see it ourselves.

Finally, note you can double up the redirect-to-file character (>>) to *append* to an existing file instead of overwriting it; this, like >, creates a new file if none previously existed.

Environment Variables

The command-line shell has what's known as an **environment**, or namespace, just like a program's namespace in Python or any other language, wherein various strings can be bound to variable names and referred to by the user when executing commands, or even by the commands themselves (which have access to the calling user's environment). The env command prints out the current state of the environment, such as:

```
$ env
TERM=linux
SHELL=/bin/bash
USER=user
PATH=/usr/local/bin:/usr/bin:/bin:/usr/games:~/bin
PWD=/home/user
EDITOR=vim
HOME=/home/user
```

Many environment variables are used by common Unix shell utilities or by the shell itself—for example, the EDITOR variable is used by programs such as Subversion, which attempts to call the named program when they need to dump the user into a text editor temporarily. The TERM variable determines the terminal type, which many programs reference when deciding whether to use color output or how to interpret keystrokes; PWD is the current directory; and so forth.

As in Python and other languages, you can alter the environment by assigning values to these variables with an assignment character. Here, we shorten the output of env for brevity.

```
$ env
EDITOR=vim
$ EDITOR=pico
```

```
$ env
EDITOR=pico
```

In this example, the default value for EDITOR is the well known vim editor, and we've changed it to point to a less powerful editor called pico. However, environment variables—as you might expect—are initialized at the beginning of each shell session. Our change to EDITOR is temporary at best, unless we alter our shell configuration files, which are read when the shell starts, to make the change permanent. (See your shell's man page for details on how to do this.)

Up till now we've been using env to print the values of environment variables, but that's analogous to Python's globals function—it's not actually very useful unless you're troubleshooting something. The shell can automatically expand any environment variables it sees and can substitute them with their values, but only when using the $ character as a prefix. We use the echo program, which simply echoes its arguments back to the user, to demonstrate this:

```
$ env
EDITOR=vim
$ echo EDITOR
EDITOR
$ echo $EDITOR
vim
```

As you can see, echoing EDITOR by itself does nothing special—it's just a string—but echoing $EDITOR results in printing the value of the EDITOR variable. To put things another way, the shell takes any name or expression following a $ and attempts to expand it into a variable value. Those of us used to languages that use $ to denote variables for both assignment *and* expansion, generally spend a while making mistakes such as this:

```
$ $EDITOR=pico
-bash: vim=pico: command not found
$ EDITOR=pico
$ echo $EDITOR
pico
```

A final note on this topic: Environment variables aren't limited to simple one-word strings, but can hold any string whatsoever. As you saw in the previous example, the shell expanded $EDITOR and combined it with the rest of the line, and then tried to execute the whole as a command. That obviously didn't work—there's no binary called vim=pico—but it's entirely possible to utilize this to save a bit of typing, such as in the following example, where we bind most of a command string to a variable and use it multiple times, appending the argument to the end.

```
$ FINDMILK="grep -ni milk"
$ $FINDMILK groceries.txt
1:Milk
5:Powdered milk
$ $FINDMILK todo.txt
```

```
1:Search grocery list for milk
$ $FINDMILK email_from_reader.txt
3:Also, what's up with all the groceries and milk examples?
```

Our FINDMILK variable is expanded each time, resulting in commands looking like
grep -ni milk groceries.txt. However, this example is slightly contrived—in many
cases such as this, what you really want to do is *paramaterize* an otherwise static call to a
program, and in that case you're better off writing a small shell script. For example, you
could write a script that takes two arguments, not just one, and enables you to specify
both the term being searched for as well as the location to search.

Details on shell scripting are outside the scope of this chapter, but your shell's man
page has plenty of information, and as with most subjects, there's a lot of excellent material online.

The Path

One environment variable, arguably the most important, is the path, normally stored as
PATH, which is a list of directories the shell looks in to find the commands you type.

```
$ echo $PATH
/usr/local/bin:/usr/bin:/bin:/usr/games:~/bin
```

When you type a command into your shell, the shell looks at each of the listed directories in turn until it finds an executable file with the name you asked for; at that point, it
executes that file with the arguments and options you provided. So, when we type echo,
for example, the shell is really executing /bin/echo, and when we type man, it finds and
executes /usr/bin/man. (See the following sidebar for an explanation of these different
bin directories.)

Unix Binary Directories

Unix systems traditionally have multiple directories for different classes of programs, such
as /usr/bin for normal user binaries (executables, just like the utilities that we've looked
at so far in this appendix) or /usr/local/bin for programs installed by the user (as
opposed to ones installed with the operating system's package manager). Still more binaries, intended for use by the system administrator and not by regular users, can live in
/sbin and /usr/sbin.

Some third-party applications, such as Java implementations or older versions of the Mozilla
suite, place their data into /opt/mozilla/, for example, with binaries being in
/opt/mozilla/bin. Paths typically contain a subset of the system binary directories, these
third-party binary directories, and potentially others as well.

It's possible to add things to your path to save time typing. In the previous example,
the user in question has added ~/bin to their path; because ~ is a shortcut for one's home
directory, this means the user can now type the names of scripts in their personal binary
directory, and they can be easily found by the shell.

Note you can easily execute programs not in the path by specifying the full or relative path when you want to execute it. The shell's path capability is simply a handy shortcut to doing this, in fact.

```
$ /tmp/packagename-2.0.1/bin/program
```

Because `/tmp/packagename-2.0.1/bin/` (a potential place for binaries if you're trying out a program not fully installed yet) is not likely to be in your PATH, you have to tell the shell exactly where to find it. In fact, the entire concept of paths is simply a shortcut, albeit a very pervasive one.

Finally, keep in mind you want the containing directory of your binaries in your PATH and not the binaries themselves—the same is true for other paths such as Python's own module path (see Chapter 1). Think of a path as a list of containers and not a list of things to reference.

Summary

You've learned a lot already by this point: how to execute programs with various kinds of options and arguments, making those programs work together and with files via pipes and redirection, and how environment variables and pathing can save you a lot of time.

However, there's a lot more to the average Unix shell program than what we've covered here—most of them are full-fledged programming environments in their own right, including conditional statements, loops, and so forth. Once you're comfortable navigating around a filesystem and running commands, you can find it worthwhile to explore the depths of the shell your system uses—it can save you a lot of time, just like any other programming tool.

Appendix B

Installing and Running Django

To develop with Django, you need to have it installed, the manner of which depends on your choice of operating system and the tools at hand. The simplest environment needed to run Django consists of Python 2.5, a light SQL database package, and Django's built-in development Web server.

However, the average Django deployment typically has a more robust set of applications behind it, using industry greats such as Apache or PostgreSQL. This appendix introduces you to the range of Django deployment options, including some specific pointers about the most common configurations, and is broken down into the necessary core parts: Python and Django themselves, a Web server, and a database engine.

Python

As with most programming languages, newer versions of Python are better. Django runs on any version of Python 2.3 or newer, but we recommend the most current and stable version you can get your hands on. (At the time of writing, that was Python 2.5.2 with 2.6 approaching fast and in parallel with the next generation, 3.0.) See Chapter 1, "Practical Python for Django," for details on the differences between these recent major revisions of Python.

Installers for all major platforms can be obtained from the official Python site at http://www.python.org/download/. Next, we outline some platform-specific notes of interest.

If you're not sure what version of Python you have installed (if any), open a command shell and type `python -v` (note that's a *capital* "V"). If Python is available, it reports its version number and exits.

```
$ python -V
Python 2.5.1
```

Mac OS X

On the Mac, Python comes installed by default, but unless you're using OS X 10.5 ("Leopard"), which comes with Python 2.5, you have Python 2.3, in which case we recommend upgrading. Python 2.4 or 2.5 can be obtained directly from python.org, which has installer packages, or via a software upgrade system such as MacPorts (http://macports.org). If you use MacPorts, you should also install the `python_select` port, so you can make the newer version your system's default.

Unix/Linux

Most open-source Unix clones such as Linux or the BSD family also come with Python installed as part of their core system; the specific version varies greatly depending on which flavor you have, as well as how up-to-date it is. Check your distribution's package management system to make sure you have the most recent Python available to you, or browse the python.org downloads page for stand-alone packages such as RPMs or source archives.

Windows

Windows doesn't come with Python by default, so you need to head to the official Python downloads page. Alternately, you can visit the Web site for the Core Python book, http://corepython.com, and click the Download Python link on the left side of the page to see a handy grid with current versions of Python for all platforms. Get the latest stable version for your system.

There is an optional Windows-only Python library known as the Python Extensions for Windows (a.k.a. `win32all`), which enables development of native Windows Python applications. Users new to Python can find the package desirable for its IDE, PythonWin, even if they don't yet need the integration with the operating system.

Updating Your Path

Once you've got Python installed, you may need to add the executable to your system's path. This is typically taken care of for you on Unix-based systems, such as Linux and Mac OS X, if Python is installed in a well-known location such as `/usr/bin`, `/usr/local/bin`, and so on. Windows users, however, need to perform this step manually to run Python scripts in the command shell, as follows:

Right-click My Computer and pull down the Properties menu item to get to the System Properties pop-up. From here, you select the Advanced tab, as in Figure B.1.

You find three main sections in the Advanced tab (see Figure B.2). Skip past these and go down to the bottom of the window and click the Environment Variables button.

After clicking on that button, you are presented with two panels (see Figure B.3) with which to alter your environment variables. Here, you can choose whether to add/edit/update the path variable for just yourself ("User variables for *USER*"), `PATH`, or

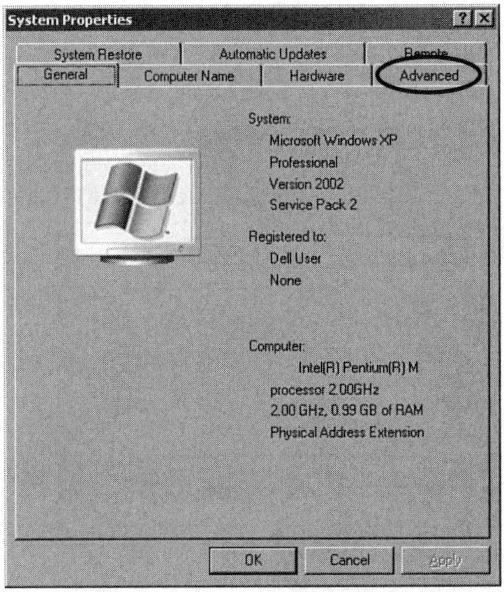

Figure B.1 System properties

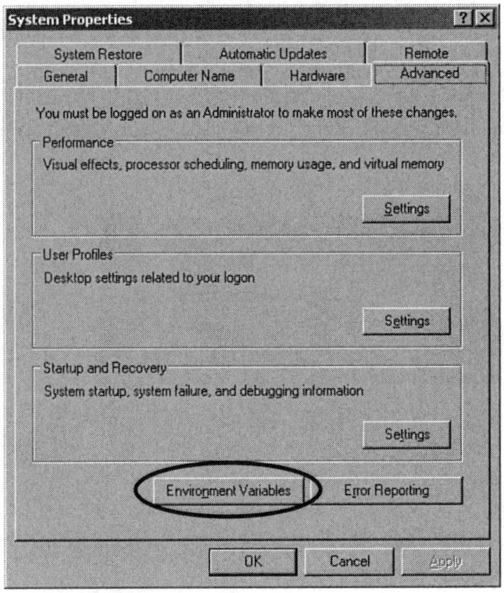

Figure B.2 The Advanced tab

for all users of the entire system ("System variables"), `Path`, provided you have the proper permissions to do so.

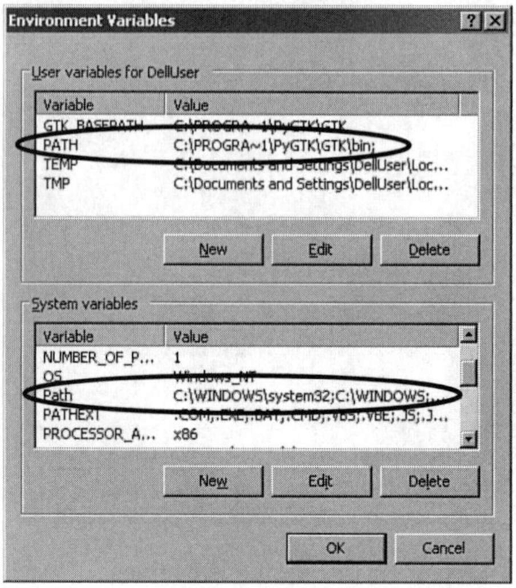

Figure B.3   Environment variables

Select the one you want to modify and click the appropriate Edit button and add `c:\Python25` to the list following the existing format, as in Figure B.4.

Figure B.4   Modifying the path

If there are already folders there, then you can just add it to any position, making sure all folders are still semicolon-delimited. If there is no such variable, then add it—it is also okay to be the only folder if such is the case.

Once you click OK and open a new DOS/Command shell, you should now be able to launch the interpreter without regurgitating the entire pathname `c:\Python25\python.exe`; just `python` by itself should work (see the following).

Testing

To make sure your Python installation went smoothly, simply load up the interactive interpreter by running the main Python program. Enter `python` in a shell/terminal window—sometimes appended with the version number, for example, `python2.4`. If everything's working correctly, opening a command prompt and executing the interpreter results in a display that looks like this in a textual context:

```
$ python
Python 2.5.1 (r251:54863, Mar  7 2008, 04:10:12)
[GCC 4.1.3 20070929 (prerelease) (Ubuntu 4.1.2-16ubuntu2)] on linux2
Type "help", "copyright", "credits" or "license" for more information.
>>>
```

Or, if you are on Windows-based system in a DOS/Command window, it looks like Figure B.5.

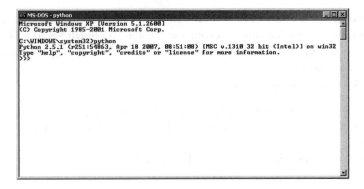

Figure B.5   Python in cmd.exe

The three "greater-than" prompt (>>>) means you are at the interactive interpreter prompt, which is waiting for you to enter some valid Python code. Exit with Ctrl-D (Unix shell or IDLE) or ^Z (DOS/Command window).

If you get an error such as "command not found" or "'python' is not recognized as an internal or external command," then you did not add the folder correctly to the PATH variable, so check it again, taking a careful look to verify your installation directory, the existence of `python.exe`, and the folder name you added to the `PATH` variable.

Finally, another useful convenience is to add the `Scripts` folder to your path, too, following the previous same steps. This enables you to run the Django administrative tool, `django-admin.py`, in a similar fashion as the Python interpreter.

Congratulations! If this is your first time using Python, and you haven't yet run through any tutorials or read Chapter 1, we suggest you do so—at least briefly—before venturing further. It's always good to do limited testing with any new tool before you start using it in earnest.

Optional Add-ons

Along with your Python installation, there are a few recommended (but optional) tools that you can consider: Easy Install and IPython.

Easy Install

One of Python's greatest strengths is that it comes with "batteries included," a rich standard library of modules and packages to help you get things done. In case this doesn't suffice for your application(s), a wealth of third-party software is available. So before you potentially reinvent the wheel, check out the Python Package Index, or "PyPI" at http://pypi.python.org to see if you can find a tool just for you.

Once you discover the additional wealth of external tools, managing your Python installation becomes more burdensome. You have to worry about things like compatibility with your version of Python, other software dependencies, integrating new packages and modules into your installation so they can be imported from your applications, and so forth.

The good news is there is a tool that does all this for you, called Easy Install, and it is available at http://peak.telecommunity.com/DevCenter/EasyInstall. You download the singular `ez_setup.py`, run it (via `sudo` or as an administrator), and it makes installing a new software package as easy as

```
easy_install NEW_3RD_PARTY_SOFTWARE
```

Easy Install uses "PyPI" to get the latest (or your specially requested) version of the desired software, downloads it (*and* all its dependencies), and installs it for you, all with one simple shell command.

Upgrading or uninstalling a software package is just as simple.

IPython

IPython is a third-party alternative to the standard interactive intepreter that comes distributed with Python. It adds many useful features on top of what Python gives you, including tab completion of variable and attribute names, command-line history, automatic indentation, easy access to docstrings and argument signatures, and much more. Because of IPython's popularity and usefulness, it is the default interpreter if you start up a shell using your Django project's `manage.py` administrative script. More information on IPython can be found at http://ipython.scipy.org.

As both an alternative to downloading it from its Web site as well as an introduction to both Easy Install *and* IPython—especially how simple it is to install third-party packages using Easy Install—here is a demo of installing IPython using Easy Install on a Linux system (and `sudo`ing to obtain superuser access):

```
$ sudo easy_install ipython
Password:
Searching for ipython
Reading http://pypi.python.org/simple/ipython/
```

```
Reading http://ipython.scipy.org
Reading http://ipython.scipy.org/dist
Best match: ipython 0.8.4
Downloading http://ipython.scipy.org/dist/ipython-0.8.4-py2.4.egg
Processing ipython-0.8.4-py2.4.egg
creating /usr/lib/python2.4/site-packages/ipython-0.8.4-py2.4.egg
Extracting ipython-0.8.4-py2.4.egg to /usr/lib/python2.4/site-packages
Adding ipython 0.8.4 to easy-install.pth file
Installing ipython script to /usr/bin
Installing pycolor script to /usr/bin

Installed /usr/lib/python2.4/site-packages/ipython-0.8.4-py2.4.egg
Processing dependencies for ipython
Finished processing dependencies for ipython
```

The process is much the same on a Windows-based system, provided you have administrator access. Here is what happens on a PC where we already have the latest version of IPython for Windows installed:

```
C:\>easy_install ipython
Searching for ipython
Best match: ipython 0.8.2
Processing ipython-0.8.2-py2.5.egg
ipython 0.8.2 is already the active version in easy-install.pth
Deleting c:\python25\Scripts\ipython.py
Installing ipython-script.py script to c:\python25\Scripts
Installing ipython.exe script to c:\python25\Scripts
Installing pycolor-script.py script to c:\python25\Scripts
Installing pycolor.exe script to c:\python25\Scripts

Using c:\python25\lib\site-packages\ipython-0.8.2-py2.5.egg
Processing dependencies for ipython
Finished processing dependencies for ipython
```

Django

Now that you've got Python up and running, the next step is to obtain Django's own codebase. At the time of writing, Django 1.0 was recently released with version 1.1 in the works. We recommend that you use version 1.0, as this book is largely 1.0-compatible, and because using the latest stable version is generally a good idea. If you're willing to live on the edge, however, see the following for information on using Django's development version.

Packaged Releases

Packaged releases of Django can be obtained on the project's Web site at http://www.
djangoproject.com/download/ (or via some package managers—check your system's
packaging system for availability). Official releases from the Web site come in the common Unix package format of `.tar.gz`—Unix and Mac systems are able to open these
natively, and Windows users require additional software, such as 7-Zip (http://7zip.org),
the command-line LibArchive (http://gnuwin32.sf.net/packages/libarchive.htm), or a
"Unix-on-Windows" environment such as Cygwin (http://www.cygwin.com/).

Development Version

Django's development version, which will have the latest features not found in the most
recent stable version, requires use of the Subversion version control client program. Like
Python, Subversion is typically available via package managers (on Unix) or MacPorts (on
OS X) and requires a direct download otherwise—see the Subversion Web site (http://
subversion.tigris.org/) for that.

Once you have Subversion, fetching the latest version of Django is a one-liner.

```
$ svn co http://code.djangoproject.com/svn/django/trunk django_trunk
```

Installation

After unpacking the `.tar.gz` file (for packaged releases) or checking out Django's trunk
(for the development version), there is a new directory at your current location named
`Django-1.0` or `django_trunk`. Inside that directory are all the pieces of Django—not
only the framework (the Python module itself, the `django` directory), but documentation
and tests, as well as other scripts and bits of information.

To get Django working, you can take one of three options:

- Add the new directory to your `PYTHONPATH`. If you did a trunk checkout in
  `/home/username/`, for example, you would want to add `/home/username/`
  `django_trunk`—not the `django` subdirectory—to your `PYTHONPATH`.

- Move, copy, or symlink the `django` subdirectory into your Python `site-packages`
  directory.

- Enter the new directory and execute `python setup.py install` (as an admin
  user), which installs Django to the proper location automatically.

For details on Python's path mechanisms, see Chapter 1. We note here if you plan on
using Subversion to keep a development checkout up-to-date, the first or second option

(and only the symlink version of the second option) is preferable. Running `setup.py install` on a trunk checkout works fine, but you'd have to do it again every time you update from Subversion, so it's not recommended.

Testing

To make sure Django is installed in your `PYTHONPATH` correctly, enter the Python interpreter and simply attempt to `import django`. If you see no errors, you're all set! If you get a message such as `ImportError: No module named django`, double check your work, or try a different option from those described previously.

Web Server

Having Python and Django installed is the first big step to actually using Django. The next most important aspect is the Web server, which takes care of delivering your dynamically generated HTML to browsers. Your Web server is also responsible for serving up static media files such as images and CSS, not to mention being a platform for the sorts of system-level things that crop up in Web development (load balancing, proxying, and so on).

The Built-In Server: Not for Production

The simplest Web server you realistically use with Django is its built-in "runserver" or development ("dev") server, which is based on Python's built-in `BaseHttpServer` (a good example of how to leverage the Python standard library). You've seen it in action in Chapter 2, "Django for the Impatient: Building a Blog," where it was used via `manage.py` to rapidly test the beginnings of a simple Web application. That's where the dev server shines: testing out new ideas and getting off the ground quickly. It's also great for debugging, as it runs in the foreground of your terminal and thus all Python `print` statements show up in its output.

However, building Web servers that have performance, reliability, and security is no easy task, and the Django team has wisely declined to try and reinvent the wheel in this area. The development runserver hasn't undergone the testing and refinement of a Web server suitable for deployment on the public Internet and is absolutely not to be used for anything but testing or simple development. The Django documentation used to joke about "revoking your Django license" if you so much as considered using it in production environments, and that sentiment is still quite true.

Finally, although the runserver does enable static file serving (see the official documentation or withdjango.com), we strongly recommend that once you're at this point in your development, you invest in setting up one of the following server environments instead. There's no real point in putting off the inevitable, and as a plus, you are developing in a close-to-production environment—always good for discovering potential deployment issues sooner instead of later.

The Standard Approach: Apache and `mod_python`

The Apache Web server, along with its `mod_python` module, has long been the preferred method for deployment of Django sites. This is the combination that the Lawrence team who originated Django used in their busy public sites, and to date, it is still the most well-tested and well-documented deployment option.

If you have requirements that make `mod_python` unsuitable for you—a shared hosting environment or a non-Apache server, for example—see the following sections on WSGI and Flup for alternatives. However, if you control your own server (or virtual server instance) or otherwise have stable support for `mod_python`, then it's a safe way to go.

You need Apache 2.0 or 2.2 (sometimes referred to in package managers as `apache2` to differentiate them from Apache 1.3, which is much older) along with `mod_python` 3.0 or newer to use Django. As with Python, the actual installation of these packages varies between platforms, with Mac users on 10.4 or older needing to use MacPorts (only Leopard has Apache 2). Windows users can find prebuilt binaries at http://httpd.apache.org and http://www.modpython.org, respectively.

In terms of post-install configuration, there are two core issues to consider when deploying Django with `mod_python`: where to hook in Django itself and where to serve your static files.

Hooking Django into Apache

The first thing you need to determine is how much of your domain's URL space Django is handling—the entirety of one's site, such as www.example.com, or only a subsection or subsections, such as www.example.com/foo/ (where www.example.com/ or www.example.com/bar/ are handled by, for example, PHP or static HTML). It's also possible to use multiple Django projects, each attached to their own subsections.

Hooking up a Django project requires the following Apache configuration snippet, which would typically live inside a `<VirtualHost>` block, or within your main `apache2.conf` (`httpd.conf` on some systems) if you're not using virtual hosts.

```
<Location "/">          " Hooking up python code to use entirely of ru site "
    SetHandler python-program
    PythonHandler django.core.handlers.modpython
    SetEnv DJANGO_SETTINGS_MODULE mysite.settings    # django project mysite
    PythonDebug On                                   # is on the PYTHONPATH
</Location>
```

The previous `<Location>` block sets up the Django project `mysite` to handle the top level of whatever domain is controlled by the configuration file it lives in. To set up Django to cover only one section of the URL space, just update the location, like so:

```
<Location "/foo/">
```

There are also a few variations on this theme: One is when you don't have your Django project on the global system `PYTHONPATH` and need to grandfather it in at the time that Apache is loading up Python modules. For this, just add an extra `PythonPath` directive. If your `mysite` Django project (the directory containing your `settings.py`, root URLconf, and app directories) was `/home/user/django-stuff/mysite/`, you need to add its containing folder to the Python path, as follows:

```
<Location "/">
    SetHandler python-program
    PythonPath "['/home/user/django-stuff/'] + sys.path"
    PythonHandler django.core.handlers.modpython
    SetEnv DJANGO_SETTINGS_MODULE mysite.settings
    PythonDebug On
</Location>
```

[handwritten margin note: lst = [a, b, c] newlst = [x] + lst]

If you want to have multiple Python projects on the same domain, you can simply define multiple such `<Location>` blocks with one major caveat: You need to tell `mod_python` to keep them separate in memory, or else you can get unexpected behavior. This is done by giving each Python handler a distinct (but otherwise arbitrary) `PythonInterpreter` directive.

```
<Location "/foo/">
    SetHandler python-program
    PythonHandler django.core.handlers.modpython
    SetEnv DJANGO_SETTINGS_MODULE foosite.settings
    PythonInterpreter foosite
    PythonDebug On
</Location>

<Location "/bar/">
    SetHandler python-program
    PythonHandler django.core.handlers.modpython
    SetEnv DJANGO_SETTINGS_MODULE barsite.settings
    PythonInterpreter barsite
    PythonDebug On
</Location>
```

As you can see, there's some flexibility with how you can use `mod_python` to serve your Django code. For details on these and other `Python*` Apache directives, see `mod_python`'s documentation at http://modpython.org.

"Poking a Hole" for Static Media

We've got Django successfully served up by Apache, but there's still something missing: our images and JavaScript/CSS (and possibly our videos or PDFs or whatever else our Web site has to serve up). Typically, you want to host these files in the same URL space as your application, so if your app lives at `/foo/`, your images and stylesheets might be `/foo/media/`. However, if we've just hooked up our Python code at `/foo/`, we've now got to make way for the media to get through.

This is a simple task: You just need to tell Apache to turn off the mod_python handler for a specific location by using another `<Location>` block following the one for your Django project.

```
<Location "/foo/media/">
    SetHandler none
</Location>
```

With this in place, requests to, say, `/foo/users/` hit our Django code without issue, but requests to `/foo/media/images/userpic.gif`, for example, end up looking in Apache's document root (defined elsewhere in your configuration or virtual host block). As you can expect, it's also possible to specify multiple such "holes" in your mod_python URL space, meaning you could have distinct directories for images, CSS, and Javascript such as:

```
<LocationMatch "/foo/(images|css|js)/">
    SetHandler none
</LocationMatch>
```

`<LocationMatch>` enables the use of regular expressions in an otherwise normal `<Location>` block, and so here we've simply used regular expression branching to state we want the handler off for any of the specified three directory names. This is functionally equivalent to defining three `<Location>` blocks, but is of course a bit neater. There's no reason to leave DRY in your Python code—apply it liberally to your system configuration, too!

The Flexible Alternative: WSGI

WSGI (Web Server Gateway Interface) and mod_wsgi are the rising stars in Python Web hosting technology. Django has fairly complete support for WSGI, and an increasing number of Django programmers (and Python Web programmers in general) prefer it more than mod_python. WSGI is a flexible protocol intended to bridge Python code with any compatible Web server, not only Apache, but also alternatives such as lighttpd (http://lighttpd.net/), Nginx (http://nginx.net), CherryPy (http://cherrypy.org), and even Microsoft's IIS.

Although WSGI is still relatively new, it works on all the previously mentioned Web servers and has been tested to work with a large number of Python Web frameworks, including Django, as well as popular stand-alone Python Web applications such as the MoinMoin wiki engine and the Trac software project manager.

The major selling points of mod_wsgi (besides the Web-server-agnostic aspect) are a reduced memory footprint and increased performance over mod_python; a single interface standard for all WSGI applications, including those outside Django; and a daemon mode that enables you to easily make a WSGI process "owned" by a particular user on your system.

The most significant downside to mod_wsgi at the time of this writing is it is not yet widely available in package managers, so chances are you have to compile and install it yourself. However, this is bound to change in the relatively near future, and Windows users can currently take advantage of some unofficial Windows binaries linked to from the main mod_wsgi Web site.

If no precompiled version exists for your operating system, you can fetch the source code from the mod_wsgi Web site, http://modwsgi.org/, and follow the installation instructions. After it's installed, it's not hard to get it running; a bit easier than mod_python in most cases, in fact. First, configure Apache to use the module. For Apache 2, that means a line such as this in your httpd.conf:

```
LoadModule wsgi_module /usr/lib/apache2/modules/mod_wsgi.so
```

And a configuration block such as this:

```
Alias /media/ "/var/django/projects/myproject/media"
<Directory /var/django/projects/myproject/>
    Order deny,allow
    Allow from all
</Directory>
WSGIScriptAlias / /var/django/projects/myproject/mod.wsgi
```

Then, finally, create the mod.wsgi script referenced in the previous last line:

```
import os, sys
sys.path.append('/var/django/projects')
os.environ['DJANGO_SETTINGS_MODULE'] = 'myproject.settings'

import django.core.handlers.wsgi

application = django.core.handlers.wsgi.WSGIHandler()
```

In all the previous code you would need to replace /var/django/projects with the path to the directory where your Django project or projects live. With the previous sys.path.append, the important thing, as always, is to use a path that *contains* your project directory; /var/django/projects rather than /var/django/projects/myproject.

Another Approach: Flup and FastCGI

The last potential Web server deployment method we cover here is the flup Python module, which is not only an alternate bridge to using WSGI (flup's original goal), but supports a somewhat similar protocol known as **FastCGI** (sometimes abbreviated **FCGI**). FastCGI, such as WSGI, is intended to act as a bridge between one's application code and a Web server, and has the same benefits: potentially better performance, due to running as a separate process, and potentially increased security by running as a user account separate from that of the Web server.

As things currently stand, FastCGI has more support on shared hosting platforms than WSGI does, partly because it supports multiple languages, and partly due to having been around a bit longer. As such, if Apache's not an option and your environment doesn't support the use of WSGI, FastCGI is an excellent choice.

The official Django documentation (see withdjango.com for a direct link) has an excellent tutorial on how to set up FastCGI, which we don't replicate here. As that document mentions, `flup` provides support for a couple of additional protocols on top of WSGI and FastCGI—SCGI and AJP—which can be important to you if your deployment needs are a bit out of the ordinary.

SQL Database

Finally, we come to the last piece of the puzzle: You've got your Python code (Python, Django), and it's hooked into your Web server (Apache, lighttpd, and so on) to serve dynamic requests. However, you still need persistence for your data, and that's where a SQL database comes in. There are multiple options when it comes to running a database for Django, and each one typically requires both the database software itself, as well as a Python library for interfacing with it.

In addition to the following notes, the official Django documentation has specific notes and gotchas concerning these various platforms (see withdjango.com for a direct link). Make sure to check it out if you find yourself with questions or problems about your database of choice.

SQLite

SQLite is well named; it's a "light" SQL database implementation. Unlike PostgreSQL, MySQL, and various commercial databases such as Oracle or MS SQL, SQLite doesn't run as a stand-alone server, but is simply a library interface to on-disk database files. As with other "light" implementations of typically complicated services, SQLite has its pluses (ease of use and setup, low overhead) and minuses (less functionality, poor performance for large amounts of data).

Therefore, SQLite is great for getting off the ground quickly (as you have already seen in Chapter 2) or for small sites where you don't want or need the overhead of a full database server. However, once you're past the learning phase, and certainly for any serious deployment, you want to upgrade to something more suitable.

To interface with SQLite, you need a Python library; if you're on Python 2.5, the built-in `sqlite3` module is the one to use, or for those on Python 2.4 and below, visit http://www.initd.org (or, always, your package manager) to obtain the `pysqlite` module.

Unlike the following database servers, SQLite doesn't require explicit database creation or any user management; instead, simply choose a filesystem location for your database to live (one that your Web server can read from and write to) and record that as the `DATABASE_NAME` option in your `settings.py`. Once you've done this, normal use of Django utilities such as `manage.py syncdb` writes to a SQLite database file in that location, and you're all set.

SQLite's SQL shell is the `sqlite3` program (sometimes just `sqlite`, especially if your system only has SQLite 2.x installed) and should be run with your database file as its argument, for example, `sqlite3 /opt/databases/myproject.db`.

PostgreSQL

PostgreSQL (often abbreviated as "Postgres") is a full-fledged database server, providing a wide range of features and with a well-respected history as one of the leading open-source database applications. It's recommended by the Django core team, which speaks pretty highly about its quality. Postgres is currently at version 8 (although version 7 is supported for use with Django) and is available for all major platforms, although it's not quite as ubiquitous as MySQL on shared or managed servers.

The official Postgres Web site is http://www.postgresql.org, and the best place to start for downloading it (if you're on Windows or it's not in your package manager) is, at the time of writing, http://www.postgresql.org/ftp/binary/. Navigate to the latest version, then your platform, and go from there.

To use Postgres from Python, you need the `psycopg` library, ideally version 2, sometimes called `psycopg2`. `psycopg` can be downloaded from http://initd.org/pub/software/psycopg/ or your package manager. One minor note to keep in mind is Django has two separate database backends, one for each version of `psycopg`. Make sure you're using the right one!

Creating databases and users with Postgres is easy; the default installation includes stand-alone command-line utilities such as `createuser` and `createdb`, and it's obvious what these do. Depending on your system and method of installing Postgres, a database-level superuser could have been created for you—sometimes it's a `postgres` system-level user, and other times it can be your own username. Check out the relevant documentation to make sure—either on the official Postgres Web site or that of your operating system (if you installed through a package manager).

Once you know the Postgres superuser name and password, you want to do something similar to the following example to set up a new database and user for your Django project:

```
$ createuser -P django_user                    person running these cmds is a/the Postgresql superuser
Enter password for new role:
Enter it again:
Shall the new role be a superuser? (y/n) n
Shall the new role be allowed to create databases? (y/n) y
Shall the new role be allowed to create more new roles? (y/n) n
Password:
$ createdb -U django_user django_db
Password:
```

The previous creates a new passworded Postgres-level database user, `django_user` with the permissions to create new databases, who is then used to create a new database, `django_db`. Once you've done the previous and entered the username and database name in your `settings.py` (along with the password you assigned the user), you should be all set to start using `manage.py` to create and update your database.

Note the final "`Password:`" prompt in our example was Postgres prompting us for our Postgres-level password—our system user is also our Postgres superuser. If that weren't the case, we would have used the -U flag to createuser to specify that superuser account name, similar to what was done in the call to createdb.

Finally, PostgreSQL's SQL prompt program is called psql and supports many of the same options as createdb and createuser, such as -U for choosing a username.

MySQL

Another mainstream, open-source database server is MySQL, now at version 5 (4 is also supported). MySQL lacks some advanced functionality present in Postgres, but is also a bit more common, partly due to its tight integration with the common Web language PHP.

Unlike some database servers, MySQL has a couple of different internal database types that determine the effective feature set: One is MyISAM, which lacks transactional support and foreign keys but is capable of full-text searching, and another is InnoDB, which is newer and has a better feature set but currently lacks full-text search. There are others, but these two are the most commonly used.

If you're on Windows or your package manager doesn't have a recent version of MySQL, its official Web site is http://www.mysql.com, and offers binaries for most platforms. Django's preferred MySQL Python library is MySQLdb, whose official site is http://www.sourceforge.net/projects/mysql-python, and you need version 1.2.1p2 or newer. Take note of that exact version number—some older Linux distributions can have versions such as 1.2.1c2, which are too old and *not* compatible with Django.

Creating databases with MySQL is typically accomplished with the all-purpose admin tool mysqladmin. As with Postgres, you need to figure out your installation's database superuser name and password before you can create a new user for your Django project. This superuser is typically root and is also often set up with no initial password (something you should change as soon as you can), leading to a fairly quick database creation such as

```
$ mysqladmin -u root create django_db
```

Unlike Postgres, MySQL's user management is done entirely within the database itself, so to create our django_user DB user we need to use MySQL's SQL shell right away. It's sensibly named mysql.

```
$ mysql -u root
Reading table information for completion of table and column names
You can turn off this feature to get a quicker startup with -A

Welcome to the MySQL monitor.  Commands end with ; or \g.
Your MySQL connection id is 6
Server version: 5.0.51a-6 (Debian)

Type 'help;' or '\h' for help. Type '\c' to clear the buffer.
```

```
mysql> GRANT ALL PRIVILEGES ON django_db.* TO 'django_user'@'localhost' IDENTIFIED
BY 'django_pass';
Query OK, 0 rows affected (0.00 sec)

mysql>
```

That's it! You're now all set to update `settings.py` and start issuing database-related `manage.py` commands.

Oracle

The final database currently supported by Django at the time of writing is a commercial offering, Oracle. If you're new to database-driven development, you're not likely to be considering this option, as Oracle itself is not as commonly available or deployed on shared hosting or Linux package managers. However, Oracle does have free versions available, and Django can interface with versions 9i and up.

Python's Oracle bridge is `cx-oracle`, available at http://cx-oracle.sourceforge.net/.

Other Databases

Django's database support is continually evolving. The best source of up-to-date information is the official Web site and the Django-users mailing list. Two options that are not currently supported by Django directly are Microsoft SQL Server and IBM DB2. An independently maintained project that gives Django MS SQL support is available on Google Code: http://code.google.com/p/django-mssql/. There is also Python-DB2 support on Google Code at http://code.google.com/p/ibm-db/, though as of this writing, it is not plug-and-play with Django.

Summary

We're hopeful that by now you've gotten completely up and running with Django and all its constituent parts—Python, Django, a Web server, and a database. If you've run into trouble, keep in mind some advice we share in Chapter 2—back up, try things over again, and make sure you don't miss any steps in the documentation you're following.

Finally, Django's own installation documentation (which covers all components and not just the Python library itself) is an excellent resource. See withdjango.com for a direct link.

Appendix C

Tools for Practical Django Development

Web development, at anything but the smallest scale, is software development. If your site takes input from users in some form and does something with that input, it's a Web application, and its development is—or should be—similar to the development of other kinds of software.

If you came to Web development from the software side, it's probably obvious to you to use established software development tools and techniques such as version control, bug tracking, and powerful development environments. You can just skim this appendix to make sure you're not forgetting anything that could make your life easier.

If you're arriving from the design side of things, some of the things presented can be new to you. The good news is, we guarantee any effort you invest in learning and using them pays off many times over in increased productivity, flexibility, and peace of mind.

Version Control

If you're developing any kind of software at all, and you're not using version control, you're missing out. Version control systems keep a complete revision history of your project, enabling you to rewind your code to any point in time (for example, to the hour before you made that innocent-looking change that broke something you didn't notice for a week).

Older version control systems such as **SCCS** (Source Code Control System) and **RCS** (Revision Control System) were simple, either maintaining the original versions of files plus deltas (minor changes to files between versions) or vice versa—keeping the latest editions of files and applying "backward deltas." One limitation of such systems was the controlled files lived on and were modified on the same server.

As software development has progressed, especially in the open source community, it became clear the existing systems were awkward for distributed group development, hence leading to more modern version control systems such as **CVS** (Concurrent

Versions System), an improved and distributed offshoot of RCS, and later, the **Subversion** project, which was meant to be "a better CVS" and a compelling replacement for it.

The Trunk and Branches

Version control systems generally follow a tree analogy, where the original or primary line of development is called the **trunk**, of which copies can be made—becoming distinct entities in their own right—and then which tend to go off in their own direction. These copies are known as **branches**, and the decisions about what work belongs in branches and what belongs in the trunk varies from project to project.

One methodology keeps all feature development—development that can break backward compatibility or be otherwise unstable—in the trunk and uses branches to represent releases of the software, which only receive bug-fixes after they diverge from the trunk. Another "opposite" approach keeps the trunk stable and puts all new feature work into branches, which has the benefit of enabling more than one big, earth-shattering feature to be worked on at the same time.

Django itself uses a methodology that exists somewhere in-between these two approaches: It keeps both release branches *and* feature branches, and the trunk is in a middle ground—neither completely stable nor terribly unstable. Changes that have a large effect on the stability of the framework get their own branches with simpler, less disruptive alterations being performed directly on the trunk.

Merging

Having branches diverge from the trunk is useful for segregating copies of the codebase, but it wouldn't be very useful without a way to get those changes back into the trunk! This is where the tree analogy breaks down a bit: The other main concept in source control is that of **merging** changes from one branch into another branch.

For example, Django's forms framework received a major overhaul recently and because it consisted of a large series of changes, it got its own branch. Work went on for some time, resulting in a much-improved version of the framework. During that time period, the trunk kept receiving its own updates in various areas, so not only did the "newforms" branch have its own list of changes compared to the point it diverged at, but there was another list of changes that occurred on the trunk between that point and the present.

There's a lot of theory surrounding how to reconcile nontrivial sets of changes such as these, but the basic gist is version control tools provide commands to merge such changes together and apply them to one side or the other. In Django's case, the maintainers ran a couple of commands to update the trunk with the changes from the "newforms" branch, manually dealt with a few places where the version control program was unable to reconcile things, and they were all done.

Now that you've got a general idea of what version control entails, let's explore the two main paradigms in today's source control techniques, including a brief look at one or two specific version control systems from each.

Centralized Version Control

The big names in open source centralized version control are CVS and Subversion—with the latter steadily supplanting the former. Older systems you can see mentioned include RCS and SCCS. Commercial alternatives in this category include Perforce, IBM Rational ClearCase, and Microsoft Visual Studio Team System.

Subversion

Subversion (http://subversion.tigris.org/) is the closest thing we have to an industry standard version control system. It's open source, available for many platforms, has good performance and stability, and is well proven in the real world.

Subversion operates on a **centralized** model with one master repository that all users connect to. Your checkout of the code can be worked on without a network connection—as in, you can edit the files—but recording your changes to or receiving changes from the repository requires you to be online. Subversion can keep track of what you've changed since the last time you fetched an update from the central server, but it doesn't give you any way to record multiple sets of changes without a connection to the server.

Subversion is the version control system that is currently used for the main Django code repository at http://code.djangoproject.com, as well as by the many Django-related projects hosted at Google Code and elsewhere. Subversion also has excellent integration with the Trac wiki and issue-tracker (see the following for more on Trac).

Decentralized Version Control

Decentralized version control is the future. A decentralized system can do everything that a centralized one can, but with the powerful additional feature that every "checkout" of a project is also a full-fledged repository. With distributed version control, you don't need a connection to a central server to record sets of changes. You simply record them in your local repository. Later, if someone else wants the changes, they can be pushed or pulled across the network.

Open source decentralized version control systems include Git, Mercurial, Darcs, Bazaar, SVK, and Monotone. Commercial systems include BitKeeper and TeamWare.

Mercurial

Mercurial (http://www.selenic.com/mercurial/) is one of the most popular distributed systems in use today. Mercurial is largely written in Python with a bit of C in performance-critical portions. Performance is something that the Mercurial developers take very seriously, which has led to the adoption of Mercurial by some very large projects, including the Mozilla Web browser and Sun's OpenSolaris effort.

Git

Something of a rival to Mercurial, in that both tools vie with Bazaar for open-source DVC mindshare, is Git (http://git.or.cz). Written in C, by Linus Torvalds and other Linux kernel team members, Git is a Unix-inspired tool and was originally created to help deal with the extremely complex source-control needs of the Linux kernel project, which uses it today. Git has also been embraced by the Ruby on Rails project and many other projects in Rails' sphere of influence, in addition to the WINE project, X.org (the Linux graphics system), the Fedora Linux distribution, and others.

Version Control for Your Project

Here's a basic walkthrough for the uninitiated of using version control on a Django project. In this example we use Mercurial (the `hg` command).

We start with a skeletal Django project.

```
$ django-admin.py startproject stuff_dev_site
$ cd stuff_dev_site
$ ./manage.py startapp stuff_app
$ ls stuff_app
__init__.py   manage.py     settings.pyc urls.py
__init__.pyc  settings.py   stuff_app
```

Now we turn this working directory into a repository.

```
$ hg init
```

And make a basic `.hgignore` file (either with `echo`, as the following, or with a text editor) that tells Mercurial to skip over those `.pyc` bytecode files because they are automatically generated by the Python bytecode compiler and not something we need to separately track.

```
$ echo "\.pyc$" > .hgignore
```

By default, patterns in an .hgignore file are regular expressions. Now we can go ahead and add files:

```
$ hg add
adding .hgignore
adding __init__.py
adding manage.py
adding settings.py
adding stuff_app/__init__.py
adding stuff_app/models.py
adding stuff_app/views.py
adding urls.py
```

Then, we commit our changes with `hg commit` and verify that Mercurial recorded them with `hg log`.

```
$ hg commit -m "Initial version of my project"
No username found, using 'pbx@example.org' instead
$ hg log
changeset:   0:e991df3d3205
tag:         tip
user:        pbx@example.org
```

```
date:        Sun Oct 07 13:49:14 2008 -0400
summary:     Initial version of my project
```

Every time you commit to a Mercurial repository, Mercurial records a changeset identified with two different numbers: an incremental integer that is only valid in this repository and a hexadecimal hash that uniquely identifies this changeset no matter where it is pushed or pulled to.

Let's make a simple change, inspect it, and commit it.

```
$ echo "I_LIKE_CANDY = True" >> settings.py
$ hg status
M settings.py
$ hg commit -m "Apparently someone likes candy."
No username found, using 'pbx@example.org' instead
$ hg log
changeset:   1:65e7cda9f64b
tag:         tip
user:        pbx@example.org
date:        Sun Oct 07 13:57:53 2008 -0400
summary:     Apparently someone likes candy.

changeset:   0:e991df3d3205
user:        pbx@example.org
date:        Sun Oct 07 13:49:14 2008 -0400
summary:     Initial version of my project
```

Once you have recorded a changeset, it remains available as a "snapshot" of your project from that point forward. If you decide that everything you did after changeset 0 was a terrible mistake, then the command `hg revert --rev 0 --all` rewinds your working directory to that point.

So at this point you are off and running with your project. You write code, you test with the development server, and you record your changes with concise yet meaningful commit messages. Soon it's time to deploy your project.

You could just tar all the files into an archive, copy that archive to the server where your live application is deployed, and extract the files from the archive. That wouldn't be so bad—if you never made any changes to your application ever again. But assuming you are actually developing software rather than creating marble busts, it's likely that you'll want to correct and enhance your handiwork, and for repeated rounds of updates the tar-copy-untar cycle is a pain.

It would be much better if you could make a quick copy of the repository, but have Mercurial remember where the copy came from so you could incrementally fetch any updates that were made to the original. That's exactly what the `hg clone` command does.

For simplicity in this example, we assume the deployed copy of the Web site lives on the same server as the development copy. This means that making the clone is as easy as changing our working directory to the spot we would like to create the clone, and then typing `hg clone` and the path to the original (development) directory. For example, if we were still inside the original directory and wanted the deployment version to be a copy on the same level as that original directory, our commands would be like this:

```
$ cd ..
$ hg clone stuff_dev_site stuff_live_site
8 files updated, 0 files merged, 0 files removed, 0 files unresolved
```

This gives us a perfect copy ("clone") of our original repository and working directory.

```
$ ls stuff_live_site/
__init__.py  manage.py  settings.py  stuff_app  urls.py
```

Wait, where are our .pyc files? Well, we told Mercurial to ignore them, so they didn't get added to the repository, and they don't show up in this list.

Now let's make some changes to the original (development) directory.

```
$ cd stuff_dev_site
$ echo "I_LIKE_DOGS = True" >> settings.py
$ hg commit -m "Also, dogs are liked."
```

When we've sufficiently tested those changes and are ready to deploy, we switch to the "live" branch and pull them in:

```
$ cd ../stuff_live_site
$ hg pull -u
pulling from /stuff_dev_site
searching for changes
adding changesets
adding manifests
adding file changes
added 1 changesets with 1 changes to 1 files
1 files updated, 0 files merged, 0 files removed, 0 files unresolved
```

We can use the same hg `revert` command to undo changes to the live site—for example, we can do that if the change we just pulled turned out to cause unexpected problems on the live site despite our testing on the dev site. Every clone of the project has the same content and the same history.

That's just the surface, but hopefully it has at least whetted your appetite. There is, of course, much more to using version control in general, and Mercurial in particular, than we have hinted at here. For more, including links to excellent free manuals for Subversion, Mercurial, and other systems, see withdjango.com.

Project Management Software

Version controlling your source code is useful, and some developers make do with a version control system and nothing more. However, many others use a breed of Web applications typically designed to "partner" with a version control system, providing not only a

Web interface to the source repository and its history, but issue or todo-item tracking, documentation, and so forth.

There are a number of such packages in existence; many are hosted services, such as Google Code, SourceForge, Launchpad, and Basecamp. Others are stand-alone applications you can host yourself; the one favored by the majority of open-source developers is named Trac, which is—not too surprisingly—written in Python.

Trac

Trac is an open source wiki, issue-tracking, source code, and project management system, maintained by Edgewall Software. We admit a bias right now: Trac is our favorite in the field of project management software. It works wonderfully out of the box, especially its excellent integration with Subversion and other version control systems. It also has pervasive wiki markup that can be used to easily link code revisions, bug tickets, and pages of documentation and notes.

If that's not testimonial enough, you should know that the Django code repository itself at http://code.djangoproject.com/ is running on Trac. (You just might not have recognized it due to the lovely style customizations.)

Note
Trac was a central tool in the process of writing this book—learn more in the Colophon.

We should also mention that although Trac ships with Subversion support as the default, it is possible to use other systems (such as the ones we described previously) with Trac via plugins. You can download Trac and read the full documentation at http://trac. edgewall.org/. If you find yourself wanting to extend Trac, make sure you check out http://trac-hacks.org/ for extra plugins and other "hacks."

Text Editors

You don't need any special software to work on a Django project. Any coder's text editor will do. Here are some tips for some popular editors.

Emacs

The most important piece of equipment you need to be a happy and productive Django coder using Emacs is **python-mode**, which enables syntax highlighting, intelligent indentation, and various other niceties that streamline the production and editing of Python code. Emacs versions 22 and newer come with a built-in version of python-mode. For older versions, or Emacs variants such as XEmacs, see the Emacs page on the official Python Web site (http://www.python.org/emacs/).

There's also a user-contributed mode for Django templates, which you can find on the Django wiki (http://code.djangoproject.com/wiki/Emacs).

Vim

Vim is a text editor based on the old vi Unix tool and provides an incredible number of enhancements and improvements to the original tool. You can read more about it and download it at the main vim Web site at http://www.vim.org/. As with Emacs, there is a Python syntax mode. A comprehensive page of tips on using the vim editor (and its variants) with Python can be found on the Django wiki (http://code.djangoproject.com/wiki/UsingVimWithDjango).

TextMate

TextMate is a popular commercial editor for OS X that has excellent support for Django. TextMate organizes its support for particular languages and syntaxes into "bundles" and ships with a Python bundle that speeds up working with Python code and makes it more readable through syntax coloring. In addition, in TextMate's public bundle repository, there are two special bundles for Django: one for Python code and one for Django template code. More information can be found via the Django wiki (http://code.djangoproject.com/wiki/TextMate).

Eclipse

The Eclipse IDE offers a powerful Python development module called PyDev. You can fetch the code and learn more about PyDev via its SourceForge page (http://pydev.sourceforge.net/).

Appendix D

Finding, Evaluating, and Using Django Applications

It's fun to write applications in Django, but you don't always want to make everything yourself. As the framework has grown in popularity, an ecosystem of open source Django-powered applications has sprung up around it. This is boosted by the fact that Django itself is open source; it leads by example, creating an ethic that says, when in doubt, release your application as open source.

Even better, most of these further follow Django's example in using the unrestrictive BSD/MIT-style license. This can make adoption of those applications an easier sell inside organizations that are shy of the most common open source license, the GNU Public License or GPL. The GPL mandates if a product based on GPL-licensed code is used in an application that gets redistributed (as opposed to merely being offered as a service via the Web, for instance), the code of that application must be publicly released. The BSD/MIT style licenses certainly enable this, but don't require it. No judgement is implied on the relative merits of the two approaches, but the fact that BSD/MIT-style licenses are more "business friendly" is well accepted, and so the license issue can affect your choices.

Whether it's something simple such as user-registration features, something more complex such as a full-featured blog engine, or a full-on e-commerce solution for running your Web store, there is likely to be an open source Django application out there that does it. But how do you find it? How can you tell if it's good? And how can you make using it (and keeping up with updates) as easy as possible?

Where to Look for Applications

Some developers run their own Web sites and/or their own project management systems, and thus you often find Django applications listed in their creator's blog or personal Trac instance. However, many (if not most) developers congregate at centralized listing sites to achieve higher visibility, and we list some of the more popular such sites here.

- The DjangoResources page on the Django project wiki: This is where many application authors let the world know about the availability of their application. The direct URL is http://code.djangoproject.com/wiki/DjangoResources.

- Google Code: With its free hosting and clean interface, Google Code has become a popular spot for Django-powered projects. Searching for projects tagged "django" yields a nice long list.

- Djangopluggables.com: Relatively new at the time of writing, djangopluggables.com is a nicely designed site that aggregates information on a wide variety of Django applications.

- DjangoSites.org: This simple directory of Django-powered sites has a "sites with source" category that shows you only the listed sites whose authors have released the source code.

- GitHub.com: A popular source-repository-and-social-networking site using the Git version control system, which hosts a few Django apps and is growing in popularity along with Git itself.

Just as the ecosystem of Django applications is constantly evolving, so are the best ways to find them. Check withdjango.com for an updated list of links and recommendations.

How to Evaluate Applications

Here are some questions you can ask of a prospective application or project that you've found.

- Is it alive? When were the most recent feature updates or bug fixes? Not every project needs to be updated every week, but a project that last saw activity in a flurry of commits a year ago could have been abandoned. Anything developed against a pre-1.0 release of Django needs to be kept up to date, or it quickly becomes useless.

- How's the documentation? *Is* there documentation? Is it organized and readable? Is it relatively free of red-flag warnings such as "NOTE: This section is out of date!"? Does it seem to be actively maintained? (For example, is the documentation managed via source control and distributed as part of the project download?)

- Who are the authors? Google the author name(s) to get a sense of how experienced they are and how their work is regarded in the community. If you come up with a lot of helpful replies on the project mailing list, for example, that's good.

- How's the code? If you have some experience as a Python programmer, one of the best ways to get a quick feel for a project is to download its source code and just start reading. Are the source files organized? Are there docstrings that explain the intent and use of functions and methods? Is there a test suite, and does it pass?

- Is there a community? Many Django projects that were started to fulfill a particular person's or organization's needs have grown to have user and development communities of their own. The more complex the application, the more likely that it has its own community of experienced people who can help you solve problems. Not every application needs a vibrant community to be considered viable, of course, but social infrastructure should be present in rough proportion to the complexity of the application.

How to Use Applications

Third-party Django applications, just like yours, are simply Python modules. To use them in a project, simply add a string containing the application's path (in Python dot-delimited form) to your project's `settings.py` in the `INSTALLED_APPS` setting.

Although you can put them anywhere you want, you essentially have three choices:

- Embedding: If you only need the application for a single project, you can decide to simply add it inside your project directory alongside your other applications. In some ways this is the simplest approach. The downside comes when you decide you want to start using it in other projects on the same server.

- Creating a "shared apps" directory: Another option is to create a directory for shared apps—you could call it `shared_apps`—and add this directory to your Python path. This keeps the third-party code in a single place, but makes it easy to import across projects. To add an application to a given project, you'd simply add its name (no dotted prefix needed) to that project's `INSTALLED_APPS` setting.

- Installing to your site-packages directory: You can also add Django applications to your system-wide Python library, usually found in a directory called `site-packages`. (Type `import sys; sys.path` at a Python prompt to find the exact path on your system, as well as the other directories on your Python path.)

If you are following an evolving project, you can work with a checkout from that project's version control system rather than simply downloading archived files. In that case, you can simply check out the latest version of the code into your project, your shared apps directory, or your system's `site-packages`, depending on which of the previous methods you are following. Just keep in mind that you need to use caution when upgrading any such external applications to make sure you don't break your projects that depend on them.

Sharing Your Own Applications

Hopefully, as you continue progress as a Django application developer, you can find that some of your creations have the potential to be useful to other people. We encourage you to consider releasing these applications under an open source license and to allow other Django users to use them and improve them. Code hosting services such as Google Code, SourceForge, GitHub and others can make it easy for you to get your code out there (without creating a whole new Web site for you to administer). Be sure to tell us, too!

Appendix E

Django on the Google
App Engine

This appendix introduces you to porting your Django application to the Google App Engine, a scalable Web application platform that is based in part on Django and embodies many Django features. Although we try to cover the basics, we cannot go over every aspect of this technology; you can find links to more information at the end of the appendix.

There are several ways of developing apps with App Engine with a varying degree of "Django-ness:"

- A new/pure App Engine app
- An existing Django app ported to App Engine
- A new Django app written specifically for App Engine

The first method uses only the (minimal) Django features and components that come with every App Engine application—we discuss these in the next section. The other two methods bring more Django into the picture and are the focus of this appendix. Again, if you want to learn more about "pure" App Engine applications, check out the related links at the end because we aren't covering those details here.

Our purpose is to focus on Django—developing applications with Google App Engine by itself warrants its own book!

Why the App Engine Matters

The launch of Google App Engine represents an exciting development for those using or planning to use Django. Its release is a welcome boost to the profile of both Python and Django within the larger software development community, generating a lot of interest from folks who previous could not have considered using either technology.

Perhaps the most significant promise of App Engine is it aims to make deployment and server upkeep a nonissue. We deal with Web server setup—Apache or nginx deployment, whether to use mod_python or FCGI, and so on—because we *have* to, to make Web sites using Python.

Contrast this to PHP, which—while suffering from many problems, the language itself not least among them—is generally free of such worries. The App Engine allows Python Web developers a similar sort of care-free programming platform. On top of that, it enables us to leverage Google's existing (and massive) infrastructure.

Pure Google App Engine Applications

Pure App Engine applications are created in a single directory and use the toolset App Engine provides: the SDK's development Web server (`dev_appserver.py`) and the application uploader (`appcfg.py`) used for deployment to the App Engine "cloud" when your code is ready for release.

Configuration of an App Engine application is defined in a YAML file (`app.yaml`) that can look something like:

```
application: helloworld
version: 1
runtime: python
api_version: 1

handlers:
- url: /.*
  script: helloworld.py
```

You notice the `handlers` section looks similar in function to a Django URLconf, hooking up a URL-like string with a specific script to execute. Another Django or Django-like feature of App Engine development is its templating system, which is essentially a wholesale reuse of Django's own.

Limitations of the App Engine Framework

From the perspective of a Django developer, the biggest missing piece in Google's implementation is Django's ORM. Instead of a relational database, Google relies on its proprietary BigTable system for storage—see http://labs.google.com/papers/bigtable.html and http://en.wikipedia.org/wiki/BigTable for more information. There are no SQL statements, no relations, no JOINs, and so on.

Although you can write brand-new apps that use the other parts of Django and substitute Google's BigTable-based ORM for your data models, this limitation scratches virtually all existing Django apps off the list. You can conceivably rewrite parts of your own apps to work around this, but you are not going to do that for existing Django apps and components such as the admin, the authentication system, the generic views, and so forth.

We discuss reworking your own apps for App Engine in the next section.

With those portions of Django out of the picture, we're left with the core functionality: URLconfs, views, and templates. Although these components are enough to build any sort of Web site, they aren't entirely satisfying if you want to use existing Django applications on the App Engine or build applications capable of deploying both normally and as App Engine.

> **Note**
>
> At the time of this writing, the Django components that App Engine ships with are part of an outdated yet stable release of Django (0.96.1).

Google App Engine Helper for Django

The key to making your experience with App Engine a bit more like "real" Django development is the Google App Engine Helper for Django. This is an open-source Google-sponsored project (with Python creator Guido van Rossum being listed as one of its contributors) that aims to make App Engine a more comfortable environment for those with Django experience. It even enables you to swap in a more current version of Django instead of the one that App Engine ships with.

Getting the SDK and the Helper

Before we go any further, we need to get the necessary software. You can download the Google App Engine SDK for your platform at http://code.google.com/p/googleappengine/, the SDK Project home page. An `.msi` file is available for Windows users along with a `.dmg` file for OS X. For everyone else, just download the general source ZIP file. Similarly, the helper is available for download at http://code.google.com/p/google-app-engine-django/.

Follow the instructions on installing both. Once completed, you are welcome to start playing around with the App Engine on its own; for example, we suggest following its tutorial to build a simple application solely on that platform. Google provides good documentation on how to get up and running with App Engine, so we don't rehash it all here. The App Engine tutorial can be found at http://code.google.com/appengine/docs/gettingstarted/.

It's advantageous to know how to create simple apps on both platforms so when we try integration such as bringing Google App Engine to an existing Django app or building a new App Engine application with more of a Django flavor, things come easier to you.

More on the Helper

At the time of this writing, the Helper is in a fairly primitive state. Its primarily goal is to round off the sharp corners of App Engine from a Django developer's perspective, but it has a long way to go. If you go poking around in the Helper source, be prepared to learn a bit about the internals of both App Engine and Django.

The Helper does not turn App Engine *into* Django, but it does ease the transition a bit. Although our following example presumes you are using the Helper, choosing to simply use the stock App Engine functionality is also perfectly acceptable. As is commonly said about Django, "It's just Python." Don't let the rough edges of App Engine prevent you from exploring its potential. In the words of one observer, App Engine "makes it hard not to scale." Assuming you are willing to trade the previous limitations for deployment convenience and the promise of immense scalability, then please read on.

The Helper is delivered in the form of a skeletal Django project containing a single application called `appengine_django`. You can use the skeleton as the basis of a new project or copy the `appengine_django` application folder into an existing project.

App Engine provides a minimal administrative back-end called the **Development Console**. Once you've installed the Helper, this admin app resides at a URL similar to http://localhost:8000/_ah/admin (assuming you have the App Engine server running on port 8000). Unlike the regular admin, this tool can only work with models that already have some records saved in the data store. If you have a model that has not yet been used to save any data, you are not able to create records of that type via the Development Console.

Integrating the App Engine

In this section, we are going to take our simple blog, as developed in Chapter 2, "Django for the Impatient: Building a Blog," and turn it into an App Engine application. We are going to follow the steps as outlined in the Google App Engine Helper for Django README file, located at http://code.google.com/p/google-app-engine-django/source/browse/trunk/README. For the following example, we are assuming you called your project `mysite` and your application `blog`.

Copying the App Engine Code to Your Project

After downloading the Helper and unzipping it, you have a directory named `appengine_helper_for_django`. Copy the contents of that directory into the root folder of your existing Django blog project, so the `app.yaml`, `main.py` files, and the `appengine_django` folder are now coexisting with your Django files such as `urls.py` and `settings.py`.

Now, edit your `app.yaml` file and change the application name to the one you registered your application under in the App Engine's Admin Console. The next step is to give your project access to the App Engine code itself.

> **Note**
>
> Updating `app.yaml` with an App Engine-registered name is not actually required; it's only necessary when and/or if you decide to upload your code to the App Engine itself. It's entirely possible to run your code with the SDK runserver without this information entered.

If you did not install the App Engine SDK using the Windows or Mac OS X installers, you need to manually link to the App Engine code. On a POSIX system (Linux or Mac OS X), the call to the `ln` command looks something like this:

```
$ ln -s THE_PATH_TO/google_appengine ./.google_appengine
```

Integrating the App Engine Helper

Our next step is to integrate our helper into our command-and-control file `manage.py`. This enables us to manage our app almost like a stand-alone Django application. The way to do this is to add two new lines to the very top of the file (after the "sh-bang" line) right before the import of `execute_manager`, so the first four lines of `manage.py` look like this:

```
#!/usr/bin/env python

from appengine_django import InstallAppengineHelperForDjango
InstallAppengineHelperForDjango()

from django.core.management import execute_manager
```

This enables App Engine to take partial control over some of the Django management commands, as well as adding App Engine-specific code and making the Helper's add-ons accessible. However, even with a modified `manage.py`, you still have access to many of the more important commands.

Now that we have a "new" `manage.py`, let's use our first new command to generate a new `settings.py` file. (We recommend backing up the original in case you want to revert everything afterward!) Why are we doing this? Sadly, we have to remove all Django functionality that's incompatible with App Engine—all the stuff we described previously. The way you do that is with the `diffsettings` command.

```
$ manage.py diffsettings
WARNING:root:appengine_django module is not listed as an application!
INFO:root:Added 'appengine_django' as an application
WARNING:root:DATABASE_ENGINE is not configured as 'appengine'. Value overridden!
WARNING:root:DATABASE_%s should be blank. Value overridden!
WARNING:root:Middleware module 'django.middleware.doc.XViewMiddleware' is not
compatible. Removed!
WARNING:root:Application module 'django.contrib.contenttypes' is not compatible.
Removed!
WARNING:root:Application module 'django.contrib.sites' is not compatible. Removed!
DATABASE_ENGINE = 'appengine'
DEBUG = True
INSTALLED_APPS = ('django.contrib.auth', 'django.contrib.admin', 'mysite.blog',
'appengine_django')
MIDDLEWARE_CLASSES = ('django.middleware.common.CommonMiddleware',
'django.contrib.auth.middleware.AuthenticationMiddleware')
ROOT_URLCONF = 'mysite.urls'   ###
```

```
SECRET_KEY = 'w**sb^(p($wzxra*a9_@4_z0s(9i(9x3(w—aribbaaa4(r^wi'
SERIALIZATION_MODULES = {'xml': 'appengine_django.serializer.xml'}  ###
SETTINGS_MODULE = 'settings'  ###
SITE_ID = 1  ###
TEMPLATE_DEBUG = True
TIME_ZONE = 'America/Los_Angeles'
```

In the output, all lines that start with "WARNING" usually indicate something is not compatible or is an incorrect setting and removed. All lines that come *after* the final line of WARNINGs and INFOs make up the contents to the new `settings.py` file.

Porting Your Application to App Engine

We need to tweak our application to use App Engine objects now, so the first place is in `models.py`. Instead of using `django.db.models.Model`, we need to use `appengine_django.models.BaseModel`. Back up your original models file, and then modify `models.py` so it looks like:

```
from appengine_django.models import BaseModel
from google.appengine.ext import db

class BlogPost(BaseModel):
    title = db.StringProperty()
    body = db.StringProperty()
    timestamp = db.DateTimeProperty()
```

The similarities are definitely there—these are now equivalent objects to what you had before. One notable difference is we no longer need the `max_length` setting for our `title`. The App Engine `StringProperty` has a maximum of 500 bytes. For simplicity, we use the same property for `body` in our example.

If there is a chance that a blog entry exceeds this size, then you can use `TextProperty` instead. `TextProperty` can hold more than 500 bytes, but the downside is these values are not indexed and cannot be used in filters or sort orders. Of course, chances are you wouldn't be filtering or sorting on your `body` attribute anyway, so it wouldn't be a big loss in this case.

Because App Engine does not use the Django ORM, you have to change your view code to use BigTable queries. You discover the App Engine database API gives you two different ways of querying for data: a standard `Query` or a SQL-like `GqlQuery`. In our case, we love the ORM-ness of Django and want to preserve a high-level of data access, so we just use `Query`s.

Taking a Test Drive

We're now ready to give our overhauled application a test drive. When you use `manage.py runserver` to start up the development server, you no longer see Django validating models, letting you know which settings file it's using, and the friendly startup message. Instead, you see the App Engine server output.

```
$ manage.py runserver
INFO:root:Server: appengine.google.com
INFO:root:Running application mysite on port 8000: http://localhost:8000
```

Open a web browser window to http://localhost:8000/blog. You should see the familiar blog entry screen as shown in Figure E.1. Of course, no entries are showing up because you are now using the App Engine datastore instead of the original Django ORM's database and have nothing in there (yet)!

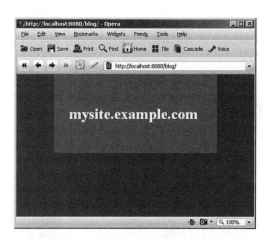

Figure E.1   No entries yet in our "new" blog app

Adding Data

As we've mentioned previously, the Django admin app is not available on the App Engine. With no admin application, we need to add our first blog entry manually (via the Python shell) so the App Engine's data-entry mechanisms is aware of that particular model. On this machine, we have IPython installed, so we see its startup message and prompts.

```
$ manage.py shell
Python 2.5.1 (r251:54863, Mar  7 2008, 04:10:12)
Type "copyright", "credits" or "license" for more information.

IPython 0.8.2 — An enhanced Interactive Python.
?         -> Introduction and overview of IPython's features.
%quickref -> Quick reference.
help      -> Python's own help system.
object?   -> Details about 'object'. ?object also works, ?? prints more.
```

Once we have the prompt, we can import our `BlogPost` class, instantiate it, and fill in the details.

```
In [1]: from blog.models import BlogPost
In [2]: entry = BlogPost()
In [3]: entry.title = '1st blog entry'
In [4]: entry.body = 'this is my 1st blog post EVAR!!'
In [5]: from datetime import datetime
In [6]: entry.timestamp = datetime.today()
```

App Engine's `DateTimeProperty` accepts a `datetime.datetime` object, hence our import and usage of that particular Python library. We then use the `today` function to get the current date and time and assign it as our `timestamp`. From here, to store the object, we just issue a call to `put`.

```
In [7]: entry.put()
Out[7]: datastore_types.Key.from_path('BlogPost', 1, _app=u'mysite')
In [8]: query = BlogPost.all()
In [9]: for post in query:
   ....:     print post.title, ':', post.body, '(%s)' % post.timestamp
   ....:
1st blog entry : this is my 1st blog post EVAR!! (2008-07-13 12:28:52.140000)
```

As stated in the database API documentation, "The `all()` method on a `Model`... class returns a `Query` object that represents a query for all entities of the corresponding kind." (This quote is from the high-level documentation on data manipulation that can be found at http://code.google.com/appengine/docs/datastore/creatinggettinganddeletingdata. html.) As you can see, we are able to open our newly-added data from within the shell. What remains is to go full circle and be able to view this new data in our app.

Make sure your server is up, and then refresh your Web browser pointing to http://localhost:8000/blog. You should now see your entry as shown in Figure E.2.

Hopefully this short experience has made you appreciate Django's admin more than you could have before. At the same time, of course, you notice the Python shell can be an invaluable tool for working with data regardless of the state of your Web site.

Figure E.2   Our blog entry now shows up!

Creating a New Django Application That Runs on App Engine

By porting an existing Django application to the App Engine, you've actually performed the more difficult task first. Creating a new application is, for most part, simpler—because you do not have the "baggage" of an existing Django application. The following steps, which apply to creating a brand new App Engine-centric Django application, can be easily followed if you keep the previous section in mind:

1. Create your Django project using `django-admin.py` as usual.

2. Copy the App Engine code (`app.yaml`, `main.py`, `appengine_django`) into your project directory.

3. Edit your `app.yaml` file with the new application name (the one registered with the App Engine Admin Console).

4. If necessary, link to the Google App Engine code.

5. Run `manage.py startapp NEW_APP_NAME`.

6. Build your application!

When building your application, you have to keep in mind not to write "pure Django," such as remembering to use the App Engine Helper's models instead of Django's. On the plus side, you now have access to all App Engine's powerful APIs.

- Python Runtime
- Datastore API
- Images API
- Mail API
- Memcache API
- URL Fetch API
- Users API

We suggest reading the App Engine documentation to see what's possible with these frameworks.

Summary

In this appendix, we introduced you to the Google App Engine, what its capabilities are, and how it presents an alternative environment to develop Django applications. In exchange for new functionality, some Django features had to be sacrificed, making it more of a challenge for existing Django programmers to jump directly into App Engine-based development. Thankfully, the App Engine helper makes this task a bit easier.

We then went in-depth, showing you how to port one of our example applications to the App Engine. Creating a new application from scratch involves similar steps, except without any worries about preexisting code. As an exercise in getting up-to-speed with App Engine, we invite you to recreate the blog app completely from scratch, as a 100 percent App Engine application.

The bottom line for you as a Django developer is you can still program (mostly) in Django, but be able to take full advantage of all the benefits that Google App Engine has to offer: simple deployment, massive scalability, and the capability to leverage Google's existing production infrastructure.

Online Resources

Following are some of the key online resources that we'd like to share with you. For a more comprehensive list, please visit the book's Web site, withdjango.com.

- Google App Engine

  http://code.google.com/appengine/

- App Engine SDK Project

  http://code.google.com/p/googleappengine/

- App Engine Tutorial

  http://code.google.com/appengine/docs/gettingstarted/

- Google App Engine Helper for Django

  http://code.google.com/p/google-app-engine-django/

- Using the Google App Engine Helper for Django (Matt Brown, May 2008)

  http://code.google.com/appengine/articles/appengine_helper_for_django.html

VIDEOS

- Rapid Development with Python, Django, and Google App Engine (Guido van Rossum, May 2008)

  http://sites.google.com/site/io/rapid-development-with-python-django-and-google-app-engine

- Introducing GAE at Google Campfire (various, Apr 2008, 7 videos) http://innovationstartups.wordpress.com/2008/04/10/google-app-engine-youtubes/

Appendix F

Getting Involved in the Django Project

Django is not just a Web framework. It's not just a great design and 50,000 lines of code. It's also a community of coders, testers, translators, question-answerers, and a global collective of volunteers. The Django AUTHORS file lists more than 200 contributors, and there are many, many others who contribute in large and small ways to keep the project going.

Django is an exemplary open source project—Python creator Guido van Rossum has said as much—and among other things that means it offers many ways for interested people to get involved. It's likely that, like many others, you find Django makes your life as a Web developer easier and more fun, and you may find your incredible surplus of leisure and happiness inspires you to give something back. Next are some examples of contributions you could make.

The easiest ways to contribute don't even require any programming whatsoever:

- Submit a correction for a typo you found in the documentation
- Help answer newbie questions on the IRC channel or the django-users mailing list
- Help with ticket triage at code.djangoproject.com, closing invalid tickets and clarifying (or verifying) valid ones

If you're willing to get your hands a little dirty, then there are options involving actual code that still don't require Herculean effort:

- Submit a patch that fixes a known bug
- Run Django's test suite on a less popular system or an unusual (but supported) software configuration to help identify potential problems
- Join work on a "branch" of Django where new features are being developed

Finally, speaking of Herculean effort, these tasks would have a significant impact on the Django community:

- Perform Django localization for a language that hasn't been done yet (if you can find one!)
- Find a feature that is widely considered desirable but hasn't been implemented, and implement it
- Create a high-quality application based on Django and release it as open source

If you're unsure, an easy way to test the waters without commitment is to join the **django-users** or **django-developers** mailing lists or spend some time in the #django IRC channel at irc.freenode.net. Before long you may find yourself contributing as well. And if you see one of us there, say hello!

Note
The Django documentation (see the official site or withdjango.com for a pointer) covers the details of contributing in great detail from coding style to mailing list protocol.

Aside from joining the mailing lists and/or the IRC channel, another way to establish yourself in the Django ecosystem is to register yourself at http://djangopeople.net, a worldwide directory of Django developers (which can also be used to find other developers if you're interested in forming a team project). Another site attempting to pair up developers with those trying to hire them is http://djangogigs.com, which also has its own developer listing (http://djangogigs.com/developers/).

Finally, you want to make sure you subscribe to the official Django blog aggregator, which can be a great way to get news on what's going on in the world of Django development. The aggregator, along with plenty of links to other community tools, can be found at http://djangoproject.com/community/.

Index

B

Form, 142

Http404, 131

ImageField, testing, 163–165. *See also* photo gallery example

ImageFieldFile, 167–168

IPAddressField, 91

Manager, 104–105

ManyToManyField, 95

Meta, 100–101

ModelChoiceField, 146

ModelForm, 143

ModelMultipleChoiceField, 146

NullBooleanField, 92

OneToOneField, 96

Q, 109–110

QueryDict, 123

QuerySet, 104–105

   as database query, 105–106

   joining databases, 108–109

   keyword composition with Q and ~Q, 109–110

   as list container, 106

   modifying SQL queries, 111–112

   as nested queries, 106–107

   removing duplicates, 108

   sorting query results, 108

TextField, 91

URLField, 91

Widget, 152

classes (Python)

   creating, 44–45

   Django models and, 46–47

   dynamic instance attributes, 52–53

   inner classes, 46

   instantiating, 45, 52

   subclassing, 46

clean up. See cron jobs

clear method (Python), 28

CMS (Content Management System)

   custom example application, 185

      admin views in, 193–195

      custom managers for, 189

      displaying stories, 198–199

      enhancement suggestions, 202–203

      imports for, 188

      Markdown usage in, 190–192

      model definition for, 186–189

      search functionality in, 199–201

      templates for, 196–198

      urls.py file, 192–193

      user management, 201

      views.py file, 196

      workflow management, 202

   explained, 181

   Flatpages application, 182

      enabling, 182–184

      error handling, 184

      templates, creating, 184

      testing, 184–185

D

F

J

N

X–Z

Colophon

We tried to approach the development of this book like we would a software project. We wanted to make our lives easier by using well-tested open source tools, especially ones that enable group collaboration. None of what we did is radical or fancy, but in the world of print publishing, there's still a surprising reliance on a workflow that boils down to e-mail attachments in a certain proprietary word processor format, and we wanted to break free from that. For the curious, here's a list of the most important open source tools we used during the preparation, writing, and editing of this book.

For version control of our manuscript and project files, we used **Subversion** (with a little **Git** and **Mercurial** for flavor). It's hard to list all the ways in which using version control makes this sort of work better, but here are some of them: complete history of the project; ability to work in parallel, even in different sections of the same file, without stepping on each other's toes; and the security of a complete copy of the project in at least four places at all times.

Trac, the lightweight software project management system written in Python, gave us convenient tracking of changes, as well as wiki-based shared notes. The combination of Trac and Subversion (or any one of the other version-control backends supported through contributed plugins) is very powerful, even for a (largely) non-code project like ours. There's nothing like a colorized diff to give you a feeling for how much work you got done that day or to help you see exactly what got changed in the latest round of edits.

Our manuscript was made up of multiple plain text files created and edited using **Vim** on Win32 or Linux machines and **TextMate** on Macs. They were written using the **Markdown** text markup system, which made it easy to generate HTML, PDF®, and other output formats as needed. Markdown was chosen because it focuses on readability and minimalistic semantic markup, both of which really matter when you are writing. To compile our text files (`.txt` or `.mkd`), we ran the seminal `make` utility, which executed Markdown-Python (along with the Wrapped Tables [`wtables`] extension), compiling all the text files into HTML.

For internal communication, we used a mailing list powered by **Mailman**, the mailing list manager written in Python. In addition to providing the core mailer services, Mailman also archived each message, so we could go back and refer to them without having to worry about keeping them within our e-mail clients.

Operating systems with sophisticated package management are a blessing when writing about a complicated software ecosystem. Need to install SQLite? Memcached? Mako? PostgreSQL? Apache? No problem. We benfitted from the excellent package management systems built into the **Debian**, **Ubuntu**, and **FreeBSD** operating systems, as well as the **MacPorts** system for OS X.

That the **Python** language is a key player here too almost goes without saying. In addition to the obvious, we also used Python in support of our quality control efforts. Simple Python scripts parsed our manuscript files, testing interactive Python examples embedded in manuscript files using the `doctest` module, and updating the code samples we drew from larger, working applications. Python code was also used to scan all manuscript files and generate updated Table of Contents text files so at any time we could see our progression. Python was also used to execute the Markdown-Python compiler that coverted our text files to HTML. All three of us have been lucky enough to be able to use Python extensively in our professional work, and we wish you the same.

Our `Makefile` also contained directives to collate the produced content, such as combining all the HTML into a single manuscript file, compressing content into ZIP archives, opening each HTML file in separate Web browser windows, and also generating PDF files (with the help of the `html2ps` [not the PHP one; the other one] and Ghostscript's `ps2pdf` filters).

Last but not least, we "ate our own dog food" by creating the book's Web site with Django!

The bridge on the cover is Erasmus Bridge in Rotterdam, Netherlands.

Software	Link
Subversion	http://subversion.tigris.org
Trac	http://trac.edgewall.org
Mailman	http://www.gnu.org/software/mailman
Markdown	http://daringfireball.net/projects/markdown
Markdown-Python	http://freewisdom.org/projects/python-markdown
`wtables`	http://brian-jaress.livejournal.com/5978.html
`make`	http://www.gnu.org/software/make/
TextMate	http://macromates.com
Vim	http://www.vim.org
Ghostscript	http://pages.cs.wisc.edu/~ghost/
`html2ps`	http://user.it.uu.se/~jan/html2ps.html
Firefox	http://mozilla.com/firefox
Ubuntu	http://ubuntu.com
FreeBSD	http://freebsd.org

Software	Link
Macports	http://macports.org
Python	http://python.org
Django	http://djangoproject.com

The Netherlands is also the birthplace of Guido van Rossum, creator of the Python language. Django, too, serves as a bridge connecting the potentially wild world of Web application development to everyday people who want to publish online without having to worry about writing complex server code, SQL statements, or what "MVC" stands for.

Developer's Library

ESSENTIAL REFERENCES FOR PROGRAMMING PROFESSIONALS

**Programming in Python 3:
A Complete Introduction
to the Python Language**

Mark Summerfield

ISBN-13: 978-0-13-712929-4

**Python Essential
Reference, Third Edition**

David M. Beazle

ISBN-13: 978-0-672-32862-6

Python Phrasebook

Brad Dayley

ISBN-13: 978-0-672-32910-4

Other Developer's Library Titles

TITLE	AUTHOR	ISBN-13
MySQL, Fourth Edition	Paul DuBois	978-0-672-32938-8
Zend Studio for Eclipse Developer's Guide	Peter MacIntyre / Ian Morse	978-0-672-32940-1
Dojo: Using the Dojo JavaScript Library to Build Ajax Applications	James E. Harmon	978-0-13-235804-0
Programming in Objective-C 2.0	Stephen G. Kochan	978-0-321-56615-7

Developer's Library books are available at most retail and online bookstores. For more information or to order direct, visit our online bookstore at **informit.com/store**.

Online editions of all Developer's Library titles are available by subscription from Safari Books Online at **safari.informit.com**.

**Developer's
Library**

informit.com/devlibrary

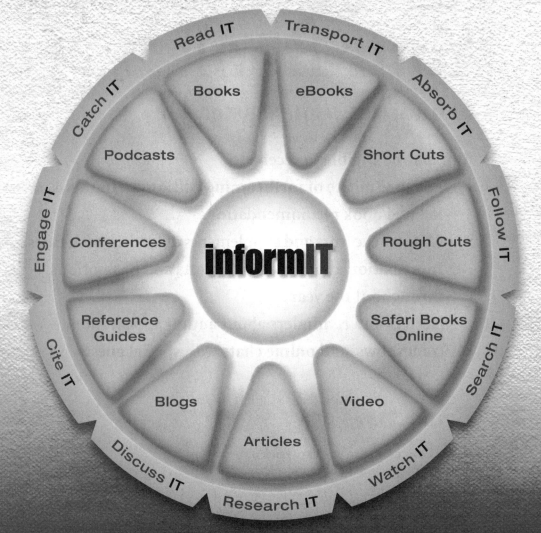